D Howard
651 The King-
T9 Crane Commission
H7

WITHDRAWN
NDSU

The King-Crane Commission

An American Inquiry in the Middle East
The King-Crane Commission
HARRY N. HOWARD

Beirut

1963

Copyright 1963 by Harry N. Howard. All rights reserved.

D
651
T9
H7

Published by KHAYATS 92-94 Rue Bliss, Beirut, Lebanon
Distributed in the U.K. and Canada by Constable & Co Ltd.
10-12 Orange St., London W.C.2

*To Virginia
and our family*

Contents

Preface — page xiii

CHAPTER I

SOME ORIENTAL BACKGROUNDS OF THE PARIS PEACE CONFERENCE

The Inter-Allied Secret Treaties — 1
   Negotiations with the Arabs — 2

   The Balfour Declaration — 4
   Additional Pronouncements — 5
   The End of the War — 8

The Opening of the Peace Conference: The Position of the Powers — 9
   The French Position — 9
   Development of the American Position — 10
   The American Intelligence Report — 10
   British Views — 12

Conflicting Aspirations at Paris: The East Speaks — 20
   The Decision of January 30, 1919 — 20
   Conflicting Claims — 22
   The Arab Position — 22
   The Case for a Commission of Inquiry — 24
   The Armenian Case — 26
   The Zionist Position — 27
   The Turks at Paris — 28

CHAPTER II

AN INTER-ALLIED COMMISSION?

The Origins of an Investigation — 31
   The Resumption of Discussion — 31
   The Commission's Instructions — 34

Appointment of the American Section of the Inter-Allied Commission on Mandates in Turkey — 37
   The Choice of King and Crane — 37
   Who's Who in the King-Crane Commission — 38
   Preparation, Confusion and Delay — 41
   Preparing a Program of Work — 42
   French Reluctance — 43
   The Critical Period — 45
   Continued Confusion — 50

The Americans Get Ready · 52
Further Discussion · 52
Further Obstacles? · 54

CHAPTER III

PREPARATIONS FOR A NEAR EASTERN JOURNEY

The Last Month in Paris · 57
Additional Instructions · 57
Importance of the Problem · 58
The Dangers of Selfish Exploitation · 59

The Paris Conference and the Turkish Problem · 63
Mandates or Spoils? · 63
The Difficulties with Italy · 65
Troubles with the Greeks · 68

The End of Delay and Confusion · 69
Conference and Study · 69
Zionist Opposition · 72
Doubts and Decisions · 74
Conference with the President · 78
Final Preparations to Leave Paris · 80
The French Refusal · 82

The Beginnings of an Adventure · 84

CHAPTER IV

AN INQUIRY INTO ZIONISM : PALESTINE

Towards the Holy Land · 87
The Investigation in Palestine Begins · 88
Preliminaries · 89
Some Differences of Opinion and Tentative Conclusions · 92
In the Region of Jerusalem · 95
The Zionist Commission · 96
End of the Work in Jerusalem · 98
The End of the Palestine Journey · 100
Conflicting Views · 100
The Majority View · 102

CHAPTER V

SOME ANSWERS TO THE SYRIAN RIDDLE

A Visit to Damascus · 106
The Beginnings in Damascus · 107
A Visit to Amman · 111

Some Tentative Impressions of the Syrian Situation 113
   The Yale Impression of Syria 113
   The Lybyer Estimate of the Syrian Situation 115

The General Syrian Congress, July 2-3, 1919 118
   The Syrian Congress and the King-Crane Commission 119
   End of the Investigation in Damascus 123

The French Occupied Region (O.E.T.A. West) 125
   Some Lebanese Testimony 125
   Some Christian Views 127

A Report to President Wilson and the Peace Conference 129
   Captain Yale's Views of the Problem 129
   Communications to the President 133

The Commission Leaves Beirut 135
   Incident at Tripoli 135
   Alexandretta and Latakia 136
   Homs and Aleppo 137

A Day in Old Cilicia 140

The End of the Syrian Journey 142
   The Petitions 142
   Some Observations on the Syrian Problem 145
   Bases of the Position Relative to France 148
   The Possibilities 148
   Feisal and Independence 150

The Syrian Journey's End 153

CHAPTER VI

THE PROBLEM OF THE TURKISH HOMELANDS — MANDATE OR INDEPENDENCE

Some Views of the Situation in Turkey: Admiral Bristol's Reports 155
   The Turkish Issue at Paris 156
   Further Reflections on the Turkish Problem 160

The Inquiry at Constantinople 161
   The Turkish Interviews 163
   Some Turkish Views of the Armenian Problem 164
   The Plea for Turkish Unity 167
   Some Representatives of the Eastern Vilayets 172
   Closure of the Turkish Case 174

The Greek Interviews 179
Some Other Christian Groups 181

The Armenian Problem 182
   The Basic Armenian Position 182
   End of the Armenian Case 184

The American Witnesses 185
   Some American Views 187

CHAPTER VII

PROJECT FOR AN AMERICAN POLICY: THE KING-CRANE REPORT AND RECOMMENDATIONS

The Montgomery and Yale Memoranda 195
   The Montgomery Report 195
   The Yale Recommendations Concerning Syria 198

The Preparation of the King-Crane Report 209
   The Lybyer Views 210
   Views on the Armenian Problem 211
   A Constantinopolitan State 213
   The Disposition of Anatolia 214
   The Desirability of a Single Mandatory 216
   Completion of the Commission's Work 217

The King-Crane Report 220
   Syria and Palestine 221
   The Report on Mesopotamia 227
   The Non-Arabic-Speaking Portions of the Ottoman Empire 228
   The Problem of an Independent Armenia 231
   Constantinople and the Straits 232
   The Turkish Homelands 233
   The Problem of the Greeks 234
   The Recommendations 235

CHAPTER VIII

TOWARDS AN AMERICAN POLICY IN THE NEAR EAST

The American Government and the Near East 239
   The Bristol Despatches 239

American Fears Concerning Turkey 244
   Policies Concerning Syria 249

The Immediate Aftermath of the King-Crane Report 256
   Delivery to President Wilson 257
   Some Attitudes Toward the Report 258

The Plan of Captain William Yale 263
   The Yale Memorandum of September 16, 1919 263
   The Yale Visit to London 265

CONTENTS

The American Military Mission to Armenia	270
The Failure of an American Policy	276
British Negotiations with Feisal and the French Concerning Syria	276
The Proposals of the American Commision to Negotiate Peace	281

CHAPTER IX

THE ROAD TO LAUSANNE

The Turkish Nationalist Movement	287
Some Anatolian Origins	287
The Nationalist Meeting at Erzerum, July 23-August 17, 1919	289
The Congress at Sivas, September 4-11, 1919	291
American Policy Concerning the Near East	294
The "Open Door" in the Near East	294
Other American Interests	295
The United States and the Treaty of Sèvres	296
American Interest in the Treaty	297
The San Remo Agreement	298
The Turks and Sèvres	299
The Controversy over Economic Rights	300
American Policy at Lausanne	301
Formulation of the United States Position	302
The United States Position on the Eve of the Lausanne Conference	303
The United States Position at Lausanne	305
The American Treaty of Lausanne	308
The Negotiations	308

CHAPTER X

WAS THE EXPERIMENT WORTH WHILE?

The Publication of the King-Crane Report	311
Some Estimates of the King-Crane Report	313
The Press	313
Conflicting Opinions	316
An Evaluation of the King-Crane Report	320
The Recommendations Concerning Palestine	320
The Recommendations Concerning Syria	321
The Recommendations Concerning Iraq	322
The Turkish Nation	323
The Validity of the King-Crane Recommendations	324
The Question of Method	325

Bibliography 329
Appendix 345
Maps
  Partition of Ottoman Empire, 1915-1917 8
  Middle East After Lausanne, 1923 308

Preface

This study, in general, grew out of the author's background in the writing of *The Partition of Turkey*, published in 1931. In a certain sense, and without repeating the materials in the earlier volume, it is a long, extended note to that study. This new work on the dissolution of the Ottoman Empire is intended to serve a four-fold purpose. First, it brings additional light to the problem of the partition of the Ottoman Empire during the period of the Paris Peace Conference. Second, American policy concerning the Near and Middle East is especially highlighted, for the materials examined have been concerned primarily with the development of American interest in that troubled region. Thirdly, the book deals with the origins, organization, investigation and report of the American Section of the Inter-Allied Commission on Mandates in Turkey, or King-Crane Commission, appointed by President Woodrow Wilson to find out the facts in and about the Ottoman Empire for the purpose of laying the essential foundations for peace-making in the Near East. Finally, it is hoped that this work will throw some light, at least, on the use of expert commissions in the technique of peace-making.

Although the author assumes full responsibility for the form and substance of the volume, and for all its shortcomings, the work has been a genuinely cooperative enterprise. So many people have been of such generous assistance in its preparation that it is difficult to find words to express adequately the deep sense of gratitude which the writer feels toward them all. The book owes its particular origin to Mr. E.W. King, the Librarian Emeritus of Miami University, Oxford, Ohio. In the fall of 1939, Mr. King placed the papers of his late father, President Henry Churchill King, of Oberlin College, at the disposal of the writer. The Office of the President at Oberlin kindly made available many of President King's private letters, written during the period of 1919-1923. The wealth of those papers is well attested by a glance at the bibliography. From that time to the completion of the task, the writer has had an almost unique experience of literally having the archives brought to his desk—the Mountain was brought to Mohammed!

Following an analysis of the King Papers the writer proceeded to gather all the available papers of other members of the King-Crane Commission. The late Professor Albert Howe Lybyer, of the University of Illinois, General Technical Adviser of the Commission, most generously permitted use of his extremely rich collection of papers and gave valuable criticism of the original manuscript. Professor William Yale, who served as Technical Adviser for the Southern Regions of Turkey, kindly allowed access to his collection of papers, and read a copy of the manuscript during 1941, when it was originally prepared. Dr. George R. Montgomery, Technical Adviser for the Northern Regions of Turkey, unfortunately kept no papers. Mr. Donald M. Brodie and Mr. Walter S.

Rogers, of The Institute of Current World Affairs, New York, permitted the writer to consult the unpublished *Memoirs* and other papers of Mr. Charles R. Crane, who, with Dr. King, was co-chairman of the American Commission. In addition, Mr. Brodie, Secretary of the Commission, allowed the writer to use his own papers.

Other manuscript materials were opened to the author. President Charles Seymour, of Yale University, very kindly facilitated the task of research by permitting use of materials from the papers of Colonel E. M. House. Mrs. Woodrow Wilson generously permitted access to and use of the papers of President Wilson on file in the Division of Manuscripts in the Library of Congress. The writer is grateful to her and to Miss Katharine Brand, Special Custodian of the Woodrow Wilson Collection at the time of his research. Mr. Allen W. Dulles kindly permitted citation of certain materials from the Lansing Papers.

The late Professor Westermann, of Columbia University, Chief of the Division of Western Asia, The American Commission to Negotiate Peace, was kind enough to permit use of certain British documents dealing with the problems of the Near East, photostatic copies of which are on file in the Hoover Library on War, Revolution and Peace at Leland Stanford University. The writer is obligated to the Director of the Hoover Library, Professor Ralph H. Lutz, and his staff for all their services and courtesies while working on these and other important materials in the summer of 1940.

The late Professor Robert J. Kerner, Sather Professor of Modern European History at the University of California, member of The House Inquiry into the Terms of Peace and of the staff of The American Commission to Negotiate Peace, under whom the writer was privileged to study, furnished much information concerning the origins of the King-Crane Commission and made many valuable suggestions in the preparation of the original manuscript.

The writer also wishes to thank Dr. G. Bernard Noble, Director of the Historical Office, Department of State, for reading the manuscript. Finally, the writer is most grateful to his wife, Virginia B. Howard, for all her encouragement and helpfulness in the preparation of the volume.

Beirut, Lebanon   HARRY N. HOWARD
November 1962

Acknowledgements

The writer gratefully acknowledges the special permission of the following publishers to quote from works copyrighted by them:

George ANTONIUS, *The Arab Awakening: The Story of the Arab National Movement* (Philadelphia, Lippincott, 1939; Beirut, Khayat, 1961).

Ray Stannard BAKER, *Woodrow Wilson and World Settlement* (New York, Doubleday, Doran, 1922), 3 volumes.

Halidé EDIB, *The Turkish Ordeal: Being the Further Memoirs of Halidé Edib* (New York, Appleton-Century, 1928).

David GARNETT, *The Letters of T. E. Lawrence* (New York, Doubleday, Doran, 1939).

David Lloyd GEORGE, *The Truth About the Treaties* (London, Gollancz, 1938), 2 volumes.

Hans KOHN, *Revolutions and Dictatorships: Essays in Contemporary History* (Cambridge, Harvard, 1939).

T. E. LAWRENCE, *Oriental Assembly* (New York, Dutton, 1940).

David Hunter MILLER, *My Diary at the Conference of Paris, with Documents* (New York, Appeal Printing Company, 1928), 22 volumes.

Allen NEVINS, *Henry White: Thirty Years of American Diplomacy* (New York, Harper, 1930).

Harold NICOLSON, *Peace-Making. 1919. Studies in Modern Diplomacy* (New York, Harcourt, Brace, 1939).

James T. SHOTWELL, *At the Paris Peace Conference* (New York, Macmillan, 1940).

Arthur D. Howden SMITH, *Mr. House of Texas* (New York, Funk and Wagnalls, 1940).

Sir Ronald STORRS, *The Memoirs of Sir Ronald Storrs* (New York, Putnam's, 1937).

CHAPTER I

Some Oriental Backgrounds
of the Paris Peace Conference

THE INTER-ALLIED SECRET TREATIES

One of the most intricate and perplexing problems before the Paris Peace Conference of 1919 was that complicated set of issues involved in the fate of the Ottoman Empire, a polyglot medieval structure at the crossroads of Eurasia and Africa. It was natural that the destiny of the Sultan's Empire, an ally of Germany in the socalled First World War, should concern all the great world powers, including even the United States of America.

Some of the decisive campaigns of the war were fought in the Near East, and from the very beginning there were serious discussions as to the future of that region and its peoples. By 1915 these discussions led to a number of secret Inter-Allied agreements.[1] The first was the Anglo-Russian accord of March 12, 1915, by which Great Britain accepted the Russian demand for control of Constantinople and the Straits, with the necessary European and Asiatic hinterlands. In return Constantinople was to be a free port and the Straits were to be open to commercial vessels. Moreover, control over the 1907 neutral zone in Persia was to pass to the British. It was not until April 10 that France reluctantly agreed to the Russian proposition, partly in return for approval by Petrograd of French control over Syria. The agreements concerning Constantinople and the Straits, therefore, were to inaugurate the deliberations and bargains concerning the rest of the Ottoman Empire.

Meanwhile, Italy was preparing to enter the war on the side of the Entente Powers, and by the Treaty of London of April 26, 1915, was to be given its share, among other things, of the Ottoman estate. Rome was not only to retain the Dodecanese Islands, occupied since 1912, but was also to have the *vilayet* of Adalia, on the coast of Asia Minor.[2] Exactly a year later, more definite blue-prints for the partition of the Ottoman Empire were ready. On April 26, 1916, a tripartite agreement among France, Great Britain and Russia was signed during the visit of

[1] In general see Harry N. HOWARD, *The Partition of Turkey: A Diplomatic History, 1913-1923* (Norman, University of Oklahoma Press, 1931), Chs. IV, V, and VI; Robert J. KERNER, "Russia, the Straits, and Constantinople, 1914-1915," *Journal of Modern History*, Vol. I, No. 3 (September, 1929), 400-415 "Russia and the Straits, 1915-1917," *The Slavonic Review*, Vol. VIII, No. 24 (March, 1930), 589-593. See also E. A. ADAMOV, *Konstantinopol i prolivy* (Moscow, 1925-1926), 2 volumes [French Translation: *Constantinople et les Détroits* (Paris 1930), 2 volumes]; *Razdel Aziatskoi Tursii* (Moscow, 1924). For a more recent study see Zeine N. ZEINE, *The Struggle for Arab Independence: Western Diplomacy and the Rise and Fall of Faisal's Kingdom in Syria* (Beirut, Khayat's, 1960), Ch. I.

[2] See René ALBRECHT-CARRIE, *Italy at the Paris Peace Conference*, (New York, Columbia, 1938), Ch. I, 334-339.

Sir Mark Sykes and M. Georges Picot to the Russian capital. This important diplomatic exchange stipulated that Imperial Russia should have Armenia, a portion of Kurdistan and northern Anatolia west of Trebizond. The French sphere of influence included Syria, the *vilayet* of Adana, southern Kurdistan and Cilicia, together with Harput. If an independent Arab community were established, Great Britain was to have a sphere in Mesopotamia, with Baghdad, and access to the ports of Acre and Haifa in Syria. Palestine, or southern Syria, was to be placed under some sort of international régime. By the Sykes-Picot agreement of May 9-16, 1916, between Great Britain and France, the Anglo-French spheres were more specifically delineated, though the general outlines of the earlier tripartite accord were observed and the agreement looked forward to the establishment of an Arab state or confederation within the Anglo-French spheres. Italy recognized the Sykes-Picot accord in return for concessions in Smyrna and Adalia, embodied in the agreement of St. Jean de Maurienne of April 19-21, 1917.[1]

These secret agreements were later to plague their authors, embarrass the governments, and confuse the uninitiated. In certain respects they conflicted with each other. But, more serious, they seemed incompatible with the specific agreements which Great Britain and the Government of India had made with the Arabs.

Negotiations with the Arabs

Negotiations with the Arabs began as early as October 31, 1914, when Lord Kitchener gave the Emir Hussein, the Grand Sherif of Mecca and the ruler of the Hejaz, a guarantee of independence, but it was not until July 14, 1915, that fruitful discussions between Great Britain and the Hejaz, through the office of Sir Henry McMahon, the British High Commissioner in Egypt, really got under way.[2] In the first note, Hussein expressed his willingness to fight the Turks provided Great Britain recognized Arab independence south of the thirty-seventh parallel. After some inconclusive negotiations in the summer, the British reply came on October 24. Sir Henry opposed Hussein's claims to the Mersina

[1] *Ibid.*, 345-346. Sir Ronald Storrs, who had much to do with the Arab negotiations, from the British Agency in Egypt, says that "until Mark Sykes appeared in Cairo in 1916 we had but the slightest and vaguest information about the Sykes-Picot negotiations...; and there was far too little realization of Indian operations in Iraq and of Indian encouragement of Ibn Sa'ud.... It seemed to be nobody's business to harmonize the various views and policies of the Foreign Office, the India Office, the Admiralty, the War Office, the Government of India and the Residency in Egypt." Sir Ronald STORRS, *The Memoirs of Sir Ronald Storrs* (New York, Putman's 1937), 168. Quoted by permission of the publishers.

[2] See Great Britain, Foreign Office, Miscellaneous, No. 3, (1939). *Correspondence between Sir Henry McMahon, G.C.M.G., G.C.V.O., K.C.I.E., C.S.I., His Majesty's High Commissioner at Cairo and the Sherif Hussein of Mecca. July 1915- March 1916. With a Map.* Cmd. 5957.

Alexandretta region and to that portion of Syria west of Damascus, Hama, Homs, and Aleppo. In general, however, the rest of the future Arab boundaries were accepted "within those frontiers wherein Great Britain" was "free to act without detriment to the interests of her ally, France." Naturally, too, agreement with Hussein was to be without prejudice to "existing treaties with Arab chiefs." In a letter of November 5, 1915, Hussein accepted the British proposition concerning Mersina and the Alexandretta region, but still held out for Aleppo and Beirut, not to mention Basra and Baghdad, though he was willing to recognize a temporary British occupation of those two cities. By January 30, 1916 the British had substantially accepted Hussein's terms, leaving the definitive position of Basra and Baghdad, as well as the French claim in Syria, undetermined.

By this time the Government of India had begun negotiations with the Emir Ibn Saud of the Nejd leading to an agreement which was ratified on July 18, 1916. The accord with Ibn Saud, which was to cause grave difficulties in the years to come, seemed clearly in opposition to the agreement between London and Hussein, for it recognized Ibn Saud's sovereignty over the Nejd, Qatif, Jubail, and lands along the coast of the Persian Gulf. [1]

Such were the so-called "secret treaties" partitioning the Ottoman Empire and the conflicting agreements made with the Emir Hussein and Ibn Saud. T.E. Lawrence, one of the leaders responsible for the Arab revolt against the Ottoman Empire, later complained bitterly, without complete justification, that the British Government had encouraged the Arabs to fight by deliberate, false promises of self-government. Lawrence had accepted the "fraud" in the conviction that Arab help was necessary to a quick and inexpensive victory, and felt that it was better that the Allies win and break their word than lose the war. The colorful and energetic Lawrence believed, too, that if he could defeat the Turks on the battlefield he might be able to conquer his own countrymen and their Allies at the Peace Conference.[2]

[1] HOWARD, 188-193. See also H. C. ARMSTRONG, *Lord of Arabia: Ibn Saud: An Intimate Study of a King* (Penguin, 1938), *passim*; H. St. John PHILBY, *Saudi Arabia* (New York, Praeger, 1955), Ch. X.

[2] T. E. LAWRENCE, *Oriental Assembly* (New York, Dutton, 1940), 144-146. See also his *Seven Pillars of Wisdom* (New York, Doubleday, Doran, 1936), 672 pp. Curiously enough, Lawrence wrote William Yale, October 29, 1929, expressing partial approval of the Sykes-Picot Agreement. See David GARNETT, *The Letters of T. E. Lawrence* (New York, Doubleday, Doran, 1939), 670-672. After examining the Hussein-McMahon correspondence in 1939, Lord Maughan, the Lord Chancellor, said that the Arab point of view had been shown to "have greater force than has appeared hitherto," although he did not "agree that it is impossible to regard Palestine as covered by the phrase 'portions of Syria, etc.'" *Report of a Committee Set Up to Consider Certain Correspondence between Sir Henry McMahon (His Majesty's High Commissioner in Egypt) and The*

THE DENOUEMENT

This was not the end of conflicting promises, disillusion and disappointment. The publication of the " secret agreements " by the Bolsheviki shortly after the November revolution in Russia shocked liberals throughout the Allied nations. The world would now know the whole, "sordid" story of Allied diplomacy, though it was not necessarily to understand the political and military exigencies which had dictated it.

The Balfour Declaration

The controversial Balfour Declaration, announced by the British Government on November 2, 1917, was a further act beclouding the situation. It viewed with favor the establishment in Palestine of "a national home for the Jewish people" and stated that the British Government would strive toward this end, with the understanding that nothing should be done which might prejudice "the civil and religious rights of existing non-Jewish communities in Palestine of the rights and political status enjoyed by Jews in any other country."[1] The policy concerning Palestine, under discussion for a long while, was launched in 1917, partly for the propaganda value it might have in the Jewish world. David Lloyd George, the British Prime Minister, tells us that it was officially communicated to the Emir Hussein as early as January 1918 and that the Arab leaders offered no objections, "so long as the rights of the Arabs in Palestine were respected."[2]

There is no doubt, however, that the Arabs were disturbed by the Balfour Declaration. Partly because of their uneasiness, Commander David Hogarth, the distinguished authority on the Near and Middle East, was sent on January 4, 1918 to convery a message of assurance to Hussein, now King of the Hejaz, whose forces had rendered excellent

---

Sherif of Mecca in 1915 and 1916, March 16, 1939, Cmd. 5974. In general, see also David LLOYD GEORGE, *The Truth About The Peace Treaties* (London, Gollancz, 1938), II, Ch. XXIII.

[1] *Parliamentary Debates, House of Commons*, Vol. 99, col. 838, November 2, 1917. See also Chaim WEIZMANN, *Trial and Error: The Autobiography of Chaim Weizmann* (New York, Harper, 1949), Ch. XVIII; William I. CARGO, "The Origin of the Balfour Declaration," *Papers of the Michigan Academy of Science, Arts and Letters*, XXVIII (1942), 497-612; Leonard STEIN, *The Balfour Declaration* (London, Vallentine, Mitchell, 1961), 681 pp.; Christina P. HARRIS, "The Balfour Declaration Today — A Warning," *Issues*, Vol. XV, No. 1 (Winter 1961), 18-30; Alan R. TAYLOR, *Prelude to Israel: An Analysis of Zionist Diplomacy, 1897-1947* (New York, Philosophical Library, 1959), 9-25; William YALE, "Morgenthau's Special Mission of 1917," *World Policies*, Vol. I, No. 3, pp. 308-20; see also J. C. HUREWITZ, *Diplomacy in the Near and Middle East: A Documentary Record*, Volume II, 1914-1956 (New York, Van Nostrand, 1956), 25-26.

[2] David LLOYD GEORGE, *Memoirs of the Peace Conference* (New Haven, Yale, 1939), II, 724, 738, 744-746; *The Truth About the Peace Treaties* (London, Gollancz, 1938), II, 1142.

service in the struggle against the Ottoman Empire.[1] Hogarth announced the determination of the Entente Powers to give the Arabs "full opportunity of once again forming a nation in the world," with a special régime in Palestine. Jewish friendship would bring support to the Arabs in all states where Jews had political influence. Zionist leaders, desired to achieve success for their movement through friendly cooperation with the Arabs, and such an offer should not "be lightly thrown aside." Hogarth found that Hussein tended to confuse his own royal ambitions with Arab unity. Moreover, he considered international control of the Holy Places in Palestine a problem to be solved after the Peace Conference. Somewhat later, in June 1918, Hogarth gave further assurances of independence to seven Arab representatives in Cairo.

Additional Pronouncements

Additional pronouncements concerning the Near and Middle East came from British, French and American spokesmen. On January 5, 1918, David Lloyd George, in an important address to the British Labor Conference, declared that the Allies, were not fighting to deprive the Turkish people of their homelands in Anatolia and Thrace or their capital at Constantinople, provided the Straits were internationalized and neutralized. But Arabia, Armenia, Syria and Palestine were "entitled to a recognition of their separate national conditions."[2] Point XII of President Wilson's famous address of January 8, three days later, was devoted to the Ottoman Empire:[3]

> The Turkish portions of the present Ottoman Empire should be assured a secure sovereignty, but the other nationalities which are now under Turkish rule should be assured an undoubted security of life and an absolutely unmolested opportunity of autonomous development and the Dardanelles should be permanently opened as a free passage to the ships and commerce of all nations under international guarantees.

Late in the summer, on September 21, Secretary of State Robert Lansing prepared a memorandum for the guidance of the American,

---

[1] See Great Britain, Foreign Office, *Miscellaneous No. 4 (1939). Statements made on behalf of His Majesty's Government during the year 1918 in regard to the Future Status of Certains Parts of the Ottoman Empire.* Cmd. 5964; see also *Conférence des Préliminaires de Paix.* British Delegation. *Memorandum on British Commitments to King Hussein.* See also Hurewitz, II, 28-30, 20 pp. Sir Ronald Storrs, *Memoirs,* Chs. 12-13, is also excellent. See also the reports of Captain William Yale in *U. S. Foreign Relations, 1018;* Supplement 1, Vol. I, 237-238, 241-244, 282.

[2] G. Lowes Dickinson, *Documents and Statements Relative to the Peace* (New York, Macmillan, 1919), 108-151.

[3] R. S. Baker and W. E. Dodd, *The Public Papers of Woodrow Wilson* (New York, Harpers, 1927), III, 160-161. See also Report made in January 1928 by the American Inquiry to President Wilson on "War Aims and Peace Terms," in R. S. Baker, *Woodrow Wilson and World Settlement* (New York, Doubleday Page, 1922), III, 23-41.

peace commissioners, suggesting that the Ottoman Empire should be reduced to Anatolia, perhaps with no possessions at all in Europe.[1] Constantinople and the region of the Straits were to be placed under an international protectorate or a government acting as a mandatory. Greece was to have the Dodecanese Islands, and possibly territory on the coast of Asia Minor. Both Armenia and Syria were to be placed under the protectorate of such powers as seemed "expedient from a domestic as well as an international point of view." Palestine was to be put under an autonomous or international protectorate or under a mandatory power. Great Britain was to be full sovereign over Egypt or to exercise a complete protectorate, while the Arabs were to receive consideration as to full or partial sovereignty over such state or states as they might establish.

The official American commentary on President Wilson's Fourteen Points dealt in detail with the Turkish problem. Constantinople and the Straits were to be internationalized, the Turks were to be restricted to Anatolia, and the coastal region, "where the Greeks predominate", was to be placed under international control, with Greece as the probable mandatory.[2] Armenia should be given a Mediterranean port, under some protecting power. Despite the French claim, it was felt that the Armenians might prefer a British protectorate. Syria had already been allotted to France. The best mandatory for Mesopotamia and the Arabs seemed to be Great Britain, whose armed forces already had conquered most of these territories. Palestine, likewise, would probably go under a British mandatory. Guarantees for the mandatories in Asia Minor were to be written into the peace treaties, with protection for minorities, the principle of the open door and provision for the internationalization of the railway trunk lines.

An interesting and valuable set of suggestions for the preservation of the unity of the Ottoman Empire came from a committee of the American Near East Relief organization, headed by Dr. James L. Barton, and thoroughly acquainted by long residence with conditions throughout the Empire. In its *Report*,[3] edited by William H. Hall, the committee

[1] Robert LANSING, *Peace Negotiations* (Boston, 1921), 192-197.
[2] See Charles SEYMOUR, *The Intimate Papers of Colonel House* (Boston, 1928), IV, 199-200. See also David Hunter MILLER's draft memorandum of July 31, 1918, a portion of which deals with Turkey. Miller argued that Point XII excluded complete sovereignty over certain portions of the empire but did not necessarily require its abandonment over Armenia, Syria, Palestine and Arabia. "Possibly one or more states may be created from what has been Turkish territory." Internationalization of the Straits was recommended. David Hunter MILLER, *My Diary at the Conference of Paris, with Documents* (New York, Appeal Printing Company, 1928), 22 volumes. Document 85, pp. 428-457. Hereafter cited as *Miller Diary*.
[3] William H. Hall, Editor, *Reconstruction in Turkey. A Series of Reports Compiled for the American Committee of Armenian and Syrian Relief*. For Private

declared that the Turkish official class should be "absolutely and completely deprived of power." But it also contended that "the territory comprised within the Turkish Empire should not be divided amongst the various European nations, 'Spheres of Influence' to be exploited by them or to satisfy colonial ambitions, no matter of how long standing." The natural resources of the old Empire should be "preserved for the enrichment of and the development by the people" to whom they rightfully belonged.

The Americans thought a division of the Ottoman Empire into a number of autonomous states would only complicate an already difficult problem. The majority population of an autonomous Armenia, for instance, would be Moslem. There would be no "democracy on such a solution", nor "the slightest hope of stability." But neither was the establishment of an autonomous, limited Turkey in Anatolia a proper solution. Each autonomous, or independent, political unit would build up its own military establishment, and racial and religious jealousies would be perpetuated, within and between the artificially created boundary lines. The American group recognized that some Armenians, Syrians, Greeks and Jews had nationalistic ambitions. But the committee felt that a fundamental solution, could best be achieved "by treating the whole together and granting to each nationality, under some provincial arrangement, the opportunity of working out its problems while the central control would give to the whole a uniform development."

With the Ottoman Government removed, either the Peace Conference or a League of Nations should appoint a "Tutelary or Reconstruction Government", which should act as the agent for the "the reorganization of the Turkish Empire" until the foundations for self-government "could be securely laid and the Empire, reorganized and democratized, would be fitted to assume its place in the great commonwealth of nations." One power, rather than several, should undertake the task of reconstruction in Turkey, since it would be more efficient in the execution of its work. The American group felt that a committee or commissions "familiar with the Turkish situation" should be formed to study on the ground and recommend in detail the framework for a reconstruction government in the Ottoman Empire.[1]

Distribution Only. 1918, 243 pp. Also Harold A. HATCH and William H. HALL, *Recommendations for Political Reconstruction in the Turkish Empire*. For Private Distribution. November 1918. 7 pp. Lybyer's Copy was received November 27, 1918 and marked confidential.

[1] Mr. Hall also wrote an article on "Reconstructing Turkey" (*Asia*, XVIII, No. 11 [November 1918], 945-951), urging that the Ottoman Empire be kept intact and stressing its vast wealth. Hall suggested the formation of an American syndicate, with $ 100,000,000 capitalization, to buy up the privilege of "reorganizing the present Turkish Empire", thereby putting humanitarianism on a strictly business basis." According to Jacob de HAAS, *Palestine: The Last Two Thousand Years* (New York,

The End of the War

The World War was now drawing to a close. Bulgaria's surrender at the end of September 1918 and the signing of the Mudros armistice by the Ottoman Empire one month later foreshadowed the end of the great conflict. On November 8, Great Britain and France issued a joint declaration stating that their aim in the Near and Middle East was [1]

> the complete and definite emancipation of the peoples so long oppressed by the Turks and the establishment of national governments and administrations deriving their authority from the initiative and free choice of indigenous populations. In order to carry out these intentions France and Great Britain are at one in encouraging and assisting the establishment of indigenous Governments and administrations in Syria and Mesopotamia, now liberated by the Allies, and in the territories the liberation of which they are engaged in securing and recognizing these as soon as they are actually established.

The Emir Feisal, son of King Hussein, had entered Damascus with his forces on October 1, and it now appeared that at last the Arabs, were to come into their own. Undoubtedly, in their enthusiasm they were misled by the Anglo-French declaration, for they took it to be more or less an exact definition of their status when the Peace Conference met in January 1919.

Meanwhile, at a meeting of the British Cabinet in December 1918, the problem of Palestine was very thoroughly discussed on the basis of a detailed memorandum submitted by the Foreign Office.[2] Rejecting

---

Macmillan, 1934), 489-492, this proposal forced on President Wilson the formation of the King-Crane Commission. American financiers and Christian missionaries and relief workers were in a conspiracy to defeat the Armenians in Armenia, the French in Syria and the Zionists in Palestine. The flaw in the scheme was that "it called for the exercise of an American mandate." Wilson, according to de Haas, "yielded only to the wishes of the sponsoring group, when it pressed upon him the advisability of ascertaining the wishes of the population of Syria and Palestine, in accordance with his own theory of 'self-determination'." There is no support whatsoever for the de Haas story in the documents available to the author. There is no reference to the episode in James L. BARTON, *Story of Near East Relief* (New York, Macmillan, 1930), 138-141.

[1] For text see Cmd. 5974 (1939), 50. On October 17, 1918, General Sir Edmund Allenby advised Feisal that measures taken under the military administration were "purely provisional" and would not "prejudice the final settlement by the peace conference...." He reminded Feisal "that the Allies were in honour bound to endeavour to reach a settlement in accordance with the wishes of the peoples concerned, and urged him to place his trust whole-heartedly in their good faith." *Loc. cit.* See also, George ANTONIUS, *The Arab Awakening* (Philadelphia, Lippincott, 1939), 435-436.

[2] See David LLOYD GEORGE, II, Ch. XXIII, especially pp. 1142 ff. For other aspects of British policy see Royal Institute of International Affairs, *Great Britain and Palestine*, 1914-1945 (London and New York, 1946), 1-17; Herbert SIDEBOTHAM, *Great Britain and Palestine* (London,

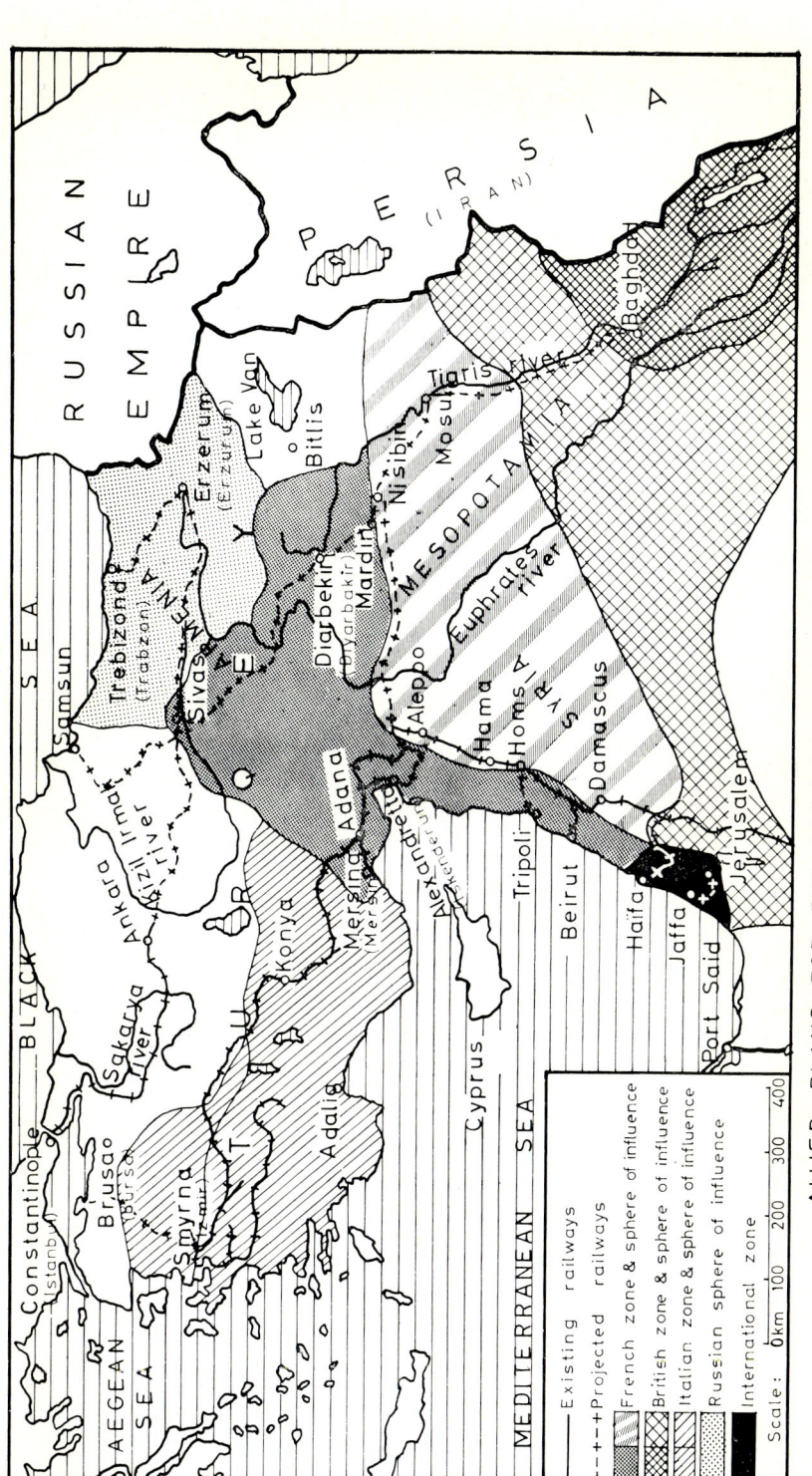

ALLIED PLANS FOR THE PARTITION OF THE OTTOMAN EMPIRE 1915-1917
[Modified from Harry N Howard, The Partition of Turkey, 1913-1923 (Norman University of Oklahoma Press. 1931). 48]

an international administration over Palestine, or continued Ottoman sovereignty, the Foreign Office favored the nomination of a single Great Power, preferably the United States or Great Britain, to act as the representative of the nations in Palestine. The boundaries of the country should be adjusted at the Peace Conference and pledges concerning the Holy Places should be "effectively fulfilled." It was after the Cabinet meeting that Lloyd George made an arrangement with Premier Clemenceau whereby the *vilayet* of Mosul was transferred to the British from the French sphere of influence and Palestine was to come under the control of Great Britain instead of being internationalized. The formal consent of France to these changes, was completed on February 15, 1919.[1]

The Opening of the Peace Conference: The Position of the Powers

At the Paris Peace Conference, which was formally opened on January 18, 1919, the secret agreements of 1915-1917 and the declarations which had followed in the last year of the war were to form the basis for the discussions concerning the future of the Near East. The magnitude of the problem is reflected in the fact that it was not until July 24, 1923, after the abortive Treaty of Sèvres and the disastrous Greco-Turkish war, that a final solution was reached in the Treaty of Lausanne.

The French Position

The French position seemed fairly clear. M. Briand had declared in the Chamber of Deputies on December 27, 1918 that the secret agreements would be brought before the Peace Conference and "would become treaties only when ratified by the conference and become definitive for France only when its representatives, after public discussion, had been asked to vote on them and ratify them...."[2] Yet it was evident from a statement by M. Pichon, the French Foreign Minister, that France felt that it had "incontestable rights" to safeguard in Syria, the Lebanon, Cilicia, and Palestine. Both Pichon and Briand, while seeming to recognize the freedom of the Peace Conference, insisted that the agreements with Great Britain were binding on both countries.[3]

Macmillan, 1937), 310 pp., *passim*; Chaim WEIZMANN, *Trial and Error* (New York, Harper, 1949), Ch. 18; Alpheus Thomas MASON, *Brandeis: A Free Man's Life* (Princeton, 1946), 451-458.

[1] See *Secret Minutes of the Conference*, March 20, 1919; Baker, III, 1-19; Republic of France, *Journal Officiel*. Sénat (1920), 1525, and Briand's address to the Chamber, June 25, 1920, *Journal Officiel. Débats Parlementaires* (1920:2), 2434-35. See also André TARDIEU, "Mossoul et le pétrole", *L'Illustration*, Vol. 155, No. 4033 (June 19, 1920), 380-382.

[2] Quoted from Georges CLEMENCEAU, *Discours de Paix* (Paris, Plon, 1938), 14-15.

[3] *Journal Officiel. Chambre* (1928:2), 3716.

France, in other words, was to stand on the basis of the secret agreements and to insist on the full letter of its rights.

Development of an American Position

As soon as they arrived in Paris, the Americans were asked about their position toward a Turkish settlement. The question of internationalizing Constantinople and the Straits was raised by Lord Eustace Percy, of the British Foreign Office, in a conversation on December 3, 1918 with David Hunter Miller, Legal Adviser to the American Delegation, and Lord Eustace more than hinted that the Panama Canal would fall in the same category, but failed to mention the Suez Canal in that connection. Miller had another discussion at dinner with Lord Robert Cecil in which the British guests unanimously approved an American mandate for Constantinople. Even Colonel T.E. Lawrence, whom Miller describes as "distinctly anti-French,"reluctantly agreed that the United States should take Armenia, and hoped that it would also administer Syria. [1] Harold Nicolson, of the British Delegation, reported that Professors Albert H. Lybyer and Clive Day, of the American Peace Commission, had evidently made up their minds that the Turks should be turned out of Europe, but were in doubt as to who should be the successor in the Constantinople zone. Nicolson gathered from the conversation that President Wilson wanted "some small power, or some group of small powers, to administer this Constantinople or Straits Zone." The American experts, however, objected and wanted "either U.S.A. or Great Britain to assume the mandate," recognizing, however, that American opinion might not approve a mandate for the United States. They evidently expected to have to take over Armenia, but were vague about the rest of the Ottoman Empire. [2]

The American Intelligence Report

By January 21, the Intelligence Section of the American Commission

---

[1] *Miller Diary*, I, 27-28, 74.
[2] Harold NICOLSON, *Peace-Making*, 1919. *Studies in Modern Diplomacy* (New York, Harcourt, Brace, 1939), 228-229. Nicolson was incorrect about the American attitude toward turning the Turks out of Europe. He noted that the Americans "would be quite prepared to see us at Constantinople as Mandatory—but less prepared to act in that capacity themselves. U. S. opinion not ready for this responsibility, but they 'might' be ready to assume responsibility for Armenia. They are very keen on a Greek zone at Smyrna." Arthur D. Howden SMITH, *Mr. House of Texas* (New York, Funk and Wagnalls, 1940), 164-165, says that he suggested to House in January 1919 "a permanent solution of the Question of Constantinople and the Straits." The plan was to internationalize the city and the region of the Straits, making Constantinople the seat of the League of Nations. House finally disapproved of the idea because of the climate—he was counting on being the American representative to the League of Nations. "So he plumped for Geneva, where he had always been comfortable."

to Negotiate Peace had worked out a series of recommendations for the President and the American Commissioners, a considerable portion of which was devoted to the problems of the Near and Middle East.[1] The report is especially interesting because of its bearing on the later recommendations of the King-Crane Commission. It proposed that an international state be established in the Constantinople region under a mandate and that it receive such governmental organization as seemed "most expedient to the peace conference." It was also recommended that "the Bosphorus, Sea of Marmora, and Dardanelles be permanently opened as a free passageway to the ships and commerce of all nations, under international guarantees." As to Turkey proper, it was suggested that a Turkish state be established in Anatolia and that the mandatory principle be applied, though no recommendation was made as to the governing power. It is interesting to observe that the Intelligence Section did not recommend assignment of Smyrna to Greece.[2] To give Greece

> a foothold upon the mainland would be to invite immediate trouble. Greece would press her claims for more territory; Turkey would feel that her new boundaries were run so as to give her a great handicap at the very start. The harbor of Smyrna has been for centuries an outlet for the products of the central Anatolian valleys and upland.

From the non-Turkish portions of the former Ottoman Empire, it was suggested that an Armenian state be established, under a mandatory, with outlets on the Mediterranean through Cilicia and on the Black Sea through Trebizond. A Mesopotamian state should be set up under mandate, but no suggestion was made as to the mandatory. Moreover, no solution should be adopted which "would preclude the incorporation of this state in an Arab confederation if a desire for such incorporation should take actual form in Mesopotamia." A Syrian state was also advised. It, too, was to be under a mandate, but again no recommendation was made as to the mandatory. No obstacle was to be placed in the way of Syrian membership in an Arab confederation. A separate state of Palestine was urged, with Great Britain as the mandatory. It was suggested [3]

[1] Document 246, *Miller Diary*, IV, 249-265. The original is in the Woodrow Wilson Collection, Library of Congress, IX-A, Box 19.
[2] The Dodecanese Islands and Rhodes were assigned to Greece.
[3] This recommendation for the Jewish National Home in Palestine practically endorsed the basic Zionist position. The French Government had endorsed the 'National Home' in Palestine as early as February 9, 1918. President Wilson expressed his "satisfaction" to Rabbi Wise concerning the Balfour Declaration on August 31, 1918; Baker and Dodd, III (i), 243. David Hunter Miller had pointed out to President Wilson in January 1919 "that the rule of self-determination would prevent the establishment of a Jewish State in Palestine", even as it would preclude "the establishment of any autonomous Armenia", since both peoples were in a decided minority. See HOWARD, 226; *Miller Diary*, XV, 104-108.

that the Jews be invited to return to Palestine and settle there, being assured by the Conference of all proper assistance in so doing that may be consistent with the protection of the personal (especially the religious) and the property rights of the non-Jewish population, and being further assured that it will be the policy of the League of Nations to recognize Palestine as a Jewish state as soon as it is a Jewish state in fact.

The Holy Places of Judaism, Christianity and Islam were to be placed under mandatory protection. The desert portion of the Arabian peninsula, exclusive of Syria and Mesopotamia, was to be treated separately. No definite action was to be taken concerning the "present tribal states". Nevertheless, "the policing of the Red Sea, Indian Ocean, and Persian Gulf coasts of Arabia, and the border lands behind these" was to be left to the British Empire.

British Views

Like their American colleagues, the British experts were also outlining the British position, and their memoranda on the subject deserve considerable study. [1] In the definitive analysis, the term "Middle East" was taken to refer to those "Middle Eastern" countries which had been in the war and which, as a result of the war, were subject to "re-settlement at the hands of the Peace Conference." These included all European and Asiatic territories formerly under direct or indirect Ottoman Sovereignty and former Russian territories "between the Russo-Turkish and Russo-Persian frontiers and the Caucasus Mountains." The principles to be applied included the Wilson Fourteen Points and other pertinent declarations in 1918 and the armistice of November 11. It was noted, however, that technically the Allies had pledged themselves to the United States to make peace on the basis of the Fourteen Points only with Germany, and were not obligated concerning Turkey, with which they had previously concluded an armistice on different terms. Nevertheless, they were bound towards Germany, the United States and each other to base the settlement of the Turkish problem on the Fourteen Points and the other Wilson pronouncements.

Point XII of Wilson's address of January 8, 1918 specifically referred to the Ottoman Empire. Other points of more general bearing had to

---

[1] See especially Great Britain, Foreign Office, *Statement of British Policy in the Middle East for Submission to the Peace Conference (if required).* February 18, 1919, 18 pp.; *Statement by the British Government for the Peace Conference Concerning the Settlement of the Middle East (1st Proof for Revision),* February 7, 1919, 17 pp.; *Maps Illustrating Memorandum Respecting the Settlement of Turkey and the Arabian Peninsula; Appendix on Previous Commitments of His Majesty's Government in the Middle East; Memorandum on British Commitments to King Hussein.* These important documents, written by or prepared under the supervision of Professor Arnold J. Toynbee, are in the papers of Professor W. L. Westermann, the Hoover Library, Stanford University. The second is also in the papers of Henry Churchill King.

do with open diplomacy, removal of economic barriers, reduction of armaments, and the League of Nations. The Mount Vernon address of February 4, 1918, calling for a settlement on the basis of the free acceptance of the peoples involved, was also applicable in general to the Near and Middle East. While the British Government and the Allies were pledged to make these principles the basis of the settlement, Britain was also bound by certain previous treaties, agreements and understandings, "entered into before or during the war, but all in circumstances very different from the present, which it might be difficult or impossible to harmonise with the new situation and the new principles governing the settlement."

In applying President Wilson's principles to the Ottoman Empire, the British statement insisted that non-Turkish populations, or populations in which the Turkish element was in a minority, "ought to be liberated completely from Turkish rule," with the reservation that equitable participation in the pre-war Ottoman debt be required. But where the Turks were in a majority and had not given "the minority elements security of life, separation should follow." This principle was understood to apply to Armenia and possibly even to Thrace and Smyrna. The rest of Turkey should be independent, though it should be required to accept foreign advisers, nominated by the various Powers under the authority of the Peace Conference, for the "more important financial and administrative departments." The peoples of the independent states "should be at liberty to opt for the assistance of a foreign Power", but the Conference, "with due consideration for the wishes of the peoples", should define the conditions of assistance, and the mandatory should act as the agency of the Conference "or ultimately of the League of Nations." Subject to certain limitations, the principle of self-determination should be accepted. An exception might be made in such areas as Thrace, Constantinople, and Armenia, in which the population could not "speak with one voice", and in which the assisting Power would have to be chosen by the Conference "rather than by the people themselves." Armenia and the Zionist Jews had claims "to special consideration out of proportion to their present numerical strength in the Middle Eastern countries." Also there were

> world interests such as the "permanent opening of the Black Sea Straits as a free passage to the ships and commerce of all nations under international guarantees", or access to Holy Places in Palestine for all religions or denominations legitimately interested in each of them, which are so important that they must, if necessary, take precedence over the wishes of the inhabitants of the localities in which they are situated.

The British memorandum then proceeded to examine specifically the disposition of Ottoman territories, taking up first the problem of Thrace, Constantinople and the Straits:

His Majesty's Government consider that the free passage of the Black Sea Straits, on a footing of equality for the ships of all nations, in peace or war, under international control (as stipulated in the Twelfth Point of President Wilson's Address of the 8th January 1918), can be secured only by removing the shores of the Bosphorus and Dardanelles, and part, at least, of the littoral of the Sea of Marmora, from Turkish sovereignty, dismantling all fortifications, and introducing some external authority to secure the maintenance of the desired conditions.

The necessary authority could be provided in either of two ways. A mandatory power might be appointed to assist the administration of the region and keep the peace among the different nationalities, maintaining "the freedom of the Straits in the name of the Conference or ultimately of the League of Nations." Or, the same authority might be delegated to an international body by the Conference or the League of Nations, "the executive functions being exercised by a High Commissioner."

But the settlement of the Straits problem would affect that of Eastern, or Ottoman, Thrace. If the zone of the Straits, including the entire shoreline, were placed under a mandatory, a portion of Ottoman Thrace would be involved. The whole province, with a mixture of Turkish and Greek elements, "might possibly be thrown in, a few frontier districts being assigned, on geographical and to a less extent on ethnographical grounds, to Bulgaria." But if the zone of the Straits were limited to Constantinople and the immediate shoreline of the Bosphorus, "the rest of the Asiatic littoral would naturally remain to Turkey, while the least objectionable solution of the European littoral of the Sea of Marmora and its Thracian hinterland would be to assign it to Greece."

It was hoped that the Italian and Greek Governments would arrive at an agreement concerning the Dodecanese Islands, by which the wishes of the islanders would be given effect. Despite the Turkish character of the Anatolian hinterland, the problem of Smyrna, with its large Greek element, should be examined separately, and

> the question of its union with Greece ought to be considered by the Conference....His Majesty's Government suggest that the question ought not to be decided without consultation of the various sections of the local population and expert investigation of the geographical problem.

Since the major part of the population in Anatolia was predominantly Turkish, the British felt that "an independent Turkish national State should be left in existence in this area." The boundaries of the new Turkey

> would depend on the west upon the disposal of the Asiatic littoral of the Straits and the Sea of Marmora, and on the decisions of the Conference in regard to Smyrna. On the east, His Majesty's Government consider that the frontier should be drawn where the more or less homogenous Turkish population of Anatolia gives place to the mixed Turkish, Armenian, and Greek population of the northeastern vilayets of the former Ottoman Empire. They would propose a line leaving Selefke, Kasaria, and Samsun in Turkey, but excluding Mersina, Sivas and Kerasund.

In view of its bankruptcy, the Ottoman Government would be required "to appoint foreign advisers to the more important financial and administrative departments, such as those of Finance, Customs and Internal Revenue, the Post Office, and the Audit, and Establishment Office." Such advisers should be nominated by certain governments represented at the Conference, and should not be removed without their consent. The Ottoman Government should be bound "on their advice." On the other hand, the British believed assistance could be fruitful only if it aimed "at promoting the prosperity and productive capacity of the country." Aid might extend to such departments as agriculture, woods and forests, and communications. This would mean a mandatory power for the Ottoman state.

In the event of any Power being opted for by the Turkish people, the Conference should define the conditions on which that Power should co-operate in the reconstruction of Turkey with the advisors proposed above and should appoint the Power to be its mandatory, or ultimately of the mandatory of the League of Nations, within these limits.

The "Six Vilayets" of Armenia should be independent. The Armenians were a prolific as well as an intelligent people, and there would be an "immigration of Armenians from abroad" who were "likely to play the leading part in the future." But, the Armenians were in a "numerical minority" even before the series of massacres which began in 1895, and at the close of the war they might conceivably "form a considerably smaller fraction of the population." The country could not, therefore, simply be handed over "to the Armenian element and organised as an Armenian national state." The Conference would have to intervene "to keep the peace between the nationalists and to reconstruct the country materially after the depopulation and devastation of the war." A mandate was recommended to promote justice between the nationalities, reconstruction of the country and the establishment of political institutions to train the population politically for independence.

The problem of Armenia naturally raised the question of the Trans-Caucasian countries, Georgia, Azerbaijan and Daghestan. It is not without interest to find the British document declaring that

the future revival of Russia ought not to be left out of account, and His Majesty's Government hold that the Conference ought not to prejudice the future relations of these countries with Russia or to take steps which might impede their federation with her by the free consent of all parties concerned.

While Georgia had "all the makings of an independent state", and only one nationality problem, that of the Moslems, Azerbaijan presented a more difficult question. In both cases some sort of assistance was approved. But Daghestan had not "even the elements of a state", but was inhabited by a number of wild Moslem mountain tribes, "without cohesion and now released from the former Russian control which alone held them together." It was thought best to leave Daghestan to itself, "merely instructing the mandatory Power in Azerbaijan to maintain a military cordon if necessary between the tribes of Daghestan and the oil-fields of Baku." The ports of Batum and Polti should be made free, and for a number of years, at least, the allocation of the produce of the Baku oil-fields should be regulated "by an international commission." [1]

The problem in the Arabic speaking countries was, if anything, more complicated than in the non-Arabic speaking portions of the former Ottoman Empire. In general, the British Government held that in the Arab lands "the wishes of the inhabitants would best be met, and peace and stability best be secured, by the establishment of a series of independent states." Some of these nations had already declared their independence and had been recognized, and others still remained to be created. Ultimate federation of these states was a "question for the Arabs themselves", but "out of the question", thanks to state of communications and existing economic, social and historical differences among the various Arabic peoples. It was recommended that the Arabic countries be placed under a mandatory of the League of Nations.

The Kingdom of the Hejaz was already recognized, though its boundaries were not yet defined. These should include, however, Mecca and Medina and their ports, the independent nomad tribes, and such other Arab principalities as had placed themselves under the sovereignty of the Hejaz. Trade would be on equal terms to the nationals of foreign states, though the restrictions against non-Moslems visiting Mecca and Medina might still hold. Moreover, the Hejaz should abstain from granting foreign concessions and public works "should be carried out directly by the government itself." The Hejaz should not be required to participate in the Ottoman Public Debt.

Generally speaking, the Arabian Peninsula outside the Hejaz included territory under the Sheikh of Koweit, the Emir Ibn Saud of the Nejd, and Idrisi Sayyid of Northern Tihama, all of whom had entered into treaty engagements with Great Britain, which controlled their foreign relations. The British proposed that these relations be recognized. In view of the nearness of the Arabian Peninsula to "important portions of the British Empire, and of the special political interests of Great Britain in the peninsula", the Peace Conference or ultimately the League of Nations should recognize Britain's "special relations with any other independent Arab Government that may exist or come into existence

---

[1] See also Firuz KAZEMZADEH, *The Struggle for Transcaucasia* (1917-1921), New York, Philosophical Library, 1951), 356 pp.; Sir Olaf CAROE, *Soviet Empire: The Turks of Central Asia and Stalinism* (London, Macmillan, 1953), *passim*; Charles Warren HOSTLER, *Turkey and the Soviets* (London, Allen and Unwin, 1957), *passim*.

in the remainder of the area." In turn, Great Britain would assure the observation of the regular rules of international trade in the region.

Mesopotamia, which included the basin of the Tigris-Euphrates river system and the *vilayet* of Mosul, inhabited predominantly by an Arabic-speaking people, was to be accepted "as an independent Arab unit or confederation of provinces." The desires of the inhabitants should be followed in the selection of the mandatory, which was to assist in the economic reconstruction of the country and the political training of the peoples. Finally, the relations of the different provinces of Mesopotamia to one another, and of the whole country to the other Arab lands, "should be settled, as far as possible, by the wishes of the people themselves." The mandatory for Mesopotamia, with the consent of the inhabitants, might be extended to Southern Kurdistan, which might have autonomy, though all Kurdish tribes could not be included.

Syria constituted "a natural subdivision of the Arab area", which could "neither be split up internally nor separated by rigid frontiers from the neighbouring Arab units." The nomad groups were dependent on the markets of Es Salt, Akaba, Dera, Damascus, Homs, Hama and Aleppo. But nomad and settled regions depended, in turn, on such seaports as Sidon, Beirut, Tripoli and Latakia, "and the country as a whole" formed "the frontage of the Arabian Peninsula and Mesopotamia on the Mediterranean." Therefore no settlement which drew lines of division between this frontage and its hinterland would be workable. Economic relations had their counterpart in the "political tendencies of the people." The Emir Feisal, "as representative of the local Arab committee of Damascus", had worked to deliver the country, and an Arab administration had been established under General Allenby, which enjoyed the support of the Arabs. This development

> should be taken as an indication that the people of this Arab country wish to form a political unit, and that they wish to govern themselves. A partition of the country would not only do violence to its geographical and economic structure, but would break up the foundations of an existing local Arab polity.

Therefore Syria should be recognized "as an independent Arab unit", though a centralized system of government might not be suitable to the country, as in Mesopotamia. Since a mandatory power would be necessary,

> the Syrian people, or the national Government constituted by them, should be free to opt for whatever Power they choose; ...the Conference should give that Power its mandate; and ...when the terms of the mandate are defined, it should be remembered that, of all the Arab countries under consideration, Syria is politically the most mature.

The problem of local government was especially knotty, and it might be that the *vilayet* of Beirut should be given the option of going with the Lebanon or with Syria.

The extremely delicate situation of Palestine and the questions which it brought to the fore were well outlined in the British statement:

> The problems of Palestine are parallel in several respects to problems already discussed in relation to other Middle Eastern countries: (a) in Palestine, as in Thrace, the Straits, the Smyrna district and Armenia, the population is mixed, and has not a common will; (b) though the great majority of the population is Arab, the Jewish agricultural colonist in Palestine, like the Armenians and Greeks in the areas above mentioned, are a minority which, on account of the historic past, its superior vigour and ability, the barbarous methods by which its numbers have recently been reduced, and its reservoirs of potential immigrants, from which its losses can be made good, is certain of a future which entitles it to consideration out of proportion to its present numbers; (c) the Christian, Jewish and Moslem Holy Places in Palestine, like the waterway in the zone of the Straits, constitute a world interest of such importance that it should take precedence, in case of conflict, over political aspirations of the local inhabitants.

The Conference could best deal with these difficulties through a mandate conferred on a single power, which was to set up the framework of a Palestinian state, with equal rights for all citizens; to secure proportional representation for the Zionist Jews and the Arabs in the administration; to train these two elements for collaboration in self-government; and to insure equitable access to the Holy Places of the country. The governor, whose qualifications should include no religious or racial test, should be appointed by and be responsible to the mandatory, but should have the advice of a representative council. There should be cultural autonomy in public education and ecclesiastical government. Furthermore, the Zionist enterprise should be given its proportionate share of the land, but " without crowding the Arab population to the wall. " The Holy Places were to be left to "special authorities constituted for the purpose", and not placed directly under the government of Palestine.

The British statement closed with a consideration of railway questions. The former German-controlled Baghdad and Anatolian railways, were to be handed over to the Allied and Associated Governments. In turn, the railway properties were to be sold to the new states created out of the former Ottoman Empire, in which the various sections of the railways were located. In the Trans-Caucasus region the railways should be bought from the Russian governement by the various parties involved. The railways built by Great Britain in Palestine and Mesopotamia should be sold to the new nations in which they ran. But the sections of the Hejaz railway, built by Moslems the world over, should probably be held in trust by the several independent states in which they would lie and be jointly administered. Freedom of transit for trade should be secured by a general convention to which it was hoped that all members of the Conference and later of the League of Nations would be parties.

The experts who prepared this basic document on British policy were well aware that Great Britain had entered into certain commitments, some of them secret, concerning the future of the Ottoman Empire. [1] They frankly acknowledged that some of these commitments were contrary to the spirit of the Wilson principles. This was especially true of the French claim in Syria. It is curious to note that Great Britain recognized "no previous commitments" in the matter of "Thrace, Constantinople, and the Black Sea Straits". The inference is clear that the Russian defection as a consequence of the Bolshevik Revolution of November 1917 simply effaced the obligation to Russia in the agreement of March 12, 1915.[2] The British conceded that the pledge to allow the Italians to remain in the Dodecanese Islands was inconsistent with the Wilson principles. Of great interest in the analysis of the commitments to King Hussein is the seeming belief that [3]

---

[1] Conférence des Préliminaires de Paix, British Delegation. *Appendix on Previous Commitments of His Majesty's Government in the Middle East*. The commitments were: (1) *Règlement Organique* of the Lebanon Vilayet, June 9, 1861; *Règlement Organique* of the Lebanon Vilayet, September 6, 1864; (3) Treaty of Berlin, July 13, 1878, Article 61, relative to reforms in the Ottoman provinces inhabited by Armenians; (4) Agreement, January 23, 1899, with the Sheikh of Koweit; (5) Agreement, October 15, 1907, with the Sheikh of Koweit; (6) Proclamation by the Government of India, November 2, 1914, regarding the Moslem Holy Places; (7) Assurance, November 3, 1914, given by the British Resident in the Persian Gulf to the Sheikh of Koweit; (8) Assurance, November 22, 1914, given by the British Resident in the Persian Gulf to the Sheikh of the Mohamerra; (9) Assurance, February 3, 1915, given in a speech by the Viceroy of India to the Notables of Basra; (10) Treaty with Italy, April 26, 1915; (11) Treaty, April 30, 1915, ratified November 6, 1915, with the Idrisi Sayyid of Sabia; (21) Correspondence, beginning in July 1915, with Hussein Bin Ali, Grand Sherif of Mecca; (13) Treaty, December 26, 1915, ratified July 18, 1916, with Abdul-Aziz Bin Saud, Emir of Nejd and Al Hasa; (14) Agreement, May 16, 1916, with France; (15) Supplementary Agreement, January 22, 1917, with the Idrisi Sayyid; (16) Agreement, August 18, 1917, with Italy; (17) Letter, November 2, 1917, from Lord Balfour to Lord Rothschild, regarding Palestine; (18) Statements, June 11, 1917, issued by the Foreign Office, in answer to seven Syrians and subsequently communicated to King Hussein; (19) Joint Anglo-French Declaration, dated November 8, 1918 regarding Syria and Mesopotamia. See also Harold NICOLSON, *Curzon: The Last Phase*, 1919-1925 (Boston and New York, Houghton Mifflin, 1934), 76-78, for his memorandum of January 2, 1918, circulated during 1919, on the British position.

[2] David Lloyd George declared on December 20, 1917 that, "of course, the fact that Russia has entered into separate negotiations absolutely disposes of any question there may be about Constantinople." *Parliamentary Debates*. House of Commons, Vol. 100, col. 2220.

[3] See Conférence des Préliminaires de Paix. British Delegation. *Memorandum* on British Commitments to King Hussein. (vii) *Relations of Commitments under* (vii) *to British Desiderata*.

all commitments hitherto made by His Majesty's Government to the Sherif on the one part and the other independent Arab rulers on the other appear to be compatible with one another. On the other hand, the problem of retaining the goodwill of the Sherif and securing him the position required by British and French desiderata in Mesopotamia, Palestine and Syria, while at the same time retaining the confidence of the other independent Chiefs, remains unsolved.

Conflicting Aspirations at Paris : The East Speaks

As already noted, the problem of the disposition of the Ottoman estate was a very important issue at Paris, in informal exchanges of opinion between the delegations of the United States and the United Kingdom, especially on the eve of the Peace Conference, and it was generally agreed that the Ottoman Empire should be broken into its component elements. In a first draft of the Covenant of the League of Nations, on January 10, 1919, President Wilson had indicated that territories formerly belonging to the Ottoman Empire should be placed under some kind of trust under the projected League of Nations and not be the subject of annexation by any Power.[1]

The Decision of January 30, 1919

But it was not until January 30 that formal discussion of the Ottoman Empire essentially began, when Lloyd George indicated that the mandate principle already had been accepted, although, in general, mandates were to be applied only to conquered parts, either of the Ottoman or the German Empire, excluding Smyrna (Izmir), Adalia and Northern Anatolia. The British Delegation, indeed, had already circulated a draft resolution, on January 29 [2], stating that, because of Ottoman misrule over subject peoples and the Armenian and other massacres, and without prejudice to the settlement of other parts of the Empire, it was agreed that "Armenia, Syria, Mesopotamia, Palestine and Arabia must be completely severed from the Turkish Empire." Moreover, the principle "that the well-being and development" of the peoples involved formed "a sacred trust of civilization and that securities for the performance of this trust should be embodied in the constitution of the League of Nations" was to be applied. It was suggested that provisional recognition as independent nations should be extended to "certain communities", formerly belonging to the Ottoman Empire, in view of the stage of development which they had achieved, subject to mandatory assistance until they were able to stand alone, and that the wishes of these communities "must be a principal consideration in the selection of the mandatory power."

---

[1] Howard, 218-219.
[2] See United States, Department of State, *Papers Relating to the Foreign Relations of the United States. The Paris Peace Conference.* 1919 (Washington, United States Government Printing Office, 1942-1947), 13 vols. Hereafter cited as *PPC*. See especially *PPC*, III, 785-786, 795-796 ; XI, 1, 5.

President Wilson did not share entirely the views of his British colleague and did not feel that it was the proper moment to discuss the partition of the Ottoman Empire. Mr. Wilson had heard talk of an American mandate, but he felt that the American people would not be inclined to accept one: [1]

> He himself had succeeded in getting the people of America to do many things and he might succeed in getting them to accept this burden also. But even if it was suggested that American troops should occupy Constantinople, or Mesopotamia, it was evident that they could not do so as they were not at war with Turkey. Therefore, it would, in his opinion, be extremely unwise to accept any form of mandate until they knew how it was intended to work.

These comments filled Lloyd George with "despair", [2] and the discussion continued in the afternoon session, when, among other things, the British Prime Minister indicated that he had unintentionally left "Kurdistan" out of the British proposal, since he had thought that the term "Mesopotamia" had covered this area. President Wilson once more repeated the reluctance of the American people to accept a "military responsibility in Asia", and stated that if the United States were asked to assume a mandate, the request would have to be postponed until he could explain the matter to the American people, "and try to bring them to the point of view which he desired them to assume."

Meanwhile, the President's proposal that the problem of the military occupation and control of the various areas be referred to the Military Advisers of the Supreme War Council was adopted. Finally, the Supreme Council adopted the basic resolution embodying the mandate principle: [3]

> It is the purpose of the Conference to separate from the Turkish Empire certain areas comprising, for example, Palestine, Syria, the Arab countries to the east of Palestine and Syria, Mesopotamia, Armenia, Cilicia, and perhaps additional areas of Asia Minor, and to put the development of their people under the guidance of Governments which are to act as Mandatories of the League of Nations.
>
> For similar reasons, and more particularly because of the historical misgovernment by the Turks of subject peoples and the terrible massacres of Armenians and others in recent years, the Allied and Associated Powers are agreed that Armenia, Syria, Mesopotamia, Palestine and Arabia must be completely severed from the Turkish Empire. This is without prejudice to the settlement of other parts of the Turkish Empire.

---

[1] *PPC*, III, 788. Secretary of State Lansing recorded on February 4: "Lloyd George and Pres't both said to me secretly they believed in a mandatory for Turkey." See also Allan NEVINS, *Henry White: Thirty Years of American Diplomacy* (New York, Harper and Brothers, 1930), 376.
[2] *PPC*, III, 789-790, 805, 807, 817.
[3] *Miller Diary*, IV, 130-131, 302-304.

It was agreed that the Powers should apply to these territories the principle "that the well-being and development" of the peoples formed "a sacred trust of civilization", and that, as had been proposed in the British draft, provision for the performance of the trust should be written into the Covenant of the League of Nations. It was thought that the tutelage of such peoples should be entrusted to certain advanced nations, although the character of the mandate was to vary according to differing conditions. Certain peoples, formerly part of the Ottoman Empire, had already reached such a stage of development that their independence could be recognized provisionally, subject to mandatory assistance until they could stand alone. Moreover, the desires of these communities were to be a principal consideration in the choice of a mandatory.

Conflicting Claims

But what of the peoples of the Near and Middle East? It was now their turn to speak of their hopes and their fears—to present their own views concerning the reconstruction of their homelands.

The Supreme Council—the Council of Ten—was ready to hear the claims and counter-claims. First came Eleutherios Venizelos, the Greek Premier, on February 3. The wily Cretan asked for Northern Epirus (Southern Albania), the Aegean Islands, Thrace and Western Asia Minor, with the city and *vilayet* of Smyrna. The Greek demands were examined by an expert committee, which prepared a report on March 6 accepting part of the Greek claims for Northern Epirus, the Italian representative dissenting. All delegations accepted the Greek claim to Thrace. Italy would make no recommendations for Western Asia Minor, because it could not be separated from the problem of Anatolia as a whole. Moreover, Greek and Italian ambitions clashed in Smyrna. [1]

The Arab Position

The Emir Feisal, the picturesque leader of the revolt in the desert, who appeared before the Council of Ten on February 6, had already been active in Paris in behalf of the Arabs for some time. The stalwart Arab warrior, a cultured man of distinguished bearing, made an excellent impression on all he met, except the French officials, who refused to accept him as a legitimate representative, undoubtedly because of his vigorous opposition to the ambitions of France in Syria. Feisal's memorandum of January 1 [2] explained that the aim of the Arab nationalist movement was "to unite the Arabs eventually into one nation". In view of their cultural differences, however, it would be impossible to "constrain them into one frame of government." Syria was sufficiently well advanced politically "to manage her own cultural affairs", with some foreign

---

[1] *PPC*, III, 859-866, 868-875; XI, 20; HOWARD, 222-24.
[2] Woodrow Wilson Papers, Box 13. Confidential. *Memorandum by the Emir Feisal*, 2 pp. January 1, 1919. See also *Miller Diary*, IV, 297-299; reprinted in Hurewitz, II, 38-39.

assistance. In Iraq it would be necessary "to oversee the educational processes" which were to "advance the tribes to the moral level of the towns." The Hejaz, on the other hand, was still suited to patriarchal conditions, a situation similar to that in the Yemen and Nejd.

In Palestine the enormous majority of the people are Arabs. The Jews are very close to the Arabs in blood, and there is no conflict of character between the two races. In principles we are absolutely at one. Nevertheless, the Arabs cannot risk assuming the responsibility of holding level the scales in the clash of races and religions that have, in this one province, so often involved the world in difficulties. They would wish for the effective superposition of a great trustee, so long as a representative local administration commended itself by actively promoting the material prosperity of the country.

Taken as a whole, in all the Arab lands, Feisal believed that if independence were granted, "the natural influences of race, language and interest" would soon draw the different Arab groups together into one people. The Great Powers would have to insure them "open internal frontiers, common railways and telegraphs, and uniform systems of education." The Arab leader asked the Powers not to force Western civilization as a whole upon the East, but to help the Orient to pick out the best from Western experience. In return, the Arabs could offer "little but gratitude."

Feisal and Chaim Weizmann, the president of the Zionist organization, had made an agreement on January 3, pledging mutual friendship and promising that after the Peace Conference the Arabs and Jews would delimit the boundaries of the Jewish community in Palestine. There is little doubt, however, that Feisal looked upon Palestine as an Arab country which formed an integral part of Syria. [1]

In his statement before the Council on February 6, Feisal asked for the independence of all Arabs in Asia south of the Alexandretta line. The Arabs, he asserted, were a civilized people, with a common language and natural frontiers. Feisal reminded his listeners of the promises which had been made concerning the liberation and unification of his people. [2]

---

[1] Text in *Miller Diary*, III, Document 141, pp. 188-189. George ANTONIUS, *The Arab Awakening* (Philadelphia, Lippincott, 1939), 437-439, thinks the document was signed on January 4. He also questions Feisal's authorization to sign a binding obligation and notes that Feisal concurred in the statement only if the Arabs obtained their independence. If the slightest modification were made, the document would not be valid. See also WEIZMANN, 234-235, 235-236, 245-246.

[2] *PPC*, III, 888-894. At the instance of Rabbi Stephen S. Wise, President Wilson received Emir Feisal and Colonel Lawrence on January 23. See Wise to Wilson, January 15; Gilbert F. Close to T. E. Lawrence, Lawrence to Close, January 21, 1919 in *Woodrow Wilson Papers*, IX-A 19. In general see also James T. SHOTWELL, *At the Paris Peace Conference* (New York, Macmillan, 1937), 129-32, 169-70; *Documents Upon Which is Based the Right of the People of Syria to be Consulted as to Their Political*

The Case for a Commission of Inquiry

It was already apparent to some who were conversant with the Middle East that an expert investigation might well be made of the situation there. As early as February 1, there was discussion in the American Commission to Negotiate Peace of sending Dr. James L. Barton and Mr. Frederick Howe for that purpose, and later on, of sending Dr. Leon Dominian along with Dr. Barton.[1] President Howard Bliss, of the American University of Beirut, who had come to Paris to plead for a just and equitable settlement of Middle Eastern problems, wrote to President Wilson on February 7, asking to be allowed to present his views. He told the President "how earnestly and even passionately the people of Syria" were depending on his Twelfth Point and on the Anglo-French Declaration of November 1918. They wanted a "fair opportunity to express their own political aspirations", though the French censorship and suppression in Syria prevented any such presentation. Bliss had heard rumors of a possible American Commission to investigate the situation in the Near East, and voiced his satisfaction:[2]

> If such a Commission is adequately backed by the French and British authorities at home *and in Syria* the result of their investigations ought to be helpful. In my opinion an international Commission would have

Future Before Any Government is Imposed Upon Them by the Peace Conference, 2 pp. (King Papers and Lybyer Papers); *Syrian Aspirations, March 13, 1919*, 5 pp. (King Papers); *The Plan of the "New Syria National League" For the Future Government of Syria* (King Papers); A French Memorandum, March 3, 1919 (King Papers).

[1] Late in 1918 an American group, headed by President H. P. Judson of the University of Chicago, had gone to Iran, returning to Paris in December. President Caleb F. Gates of Robert College, *Not to Me Only* (Princeton, 1940), 252, tells of their visit to Constantinople and notes Judson's "prejudiced and bitter opinions about both the Armenians and Turks." Secretary Lansing had an interview with Dr. Judson on January 19 and learned that Great Britain was "not disposed to continue to control Mesopotamia." Judson opposed a " 'greater Armenia,' considering Armenians about as bad governors as Turks." By March 6 the Barton-Dominian mission, fostered by Dr. Isaiah Bowman, was dropped altogether because the American Commissioners were not "quite clear as to why such a large mission should be sent, and what the particular interest of the United States was in obtaining any more than political information for so large a tract of Asia Minor, Syria, the Caucasus, etc." Lansing noted on March 13 that "White, Bliss and I listened to Bowman, Dominian and others on Commission to Turkey. We opposed their plan as too extensive." See also SHOTWELL, 99; BARTON, 97-100; *PPC*, XI, 8, 27.

[2] Woodrow Wilson Papers, IX-A 20, 25. Memorandum for the President, January 23, 1919; Memorandum on Syria, February 8, 1919; Howard Bliss to Woodrow Wilson, February 7, 11, 1919; Wilson to Bliss, February 11, 1919; Feisal to Wilson, February 11, 1919; Wilson to Feisal, February 14, 1919; Wilson to Newton D. Baker, February 8, 1919. On Bliss see especially Zeine N. ZEINE, *The Struggle for Arab Independence: Western Diplomacy and the Rise and Fall of Faisal's Kingdom in Syria* (Beirut, Khayat's, 1960), 69-71, 74-75, 94.

certain marked advantages over a purely American Commission and perhaps the change will still be made. I believe that the report of any Commission, made up of fair, wide-minded and resourceful men, would show that the Syrians desire the erection of an independent state or states under the care, for the present, of a Power, or of the "League of Nations". I believe the Power designated by the people would be America, for the Syrians believe in American disinterestedness; or England, for the people trust her sense of justice and believe in her capacity. I believe that French guardianship would be rejected for three reasons: serious-minded men in Syria fear that the people of Syria would imitate France's less desirable qualities; they do not consider the French to be good administrators; they believe that France would exploit the country for her own material and political advantage. They do not trust her. If America should be indicated as the Power desired I earnestly hope that she will not decline.

At the same time, the Emir Feisal advised the military representatives on the Supreme Council that "the Associated Powers should send a commission to Syria to establish the facts and ascertain the wishes of the people, and that in the meantime no further troops should be sent." If this were done, it was probable that an agreement concerning Syria could be reached which would "satisfy the French claims and those of the Arab tribes." Dr. Bliss wrote to President Wilson on February 11, that if a Commission were to be sent to Syria, "no time should be lost in sending it." Like Feisal, Dr. Bliss hoped the Syrian problem would be taken up before President Wilson left for the United States on February 14.

Dr. Bliss, a "distinguished looking college president of the long, thin Yankee type", actually appeared before the Council of Ten on February 13, and presented his evidence "with a quiet but forceful and convincing manner." He called for the sending of a commission to Syria to find out the facts in the case. Syria was under martial law and it was impossible to obtain an "accurate statement of the Syrian point of view except by an examination on the spot by commissioners authorized by the Peace Conference." Since General Allenby was in control of Syria, Lord Balfour, the British representative, protested against Dr. Bliss' insinuation and wanted to know what he had meant. Bliss refused to amplify his statement because he said "they should find out the situation on the spot and not take his word for it."[1] It was the Bliss suggestion which seems to have germinated, officially, the idea of a neutral, inter-allied, or mixed commission

[1] *PPC*, III, 1015-1020; XI, 61, 63, 66-67, 72, 76, 79, 85, 87, 99, 116, 133-134, 140, 145-146, 150, 155; *Miller Diary*, XIV, 392. Charles R. Crane remarks in his unpublished *Memoirs*: "During the spring of 1919 Dr. Howard Bliss ... appeared in Paris to make an appeal for the people whom he and his father had served for so many years. He was one of the most inspiring educators and had a wonderful understanding of and sympathy for the people of the Near East .... He went to see President Wilson and urged him to appoint a commission to go to Syria and Palestine to find out what the people really wanted, and what they really feared, before their fate was determined."

to the Near East, which ultimately became the King-Crane Commission.

After hearing the Syrian problem discussed during the next several days, Secretary of State Lansing, on February 18, suggested the sending of a Commission to Syria, but the question was postponed. A commission of investigation might arouse false hopes and sow the seeds of popular discontent, whatever conclusions it might reach. By February 22 Lansing thought it "was so late in the day that he was skeptical of the wisdom of trying to send a mission to Syria." General Tasker H. Bliss suggested that the Emir Feisal ought to be called in, and that both Dr. Howard Bliss and Professor W. L. Westermann be consulted, after which a definite recommendation could be made. [1]

The result was that Dr. Bliss appeared before the American Commission to Negotiate Peace on February 26 and urgently reiterated his hope that an Inter-Allied Commission be sent to Syria and the Near East. [2] Whatever its findings, "it would satisfy the demands of honor." Secretary Lansing, whose earlier proposal had "been refused by Pichon under orders from Clemenceau", was prepared to press the matter, provided he could be sure of British support. The American Commissioners agreed with Dr. Bliss that Syria should certainly not be handed over to anyone before the wishes of the people were consulted. Mr. Henry White wondered how a commission could obtain a comprehensive view of the Syrian problem, because of British and French propaganda. Dr. Bliss recognized the difficulties, but believed that much could be accomplished if men of dignity and character were selected. If it were impossible to send an Inter-Allied Commission, Bliss strongly recommended that an American group go out, "which could talk freely to all classes of Syrians." He did not favor calling Syrians to Paris, because it would be hard to choose proper men, and he "distrusted French ideals in this matter." But at the end of the interview, Mr. Lansing informed Dr. Bliss that "no decision was imminent."

The Armenian Case

Discussion of the Arab problem led naturally to that of Armenia. The Armenian Delegation, led by Mr. Aharonian and Boghos Nubar Pasha, presented the case for an independent Armenia on February 26. [3]

---

[1] *PPC*, XI, 61, 66-67.

[2] *PPC*, XI, 76-77. Mr. H. G. Wilson advised the Commissioners that Mr. Grew had informed Dr. Bliss and Dr. Westermann concerning the question of a reliable American observer to be sent to Syria. It was decided that Mr. W. H. Buckler should not be sent to Syria.

[3] *PPC*, IV, 147-157. For British views on the problem of Kurdistan, and on Boghos Nubar Pasha, in December 1919, see United Kingdom, Foreign Office, *Documents on British Foreign Policy 1919-1939*. Edited by E. L. Woodward and Rohan Butler. First Series (London, H. M. S. O., 1952), IV, 920-24. Hereafter cited as *British Documents, 1919-1939*.

The Armenians demanded Cilicia, including the *sanjaks* of Marash and Adana, with the port of Alexandretta; the six Armenian *vilayets* of Erzerum, Bitlis, Van, Diarbekir, Harput, Sivas and the port of Trebizond on the Black Sea; the territory of the Republic of Armenia in the Caucasus, with Erivan, southern Tiflis, southwestern Elisabetpol and Kars, with the exception of northern Ardahan. Liberated from the Ottoman Empire, Armenia was to be placed under the joint protection of the Powers, with a twenty year mandate. But the problem of Armenia was complicated by the fact that for generations the Armenians had been scattered, mostly by their commercial pursuits, to the far-flung corners of the Ottoman Empire and even the world, and there was hardly any region in which they constituted a clear-cut majority of the population.

The Zionist Position

On February 27, the Zionists presented their plea for a Jewish National Home in Palestine. The problem of Palestine was a dangerously delicate one. It was as difficult of equitable solution as any before the Conference, for as David Hunter Miller had advised President Wilson in January, "the rule of self-determination would prevent the establishment of a Jewish State in Palestine", just as it would prevent "the establishment of any autonomous Armenia." [1] As outlined by Mr. Sokolow on February 27, the Jews desired a "national home" on the basis of the Balfour Declaration, in which the rights of all would be protected. A British mandatory was preferred under which Jewish immigration and local government would be preserved. When Dr. Chaim Weizmann, President of the Zionist Organization, appeared before the Council of Ten, he stated quite frankly that the Zionists wanted [2]

> merely to establish in Palestine, under a mandatory Power, an administration, not necessarily Jewish, which would render it possible to send into Palestine 70 to 80,000 Jews annually. The Association would require to have permission at the same time to build Jewish schools, where Hebrew would be taught, and in that way to build up gradually a nationality which would be as Jewish as the French nation was French and the British nation British. Later on, when the Jews formed the large majority, they would be ripe to establish such a Government as would answer to the state of the development of the country and to their ideals.

But would it be possible to reconcile Dr. Weizmann's position with the legitimate demands of the Arabs? The Jewish population of Palestine

---

[1] See HOWARD, 226. Also Arabian Representation at Paris. Palestine. *Résumé de la Requête en Arabe Présentée par les Délégués de la Syrie du Sud (Palestine) au Congrès de Paix* (Lybyer Papers). A description of the Zionist Delegations at the Paris Conference may be found in O. I. JANOWSKY, *The Jews and Minority Rights*: 1898-1919 (New York, Columbia, 1933), Ch. VII.
[2] *PPC*, IV, 169; *Miller Diary*, XV, 115-116. See also WEIZMANN, 243-245; TAYLOR, 26-34.

at the time constituted a bare 10 per cent of the people, and political Zionism was now to make its impact on a very small country, with quite limited natural resources, in which a very large Arab population, since the beginning of the First World War, had "become strongly conscious of its national aspirations." [1] Indeed, Palestine had been predominantly Arabic and Moslem almost since the Caliph Omar had carried the standards of the Prophet to Jerusalem in 638 A. D. To give justice to all parties would require all the tact, skill, knowledge and insight which men of good will could bring to the settlement.

The Turks at Paris

As the Arabs were opposed to the Jewish claims in Palestine, so the Turks rejected the Armenian position. On the eve of the Conference, the "Turkish Wilsonian League", with Professor Hussein Bey of Robert College as one of the founders, prepared a program asking President Wilson for American supervision of Turkish affairs for "not less than fifteen nor more than twenty-five years." [2] Specifically the program called for:

The preservation of the sovereignty of the Sultan and a constitutional form of government.

The protection of the rights of minorities. Eligibility of all Ottoman nationalities to all government offices.

The appointment of an American Adviser-in-Chief with staff of expert assistants to each of the following ministries: Finance, Agriculture, Industry and Commerce, Public Works and Public Instruction these advisers constituting together an American Commission.

The forming by an American Adviser-in-Chief of a Board of legal experts, selected from such countries as may be deemed advisable, for the reform of the judicial system.

The Supervision by an American Inspector-General of the Police and Gendarmerie. Prison reform by a board of American experts.

An American Inspector-in-Chief in every province in Turkey.

The assurance by international guarantee of the complete neutrality of Turkey during the period of American supervision.

The Congress of Liberal Turks, represented at Paris by General Sherif Pasha, presented a number of memoranda asking the preservation of the

---

[1] Hans KOHN, *Revolutions and Dictatorships* (Cambridge, Harvard, 1939), 321-322.
[2] From the Lybyer Papers: "The Turkish Wilsonian League", transmitted by the American Military Attaché at Rome to Military Intelligence, G. H. Q., A. E. F., January 7. Original appeal dated December 5, 1918. See also Professor Lybyer's conversation with Professor A. der Hagopian, January 24, 1919, concerning the "Turkish Wilsonian League". Hagopian contended that the principal aim was to retain a "very large area" for Turkey. The major support came from "the large majority of newspapers and the leaders of the professional and educated classes".

territorial integrity of the Ottoman Empire. A few Kurds demanded independence for Kurdistan.[1]

So the Paris Peace Conference was confronted with a veritable series of Gordian knots in the Middle East. What was to be done about the Arab lands, the Jews of Palestine, the Armenians and the Turks? Should the territorial integrity of the Ottoman Empire be preserved or the constituent elements allowed to go their own way in unlimited self-determination? Who could offer a satisfactory solution to what seemed almost insoluble problems? By what methods could the grave questions of the hour be solved? Would the seemingly reasonable suggestion that a commission be sent to investigate the facts and report with recommendations be accepted by the Powers?

---

[1] HOWARD, 226-227, fn 27, p. 451.

CHAPTER II

An Inter-Allied Commission

THE ORIGINS OF AN INVESTIGATION

The hopes and fears of the Near Eastern peoples, the clash of fundamental interests among the Great Powers, particularly between France and Great Britain, and the direct opposition of the American Delegation at Paris to the secret treaties of 1915-1917 partitioning the Ottoman Empire were enough in themselves to call for some sort of impartial investigation in the Near and Middle East.

The Resumption of Discussion

There had been many interesting discussions concerning what should be done about the peoples and nations of the East when the problem formally came before the Peace Conference again on March 20, 1919. [1] In an interview among Clemenceau, Colonel House and David Lloyd George on March 7 [2], the latter asked House "whether America would be prepared to accept a mandatory in respect of the Turkish Empire", and he pressed House especially as to an American mandate for Armenia and Constantinople. House doubted America's willingness to take the

---

[1] President Wilson was absent from the Conference and in the United States during February 14-March 14, 1919. Following a meeting with Rabbi Stephen S. Wise and Louis Marshall, on March 3, he was quoted as having declared that "the Allied Nations with the fullest concurrence of our own Government and people are agreed that in Palestine shall be laid the foundations of a Jewish Commonwealth". (See *Statement to the International Commission on Mandates in Turkey. American Section.* By Zionist Commission to Palestine, June 1919.) The statement was cited in a number of papers in the Near East and, on April 13, at the suggestion of Professor Westermann, Secretary of State Lansing inquired of the President whether he had been correctly quoted. President Wilson replied on April 16 saying that he had not used any of the words quoted, although he had used their substance. He remarked, however, that the expression "foundations of a Jewish Commonwealth" went "a little further" than his idea at the time. All he had meant to do was "to corroborate our expressed acquiescence in the position of the British Government with regard to the future of Palestine"—*i.e.* to reindorse the Balfour Declaration. See *PPC*, XI, 155. See also American Commission to Negotiate Peace, 1918-1919. Department of State, Vol. 157, National Archives (185. 5137/103-104). Nevertheless, the statement was continually used in Zionist propaganda. See, for example, Israel COHEN, *The Zionist Movement* (New York, Z.O.A., 1946), 121; Carl J. FRIEDRICH, *American Policy Toward Palestine* (Washington, Public Affairs Press, 1944), 7. See also *The Jewish National Home in Palestine.* Hearings before the Committee on Foreign Affairs. House of Representatives. Seventy-Eighth Congress, Second Session; O. H. Res. 418 and H. Res. 419: Resolutions Relative to the Jewish National Home in Palestine. February 8, 9, 15, and 16, 1944. With Appendix of Documents Relating to the Jewish National Home in Palestine (Washington, 1944), *passim*.

[2] David LLOYD GEORGE, I,189-190; HOUSE,IV,358-359; Lady Gertrude BELL, *The Letters of Gertrude Bell* (London, Benn, 1927), II, 467-69.

Turkish mandate, though it might be prepared to accept more restricted mandates for Armenia and Constantinople, to exercise some sort of general supervision over Anatolia, and would not shirk its international duties. Lloyd George supposed that France would take Syria, only to have Clemenceau add, "and Cilicia". Anxious for a settlement, the British Prime Minister urged Clemenceau to make an agreement with the Emir Feisal concerning Syria, but Clemenceau, determined on the Syrian prize, was afraid France would "have to fight him." In the end, it appeared to Lloyd George that the United States would accept a mandate for Constantinople and Armenia, and general supervision of Anatolia, that France would take over Syria and a portion of Cilicia, that Great Britain would have Palestine and Mesopotamia, and Italy, if it stood by the Treaty of London, would move into Adalia and, perhaps, the region of the Caucasus.

But the fundamental discussion did not come until the meeting of the Council of Four on March 20 in the apartment of the British Prime Minister, when there was a lengthy controversy over the secret treaties according to which the Ottoman Empire was to be carved up.[1] M. Pichon, the French Foreign Minister, stated the French case for the control of Syria and Cilicia. Great Britain, having settled the Mosul problem with France on February 15, made no objection, although the French claim in Damascus, Homs, Hama and Aleppo was contested.

As the deliberations proceeded, President Wilson explained that he was not indifferent to the secret treaties or the understandings with the Arabs, but since the mandate principle aready had been accepted on January 30, he thought it wise to find out whether the French were really wanted in Syria and the British in Mesopotamia. There were, moreover, other serious problems concerning Cilicia and Armenia. President Wilson[2]

> suggested that the fittest men that could be obtained should be selected to form an Inter-Allied Commission to go to Syria, extending their inquiries, if they led them beyond the confines of Syria. Their object should be to elucidate the state of opinion and the soil to be worked on by any mandatory. They should be asked to come back and tell the Conference what they found with regard to these matters. He made the suggestion, not because he lacked confidence in the experts whose views he had heard, such as Dr. Howard Bliss and General Allenby. These, however, had been involved in some way with the population, with special objects either educational or military. If we were to send a

---

[1] *PPC*, V, 1-14; BAKER, III, 1-19. At a meeting on February 20, the American Commissioners agreed that the United States intended completely to "ignore these agreements in the discussion of these problems unless by chance, they happen to contain certain provisions which we consider to be just and proper, in accordance with our declared principles." *PPC*, XI, 50-51.

[2] *PPC*, V, 12; BAKER, III, 16-19. See also David LLOYD GEORGE, *Memoirs*, II, 1071-1075.

Commission with no previous contact with Syria, it would, at any rate, convince the world that the Conference had tried to do all it could to find the most scientific basis possible for a settlement. The Commission should be composed of an equal number of French, British, Italian and American representatives. He would send it with *carte blanche* to tell the facts as they found them.

Mr. Clemenceau, no doubt with his tongue in his cheek, agreed in principle to an inquiry, but thought it necessary to have certain guarantees. Since other mandates were involved, and the problem was "extremely delicate", the inquiry should not be confined to Syria. Moreover, "Orientals were very timid and afraid to say what was at the back of their minds", so it would be difficult "to get the real feelings of the people" if the investigation were "merely superficial." Hence, the French Premier would need at least twenty-four hours for proper reflection on the matter. Clemenceau, however, was concerned with more basic questions. He thought the Emir Feisal "practically a soldier of England", and more French soldiers might be required in Syria. Despite obvious difficulties, Clemenceau was trying to bring himself "to agree with the principles propounded by President Wilson". He believed that the members of the Commission should be carefully chosen and should inquire into every Near Eastern mandate. Subject to these reservations, Clemenceau would accept the Wilson proposal "in principle". [1] But did he accept it "in fact"?

Lloyd George had no objection to an investigation in Palestine and Mesopotamia, where Great Britain was primarily concerned, and was not opposed to sending a Commission into Armenia. President Wilson, too, saw advantages "in a unified inquiry into Turkish mandates", while Lloyd George pointed out that if this extension were to be given to the Commission "it was essential that it should get to work at once", as the military burden fell primarily on British forces. Arthur James Balfour, on the other hand, was afraid of postponing the conclusion of peace. There was something to Balfour's point, although President Wilson did not agree with him. Lloyd George insisted that the Turks were "entitled to know who would be the mandatory", but Wilson thought that it was "rather that they ought to know how much was to remain Turkish." The President felt that Turkey was entitled to know whether it was to have territory of its own and what other parts of the late Empire were

---

[1] Clemenceau told House on March 20 that the Council of Four had accepted Wilson's idea of an investigation and House congratulated him (*House Diary*, March 20, 1919). Harold NICOLSON, (*Peace-Making*, 286-287) noted in his Diary on March 20: "Supreme Council... They ... decided to send a Commission of Enquiry and Research to Asia Minor (to obtain the wishes of the peoples themselves). Very pretty, but what about a Treaty of Peace with Turkey? Relations between French and ourselves becoming strained over Syria."

to be placed under the League of Nations. Subsequently it would be informed of the identity of its next-door neighbor. Mr. Balfour wondered whether it would be wise to include western Anatolia within the purview of the Commission. Constantinople was mainly a military question, but south of that area were regions which the Greeks were claiming. As the discussion closed, Lloyd George, who moved that President Wilson prepare the instructions for the Commission, stated that the group should not travel beyond Armenia.

The Commission's Instructions

The Armenians began immediately to set up their own section of the proposed Inter-Allied Commission on Mandates in Turkey. On March 20 the American Commission to Negotiate Peace decided that the American group should consist of five officials, with four field clerks, and it was thought that "a sum of $18,500 to pay the expenses of this Mission, would not be excessive." [1] Two days later, on March 22, President Wilson had prepared his Instructions for the Inter-Allied Commission, which were accepted on March 25, with Clemenceau agreeing, as usual, "in principle", and Lloyd George giving his "lukewarm" support. [2] After reiterating *verbatim* the resolution of January 30 embodying the principle of the mandate and repeating the Anglo-French Declaration of November 8, 1918, concerning the liberation of the Arabic peoples, the Instructions asserted:

> The Conference... feels obliged to acquaint itself as intimately as possible with the sentiments of the people of those regions with regard to the future administration of their affairs. You are requested, accordingly, to visit those regions to acquaint yourselves as fully as possible with the state of opinion there with regard to these matters, with the social, racial, and economic conditions, a knowledge of which might serve to guide the judgment of the Conference, and to form as definite an opinion as the circumstances and the time at your disposal will permit, of the divisions of territory and assignment of mandates which will be most likely to promote the order, peace and development of those peoples and countries.

But those who objected to the idea of a Commission continued their opposition. Curiously enough, on Tuesday evening, March 25, the very

[1] *PPC*, XI, 128.

[2] See *Miller Diary*, XV, SM 140, pp. 505-08; BANER, I, 77-78. See also King Papers: American Commission to Negotiate Peace, *Future Administration of Certain Portions of the Turkish Empire Under the Mandatory System*. Instructions for Commissioners from the Peace Conference to Make Enquiries in Certain Portions of the Turkish Empire which are to be Permanently Separated from Turkey and put under the Guidance of Governments Acting as Mandatories, for the League of Nations. Mimeographed, 3 pp. For correspondence see Hankey to Close, March 21, 1919; Close to Balfour, March 22; Balfour to Close, March 25, 1919 Woodrow Wilson Papers, IX-A 32.

day on which the organization and instructions of the Commission had been approved, an informal meeting of certain British and French experts took place, at which Colonel T. E. Lawrence, Miss Gertrude Bell, Sir Valentine Chirol, of the British Delegation, and Robert de Caix, Philippe Millet, Henri Brenier, and Auguste Gauvain, from the French group, were present. Called together by Mr. Henry Wickham Steed, of the London *Times*, they discussed Middle Eastern problems for nearly six hours. The French were much upset by the Emir Feisal's arrival in Paris as a delegate to the Peace Conference, but the group, for the moment at least, seemed in substantial accord. They were all opposed to sending a Commission to Syria on the ground that it might upset and unsettle the people. Colonel Lawrence did not believe that the movement for Arab unity had any serious political value for the present or the near future, and declared that there was no connection between Feisal and his father, King Hussein, of the Hejaz. In the end, there was such general agreement that Lawrence undertook to advise Feisal to remain in Paris, while the French were to get into touch with him. In this way it was hoped to avoid the necessity of sending a Commission to Syria and to settle the problem in Paris. [1]

No one could have been more pleased about the decision to send a Commission to the Near East than the Emir Feisal, who had written to President Wilson on March 24 that he could not find words to express his gratitude for the opportunity now to be given the Arabs to express "their own purposes and ideals for their national future." [2] Feisal, accompanied by Colonel Lawrence, called on Colonel House on March 29, on the eve of his intended departure for Syria, and told him he thought the idea of sending a Commission to Syria was the best thing he had ever heard. The Arabs had sent Feisal to see the different European peoples and choose the best one for a mandatory. He liked the British very much, but had since come to know the Americans and wondered whether the United States would accept a mandate for Syria, in view of the Anglo-French friction on the subject. House questioned American acceptance of a mandate, and Feisal told him that the Arabs preferred death to a French mandate, while Lawrence added that if the British took over Syria, the French would accuse them of being hypocrites. Lawrence explained that the Syrian Arabs desired a British mandate, while the Arabs in the United States wanted an American mandate over

---

[1] For the discussions at the meeting see *Miller Diary*, VII, Document No. 608, pp. 169-170; Henry Wickham STEED, *Through Thirty Years* (Garden City, N. Y., Doubleday, Page, 1925), Pt. II, 300.

[2] Woodrow Wilson Papers, IX-A, 33. The Emir Feisal to President Wilson, March 24, 1919. Feisal hoped that Mr. Wilson would "continue to encourage us forward on the path of moral and material development." For Feisal's attitude see also Lord BIRDWOOD, M.V.O., *Nuri es Said: A Study in Arab Leadership* (London, Cassell, 1959) 105.

Syria. Since the Chairman of the proposed Commission to the Near East was to be an American, Colonel Lawrence hoped he could be induced to report in favor of an American mandate in Syria, after satisfying himself as to the wishes of the people. He added that he had found serious opposition in certain Parisian quarters to sending a Commission.[1]

APPOINTMENT OF THE AMERICAN SECTION OF THE INTER-ALLIED COMMISSION ON MANDATES IN TURKEY

The problem now was to appoint the members of the Commission, and particularly the American Section, to organize its machinery, and to get it started to the Near East at the earliest possible moment. Immediately after the meeting of March 20, President Wilson began to think of the American members, and the name of Charles R. Crane had already occurred to him. Ray Stannard Baker, with whom the President had discussed the matter, had proposed the name of Mr. Georges Rublee, who had been a member of the Federal Trade Commission, as well as American delegate to the Allied Maritime Transport Council in London during 1918-1919. He was "practically unoccupied", and thanks to his experience, Baker thought Rublee would be "a valuable man to consider." Dr. W. L. Westermann, Chief of the Division of Western Asia, had also made a very favorable impression on Baker. He not only had "a thoroughgoing knowledge of the affairs of Asiatic Turkey", but was "a firm believer in the right of human beings to decide their own destiny."[2] Mr. Vance McCormick, who had been Chairman of the Democratic National Campaign Committee in 1918 and who served as an adviser to the President in Paris, was also a possibility.[3] Baker also noted that President Henry Churchill King, of Oberlin College, was in France. He had met Dr. King in Rome just before the close of the war and the two had visited some of the Italian prison camps. Wilson, too, had met Dr. King before,

---

[1] See Notes of a Conversation between Colonel House and Emir Feisal, held at Hotel Crillon, on March 29th, 6 p.m., Colonel Lawrence being interpreter; David GARNETT, *The Letters of T. E. Lawrence* (New York, Doubleday, Doran, 1939), 273-275. The Lawrence statement about the proposed Commission is somewhat curious, for he had attended the meeting of experts on March 25 at which the sending of a Commission was opposed.

[2] Woodrow Wilson Papers, IX-A 32. R. S. Baker to President Wilson, March 21, 1919. Westermann wrote House on March 28 suggesting that he be attached as an expert to the Interallied Commission while it was in Paris (File 181.91/61, National Archives).

[3] Woodrow Wilson Papers, IX-A 33. Vance McCormick to President Wilson, March 23, 1919. While willing, if the President so desired, McCormick doubted that he should go to Syria. When he talked with Lansing on March 23, the latter advised against going because of McCormick's work in Paris. McCormick felt that both Colonel House and Herbert Hoover were involved in a political manipulation to get him out of Paris. See *Diaries of Vance McCormick* (privately printed), March 21, 22, 1919.

and Baker considered him a distinct possibility. King was "a man of liberal spirit" and commanded "very high respect and esteem in America." [1]

The Choice of King and Crane

Dr. King was at Coblentz at this time, but on March 23, he had a "late telephone message" from Baker indicating that Colonel House wanted to see him, and returned at once to Paris for a conference on March 26 with House, who wanted to find out whether he would be suitable for the mission to the Near East, along with Charles R. Crane. The Texan "found King an intelligent vigorous fellow and arranged with him that he should go." Another "excited afternoon caller" on Colonel House was Professor Felix Frankfurter, of the Harvard Law School, who came in behalf of the Zionist Organization. As House recorded: "The Jews have it that the Inter-Allied Commission which is to be sent to Syria is about to cheat Jewry of Palestine." But House "assured him there was no such intention", explained "the real situation so he might take it to his fellow Hebrews", and indicated that the Balfour Declaration was to be honored. Frankfurter gained the impression that the Inter-Allied Commission was merely a device for temporarily postponing the issue. [2]

At a meeting of the American Commissioners the next day, March 27, Mr. White informed the group of President Wilson's wishes to send Dr. King and Mr. Crane "as field observers to Syria." The President "felt these two men were particularly qualified to go to Syria because they knew nothing about it." Secretary Lansing inquired whether there was any written record of the President's desires "in order that the question of the whole Mission to Turkey could be settled accordingly." [3] Two days later, however, it was impossible for the Commissioners to take any action relative to the proposed mission to the Near East, since they were unable to ascertain exactly what President Wilson desired Dr. King and Mr. Crane to do or what "their sphere of investigation" was to be. But by April 3, the American Commission to Negotiate Peace duly noted that they were to serve as "the American representatives on an Inter-Allied Committee to investigate conditions in those portions of Turkey" which were "to be permanently separated from Turkey and put under

---

[1] Baker notes that shortly after the meeting of March 25, President Wilson remarked that he wanted "to put the two ablest Americans now in Europe on that commission." Baker "suggested President Henry Churchill King of Oberlin College, a man of sound judgment and high ideals. The President immediately asked me to get in touch with President King and he was appointed, with Charles R. Crane, as a member of the commission." BAKER, I, 77-78.

[2] King Papers: King to Baker, May 6, 1922; King *Diary*, March 23, 1919; House *Diary*, March 26, 1919.

[3] *PPC*, XI, 133-134.

the guidance of Governments acting as Mandatories for the League of Nations." Now the question was that of the assignment of experts to serve with them, and it was proposed that, if they concurred in the advisability of being given expert assistance, they write a letter to the Commissioners requesting it.[1]

With arrangements evidently soon to be made for an extended leave from the active Presidency of Oberlin College, Dr. King prepared to assume his new responsibilities as one of the American commissioners in the Near East. He wrote:[2]

> In accepting the President's call to a special service for world peace in this critical time, I am counting confidently upon the loyal cooperation of Oberlin students as well as faculty in assuring that the College shall suffer no loss from my continued absence. I was guided in forming the decision, which the College expressed its willingness that I should make, not only by my own sense of duty to take this rather heavy responsibility, if the President really wanted to have me do it, but also by the clear and emphatic judgment of the two College Trustees here, Mr. H.H. Johnson and Dr. Dana Durand. The official instructions for the Commission indicate that it covers considerably more ground than I first supposed, and involves inquiry concerning Palestine, Syria, the Arab countries to the east of Palestine, Mesopotamia, Armenia, Cilicia, and perhaps additional areas in Asia Minor.

Who's Who in the King-Crane Commission

While neither President King nor Mr. Crane was an "expert" on the Near East, in the usual sense of that much-abused term, both were men of experience and sound judgment. Dr. Henry Churchill King, born in 1858, had been a professor at Oberlin College for many years and had served as president since 1902.[3] He had traveled considerably, was especially familiar with the Holy Land through his Biblical studies, and was the author of a number of books, pamphlets and articles, particularly

---

[1] *PPC*, XI, 140, 145.
[2] King Papers. From an undated letter. See also the cable, March 27, 1919, to Dean Bosworth. King noted in his *Diary*, March 27: "Conferred with H. H. Johnson on Syrian Commission. He heartily approves my going." On the next day he had an appointment with R. S. Baker and later talked with Professor Westermann, Dr. George R. Montgomery, Professor David McGee, Captain William Yale, and Dr. C. R. Watson, of the Division of Western Asia.
[3] Professor Charles H. A. WAGER, of Oberlin, (*To Whom It May Concern* [Boston, Marshall Jones, 1938], 156), wrote of him: "His frankness, directness, sincerity have produced an administrative method as unlike as possible to the sinuous and serpentine courses that many persons believe to be a necessary element in the government of an institution. There have been no backstairs to the President's office. Trojan and Tyrian have alike had entrance there and been treated in exactly the same fashion." See also King Papers, for Dr. King's letter to W. F. Bohn, November 13, 1918, for his Y.M.C.A. work with the American Expeditionary Forces. See also Donald M. LOVE, *Henry Churchill King of Oberlin* (New Haven, Yale, 1956), 300 pp.

in the field of religious literature. He had been serving with the Y.M.C.A. in the American Expeditionary Forces since August 1918.

Charles R. Crane, also born in 1858, had already had a very interesting career. A Chicago business man, he was for many years the head of the well-known Crane Company, a manufacturer of valves and fittings. President Taft had appointed him as American Minister to China in 1909, although the appointment was canceled by Secretary of State Philander C. Knox, because of an "indiscreet" speech, in which Mr. Crane had predicted war with Japan, on the eve of his departure for China. In 1912, therefore, he joined the Democratic Party in support of Woodrow Wilson, becoming the Vice-Chairman of the Finance Committee of the Wilson campaign fund. Very young in life, Mr. Crane decided to make an art and science of traveling, and he had made many trips to the Near East, beginning in 1878. As one of his associates had remarked: "Mr. Crane had been in the Near East many times and had many friends there and he had a feel for what was going on. He never was a fact gatherer, but he was extremely sensitive to movements and personalities." Thanks to their training and their complementary personalities, the two American Commissioners were to work exceedingly well together. [1]

But what of those who were to serve the Commission in a technical capacity? First of these to be selected was Professor Albert Howe Lybyer, of the University of Illinois, who became the General Technical Adviser of the Commission. Dr. Lybyer had come to Europe as a member of Colonel E. M. House's "Inquiry", serving with that body from August to November 1918, when he became an Assistant in the Balkan Division of the American Commission to Negotiate Peace, under Professor Clive Day. Lybyer had substantially completed his work in the Balkan Division during the early part of March, with a final memorandum on "The Balkan Policy of the Peace Conference", and was about to leave the Conference for some sort of educational or religious enterprise or work with the Near East Relief. He was much in doubt as to his immediate plans, when, about March 8, Professor Robert J. Kerner, the brilliant young expert on Central Europe, returned from his mission to Austria and Czechoslovakia under Dr. Archibald C. Coolidge. Lybyer and Kerner were constant companions, and, in the light of his Central European experience, the latter proposed a similar mission for the Near East. When

---

[1] The materials on Mr. Crane and Dr. King are taken primarily from the *Who's Who* of the King-Crane Commission, compiled by Professor Lybyer in *Lybyer Papers*. A further indication of Mr. Crane's many-sided activities is indicated by his membership on the Board of Trustees of Robert College, Istanbul. He was also President of the Board of Trustees of Istanbul Women's College, and President of the Marine Biological Laboratory at Woods Hole, Massachusetts. He was also President Wilson's Minister to China (1920-1921).

Lybyer called on Dr. King on March 29, he found that King was going to Syria "on a commission appointed by the President and the other governments", some of which were not very pleased about the matter. Lybyer was somewhat doubtful about the value of a Commission and skeptical about serving on it. Later on, he joined Kerner, who immediately advised him to "go out as secretary", since "it would be a great opportunity." So he was reluctantly persuaded. Within a few days arrangements were made and by the end of the first week in April, Lybyer seemed "a settled member" of the "King-Crane expedition". [1]

The two other Technical Advisers were now to be chosen. While several people were interviewed, among them Captain H. L. Hoskins, in the end, Captain William Yale, U. S. A., and Dr. George Redington Montgomery were appointed, Yale as Technical Adviser for the Southern Regions of Turkey and Montgomery for the Northern Regions. Both were placed on the technical staff from Dr. Westermann's office at his specific request. Professor Westermann did not desire personally to go to the Near East, but did insist that two of his men should accompany the Commission.

Both Yale and Montgomery appeared well qualified for the tasks which confronted them. Captain Yale was a graduate of the Sheffield Scientific School of Yale University, and had served as a civil engineer with the Isthmian Canal Commission in Panama in 1907. During 1912-1917 he was in the service of the Standard Oil Company of New York, spending a number of years in the Ottoman Empire, 1912-1913 and 1913-1917. Late in the summer of 1917, following the entry of the United States into the World War, Yale was appointed Special Agent of the Department of State and sent to Cairo to report on political developments in the Middle East. Soon thereafter he was given a commission in the United States Army, made assistant to the military attaché in London, and assigned to duty as Military Observer to the Egyptian Expeditionary Force in Palestine. He served in that capacity from June 1918 to January

---

[1] Lybyer Papers. A. H. Lybyer to Mrs. Lybyer, March 29, April 1, 1919. Lybyer noted that Dr. Kerner was "a great help to me.... He had come up since his trip to Central Europe.... He predicted the Hungarian revolution quite closely. He has much shrewd political insight, and personal evaluation of men...." For Lybyer's memorandum on "The Balkan Policy of the Peace Conference" see Lybyer Papers and Woodrow Wilson Papers, IX-A 40, 42. See also Lybyer *Diary*, March 31, 1919. Lybyer was well qualified for the position of General Technical Adviser. An historian, he had been a Professor of History at the University of Illinois and at Oberlin College, and for seven years (1900-1907) at Robert College. He was well-known for his *Government of the Ottoman Empire During the Time of Suleyman the Magnificent* (Cambridge, Harvard, 1913) and his article on "The Ottoman Turks and the Routes of Oriental Trade" in the *English Historical Review* (October 1916), not to mention other writings.

1919 in both Palestine and Syria, and was then called back to Paris, as an expert on Arab affairs, to serve under Professor Westermann.[1]

Dr. G.R. Montgomery was born at Marash, in the Ottoman Empire, and had the experience of long residence in the East. A clergyman, he had studied at the University of Berlin and at Yale, where he received the doctorate of philosophy in 1901. Dr. Montgomery had written a number of religious items, and had been appointed special assistant to Ambassador Morgenthau at Constantinople in March 1916. He had come to France in 1917 about the time of the American entry into the war.

Early in April 1919, therefore, despite all the obstacles which stood in the way, the personnel of the King-Crane Commission was being made up. In the end, the members of the American group consisted of the two Commissioners, Dr. Henry Churchill King and Mr. Charles R. Crane; Professor Albert H. Lybyer, General Technical Adviser; Dr. George R. Montgomery, Technical Adviser for the Northern Regions of Turkey; Captain William Yale, U. S. A., Technical Adviser for the Southern Regions of Turkey; Captain Donald M. Brodie, U. S. A., Secretary and Treasurer; Dr. Sami Haddad, instructor in the School of Medicine of the American University of Beirut, physician and interpreter; Sergeant Michael Dorizas, interpreter; Mr. Laurence S. Moore, Business Manager; Sergeant-Major Paul O. Toren and Private Ross Lambing, stenographers. But it should be kept in mind that neither the American nor any other section of the projected Inter-Allied Commission on Mandates in Turkey had yet been formally appointed.[2]

Preparation, Confusion and Delay

There was now to ensue a period of preparation, confusion and delay, with no little intrigue as well, before the Commission was to leave for the Middle East at the end of May 1919. The Americans, somewhat optimistically, to put it mildly, were planning to leave by April 15, and Lybyer stressed the necessity of making a "start with the problem of Turkey." He thought that Colonel Lawrence, who "started this Commission", had now "lost interest". By April 9 a plan of internal organiza-

---

[1] For Yale and Montgomery see *Who's Who of the King-Crane Commission*; Yale to Howard, September 28, October 17, 1940. Westermann was much opposed to a Commission going to the Near East since he considered that all the necessary information was already available in Paris. For Yale's later estimates of the Commission and its work see his *The Near East: A Modern History* (Ann Arbor, University of Michigan Press, 1958), 315-317, 335-337, 362.

[2] Brodie, Moore and Dorizas were all selected about April 4-5, 1919; Haddad later. Brodie was an army chaplain, a graduate of Oberlin College. The American Commission to Negotiate Peace agreed on April 3 that an allotment of $18,500 should probably be placed at the disposal of the King-Crane Commission (*PPC*, XI, 146).

tion of the American Section was ready. Lybyer and King had become "very confidential", and the former considered that Dr. King had "a very firm grasp of the situation and a great deal of shrewdness." Plans were being pushed, but the Americans had learned little or nothing of the schemes of other groups.[1]

Preparing a Program of Work

On instructions from Dr. King, Lybyer went to see Arnold J. Toynbee, of the British Delegation, on April 10, and found that while the British Delegation had made no announcement, the British Commissioners had been named. Toynbee, believing that America should occupy Armenia, thought the jurisdiction of the American Commission should be from Armenia eastward. He was to send word as soon as the British Commissioners had been formally selected, so they could meet with the American members. Lybyer showed Toynbee a proposed itinerary which he had worked out as early as April 4,[2] outlining the trip in interesting detail. In view of the climatic conditions it was thought best to depart for the Near East at the earliest possible moment and to visit Syria first. The Commission should have a ship at its disposal for safe and comfortable travel. Assuming that Syria could be reached by May, Lybyer calculated that the Commission could spend ten days in Palestine, landing at Haifa, with several days in Jerusalem, a short stay at Jaffa, sailing from that city or Haifa. Arriving at Beirut on May 10, two weeks could be spent in Syria, the Lebanon, and the city of Damascus. The Commission would then go on from Beirut to Alexandretta on May 25 and spend a week at Aleppo, "which would complete in a month a very general study of the Palestinian and Syrian questions." After leaving Aleppo about June 1 a circuit could be made through the Armenian and Cilician regions of Aintab, Marash, and Adana, to Mersina, where the ship could be taken again about June 15. If western Asia Minor were to be visited, the group might call at Adalia, make a longer stop at Smyrna, of perhaps two weeks. Another two weeks might be spent at Constantinople for conferences and the preparation of preliminary reports. The Caucasus was not to be included in the proposed itinerary, although Lybyer suggested that a month might be spent there. The Commission might go to Trebizond about July 4, and spend some two months "in a journey across Armenia to Baghdad, visiting Erzerum, Erzinjan, Harput, Diabekr, Mardin, Mosul, etc." Leaving Baghdad about the middle of September the journey might be made by rail or river to Basra, and

---

[1] See the *Lybyer* and *King Diaries*, April 7-10, 1919. The Commission had its headquarters in Rooms E-104-105, 4 Place de la Concorde. Meanwhile, the American Commission to Negotiate Peace received the Commission of the American Jewish Congress on April 2 (*PPC*, XI, 141).

[2] Lybyer Papers. Lybyer to King, April 4-5, 1919. *Preliminary Project of Itinerary for the Inter-Allied Turkish Commission.*

then by ship around Arabia, stopping at such points as Aden and Jidda. Port Saïd might then be reached, by October 1, and Western Europe a few days later.

This was a very ambitious program, and yet Toynbee liked the itinerary and the proposal to send back partial reports, and suggested coming back from Constantinople before visiting Armenia. But Professor Westermann did not like the project. He entered a marginal note ruling out any investigation outside Syria and Palestine, declared that any report to be effective must be made "certainly before August 1", and believed that a week more than the time allotted would be necessary.

French Reluctance

Professor Lybyer called on M. Jean Gout, of the French Delegation, at the Quai d'Orsay on April 10 to discuss the proposed Inter-Allied Commission.[1] He was told that the French Foreign Minister, M. Pichon, had already spoken to Gout and Senator Augagnard about the projected investigation, and "thought it would be a long time before going." According to Gout, Lloyd George was now opposed to sending the Commission because of the unrest in Egypt. Colonel Lawrence, he remarked, had encouraged the Arabs altogether too much, and the French would be hurt at the loss of Syria. If Syria were assigned to the British, the Anglo-French Entente would soon perish.[2] Gout thought, therefore, that it would be best to settle the entire problem in Paris, after which the Commission could go to study the form of Government to be established. Moreover, he thought the Moslems were gaining in strength, and believed there was great danger in a large Arab empire. The French wished to nationalize the Moslems, and Gout was certain that the Moslems of India would never adhere to King Hussein. He believed that the Emir Feisal[3] was very much interested in the preservation of the Ottoman Empire and that the Moslems could not well endure that a Christian state, Armenia, be wedged in between the Turks and the Arabs. Neither would the Turks give up Constantinople to the

---

[1] Lybyer Papers. Notes on a Conversation with M. Gout in M. Gout's Office at the Quai d'Orsay, 3:30 to 4:30 p.m., April 10, 1919. *Lybyer Diary*, April 10, 1919. See also interview of Robert de Caix in *L'Asie Française*, April 11, 1919.

[2] Curiously enough, as early as March 18, 1915, Lawrence had written to David Hogarth that in the hands of France, Syria would provide a good base for possible naval attacks against Egypt. He did not believe that Great Britain could always count on French friendship. David GARNETT, *The Letters of T. E. Lawrence* (New York, Doubleday, Doran, 1939), 193-194.

[3] See purported agreement between Emir Feisal and Mustapha Kemal, June 16, 1919, in which the two parties allegedly agreed that "they could never recognize the partition of the Turkish Empire and of Arabia, and their occupation by foreigners." From the papers of Admiral Mark Bristol, U.S.N.

Christians. M. Robert de Caix, who was also present, said that the various groups, especially the Armenians and the Jews, were by no means ready to be constituted into states. They lacked unity, the Armenians and Jews were small minorities in the territories which they claimed, and were not capable of conducting an administration. Lybyer told the two Frenchmen that they were "criticizing the resolution of the Council of Ten of January 30", and then proceeded to read it to them. But Gout merely replied that "the Council had not considered the facts carefully when it agreed to that resolution." Moreover, he noted that the principle of self-determination was being neglected in the case of the Turks, who also had their rights. The Armenian claims, for example, went deep into Turkish territory, since Trebizond and the territory to the west was Turkish.

The next morning M. Gout proceeded to tell Lybyer what he proposed to say to Dr. King when the two were formally appointed members of the Inter-Allied Commission and could get together for fruitful discussion. Once more he stated that [1]

> it would be better to agree here in Paris upon the mandates to be assigned and then the Commission could proceed at its leisure to study local conditions and fix the manner in which the mandate should be exercized. To go before that is done would arouse great disturbances down there. As soon as the Council's decision was made known, Emir Feisal prepared to go home, and said he was going in order to arrange a plebiscite, working for an American mandate for Syria.

Lybyer, naturally, could not accept that point of view. He asked whether it were not the case that no mandate could be assigned until the territories to be placed under mandate had been separated from the Ottoman Empire, a treaty with Turkey signed, and the League of Nations established. This would take some time, since the Turkish delegates would have to be summoned from Constantinople.

When Lybyer, who thought disturbances more likely in the Near East if no Commission were sent to investigate, drew out a copy of the instructions, Gout had a dossier brought from the files, containing a document prepared for M. Clemenceau. It instructed the Commissioners to consult the peoples regarding local government and to investigate social and economic conditions. Military commanders were ordered to provide for " a perfectly free investigation. " Lybyer saw little objection to these instructions, but later questioned the stress on local government. Gout noted that the resolution of March 20 did not make clear what was wanted and that "the agreement was only in principle." But Lybyer wondered whether the record should not be considered an order, since President Wilson obviously intended the Commission to go to the Near East. Gout retorted:

[1] Lybyer Papers. Conversation of Mr. Jean Gout and D. Lybyer in M. Gout's Office at the Quai d'Orsay, 10:30 a..m, April 11, 1919.

The instructions were not approved by the Council of Four; they were written up perhaps by our people and given to the British and the British gave them to us. The military authorities down there have behaved badly. Ours are bad, but the British are worse for they are brutal. Each tries to settle the occupied areas in its own direction. The American missionaries also are purchasing the population.

Lybyer entered a vigorous objection to the remark about the missionaries, insisting that Gout understood nothing whatsoever of the spirit of American charity. Moreover, he could have added that the Council of Four had definitely approved the Wilson instructions on March 25. M. Gout was also reminded that the United States could not accept a mandate unless the American people approved of it. It was well that this was true, "for otherwise the giving of relief would certainly seem like a bid for territory."

The question then turned to the Commission itself. Gout inquired whether Dr. King had ever been in the East, and De Caix thought the Americans "too honest to deal with the Orientals." Lybyer could only reply that he was sure the American Commissioners had "not reached decisions in advance." They were open to conviction and expected "to carry on a really scientific investigation." They had instructions to go, believed they should go, and hoped the French would help to arrange matters and go, too. Gout did not reply except to say that he, like De Caix, wished to talk with Dr. King.

The conversation illustrated the kind of dilatory tactics with which the French were obstructing the Commission. They were in no hurry to move, and really not anxious to move at all. The talks were duly reported to Dr. King and, partly, to Professor Westermann.[1] When Lybyer called on Signor Galli, the Italian specialist for Western Asia, on April 12, he found that no Italian member had been appointed, but might be within a few days. Toynbee told him that things were on the move, that the British Commissioners were coming and that a specialist was to be selected. When Lybyer reported these developments to King and Westermann, the latter complained that the idea of an expedition was "ridiculous".[2]

The Critical Period

There now appeared to be very little prospect of a commission of investigation ever going to the Middle East. The French, it was clear,

---

[1] *Lybyer Diary*, April 11, 1919. King was "a strong, wise man, free from jealousy, full of good will, but shrewd."
[2] *Lybyer Diary*, April 12, 1919. Lansing noted on Saturday, April 12: "Bliss, White and I listened to Westermann on our taking military control in Armenia. Explained to him that as we were not at war with Turkey, we had no authority to act in that way. Westermann's attitude shows folly of having inexperienced men attempting to outline policies of govt."

wanted no investigation in Syria, and the Zionist Organisation was opposed to an inquiry in Palestine, on the ground that the future of Palestine had already been definitely decided. But if the Commission were to be barred from both Syria and Palestine, of what purpose would it be? President King was so discouraged and disgusted that he began to clear up things in his office "preparatory to leaving work", and he wrote to his friend, Mr. W. F. Bohn: [1]

> I had expected to be off for the Turkish Empire before this, but matters are being held up, it is pretty obvious, because the other powers do not really want to have the Commission go. They prefer not to have the situation investigated, but to be allowed to bargain among themselves along the old lines. Just how the matter will come out I don't know. Of course, in the meantime I have been choosing the personnel of the staff to go with the two American Commissioners and have been working into the problem, upon which I have now done a good deal of work.... If the Commission becomes simply a Commission to stay here in Paris I shall not feel that I am bound to stay for it, for that was not what the President asked me to do and, consequently, not what I accepted. It is possible, therefore, that I may still be getting home before very long, but one can really not tell at present what will result.... If I am back, I shall probably be able to give the opening lecture for the summer school, but if I go to Turkey, in line with the official instructions, the problem will be a good deal bigger one than the Syrian problem of which I was first told, and is likely to take a good deal of time.

Professor Lybyer set down his own ideas as to the situation on April 12.[2] He did not believe that the British and French were then standing by any secret agreement. The French wanted Syria, with the city of Damascus and Cilicia as well. The British were attempting to manœuver the French out of all this, or out of all but a small portion of it. Feisal was "practically a hired stalking horse for the British." Both the British and the French were fearful that the United States wanted the mandate for Syria. Clemenceau had held up the project of the Commission on the technical point of not bringing it up again after twenty-four hours, while Lloyd George acquiesced in this strategy on account of his fears concerning Egypt. Nevertheless, the French might become convinced that the investigation would be "fair, scientific and impartial at least on the part of the Americans", and might, perhaps, appoint their members promptly. Should that happen, both the British and the Italians would follow. The British might then attempt to have the Syrian problem settled first, separately, and in their own favor. Again, the United States might obtain directly from the Ottoman Government the right to occupy Armenia, "with a view to relieving wants, preserving order and improving communications and administration." If any change were to be made

---
[1] King Papers. King to Bohn, April 12, 1919.
[2] Lybyer Papers. Lybyer to King, April 12, 1919, *Conjecture as to the Present Situation*.

in the instructions, Lybyer thought the Commission might be "authorized to proceed to Constantinople first and arrange for the above occupation." The danger was that the Italians would then insist on the recognition and extension of their occupation at Adalia.

By mid-April a crisis in the fortunes of the projected Commission had clearly developed. *Le Temps* and other French journals were writing of attempts to solve the problem of Syria, for example, before a Commission went to the Middle East. Westermann, who felt that all the necessary information was already available in Paris, asked Lybyer what the group "would expect to find there", only to be told that if they knew there would be no need of going. King and Lybyer agreed that they would take no part at all, if the Commission were simply to remain in Paris. [1] Crane was planning to go to Constantinople, whatever the fortunes of the Commission. After a conversation with Dr. King on April 15, Lybyer drew up a memorandum on "Points to be taken up with President Wilson", which he took to the President's home, where Admiral Cary T. Grayson promised to transmit it to President Wilson. Lybyer informed Grayson that the American group was anxious to go to the Middle East, that the British were moving, and that even the French seemed "to feel that if they must go", they would. [2]

But the confusion, if anything, worse confounded, continued into the next day. After talking with King, Lybyer went to see Joseph C. Grew, the Secretary-General of the American Delegation, about the formal appointments of King and Crane, and was informed that the papers would be prepared at once. [3] But in the afternoon, while King and Lybyer were going over the salary list and other matters pertaining to the American Section, Mr. Crane came in to inform them that it was all off. The President had just received a wireless message showing how the Europeans, were double-crossing him behind his back. So, "after laughing", the Americans planned to go home again! Lybyer advised Grew of the situation, and was now told to prepare a new memorandum authorizing the American Section to go to the Middle East alone.

In conformity with Grew's instructions, Lybyer conferred with Dr. King, Mr. Crane and Professor Westermann on April 16 [4] regarding

[1] *Lybyer Diary*, April 13, 1919.
[2] Lybyer Papers. Memorandum of Conversation with Grayson at 11 Place des Etats-Unis, 11:30 a.m., April 15, 1919. Even *Le Temps* now declared that the Commission would go soon. Crane, meanwhile, was inviting both King and Lybyer to go with him to Constantinople.
[3] It was now learned that Sir Henry McMahon, who had been British High Commissioner in Cairo, and Commander Hogarth, the noted authority on the Middle East, had been appointed as the British Commissioners, while Arnold J. Toynbee was to serve as an expert adviser.
[4] Lybyer Papers. Lybyer to Grew, April 16, 1919. In a note to Grew on April 18 Lybyer stressed that the failure "at the outset of this Commission", whose creation was "one of the first practical measures,

the possibility of sending a separate American commission, if an international commission proved impractical. Westermann still opposed sending a Commission because it could gather "no important information" not already available, and because "its coming might be made the occasion of disturbances, especially in Syria." In Westermann's opinion the better plan was simply "to settle all questions regarding Turkey" in Paris. Considering the attitude of the people and the position of the occupying powers in Syria, Palestine and Mesopotamia, Mr. Crane wondered whether "the appearance of an American Commission of Inquiry might not arouse hopes which it would not be possible to fulfill." Subject to President Wilson's approval, however, he thought that "an American Commission might well go and investigate the question of America's taking a mandate for certain areas, such, for example, as Constantinople and Armenia." Dr. King regarded the proposal as a "reconstitution" of the Commission, although he would be glad to serve on it if the President desired. Lybyer himself felt that in view of the constantly changing Turkish situation, and of the fact that the Peace Conference had done very little toward a solution, it was "desirable that a beginning of some sort should be made." It was regrettable that "the loyal cooperation of other Powers" was "so difficult to secure." Should the United States "eventually accept a mandate for any portions of Turkey, no time should be lost in beginning to prepare the way". In any case, if an American Commission should "do nothing more than visit Constantinople, and gather from all sources there opinions and relevant information in regard to the desirability of American action in Turkey, its work would in all probability be of great and perhaps decisive value."

Interestingly enough, just at this critical juncture a secret French document "accidentally" was left in the office of the Division of Western Asia, by Robert de Caix.[1] This important document gives an almost complete picture of the French position concerning Syria and the projected Inter-Allied Commission. The British Government, the French thought, would be eager to have an agreement between France and the

looking toward the League of Nations, would be a serious discouragement to the whole idea of the League; while its successful carrying through despite all obstacles would be an initial triumph, which might go far toward marking the League, not a failure, but a success...." See also American Commission to Negotiate Peace, 1918-1919. Department of State, Vol. 157 (181.91/109). National Archives.

[1] Woodrow Wilson Papers, IX-A 75. From the Division of Western Asia. *Abstract of Memorandum Which Accidentally Came into Our Hands*, presumably intended for the French Foreign Office, on the Syrian Matter. [From Mr. Frazier's Office. Memorandum for the President]. According to Lyber's *Diary*, April 17: "Montgomery brought to Kg. secret about the wireless, said De Caix had accidentally left behind paper showing French negotiations. King told me of it. Sounded Westermann and he didn't tell me. Kerner dining with Beneš."

Emir Feisal because it feared "the result of the Inter-Allied Commission projected for Syria." In view of American intervention the assignment of Syria was no longer "entirely in England's hands." Now the British would be forced to allow France to create a *fait accompli* in Syria which would enable the French to "meet" the Commission, if it could not be avoided, or to follow any other procedure which might be adopted "in deciding the mandate question." Great Britain would be forced to permit France to replace the British troops in Syria, and the two countries would mutually support each other in obtaining the mandates in accordance with the Sykes-Picot accord of 1916. Feisal would then have to make an agreement with France, because he knew he could not "rule certain elements in Syria", favorable to France, without French assistance.

The Division of Western Asia, in analyzing the French memorandum, was now fully aware that the French did not "want the Inter-Allied Commission to go to Syria", although that had been clear all along. It was not so certain, however, that the British were fearful of the results of an investigation. The French hoped to influence the American Commissioners, to help them "obtain Syria", and expected to settle their problem along the lines of the Sykes-Picot agreement, with the term "mandate" substituted for "spheres of influence."

But if the analysis did little more than repeat the French contention, the conclusion was equally interesting. The Division of Western Asia declared that if the Inter-Allied Commission went to Syria it would "find the cards stacked everywhere." It would "do no good" and might "do much harm." Moreover, it was contended that "all the information requisite to the settlement" was "already here in Paris". Delay would only compound the difficulties. The Near East was "the great loot of the war", and "the fight on the question of division and mandates must be fought out here in Paris—and the sooner the better."

Grew read the Lybyer letter summarizing the situation and setting forth the position of King, Crane and Westermann when the American Commission to Negotiate Peace met on April 18.[1] After some discussion, House, Lansing, Bliss and White agreed that it would be best

> to give up entirely the sending of a purely American mission to Syria at the present time inasmuch as such a mission could scarcely furnish data upon which the Commissioners could base their decisions with regard to the problems in the Near East in a sufficiently short time, and inasmuch as the arrival of such a mission in the Near East might

[1] *PPC*, XI, 155; Grew to Lybyer, April 19, 1919, with Inclosure, No. 231 in Lybyer Papers. Lybyer took King over to the President's residence but saw from "Hoover's behavior that Crane is probably right about Commission." Lybyer *Diary*, April 18, 1919. King noted on April 18: "Went with Lybyer to try to get an appointment with President. Saw Baker and Col. House. Began on sailing arrangements. Saw Col. House a second time—Commission abandoned."

be construed as indicating the special interest of the United States in certain regions and thereby arousing either false hopes or create local disturbances.

Continued Confusion

To be or not to be—to go or not to go—that was the question now for the next three days. Professor Kerner, who saw Lybyer constantly, sensed the critical situation, and advised that Dr. King ask to see President Wilson at once, a proposal with which Grew agreed. King did, in fact, see Colonel House twice, only to be told that neither the international nor the American Commission would go to Syria or the Middle East.[1] Lybyer now planned to make the trip to Constantinople with Mr. Crane, the latter nominally to be Lybyer's secretary, and arranged for tickets, letters and special passports! But by this time, Grew informed him that the Commission legally was still in existence, and on April 20, the two British Commissioners, Sir Henry McMahon and David Hogarth, who knew Arabic intimately and thought the Commission necessary, arrived. With all the confusion in the air, it was not surprising that President King wrote home on April 21:[2]

> ...It now looks as if the stir-up had all been in vain, for, after waiting nearly a month, diplomatic and other conditions are such that the President thinks it probably not wise to try to send the Commission. He thinks that he would be sending us on something of a wild goose chase, and does not feel that he has any right to ask that from us. I am planning, therefore, to sail for America on April 24th, from Marseilles, on the Steamer "Patria". That should land me in New York somewhere between the 6th and 8th. That is the earliest sailing I can get. It is possible that this letter may reach you before I do, though that is a little doubtful. I will cable someone in Oberlin (probably Mrs. King) in the meantime....
> P. S. Word has just come from the President that he is now very anxious that the Commission should go and that it seemed more important than ever. So I have once more cancelled my sailing and am planning to go to Turkey as the present place of duty.

What had happened to produce all this confusion within the space of two or three days? The French and the Zionists were particularly nervous

---

[1] House and Lloyd George, also discussed the Syrian problem on April 18. Lloyd George was certain the French would clash with the Arabs. What he wanted was "for us to accept the Mandatory for Syria and let the French have Constantinople. In discussing this with the President afterward, he was afraid the French would intrigue in Constantinople and that it would not be a wise move. He preferred them in Syria where the League could watch them. I have changed my mind about our accepting the Mandatory for Constantinople. I have looked into the matter carefully and have talked with some of our people, notably Hoover. I have come to the conclusion that with all the surrounding countries having ports of their own to develop, it would leave Constantinople a dead city on our hands. I told the President of my conclusion and suggested that we allow the French to have it or internationalize it under the League of Nations." House *Diary*, April 18, 1919.

[2] King Papers. King to Bohn, April 21, 1919.

about the sending of the Commission. President Wilson, much discouraged about the whole situation, had advised both Dr. King and Mr. Crane that they could return home. And then suddenly came the change of front. One of the factors, no doubt, was that "a sharp demand came from General Allenby in Cairo that the Commission be appointed and get to work. Word had gone all through the East that such a Commission was contemplated and the people demanded that it should come along." [1] Moreover, on April 20, the day before his departure for Syria, the Emir Feisal wrote to the President expressing his hopes about the Commission and confident that when it visited Syria, it would "find a country united in its love and gratitude to America." Finally, Colonel House, on whom Feisal had just called, wrote Wilson on April 21 that Feisal had assurances from both Lloyd George and Clemenceau that the Commission would leave within two weeks. House was now strongly of the opinion that unless the Commission went to Syria, there would "shortly be widespread trouble of a religious and racial character" in Syria and Palestine. [2]

The crisis, at last, had passed. The Commission was to be and it was to go to the Middle East. The word had definitely come from President Wilson himself. As Lybyer recorded, April 22 was "the day of the Great Change in the fortunes of the Commission." [3] Henry Churchill King was to be the Chairman of the Inter-Allied group.

[1] *Crane Memoirs* (unpublished).
[2] Woodrow Wilson Papers, IX-A 45. Feisal to Wilson, April 20, 1919; House to Wilson, April 21, 1919. Wilson thanked Feisal on April 21, and added: "My best wishes will go with you and I hope in every way that it is possible to be serviceable to Syria in whose fortunes I am deeply interested." Shortly before his departure, an exchange of letters was drawn up between Feisal and Clemenceau, although the French did not accept Feisal's conditions and the correspondence, which Lord Balfour sent to Curzon, did not become "official". The draft Clemenceau letter, April 17, 1919, accepted an independent Syria and offered French assistance. But Feisal, who had conferred with Clemenceau, made unacceptable conditions. In the draft Feisal letter of April 20, he thanked Clemenceau "for having been the first to suggest the depatch of the Inter-Allied Commission", which was leaving shortly "to ascertain the wishes of the local peoples as to the future organization of their country." M. Robert de Caix rejected the letter and did not transmit it. *British Documents*, 1919-1939, First Series, IV, 250,253.
[3] See King and Lybyer Diaries, April 22, 1919. Lybyer noted : "Saw Mr. Crane at 9:30, arranged to meet British Commissioners at 11. Could not find King at 10:40. Waited until 11:15. Had informal meeting of 2 British Commissioners w. Crane, Toynbee and myself. Crane agreed to go if Pres. wished him to. Read Gates' letter w. wh. they agreed. Also read a proposal of mine to go only to Damascus and Consple. Adjourned until 4 P.M. Met King downstairs. Had been summoned by Baker to be told that President now wanted very much that Commission should go. King much upset, had thought certainly not going, and was ready to sail. Took in copy of Gates' letter at Crane's suggestion to Admiral Grayson

The Americans Get Ready

While the Americans were to wait another six weeks before entraining for the Middle East, conditions in that end of the world appeared to demand action. Rear Admiral Mark L. Bristol, Senior United States Naval Officer at Constantinople, soon to become United States High Commissioner, reported as early as February 1919 that the situation was terrible and becoming steadily worse. He urged the raising of the blockade, and wirelessed to the Force Commander in London on February 12 that starvation and suffering were disturbing the peace of the area by driving the husbandmen off the land into the mountains as brigands. On February 20 he begged for support to the American Relief Committee and its work of mercy and goodwill, which increased American prestige. To wait until the end of the Peace Conference "to take proper action in Turkey" would be "too late and a criminal act toward all races of Turkey." Bristol earnestly recommended that the Conference authorize or direct the Allied Commission in Constantinople to occupy as much Turkish territory and the Caucasus, in cooperation with the Turkish authorities, as was "necessary to disarm demobilized soldiers, put down brigandage, combat epidemic disease and insure the planting of crops this spring." That action, however, was not to prejudice any final actions of the Peace Conference. [1]

Further Discussion

Especially important, too, was a letter from President Caleb F. Gates, of Robert College in Constantinople, which reached Professor Lybyer on April 21, and which he transmitted to President Wilson the next day. [2] Dr. Gates, who knew the Ottoman Empire well, having served as a missionary in Mardin and Harput since 1881 and as President of Robert College since 1903, told of the tragic conditions which he had found while serving with the American Relief Committee. The delay of the Peace Conference in reaching decisions regarding the Ottoman Empire, he thought, had "given opportunity for increasing bitterness, faction and intrigue", and the French policy of using Armenian troops in Cilicia had had "a very bad effect throughout all Asia Minor." Dr. Gates was fearful that the creation of an Armenian state would be "the signal for the breaking out of serious riots and massacres all over the

---

—up backstairs to his office.... 4 P.M. met with British at Hotel Majestic. Told Westermann, Grew, Kirk. 1 1/2 hours talk. British want one ship for party—can provide it. Hope to have Americans agree with them and against others. Palestine settled. We explained our plans. King to be chairman of Commission."

[1] The Bristol Dispatches (hereafter *B.D.*), fifty-three in number, are in the King Papers.
[2] Lybyer Papers. Gates to Lybyer, April 12, 1919. Woodrow Wilson Papers, IX-A 45, 46. Lybyer to Wilson, April 22 1919; Wilson to Lybyer, April 23, 1919.

country." He was still more strongly convinced that the Peace Conference should place "the whole country under the efficient control of some great power." That would assure good government and equal rights to all nationalities. He feared the decisions of the Peace Conference because he thought is was "acting without sufficient knowledge", and its decisions were likely "to create even greater difficulties."

But President Gates, who was soon to come to Paris, was even more detailed in his analysis in a letter to Mr. Cleveland H. Dodge.[1] To drive the Turks out of Europe would simply "transfer their misrule from one place to another." A permanent solution would "provide good government for the Turks as well as for the Armenians—that is, for the whole Turkish Empire." Only the United States, in Gates' opinion, could provide a satisfactory and acceptable mandatory control.

Once more the Commissioners and Professor Lybyer set definitely to work planning their journey. Lybyer sent a memorandum to Dr. King and Mr. Crane, on April 22, dealing with "Problems to be Studied First."[2] In view of conditions in the Near East, he wondered whether it might not be well "to select first, the problems of Damascus and the Arabs connected with the Emir Feisal; and second, the problem of the Armenian mandate." This would mean going as quickly as possible to Beirut and Damascus, investigating and sending back recommendations concerning Syria, then going directly to Constantinople as the center "for the question of mandates in Anatolia and Armenia." The areas occupied by European troops could await settlement somewhat better than the unoccupied lands. Moreover, the situation in regions under Arab and Turkish occupation seemed to be getting worse, and might get completely out of hand. If an explosion should occur in the Turkish Moslem areas, the possibilities for mischief would be incalculable. It was imperative that "control by the West be maintained over the Arabs and Turks", if the world were to be held steady. Finally, "Zionism, the Balkan problems, and the control of the new Straits" seemed more capable of postponement than the settlement of Western Asia.

Lybyer's letter of April 23 to Mr. Grew[3] outlined the personnel of the staff of the King-Crane Commission, though "a physician, a stenographer, and one or more orderlies" were yet to be selected. Addi-

---

[1] Quoted in Gates, *Not to Me Only*, 252-253. See also Halidé Edib, *The Turkish Ordeal* (New York, Century, 1928), 11, citing the Armenian fury against Gates because of his opinions.
[2] Lybyer Papers. Lybyer to Dr. King and Mr. Crane, Paris, April 22, 1919.
[3] Lybyer Papers. Lybyer to Grew, April 23, 1919. $ 425 per month was asked for Lybyer, but not granted, $ 350 for Montgomery, while Yale and Brodie had their salaries as Captains in the United States Army. $ 175 was recommended for Mr. Moore, while $ 166 was recommended for Dorizas. See also Lybyer *Diary*, April 23, 1919.

tions to salaries were recommended, in view of the "more dangerous service and the expense of special personal outfitting." Dr. King was on leave from Oberlin and his salary might be continued. Mr. Crane asked for no salary, since he did not need the money at all. Provided a ship were available for sea travel, it was thought that the sum of $ 20,000 should be set aside until June 30 and that after that date provision should be made on the basis of $ 10,000 per month. Special passports were also necessary. In general, these arrangements were approved at a meeting of the American Commission to Negotiate Peace on April 26.[1]

Further Obstacles ?

Appearances now indicated that the other groups were preparing to move as well. The British Commissioners were ready to leave when given their orders, and when Wilson and Lloyd George met on April 25, it was decided that the Commission should go as soon as possible. Even Clemenceau, it seems, promised to appoint the French members at once. The prospective Italian member, Captain Pallavicini, was eager to go to the Near East, but Jean Gout, who seemed less actively opposed, nevertheless, had not heard of the new decision to act.[2]

There were still attempts to prevent the Inter-Allied Commission from being appointed, and the American Commissioners from going, however. Despite Clemenceau's promise to appoint the French Commissioners immediately, he appears to have had no such intention at all. When Henry Wickham Steed returned to Paris late in April he got into touch with the French leaders at once, including Premier Clemenceau, and attempted to facilitate a solution of the Syrian problem. Clemenceau was furious with Lloyd George because of his apparent failure to force Feisal into an agreement with France. Steed saw some American experts, who were prepared to recommend a settlement in Paris, if Colonel House would agree. But House advised Steed not to begin by arranging a meeting between the various experts or prospective members of the Commission, but to return first of all to Clemenceau and try to arrange an agreement between the French Premier and Lloyd George. House added that there would be a positive basis for discussion, and that the United States would

---

[1] *PPC*, XI, 164, 166. See also King Papers for a note from Dr. King and Mr. Crane to the Commissioners, April 24, 1919. Lybyer noted in his *Diary* that he saw Jean Gout, who "had heard nothing of American decision to go. Would look it up." Ray Stannard Baker wrote to Close on April 24 asking for an appointment for Dr. King with President Wilson. Woodrow Wilson Papers, IX-A 46. At the meeting of the American Commission to Negotiate Peace on April 26, Professor Westermann presented a memorandum relative to the mandate problem, in which he proposed that an American Commission be established to consider the entire question.

[2] Lybyer *Diary*, April 25, 26, 1919.

certainly accede to any fair Anglo-French agreement. In that case, evidently, the Inter-Allied Commission would not be necessary. [1]

Meanwhile, Professor Westermann had outlined a general form for mandates over states which might be carved out of the Ottoman Empire, which Secretary of State Lansing transmitted to President Wilson on April 28. [2] According to the Westermann scheme, which was submitted to the American Commission to Negotiate Peace on April 26, the mandate was to last for twenty-five years and to be subject to the control of the League of Nations. It would prepare the people for complete self-government, "essentially popular in form", with provision for the largest measure of regional autonomy and a constitutional convention within five years. With the abolition of the capitulatory régime foreigners and citizens would be placed upon a footing of equality. Religious freedom was stipulated, as was protection for religious, educational and philanthropic organizations. Each new state was to share in the Ottoman Public Debt. Finally, there were to be no fortifications, and no troops except for the preservation of public order.

Secretary of State Lansing considered that the entire question of mandates and mandatories required extremely careful study. Like other members of the Commission, he desired President Wilson's view "as to whether an American Commission should not immediately be formed to consider this matter, and that if possible, this Commission be broadened as soon as possible into an Inter-Allied Commission for the same purpose." One may wonder, however, whether the Secretary of State intended to duplicate the work of the Inter-Allied Commission on Mandates in Turkey, or to use the one which already appeared in the offing, the establishment of which had been blocked so many times. Whatever his intention, the program of the King-Crane group appeared to be moving forward. By April 28 the personnel of the Commission was approved. Two days later, on April 30, they received formal notices of their appointment from Mr. Lansing, instructing them "to make inquiries in certain portions of the Turkish Empire" which were "to be permanently separated from Turkey and put under the guidance of the Government, acting as mandatories for the League of Nations." A copy of the instructions and a *laissez-passer* were enclosed, certifying the Commission and

---

[1] Henry Wickham STEED, *Through Thirty Years*, II, 323-324. But the Clemenceau-Lloyd George controversy continued, and nothing came of these overtures. Professor Felix Frankfurter, who had just seen Crane, wrote to Colonel House on April 30, asking him to use his influence to exclude Palestine from the scope of the inquiry as territory concerning which there was no dispute.

[2] Woodrow Wilson Papers, IX-A 48. Robert Lansing to the President, April 28, 1919. *The General Form to be Adopted for, and Certain General Clauses to be Included in, the Specific Mandates over States that may be Formed Through the Breaking Up of the Ottoman Empire*. See also *PPC*, XI, 165.

empowering the Commissioners "to perform any and all acts that may be necessary" to carry out the instructions.[1]

Soon the Americans would start on their long journey to the Middle East. There were all kinds of equipment to be purchased, and all had to be innoculated against typhoid fever. Dr. King bought some books "for atmosphere": *Talisman*, the *Rubaiyat*, Herodotus, *Arabian Nights*, *Light of Asia*, and a number of others.[2] But there was to be another month in Paris!

---

[1] *PPC*, XI, 165. King Papers: Robert Lansing to Mr. King, Paris, April 30, 1919. Grew to King, April 28, 29, 1919. King's salary was approved at the rate of $ 8,000 per year and Lybyer's at the old rate of $ 350 per month. An original allotment of $ 10,000 was made to the Commission instead of the requested $ 20,000. The transport problem was unsolved (*PPC*, XI, 170; Lybyer *Diary*, April 28, 1919).

[2] King and Lybyer *Diaries*, April 29 - May 1, 1919. For Westermann's continued opposition to Commission see American Commission to Negotiate Peace, 1918-1919, National Archives, Vol. 157 (181.781/96).

CHAPTER III

Preparations for a Near Eastern Journey

THE LAST MONTH IN PARIS

In preparing for their trip, members of the King-Crane Commission tried to learn everything possible about the situation in the Near and Middle East through careful study, research and conferences. By May 1, President King had prepared two memoranda dealing with the materials which should be taken on the journey.[1]

Additional Instructions

At the same time Professor Lybyer drew up some additional instructions for the American group requesting it to investigate and prepare

---

[1] Among the materials already gathered were: I) Official Instructions to Commission; II) Physical and political maps of the Near East, with detailed data on Asia Minor, Syria, Palestine, the Lebanon, Arabia, and Mesopotamia; III) Statistical and economic data concerning populations in occupied and unoccupied regions; IV) Material on historical backgrounds; V) A copy of Wilson's Fourteen Points and all his other utterances bearing on the Inquiry; VI) Expert's Reports; (1) Byrne's report on *Syrian Aspirations*, and their later statement; (2) Captain Yale's two summary reports on *Syrian Conditions*; (3) Butler's report on *Arabian State or States*; (4) Judgment of experts on the merits of the case: a. Armenian claims; b. Syrian aspirations; c. Arabic States; d. British, French Greek, and Italian claims; e. Zionist claims; VII) Diplomatic and similar material: (1) Pact of London; (2) Handbook "A". St. Jean de Maurienne Agreement, Sykes-Picot Agreement; (3) Collection of Secret treaties; VIII) Statements of Special Groups: (1) Statement of Zionist Organization; (2) The Armenian Question; (3) "The Plan of the New Syria National League"; The Syrian Appeal, Rihany's *America Save the Near East*; (4) Other official documents of different group; IX) Books and other similar material bearing on inquiry. Among the books listed in Dr. King's *Notebook* were: (1) BAEDEKER's *Guidebook to Syria*; (2) MURRAY's *Asia Minor*; (3) EVERSLEY, *The Turkish Empire*; (4) Gertrude BELL, *Amurath to Amurath*; (5) D. G. HOGARTH, *The Near East, The Penetration of Arabia*; (6) ZWEMER, *Arabia, The Cradle of Islam*; (7) G. A. SMITH, *Syria and the Holy Land*; (8) H. A. GIBBONS, *Zionism and World Peace*; (9) *Report of Committee on Armenian and Syrian Relief*; (10) *Recommendations for Political Reconstruction of the Turkish Empire*; (11) RAMSAY, *Impressions of Turkey, Wanderings in Turkey*; (12) Charles M. DOUGHTY, *Travels in Arabia Deserta*, 2 vols (1888); (13) BELL, *Arabs of Mesopotamia*; (14) WIGRAM, *The Cradle of Mankind*; (15) *Encyclopedia and Dictionary*; (16) Leon DOMINIAN, *Frontiers of Nationality and Language in Europe*.

Among data still desired were any further statements on the Near East. Lybyer listed a copy of the *Bryce Report* on Armenia, *The Dictionary of Islam*, and the works of Snouck-Hurgronye and Schaff-Herzog. A more prosaic list of necessities, drawn up by Lybyer, included: Candles, matches, sugar, chocolate, candy, powdered coffee, medicines, jam, insect powder, shoe nails, courier bag, crackers, sardines, salmon, tinned meat, mosquito net, toilet paper, salt, canned oysters, dysentery injection, field desks, games, alcohol, fuel, canteen kits, map cases, boxes, catsup, cologne, soup, sweet potatoes, tea, cheese, butter, cocoa, bandages, absorbent cotton, and baking powder.

reports [1] on the best solution of the Near Eastern problem and particularly on the question of an American mandate. The guiding principles which President Wilson had laid down in four great addresses of December 4, 1917, and January 8, February 11 and July 4, 1918, were embodied in the new instructions. They called for a fair and equitable treatment of all the peoples of the Balkan and Near Eastern region, not a mere reshuffling of frontiers on behalf of imperialistic interests. The address of July 4, 1918, for instance, insisted on a peace resting upon the basis of the free, popular acceptance of the settlement, and "not upon the basis of the material interest or advantage of any other nation or people which may desire a different settlement for the sake of its own exterior influence or mastery."

The Commission could use its discretion in choosing the regions to be visited, within the Ottoman Empire or adjacent areas, "which might be brought under the mandatory system." It would also be free to pursue its inquiry "either alone or in association with Commissioners appointed by other nations", and was to leave Paris at the earliest possible date. Once in the Near East, the Commission was to report from time to time to the President and after the completion of the investigation to present a final report. All officials of the United States in the area, "whether military, naval, diplomatic, or other" were to facilitate the inquiry in every possible way. The Commission was instructed to visit Palestine Syria, the Arab countries to the east, Mesopotamia, Armenia, and Cilicia, and possibly parts of Asia Minor. [2] The Commission was to assess popular opinion, study "social, racial and economic conditions, knowledge of which might help the Conference" and reach conclusions as to the best division of territory and assignment of mandates.

Importance of the Problem

Meanwhile, the American group was increasingly concerned with conditions in the Near East. In a memorandum submitted about May 1, [3] Captain Yale dealt with the specific subject of petroleum,

---

[1] Lybyer Papers: *Supplementary Instructions for the American Members of the Commission on the Future Administration of the Turkish Empire Under the Mandatory System*. About May 1, 1919. The Wilson addresses are in Baker and Dodd, III, 118-139, 155-162, 177, 184, 231-235.

[2] Lybyer Papers: *Condensation of Instructions*, about May 1, 1919, It was noteworthy that Arabia proper had been omitted in the statement of March 25, but not in that of January 30. The guiding principles were based on the Anglo-French Declaration of November 1918 and the resolution of the Council of Ten, January 30, 1919. The Commission was to keep in mind that the wishes of the peoples were to be a principal factor in determining the mandatory.

[3] Lybyer Papers: Captain William YALE, *Memorandum on Oil Interests*, about May 1, 1919. Captain Yale also prepared a "Suggested Answer to Attached Questionnaire" dealing with the oil situation and policies of the Powers, about May 1, 1919. See also Miscellaneous No. 10

stressing that "the development of the natural resources of these lands should be directed to the greatest ultimate benefit of the ward rather than to the special interest of the guardian." It was obvious that "the open door policy" was best designed to achieve this purpose. Yale outlined the petroleum situation in the world and its bearing on American interests. In the Near East especially, it was anticipated that Mesopotamia, one of the large potential oil fields, would fall under British administration. Americans would want to participate in the exploitation of Mesopotamian oil resources:

> Unless, before Mesopotamia and other territories are actually placed under British administration, there be express provision made or adequate assurance given to safeguard the free right of entry to the American petroleum industry, its exclusion must be apprehended, to be followed by the exploitation of the oil resources of these lands for the sole benefit of Great Britain and her trade.
>
> It is necessary to point out the extreme importance to the American nation of maintaining a strong position in the petroleum trade of the world. It is a fact that the native petroleum resources of the United States are becoming exhausted and that the maximum production has already been nearly, if not quite, reached. It is proper to observe that during the war, 80% of the petroleum products of the Allies were shipped from the United States. This was accomplished at a great sacrifice to the reserves above and under ground, and at prices which were fixed by the United States Government....
>
> Our national safety, the maintenance and expansion of our foreign and domestic trade, must depend in large measure upon the assurance to the United States of continued supplies of petroleum. With our requirements constantly increasing, with our own supplies about to decline and with more than half of the potential production of the world located without our territorial limits, the necessity of guaranteeing now to American industry the right to have its part in the development of the petroleum resources of the territories about to pass under British control will be apparent.

The Dangers of Selfish Exploitation

Dr. King, Mr. Crane and their technical advisers sent a statement to President Wilson on May 1 concerning the dangers to the Allies of a selfish exploitation of the Ottoman Empire. [1] Since this memorandum was basically the first report made by the King-Crane Commission and had a bearing on the final conclusions written in August, 1919, some analysis is necessary.

(1921). *Correspondence between His Majesty's Government and the United States Respecting Economic Rights in Mandated Territories.* Cmd. 1226.

[1] Woodrow Wilson Papers, IX-A 75 and Lybyer Papers: A. H. L. Mandate Commission. Copy of Note Sent to President, May 1, 1919. *Memorandum on the Dangers to the Allies from a Selfish Exploitation of the Turkish Empire,* 4 pp. The memorandum was signed by Henry Churchill King, Charles R. Crane, Albert H. Lybyer, George R. Montgomery, and William Yale.

The Commission pointed out to President Wilson that the fidelity of the Allies "to their announced aims in the war"... was "particularly to be tested" in the plans "for the division of the Turkish Empire." If the partition of the Ottoman territories was to be based primarily on the selfish interests of the Great Powers, there would be grave difficulties in the Near East, little gain for the Allies, and serious dangers for the world at large:

1. Such a division would have to be forced upon the peoples concerned—not chosen by them.
2. A large number of troops would thus be required to establish and to maintain such a division. This might prove a very serious consideration.
3. Men like President Gates of Robert College believe that the mere announcement of such a division would be likely to provoke further massacres of Christians in Turkey—a consideration of great moment.
4. Such a selfish exploitation of Turkey would not only certainly call out the resentment of the most solid portion of the American people, as emphatically illustrating the ends for which America came into the war; but would also tend to alienate the best sentiment among all the Allies. To eliminate from the cause of the Allies this weight of moral judgment would involve a loss of power not lightly to be faced.
5. Such exploitation would mean, too, the deliberate sowing of dissension of the gravest kind among the Allies themselves—threatening the moral unity of their cause and entailing serious world consequences.
6. Coupled with similar decisions already reached, it would also go far to convince men of independent moral judgment all over the world —including many previously ardent upholders of the cause of the Allies— that the aims of the Allies had become as selfish and ruthless as those of the Germans had been. That would carry with it its own consequences.
7. For one thing, when such moral condemnation became clear—as it certainly would in time—it would in itself encourage rebellious uprisings on the part of national groups, and to increase general sympathy with such uprisings.
8. For another thing, America cannot be expected to furnish financial backing for schemes of selfish exploitation — even sometimes directed precisely against herself.

On the other hand, certain considerations were involved in the division of the Ottoman estate. It was desirable that the Empire "as such should definitely cease to exist." The repeated massacres and the demonstrated age-long incapacity for good government demanded that. Moreover, "the strategic position of Constantinople and the Straits" required that Ottoman control be eliminated and that the Sultan, if he were to continue, "be removed to some other capital like Brusa." The Commission did not feel that the Moslem Indian protest against removal of the capital from Constantinople should prevail. There was danger, even under a mandate, "in keeping intact the Empire as a whole, or perhaps even the Asia Minor portion of the Empire—danger of a later revival of the Turkish Empire and repetition of its past history, on account of jealousies of the Powers." Unusual restrictions were necessary in the case of the Turks. In any event, the Ottoman Empire had not been a genuine unit "from any point of view." The non-Turkish portions, Syria, Mesopotamia and Arabia, had a unity of their own. The so-called Moslem peoples of Asia Minor did not constitute "a truly national group." The Allies should boldly break "with the whole previous Turkish situation, and build the Near East on sound principles." The Commission went on:

> It is right that the more able, industrious and enterprising groups, like the Greeks and the Armenians, should be recognized in the settlement. It is right that the long relations of Greece, France, Italy and Great Britain with various parts of the Turkish Empire should be given due weight also.
>
> If the proposed divisions can be made genuine mandatories under the League of Nations, with real regard for the peoples under the mandates, with annual reports to the League, and with limited terms, something like a generous rivalry for good government and in service of the peoples involved might result, especially if America took a significant mandate. All this may be said in recognition of the variety of interests involved in the problem of the breaking up of the Turkish Empire, and in favour of some division, on large lines, of that Empire.
>
> But if the principles of national unity and of self-determination are to be applied at all to the Turkish people, at least a large central portion of Asia Minor, sufficient to provide for the bulk of the Turks under a single mandate, and with adequate outlets to the sea, should be left to them. For the present, such a province should be under a mandatory power, in order to secure to the Turks themselves that good government which they have so notoriously lacked. "The wishes of these communities", moreover, as the Covenant of the League of Nations says, "must be a principal consideration in the selection of the Mandatory."
>
> The immemorial trade routes suggest the undesirability of breaking up the economic unity of Turkey, and so producing artificial barriers and wasteful arrangements. There should be a customs union, and other economic agreements, covering at least all of Asia Minor, and perhaps the whole of the old Empire.

In view of these considerations, a number of mandates within the old Ottoman Empire "might be justified". In the Arabic-speaking portions, Great Britain might have the mandate, for Mesopotamia, because of "British fitness and the general desires of the peoples involved." In Palestine the British should act "as Agent for an International Mandate... to guard the holy places and the entire territory for the benefit of all the peoples interested, and not simply for the Jews." In Arabia proper, King Hussein was to be recognized as king of the independent state of the Hejaz, although the right of all national and racial groups among Moslems in all countries to representation on a League of Nations Commission for the Holy Places of Islam, was to be recognized. On the other hand, the Commission would recognize Great Britain's general supervision of Arabia, provided the "open door" were maintained for all members of the League of Nations, a reservation which "would go far to remove the natural French and Italian jealousy of Britain's large territorial gains in this war." In Syria a French mandate "liberally, interpreted", might be established, though it was "frankly based, not on the primary desires of the people, but on the international need of preserving friendly relations between France and Great Britain." In the non-Arabic portions, *i. e.*, Asia Minor, the first choice of the peoples "would be for *a general American mandate*, perhaps with subsidiary mandates under the general mandate: recognizing the Greek and Armenian interests, the desirability of some provision for Turkish national unity, and the necessity of an international Constantinopolitan State." But there were obvious difficulties, and the United States might be unwilling to assume so large a task, which would "also probably arouse the jealousy of the other Powers." A composite mandate might remove some of the objections to a single, general mandate. If a single mandate for Asia Minor were set aside, the Commission proposed a four-fold division:

(1) An American Mandate for an International Constantinopolitan State—an essential world interest.
(2) A Mandate for Anatolia, under supervision still to be determined. providing for the bulk of the Turkish people under a single mandate.
(3) An autonomous Greek region within Anatolia, covering Smyrna and contiguous territory, but not so large as to shut off the Turkish portion of Anatolia from good access to the Aegean Sea.
(4) An American Mandate for Armenia and the rest of the northern portion of Turkey, including Adana in order to give access to the Mediterranean Sea.

The Paris Conference and the Turkish Problem [1]

The Conference of Paris was not delayed in the moves made concerning the Turkish problem, certainly not by the manœuvres connected with the appointment of a Commission of Inquiry. [2] Both before the King-Crane Commission went to the Near East, and shortly after it had gone, there were serious developments which were to have grave consequences in the years following the First World War. Before the Commission left, the Italians became especially nervous both about Fiume and the problem of Asia Minor. David Lloyd George and Clemenceau suggested on April 21 that Italy might compromise on the Adriatic question, if given a mandate in Asia Minor which, Clemenceau thought, might cover a portion of Anatolia bordering on the territory assigned to Greece in the Smyrna area and the Constantinoplitan and Armenian mandate. [3] President Wilson did not favor the idea for a number of reasons, while Lloyd George suggested an Italian sphere such as Great Britain had in

[1] Condensed and modified from my *Partition of Turkey*, 231 ff.
[2] *Al-Mokattal* (Damascus), May 1, 1919, much interested in the work to be done in Syria, published the names of the Commission and noted that "the date of the arrival of the Commission in Palestine has not yet been decided, but it is not far off."
[3] *PPC*, V, 106-109.

various parts of the world. Because of President Wilson's opposition on the Adriatic question, the Italians left the Conference on April 24 and did not return until May 5.[1] On April 30 it was announced that an Italian warship had gone to Smyrna, and it was suggested that all the Powers send warships to that troubled area.[2]

Mandates or Spoils?

These developments, of course, were of deep concern to the peace makers and, on May 5, at a meeting of the Council of Four, Lloyd George suggested the impossibility of an immediate settlement of the mandate problem in the Ottoman Empire and a redistribution of troops. In his view, the United States would send troops to Armenia and Constantinople, Great Britain would withdraw from the Caucasus, France could garrison Syria, and the Greeks occupy Smyrna. The Italians were not mentioned at all in this proposal and Lloyd George's announced intention to withdraw British troops from the Caucasus was made "in order to have them ready to counteract any move by the Italians." At the end of the session the Prime Minister repeated, that he was "very anxious to settle the question of the mandates before the Treaty of Peace", but President Wilson felt it could hardly be settled within two days, and remarked that "in regard to Turkey in particular, it was impossible for him to give a decision at present as to whether the United States could take a mandate", a difficulty which Lloyd George appreciated.[3]

The next day, May 6, President Wilson stated definitely that the United States could not send troops to the Ottoman Empire since it had not been at war with that country. Italy might be compelled to get out of Anatolia, however, because of its dependence on the United States for credits. An Italian mandate for Anatolia, in the President's view, would be a cause for grave friction. At the same time, Wilson thought that the only advantage in allowing Italy to keep Fiume was that it would break the Treaty of London, giving the Dodecanese to Italy.[4] On May 7,

---

[1] On May 5, 1919, Lloyd George announced Italian occupation of the harbor of Marmaris as a coaling station. A battalion was at Konia by agreement, and troops had been landed at Adalia, and possibly at Alaja. For Italian policy, January-October 1919, see *Miller Diary*, XIX, 557-559.
[2] See especially René ALBRECHT-CARRIE, *Italy at the Paris Peace Conference*, 217-225.
[3] *PPC*, V, 465-468, 472.
[4] *PPC*, V, 482-484. See also Woodrow Wilson Papers, IX-A 51. In a note of May 6, 1919 to Wilson, House suggested that Clemenceau be informed that "if Great Britain becomes Mandatory for Arabia and France Mandatory for Syria," and the two become involved in war, a very difficult situation would arise. If limitations were made concerning native troops, "it would have a tendency to prevent Asiatic and European backward countries from accepting any mandatory." See also Paul BIRDSALL, *Versailles Twenty Years After* (New York, Reynal and Hitchcock, 1941), 279.

Premier Venizelos was brought into the discussion, particularly as to the disposition of Greek troops.[1]

The Council of Four again pondered the Italian situation on May 13 when Lloyd George once more raised the mandate question, and rather naively suggested that an Italian mandate in Anatolia might solve the immigration question in the United States. President Wilson advanced a proposal favoring the uniting of the Smyrna area and the Dodecanese Islands to Greece. Mr. Nicolson, the British expert, indicated a line on the map excluding the Baghdad railway from the Italian zone. Again, Lloyd George brought forward his proposal that the United States take a mandate for Armenia and Constantinople, France one for Northern Anatolia and Italy one for Southern Anatolia, while Greece would receive the Smyrna region and the Dodecanese. But the Italians wanted Scala Nuova in addition, and President Wilson could not promise American acceptance of a mandate for any portion of the Ottoman Empire. Moreover, Wilson reminded his colleagues, that certain elements in Turkey favored a single mandate for the Turkish area and a similar principle applied to the Arabs. Lloyd George thought this would be difficult in practice, while Clemenceau could see little difference between a "mandate for development and administration, and a mandate for guidance."[2]

The next day, May 14, Lloyd George presented his plan for the reorganization of the Ottoman Empire, which had been worked out by Harold Nicolson. This proposal involved (1) an American mandate for Constantinople and Armenia; (2) full Greek sovereignty over Smyrna and Aivali, the Dodecanese and Castellorizo; and (3) spheres of influence in the rest of Asia Minor, with a Greek mandate for the territory adjacent to Smyrna. Italy was to have the mandate for the southern seaboard, from west of Makri to the point where Armenia strikes the Mediterranean. France was to receive the mandate for the rest of the "future Turkish State." President Wilson's idea was to establish a Turkish state in northern Anatolia, under a "loose" French mandate as it would be better not to have the French and Italians mixing in southern Anatolia—both with

[1] *PPC*, V, 501-505. On May 6, Lloyd George stated that "it ought to be decided that M. Venizelos should be allowed to land two or three divisions at Smyrna to protect his fellow-countrymen in Turkey." Wilson pointed out that the Greek Commission was "now unanimously in favour of giving this area to Greece" (*ibid.*, 484).
[2] *PPC*, V, 479-584, 812. It is interesting to note that Lloyd George stated personally that he "would like to add Cyprus to Greece, although there were considerable difficulties. He thought that such an act would deprive the whole transaction of any atmosphere of 'grab'." President Wilson said "it would be a great thing if Mr. Lloyd George could accomplish that." In a discussion of May 22, he noted that "it has also been proposed that we should give up Cyprus, although that was not in any bargain or treaty." See LLOYD GEORGE, II, Chs. XXIV, XXV.

advisers at the Turkish capital. Lloyd George urged this as "the great argument against dividing up Anatolia." According to Wilson, southern Anatolia should be a self-governing unit with Konia as the capital, and an elected governor-general. As an alternative, the British Prime Minister proposed that the sultan remain in Constantinople, as sovereign over all Turkey, leaving France, Italy and Greece to overlook parts of Anatolia, while the United States supervised the activities of the Sultan at Constantinople. Subject to Senatorial approval, the President now agreed to two proposals, originally drafted by Nicolson, which provided for American mandates in Armenia and Constantinople and the disposition of the rest of Anatolia. [1]

Another very important event took place on May 14. On April 12 Venizelos had reported serious trouble in Smyrna and Aidin and urged strong, immediate measures. May 14 witnessed a landing of Greek forces at Smyrna under cover of British and French vessels and the *U. S. S. Arizona* and five United States destroyers. This was the definite beginning of the terrible Greco-Turkish drama of 1919-1922 which ended so disastrously for the dreams of a greater Hellas in Asia-Minor.

The Difficulties with Italy

The Italian landings on the coast of Asia Minor in the spring of 1919 thoroughly angered President Wilson, Lloyd George and Clemenceau and the problem was discussed in detail with Orlando at the meeting of the Council of Four on May 17. A protest was presented to Orlando which he attempted to answer the next day. [2] Meanwhile, on the morning of May 17, Lloyd George circulated among the members of the Council a memorandum of Balfour, prepared on May 16, protesting against the partition of Anatolia. Mr. Balfour did not believe that the Ottoman Empire had been so rotten as to warrant such treatment and

---

[1] *PPC*, V, 614-620, 622-623, *Miller Diary*, XIX, 562. See also *House Diary*, May 15, 1919, in Seymour, IV, 467, and *British Documents*, 1919-1939, First Series, IV, 857-869.

[2] Woodrow Wilson Papers, IX-A 55. The Orlando reply of May 18 denied that the action had been taken without warrant or knowledge of the Allies, although no previous warning had been given. He cited the Greek landing at Smyrna and the general "anarchy" in the region. Lloyd George noted in his *Memoirs*, II, 1249-1250: "The question of Smyrna had been settled before President Wilson departed for America.... There was a race between the Italians and the Greeks as to which of them would be the first to land a garrison in Smyrna. Prompt action taken by Wilson, Clemenceau and myself enabled Venizelos to get a Greek force into the town whilst the Italians were hesitating. Some difficulties arose from time to time as to the limits of Greek occupation, but these were adjusted without serious trouble." See also *PPC*, V, 668-669, 669-672; *Miller Diary*, XIX, 563; BAKER, III, 302-307; ALBRECHT-CARRIE, *passim*; M. H. MACARTNEY and Paul CREMONA, *Italy's Foreign and Colonial Policy*, 1870-1935 (London and New York, Oxford, 1938), Ch. III.

was particularly afraid that the partition would "deeply shock large sections of Mohammedan opinion." He felt that "we must admit that no such scheme would ever have been thought of, if it had not been necessary to find some method of satisfying Italian ambitions." Under the Balfour scheme Turkey would remain an undivided state without a mandatory, with much diminished territories, but with substantially the same status of the old empire. The Ottoman sultan would "reign at Brusa or Konia as his predecessors had formerly reigned at Constantinople." But since something had to be found for the Italians in Asia Minor, "at the smallest cost to mankind", compensation might be given in the Adalia region. It is interesting to note, of course, that British interests were well considered in the memorandum, for Constantinople would not be the Turkish capital, Turkey would not control the Straits, and Great Britain would retain what it had gained and desired in Mesopotamia and Palestine. [1]

On the afternoon of May 17, Lloyd George introduced to the Council of Four, under the sponsorship of the Rt. Hon. E. S. Montagu, the Secretary of State for India, and a number of prominent Indian Moslems, including the Aga Khan, all of whom protested strongly against the projected partition of the Ottoman Empire and particularly, it would seem, against the detachment of Constantinople and the region of the Straits, primarily because of what it would mean to the Caliphate. [2] Partly because of this protest, Lloyd George suggested on May 19 that the Italian mandate proposal be withdrawn and the Italians get out of Asia Minor entirely. If they did not do so, he would disavow their claims. When Wilson, seemingly much impressed with the Moslem sentiment, proposed leaving the Sultan in Anatolia and perhaps even in Constantinople, under French advice, Lloyd George declared that if France were to be the single adviser of Turkey, "he would have to ask for a reexamination of the whole question of mandates in the Turkish Empire", since he could not approve a solution which would place France in prospective control of Constantinople and the Straits. [3]

[1] *PPC*, V, 686-688, 688-689.
[2] *PPC*, V, 690-701.
[3] *PPC*, V, 705-711, 716-723, 726. Harold Nicolson noted in his diary for May 19 (*Peace-Making*, 343): "Most of the Cabinet have come over from London to discuss the future of Turkey.... Curzon pressed for ejection of Turkey from Europe, and accepts Greek zone at Smyrna although with deep regret. Montagu and Miller are all against disturbing the Turks still further. Winston wants to leave him as he is, but to give America the mandate over Constantinople at the Straits, with a zone extending as far as Trebizond. A. J. B. wants Constantinople under an American mandate, Smyrna and the rest of Turkey as an independent kingdom, supervised by foreign advisers. Ll. G. is non-commital. No decision come to in so far as, through the glass darkly, I can ascertain."
See also The Woodrow Wilson Papers, IX-A 56 for the letter of Edwin

On May 21, Mr. Lloyd George came forth with another mandate scheme under which the United States would take the mandate for Constantinople, the region of the Straits, Armenia and Cilicia. Anatolia would remain undivided, except for the region which was to be united with Greece. Unless the United States would take the mandate over Anatolia, there would be none for that territory. France, on the other hand, was to have a provisional mandate for Syria until the report of the Inter-Allied Commission, while Great Britain would assume a similar provisional mandate for Mesopotamia. Until Russia's reorganization, the United States was to have a mandate for the Caucasus. Italy was entirely excluded from any mandate over any portion of the former Ottoman Empire. While Indian Moslem objection was said to have been the basic reason for excluding Italy, there was also the British desire to preserve the freedom of the Straits through an American mandate, without the interference of France or Italy. British forces had done nine-tenths of the fighting against the Ottoman Empire and Lloyd George did not consider it good policy to partition the Turkish homelands in Anatolia. However, since an independent Turkey would require some sort of foreign supervision, that control should be exercised by the United States. The Turks would distrust a European mandate, fearing that Turkey might become "a mere colony". Moreover, it was "impossible to make Italy sole mandatory in Anatolia and if France alone exercised this power Italy would be jealous." It was also perfectly clear that Great Britain would oppose any other mandatory. The United States alone must assume that obligation. [1]

While there was much truth in what Lloyd George said concerning an American mandate, President Wilson seemed to penetrate to the essence of the British project when he questioned once more American willingness to accept a mandate for Anatolia. Moreover, he declared that even "if the United States were the Mandatory of the Straits they would not in the least object if the Sultan were advised in stipulated

---

S. Montagu to President Wilson, May 7, 1919. Wilson thanked Montagu on May 19 indicating that he would now know better how to play his part "in dealing with the critical question of Turkish sovereignty."

[1] *PPC*, V, 755-766, 769-771. An undated British Memorandum in The Woodrow Wilson Papers called for an American mandate over Armenia and the region of Constantinople and the Straits, an Italian mandate over Southern Anatolia, Greek control over Smyrna region and the Dodecanese, a tripartite mandate over "the future state of Turkey," and a French mandate over the remaining portion of "Turkey". (Wilson Paper, IX-A 75). Henry Morgenthau, Sr., W. H. Buckler, and Philip Marshall Brown submitted a memorandum on *The Future Government of Asia Minor* to Wilson on May 21, which the President considered valuable, providing for a triple mandate over Armenia, Anatolia and the region of the Straits, to be assumed by the United States. Wilson Papers, IX-A, 56; Morgenthau, 337.

matters by other Powers on the subject of the government of Anatolia." Lloyd George, thereupon, replied that "if the United States could not take a Mandatory over Anatolia, it would be better for the Sultan to clear out of Constantinople." Clemenceau, like Wilson, but on entirely different grounds, also objected to the British scheme and urged that France "surely ought not to be expelled from Asia Minor on two such grounds as the Musulman question and the Italian question", and he was very bitter concerning alleged British bad faith in connection with the Syrian problem. [1]

Troubles with the Greeks

Meanwhile, the Greek occupation of Smyrna during May 14-15, 1919 was producing a furor. [2] The Ottoman cabinet had resigned and Admiral Mark Bristol, the American High Commissioner in Constantinople, telegraphed the American Commission in Paris on May 17 that everybody was surprised by the occupation, and that the Turks considered it a "humiliation", a sentiment which might be "changed to resentment and general discontent." A storm of protest from various groups of Turkish citizens went to President Wilson charging, among other things, that the Greek action at Smyrna was in flagrant contradiction to the high principles for which the United States had fought. Admiral Bristol cabled on May 22 that resentment in Turkey was increasing and he begged for a statement regarding the Greek occupation, "or else occupation (of Turkey) by associated military forces." On May 31, after a conference with leading Turkish citizens, including the former Grand Vizier, Izzet Pasha, Admiral Bristol telegraphed that if the United States were made the mandatory over Turkey, "the support and cooperation of Turkish military forces could be relied upon" and that only a small United States military force would be necessary. But he complained that while the British and French were making desperate rival efforts to control the Ottoman Delegation to the Peace Conference, nothing was being done in behalf of the United States, and stressed that in the selection "no

---

[1] When Lloyd George challenged Clemenceau concerning the naming of French members of the proposed Inter-Allied Commission, the latter indicated that he was "ready for the French representatives to go, as soon as the British troops in Syria had been replaced by French." A letter from Grew to Close, May 24, 1919 (Woodrow Wilson Papers, IX-A 58) contains a warning from Balfour against "any premature disclosures of the terms to be imposed upon Turkey unless and until time has been given to advise the Allied and Associated representatives at Constantinople."

[2] For a justification of the Greek position see A. A. PALLIS, *Greece's Anatolian Venture—and After* (London, Methuen, 1937), 239 pp. See also Harold NICOLSON, *Curzon: The Last Phase*, Ch. IV. The material which follows is based in part on the papers of Admiral Bristol, contained in the files of the King-Crane Commission, primarily those of Henry Churchill King.

American influence" of any sort was "being brought to bear." Damad Ferid Pasha, who later was to head the Ottoman Delegation, represented French sentiment.

More direct evidence of what was going on in Smyrna came from the American Consul, Mr. Ralph Y. Chesbrough, who had been detailed there during May 3 to 14, from Constantinople. Mr. Chesbrough did not doubt that "of all the foreign colonies in Smyrna the best organized for the purpose of carrying on propaganda work since the armistice was the Greek Church and the Greek Consulate." The home of the Greek archbishop and the Greek Chamber of Commerce had been the headquarters of this propaganda. Moreover, both the French and the Italians had exerted every effort to extend their influence over that section of Turkey. While Admiral Bristol did not want to question the wisdom of the Peace Conference, he felt compelled to do all in his power "to give correct information concerning the results of that occupation", because, he felt "that those who made the decision could not have known the facts beforehand." [1]

The End of Delay and Confusion

While the Peace Conference was considering the problem of mandates in the Middle East, members of the King-Crane Commission were also busy. During the latter part of April and the opening of May, they held a number of conferences for the purpose of exchanging expert opinion.

Conference and Study

As early as April 25, Professor Westermann [2] outlined the various claims which the Allied Powers had staked out, as well as the different schemes for the partition of the Ottoman Empire, with an international state in the region of Constantinople and the Straits, Mesopotamia and Palestine under a British protectorate, Syria under France, and Arabia independent. Armenia might be subdivided into four provinces, including

---

[1] Report of Operations for Week Ending 1 June 1919. Senior U. S. Naval Officer, Turkey, Part Four. On May 28 Professor Westermann wrote to Secretary of State Lansing: "The idea that the Greek people are fitted, either economically or from the standpoint of political morality, for the obligations of mandatory supervision, will not be countenanced by any person who knows the Near East, and need not be discussed. We wish to recall to the American Commissioners that our office has always opposed the Greek claims to territory in Asia Minor. We still oppose it. The incidents of the Greek occupation of Smyrna on May 15, carefully excluded from the French papers, are typical of Greek methods." Woodrow Wilson Papers, IX-A 59: Westermann to Lansing, May 28; Lansing to Wilson, May 29, 1919; *PPC*, XI, 193.

[2] Lybyer *Diary*, April 25, 1919. See also the *Notebooks* of Brodie, King and Lybyer. Westermann and Magie urged President Wilson on May 6 to do something about Armenia (Woodrow Wilson Papers, IX-A 51).

Cilicia, Kurdistan, and Armenia proper, with the United States, perhaps, taking control of the territory previously assigned to Russia. But, in any case, the United States should make its decision and inform the Armenians.

A few days later, on April 30, Mr. Heck, of the American Embassy in Constantinople, spoke to the Commission on the disposition of the Ottoman Empire, favoring a unitary solution of the problem. [1] He felt that the Ottoman Government had failed to solve its problems, and he expected a break politically between the Turks and the Arabs, although Captain Yale suggested the possibility of a Turkish-Arabic understanding at the close of the war. Heck thought that Constantinople, European Turkey and Asia Minor should all be placed under either Great Britain or the United States. While there were Christian minorities throughout this region, he did not believe that the "Turkish majorities" could be "ignored". The Sultan should be kept in Constantinople. The Turks preferred an American mandate, for they were grateful for the philanthropic and educational work which Americans had performed in the Empire, and did not want the French. He noted, however, that the Entente representatives in Constantinople were opposed to an American mandate. A separate Armenia would be a mistake. Under an American mandate the Sultan could be retained as the nominal head of state, but American officials, with local assistants, would manage the departments of justice and public order, simplify the land tenure system of the empire, rebuild the naval and military establishments, and set the country on the road to progress. About 3,000 American officials would be sufficient after pacification of the country.

Professor David Magie, of Princeton, on the staff of the Office of Western Asia, told the King-Crane group on May 2 that some kind of strong government would be necessary to preserve order between the Kurds and Assyrian Christians. Captain Yale discussed the "Arabian and Syrian Situations" on May 5-6. He traced the early separatist movements among the Arabs, outlined the influence of the "holy war" on the Arabs and the growth of Arabic antagonism toward the Turks. He stressed the bad effects of Jemal Pasha's attempts to "Turkify" the Arabs, his hanging of some two hundred Arabs, the Arab belief that the idea of the "holy war" had been misused by the Turks, and the transformation of the Syrian into the more general Arab movement. [2] On the other hand, Yale contended that religion rather than nationalism was the keynote of the Arab uprising, a position in which he disagreed with Colonel

---

[1] Lybyer *Diary*, April 30, 1919; *Notebooks* of Brodie and Lybyer.
[2] For the Turkish case see Le Commandant de la IVème Armée, *La Vérité sur la Question Syrienne* (Stamboul, Imprimerie Tanine, 1916, 168 pp.), with documents and facsimiles. See also George ANTONIUS, Chs. XI-XII; Zeine N. ZEINE, *Arab Turkish Relations and the Emergence of Arab Nationalism* (Beirut, Khayat's, 1958), 156 pp., *passim*.

T. E Lawrence and others who felt that the Emir Feisal and his followers were strong enough to break the religious hold and develop a liberal nationalism. [1]

It was not until May 7 that President Caleb F. Gates, of Robert College, Constantinople, arrived in Paris for consultation with members of the Commission and for talks with Colonel House and others. Dr. Gates was on his way home to the United States, but was very anxious about the Turkish situation, and had been urged to give his views. On arrival he found that [2]

> the Versailles Peace Conference was dragging matters along; and meanwhile the situation was getting worse and worse. I was afraid that there would be serious trouble—not in Constantinople where the Entente was strong—but in the provinces. The Armenians were asking altogether too much and French politics were very bad. In Paris, I observed that the Peace Conference was making a hopeless muddle of the Turkish question. It was proposing to send out a commission of investigation, which would take at least three months, although the facts were fully known. Meanwhile they would probably require Turkey to sign some kind of treaty which would divide their country into various zones of influence, leaving the mandates to be settled there. I felt certain that the Turks would resist this, and that disorders would break out all over the country, in which the rest of the Armenians might perish. The powers could not agree to act in concert, but neither would they agree to allow any one power to act alone. Wilson's idealism appealed strongly to the peoples, but not to the diplomats. The situation left me anxious and heartsick. I felt like advocating a new petition for the litany: "Good Lord, deliver us from wars and from peace conferences."

Whatever Gates' personal feelings about the necessity of the King-Crane Commission, he spoke at length to the group on May 8 at the Hotel de Crillon, stressing that the problems of Armenia and Turkey were inseparable and that an independent Armenia would be useless if it were a surrounded province. Moreover, he raised the question of Turkish *majorities* in Armenia and Armenian *minorities* in the rest of Turkey. Since the armistice the situation in the Near East had become increasingly difficult. The Turks, with the Committee of Union and Progress still very strong and wealthy, had misunderstood the kind treatment meted out to them and did not realize they had been beaten in the war. The French had made a serious error in using Armenian troops to occupy Cilicia, and the Armenian delegation at Paris had been all too extravagant in presenting their claims to territory which was not really Armenian in national character. A declaration of an independent Armenia without military protection of some 300,000 troops would mean

---

[1] Lybyer *Diary*, May 5-6, 1919; *Notebooks* of Brodie and Lybyer. See also ZEINE, *The Struggle for Arab Independence*, Chs. IV, V.

[2] Caleb F. GATES, *Not to Me Only*, 260-261. For the Gates presentation see the Lybyer *Diary*, May 8, 1919; *Notebooks* of Brodie and Lybyer.

the beginning of massacres. Gates favored, as did most educated Ottomans, he thought, a single mandate for all Turkey, with the United States as the mandatory. Great Britain, too, would be a satisfactory mandatory, if willing to assume the burden, but neither France nor Italy would be acceptable. If Turkey were to be divided, the Arabs should be separated from the Turks, and Great Britain should take over Armenia with Mesopotamia. But Gates was opposed to creating an international city or state of Constantinople, because it would become a literal "hornet's nest". Whatever the decision, however, speed was essential.

Dr. Gates was opposed to the sending of the Commission to the Near East because it would result in further delay and confusion and he believed the facts well enough known. No doubt this opinion was generally circulated in official quarters, for President Gates had dinner with Henry White and talked with Colonel House. At any rate, Lybyer was very fearful that Gates' ideas would kill either the Commission or force action in the direction of the partition of the Ottoman Empire. [1] There were other conferences within the Commission itself. Professor Lybyer presented an historical analysis of French relations with Syria, and conferences were held with the Reverend Abraham M. Rihany, and Dr. Leon Dominian, whose work on *The Frontiers of Language and Nationality in Europe* (1917), Dr. King had read very thoroughly.

Unfortunately, not much progress apparently was being made in the direction of actually leaving for the Near East. On May 3 Dr. King urged that American consular officers in Turkey, Syria and Egypt be instructed to prepare immediately lists of important persons and to obtain other information. [2] He wrote Colonel House on May 6 urging that French Commissioners be appointed promptly and pointing out that the continued delay might prejudice their case and "drive the American Commissioners into the arms of the British." President Wilson, to whom the King letter was communicated, tried to get Clemenceau to appoint the French members, but the French Premier "always wriggled out." [3]

Zionist Opposition

Meanwhile, the Zionist Organization was growing ever more anxious

---

[1] Lybyer *Diary*, May 11, 1919.
[2] Woodrow Wilson Papers: IX-A 52, Close to Boston, May 13, 1919; King Papers: Grew to King, May 5, 8, 1919. While desirous of helping, Admiral Boston pointed out that all suitable ships were transporting troops back to the United States, but he instructed Admiral Bristol to help.
[3] Woodrow Wilson Papers, IX-A 51. King to House, May 6, 1919. In a letter of May 8 to Lybyer, Eric Forbes-Adam, of the British Delegation, indicated British troubles about getting a ship. He hoped that the Council of Four would insist on the French appointments "being made at once", but had had no further word from the Italians. See also Lybyer *Diary*, May 9, 12, 1919.

about the situation in the Near East and fearful in particular about the King-Crane Commission. Professor Felix Frankfurter, who had already written to Colonel House on April 30, suggesting that Palestine be excluded from the scope of the inquiry as territory concerning which there was no dispute, wrote to President Wilson on May 8: [1]

> Conscious of the duty of every American not to take from your time and energy, I am nevertheless compelled to bring to your attention the conditions that now confront Jewry, above all Eastern Jewry.
>
> You are familiar with the problems and have stated their solution. The controlling Jewish hope has been—and is—your approval of the Balfour Declaration and your sponsorship of the establishment of Palestine as the Jewish National Home. The appointment of the Interallied Syrian Commission and the assumed postponement for months, but particularly beyond the time of your stay here, of the disposition of Near Eastern questions, have brought the deepest disquietude to the representatives of the Jewry of the world. As a passionate American I am, of course, most eager that the Jews should be a constructive and not a disruptive force in the new world order. I have reassured their leaders with the conviction of knowledge of your purposes. They have faith; I venture to think no people in Paris have more faith—the faith of 2000 years. But they also have the knowledge of the suffering of millions of Jews, and the hopes of Jews the world over, which nothing will assuage except the rededication, at last, of Palestine as a Jewish Homeland. Moreover, it is not merely a Jewish question. An extended delay in the Near Eastern settlement is bound to intensify the existing unrest by giving dangerous opportunities to Young Turk intrigue and to the stimulation of religious animosities.
>
> The English authorities are eager to have Dr. Weizmann and me go to Palestine to assure moderation in the Jewish population. We are doing all that can be done and I am confident the Jewish population will maintain restraint. But I dare not leave here while the Turkish issues are undetermined and while you are still in Paris to decide them.
>
> You will forgive me for writing, but circumstances have made me the trustee of a situation that affects the hopes and the very life of a whole people. Therefore I cannot forbear to say that not a little of the peace of the world depends upon the disposal, before you return to America, of the destiny of the peoples released from Turkish rule.

President Wilson did not reply until May 13 and then merely expressed his appreciation of "the importance and significance of the whole matter." This brief note, naturally, was not very satisfying, and on May 14, Professor Frankfurter wrote once more:

---

[1] These letters may be found in Woodrow Wilson Papers, IX-A 52, 53, 55. They have also been published in *British Documents*, 1919-1939, First Series, IV, 260-262. Mr. Justice Frankfurter also kindly furnished the writer with copies of the ensuing correspondence. Evidently the President authorized Frankfurter to show the correspondence to anyone interested at Paris "and use it in the way that you suggest." Lybyer quotes Dr. King as saying on May 11 that Frankfurter wanted "to go to Turkey with us."

today—how their hopes and their faith are sustained or saddened, by what you say, or fail to say. Therefore, I know you will want me to inform you, in all candor, that your note of acknowledgement to my letter of May eighth has occasioned almost despair to the Jewish representatives now assembled in Paris, who speak not only for the Jews of Europe, but also for the American Jewish Congress, the democratic voice of three million American Jews. I do not fail to appreciate the forces which confront you here, and the circumspection which conditions impose upon you. On our side the task is to keep literally millions of Jews in check. Uncertainty, indefinite delay, seeming change of policy bring a feeling of hopelessness which only those in intimate contact with the people whose fate is at stake can fully guage. We are bending every energy to avert the slow attrition of the spirit of such a people.

Therefore, you will forgive me for submitting to you the wisdom and justice of a reassuring word, written or spoken,—even though it be repetitive—that you are purposing to have the Balfour Declaration written into the Treaty of Peace, and that you are aiming to see that Declaration translated into action before you leave Paris.

You know how profoundly words, even familiar words, move people.

Two days later came the answer from the President, who had "never dreamed that it was necessary to give... any renewed assurance" of his adherence to the Balfour Declaration, and had found no one who was "seriously opposing the purpose" which it embodied. Moreover, on May 16, the President expressed his "surprise" that Professor Frankfurter had considered anything which he had written "discouraging", since he saw "no ground for discouragement and every reason to hope that satisfactory guarantees" could "be secured".

Doubts and Decisions

President Wilson was apparently making up his mind to send the King-Crane Commission to the Near East. He told Ray Stannard Baker on May 13 that Dr. King "must be wearied" by the varied fortunes of the Commission. In accordance with President Wilson's suggestion, Dr. King prepared a memorandum for the President's consideration and then went to work on other problems involved in the breaking up of the Ottoman Empire. [1] Whether there was much point to all this work was another matter, for it appeared that plans for the "settlement of Turkey" were practically complete by May 17, with the United States in Constantinople and Armenia, and, as Lybyer heard it, Turkey split through the desert east to west, the south to Italy, and the north to France.[2]

---

[1] Woodrow Wilson Papers, IX-A 54. Baker to Close, May 15, 1919. Somewhat later King asked to have a brief conference with Wilson "on the Memoranda already sent in, at the President's convenience." See Wilson Papers, IX-A 76 and Lybyer *Diary*, May 13, 1919.

[2] Lybyer *Diary*, May 14, 1919. A circular had come from Grew indicating that in making the Bulgarian and Turkish treaties, the Americans would serve only in an advisory capacity, since the United States

Once more the Commission was facing a crisis similar to that which it had met during April 20-22. Mr. King recorded on May 18 that it looked increasingly as if there were no place for the Commission, since the entire question of mandates was being taken up by the Conference and the Council of Four. Lybyer, too, was about convinced that all would be settled without the United States and the Commission would probably not leave Paris. Crane advised King on May 19 to see Colonel House "about disbanding the Commission." In general the group was somewhat indifferent about the outcome, for it was "tired of struggling." [1]

As in April, the crisis came and quickly passed, for the forces which were now in favor of sending the Commission were gathering momentum. On May 20 Colonel House received an urgent communication from the Hejaz Delegation at Paris calling his attention to fact that the Supreme Council several times had decided to send an Inter-Allied Commission to the Near East. [2] Now it had been rumored that the Commission "would not trouble to go to learn the wishes of the Arab populations concerning the fate of their country." House had assured Feisal that "as France and Great Britain had already given their assurance" as to sending the Commission, its departure was a "question of honor", especially for the United States, and "nothing in the world could prevent its departure." The Arabs had accepted "the word and good will of the Allied and Associated Governments", but now they had heard that the Supreme Council desired "to settle the Arab problems in Asia Minor without consulting the populations whose fate" they were determining. Freed from the Turkish yoke, partly by their own heroic sacrifices, the Arabs were energetically opposed to "any arbitrary decision taken without their consent", and were "now waiting impatiently for the arrival" of the Commission. The Peace Conference might "treat its enemies in any way" it pleased, but "not its friends." All the Arabs knew that the Allies had given their word of honor to send a Commission. For these reasons "and in order to put an end to the confusion arising from this question", the Hejaz Delegation begged House "to do everything possible to hasten the departure" of the Commission.

---

had not been at war with either Bulgaria or Turkey. Westermann was convinced this meant that they were to have no voice at all, and signaled an "old-fashioned grab-game method." He had "profound distrust of the English—put forward a good crowd, and then withdraw them at a critical time, and bring up old foreign office diplomats." Shotwell noted on May 15: "... This means that the United States is not going to interest itself in the settlement of Turkey in the Near East and there is great dissatisfaction in certain quarters. The League of Nations is starting with a pretty serious handicap in a world that is by no means settled...."
SHOTWELL, *At the Paris Peace Conference*, 321.

[1] Lybyer *Diary*, May 19, 1919..
[2] Woodrow Wilson Papers, IX-A 56. The Hejaz Delegation to Colonel House, Paris, May 20, 1919.

When Dr. King told Colonel House on May 20 that the King-Crane group was "ready to drop out", he was advised to "stand pat for a time", because President Wilson had decided definitely to send the Commission to Syria on Monday, May 26. Colonel House, who already had transmitted the Hejaz letter to President Wilson, recorded: [1]

> Dr. King came to-day about the Syrian Commission, and I told the President it was something of a scandal that this commission had not already gone to Syria as promised the Arabs. The honor of Great Britain, France, and the United States was at stake, and I hoped he would insist that the commission leave at once. The President assured me that he had done everything he could in the direction indicated. I then suggested that he set Monday as the time when our commission would start, regardless of the French and English. He adopted the suggestion and said he would tell Clemenceau and Lloyd George tomorrow.

Everything seemed settled now; once more the Commission was to be and it was to go to the Near East. The British group, too, was making preparations to leave. But David Hogarth was assuming that President Wilson was intent on immediate action in three matters: "1. Suspension of assignment of Turkish mandates, leaving us some honest purpose and character; 2. Insistence on the French appointing their Commission and joining up without delay; 3. Provision of transport to Palestine." On the success of all these measures would depend the final British decision. [2]

Dr. King evidently shared the views expressed by Commander Hogarth, and in two letters to Colonel House on May 21 and 22, [3] he set forth the situation admirably. The first note declared:

> In accordance with the instructions of the President... the American members of the Commission on Mandates in Turkey are preparing to leave for Syria on Monday next, May 26th, or as soon thereafter as possible. I am assured that the British Commissioners would wish to go with us but would find it difficult to complete their arrangements and

---

[1] King *Diary*, May 20, 1919; Seymour, IV, 468, for House note. The Lybyer *Diary*, May 20, notes that King went to see House in the morning and suggested disbanding of the Commission, "since it looked as though all its work would be done here. Col. said 'No, wait five or six days.' Arabs say Commission has been definitely promised. Fact is Haidar Pasha, representative of Feisal, wrote very strong letter, stating House had given word of honor Commission would go. Col. had King read letter aloud—sent word to Haidar to have personal allusions removed." That evening Dr. King remarked: "I have startling news for you. Col. House sent for me again and told me that the Pres. wishes us to start Monday, whether any others go or not."

[2] Lybyer Papers. David Hogarth to A.H. Lybyer, May 20, 21, 1919. Hogarth hoped to get off and have the thing settled, however unsatisfactory be our mandate, but agree that things are coming to a pass out there."

[3] King Papers: King to E. M. House, May 21, 22, 1919.

get back to Paris, before the middle of next week. Manifestly it is particularly desirable, in the visit to Syria, that the French Commissioners should go with us, or join us shortly; and no doubt all possible will be done to insure that result.

The chief concern of our Commissioners is that we do not see how the Commission, in now going, is to have an honest purpose and character, unless there is suspension of assignment of Turkish mandates here in Paris in the meantime, in view of the fact that our Commission is known to have been expressly appointed to recommend concerning mandates in the Turkish Empire. The Commission has no desire to urge its own continuance; but if it is to continue, then for the sake of honest relations with the peoples to whom we go, and for the sake of all the delicate interests involved, it is of essential importance that our precise task, whether in Syria or in other portions of the Turkish Empire, should be clearly delimited and understood.

Colonel House added a penciled note to King's letter indicating President Wilson's position that all the mandates were provisional until acted on by the Senate. Dr. King again set forth his views in the second letter:

You already know, from my conversation of day before yesterday with you, that Mr. Crane and I had come to feel that the Peace Conference had reached a point where it was practically inevitable that they should seek early decisions upon them; and that under those circumstances there was no further reason for the continuance of the Commission on Turkish mandates.

But if now, in the judgment of the President, there are special reasons why the Commission—so much of it as can be gotten together—should still go, at least to Syria, it is then the clear and unified judgment of both the British and the American Commissioners, that the assigning of mandates, at least in the Arabic-speaking portions of the Turkish Empire, should be suspended in the meantime, in order that the Commission may not be put in the false and intolerable position, in the view of the peoples of the Near East, of professedly examining a situation, with a view to recommendations, which has already been determined, or is in the process of being determined, by the Conference at Paris. Can that difficulty be resolved?

It should also be borne in mind that the French opposition to the Commission has been, in considerable part, due to their feeling that the British claims were to be taken as settled while the French claims were to be regarded as under investigation.

In the last analysis, of course, President Wilson himself would have to make the final decision, and the stage was being set for a last conference with him. On May 22 Mr. Wilson received a telegram from the Emir Feisal declaring that he had found everybody in Syria "anxiously awaiting the arrival of the Commission." [1] In addition, Mr. Henry White was lending his support to the sending of the Commission, although

[1] Woodrow Wilson Papers, IX-A 57. The telegram came from General Clayton at Cairo, May 6 [Damascus, May 4], and was transmitted from Grew to Close for the President.

he had his doubts concerning an American mandatory, particularly if the Sultan-Caliph remained in Constantinople, with different foreign advisers, and continued as the sovereign of Anatolia. White had received a letter from Lord Bryce on May 19 suggesting "small impartial commissions" to examine certain Balkan questions, and he thought so much of the idea that he wrote to Wilson on May 22 urging that there was "a good deal to be said for his suggestion" of impartial commissions to investigate such problems during the summer, "with a view to reassembling of the Conference in the autumn, to receive and act upon the reports of these commissions." [1]

Conference with the President

It was with this background that Dr. King, Mr. Crane and Professor Westermann called on the President on the afternoon of May 22. [2] First Dr. King discussed several questions with the President concerning "the position of the Commission". Was it certainly going, and if so, how soon? Were the official instructions to be changed, so as to include Turkey proper? Was the Commission to have an American ship at its disposal, a matter which would give it added prestige? If the Peace Conference dissolved before the group's return, to whom should it report? What effect would the conclusion of a peace with Turkey have on the Commission? What about funds, yachts, etc.? The President replied that, regardless of the British and French, the Americans were to make the journey to the Near East and report to him. Second, what were "the President's personal desires and purposes as to the Commission"?

---

[1] Woodrow Wilson Papers, IX-A 57. Henry White to the President, May 22, 1919. In a letter of May 21 (Wilson Papers, IX-A 56) Professors Westermann and Magie complained to the President that they had no idea as to what was being done, for apparently the only technical advice which was being heard was that of the British and M. Venizelos, all of whom were interested parties. They feared that the decisions based on such advice would "result in the looting of the Ottoman Empire in violation of the principles which both you and the American people desire to see enforced." Westermann and Magie felt that their own advice was "purely disinterested" and that they might be of assistance in bringing about a more equitable solution of some of the problems involved, and therefore asked for an opportunity to see the President.

[2] King *Diary*, May 22, 1919. King Papers: Memorandum of Points Desired to be Taken Up with the President (Memorandum also in Wilson Papers, IX-A 54). Dr. King noted President Wilson's answers in his penciled marginal notes. Lybyer recorded on May 22: "3 P. M. King returned—President very pleasant—wishes Commission to go. Chose men in whom he had confidence, wants them to see people and report to him, will rely on their report. To be done for League of Nations—no matter if mandates are temporarily assigned meantime. Americans to go anyhow, others if they wish. Westermann pleased by his talk—President has good knowledge of facts. Will do all he can for a good solution." See also Wilson Papers, IX-A 57: Crane to President, May 22, 1919.

What points did "he desire especially to emphasize"? Could the United States be expected "to accept a mandate for Armenia, or Syria, or Constantinople, or for the whole of Asia Minor", if that seemed best? Third, what about "limitations of time and territory"? The President declared there were no definite limitations of time, and, in his view, the Commission was to visit such places as seemed "most vital". Finally, there was the problem of "existing agreements or understandings". The President indicated that both the Zionist question and the problem of Mesopotamia were "virtually" closed by the Powers. But the Arabian question appeared to be open. The Commission was not "bound by any pre-Conference or other agreements". In conclusion Wilson informed his callers that there were no Conference understandings which closed any part of this question, and no mandatories had yet been decided.

Dr. King left a draft memorandum of recommendations with President Wilson, [1] which called for a "definite American policy in regard to Turkey" and asserted that "the plan of the Peace Conference" as projected in March was "no longer feasible." That was true primarily because Turkey would "not consent to be dismembered into four or five parts without the presence of a larger occupying force" than could then be provided. Moreover, if preliminary announcement of American acceptance of a strictly Armenian mandate were made, the Armenians "would be destroyed long before American occupying troops could be provided." Italy could not control Anatolia "without great disorder", and Greece did not have the power to take "Western Asia Minor from the Turks." But even if such a plan were feasible it would be undesirable. It would be imposing on the Turks their third or fourth choice, it was not a plan based on ethnographical conditions, and since the Turks were in a majority in the four or five areas involved, this would be the very negation of "self-determination and the rights of peoples."

It was recommended that the United States "should adopt the policy of taking the whole non-Arabic-speaking portion of Turkey", under a mandate from the League of Nations, for a term of years. Neither the territories nor the people were readily divisible, economic interests demanded "unified handling for a time at least", and "the consent of the Turks" could be obtained for such a plan. The proposition, therefore, was immediately feasible. However, the area was not to be placed under

[1] Lybyer Papers. A. H. LYBYER, *Suggestions in Regard to the Turkish Situation*, May 20, 1919, Lybyer had worked out this memorandum, which Westermann approved, substantially by May 13. It is interesting to note the changes in attitude in the memorandum. Lybyer wrote on August 4 on this memorandum that investigation on the spot had shown that a satisfactory arrangement between France and the people of Syria was "impossible". Moreover, he noted that "Palestine would be better off united with Syria, under an American mandate." Italy seemed to have declined the offer of a temporary mandate in the Caucasus.

a single American mandate, but under a composite or group of mandates, involving the setting off of an Armenian, a Greek and a Turkish area, with a separate territory for the Straits. In view of the past, world opinion demanded that " 'Armenia' should be forever separated from Turkish rule". The weakening of Turkish prestige and that of the Sultan-Caliph by the removal of the Government to Brusa would be desirable. Moreover, "the command of the Straits" was "an interest of all the world."

On the other hand, France might well "have a mandate for a fairly large 'Syria'." The essential problem for France was to reach an agreement with the "peoples under mandate." Great Britain, too, "might well have a mandate in Mesopotamia, Palestine, and Arabia", although "in Palestine the rights of non-Jews must be thoroughly safeguarded." Finally, if it were necessary to provide for a compensatory Italian mandate, since there was no place for Italy within the Ottoman Empire, "a temporary mandate might be provided for her in the Caucasus region." This would exclude Russian Armenia, however, which was to be joined with the Armenian districts set off from the old Empire.

Final Preparations to Leave Paris

Following his conference with President Wilson, Dr. King began to make definite preparations for getting away to the Near East, for there was no longer the slightest doubt about going. He called a staff meeting on May 23 to complete arrangements and in the afternoon he saw Colonel House, "for advice as to many matters connected with his duties." In a letter of May 23, King summed up his attitude: [1]

> ... It seemed to me so plain, the first of this week, that the reason for the existence of our Commission had ceased, that I made tentative arrangements for passage home on May 31st. But the same night I received word from the President that, whether the other national representatives on the Commission went or not, the President wanted the American Commission to go, and as soon as possible; so that we are trying to arrange to get off as early next week as we can, and I suppose this may be regarded as fairly decisive. However, there have been so many ups and downs in this business, that I shall not feel quite sure until we are actually in Syria. I think you know that our instructions include not only Syria and Palestine, but other portions of the Turkish Empire as well, so that the inquiry is a broad one. And the President feels that, in spite of the fact that the Conference is already going over the various mandates, he wants further ground for his own personal judgment, from our Commission, and he believes that America is entitled to such ground for independent judgment, as a nation peculiarly interested in the whole problem of the League of Nations. Mr. Crane and I had a very satisfactory interview with him yesterday. In the light of what he then said, we feel ready and glad to go....

> I have turned my back rather reluctantly, again, on home, but there

[1] House, King and Lybyer *Diaries*, May 23, 1919. King Papers: King to W. F. Bohn, May 23, 1919.

has really seemed nothing else for me to do, under the circumstances, but to go ahead with what I had once undertaken. I had thought that by sailing May 31st I could just about get Commencement week in, but evidently I am not going to have that pleasure.

It was well that the decision to send the Americans to the Near East had, at last, been reached, for serious disorders had been threatened as a result of the unfortunate Greek landing at Smyrna on May 14, which served to precipitate a long struggle which did not end finally until the Greek defeat in the middle of September 1922, three and one half years later. Admiral Bristol, the American High Commissioner in Constantinople, who was especially fearful as to the consequences of the Greek action, cabled Paris on May 23 that the Commission should "proceed as soon as possible", for its coming would be the "greatest safeguard against unnecessary bloodshed." Admiral Bristol believed that the Ottoman Empire should not be split up, and he reported an almost unanimous sentiment among representative Americans and many prominent Turks favoring an American mandate over the country. [1]

A number of things had to be done before the final departure of the Commission. Mr. Crane, who was anxious to be present at the commencement services of Istanbul Women's College, left Paris on May 25. Dr. King saw Secretary of State Lansing and drew the rest of the $10,000 which had been set aside for the use of the Commission until June 30. [2] On May 27 Mr. Grew sent King the necessary documents for the Commission certifying their appointment as the "American delegates of the Inter-Allied Commission to proceed to Turkey for the purpose of studying conditions, political and economic, therein, for the benefit of the Peace Conference" and requesting "proper courtesies and facilities enabling them to fulfil the duties incumbent upon them." [3]

The King-Crane Commission was now ready to leave, although a few last minute items had to be cleared. On May 28, the Palestine Syrian Delegation at Paris told the Commission that they did not want and would "never accept Zionist rule", but asked that President Wilson's views on self-determination be applied to Palestine, "without outside interference." They desired that no decision be taken before the people had been "seen on the spot and consulted." [4]

It was clear, of course, that the Americans were now going alone.

---

[1] King Papers: Bristol to Ammission, Paris, May 23, 1919.
[2] *PPC*, XI, 177, 189, 195, for financial arrangements. Grew informed King on May 27 that after July 1 some new appropriation, if necessary, would have to be found. Like King, Lybyer had a number of conferences, with Kerner, Westermann and others. He noted on May 27 that King had talked with all five American Peace Commissioners, and consulted Lybyer "on all important points."
[3] King Papers: Grew to King, two letters, May 27, 1919.
[4] Lybyer Papers: Lybyer *Notebook*.

The British were willing to help, but did not feel they could go unless the French went along as well. It would look too much like an Anglo-American combination and conspiracy against the French in Syria. In bidding Lybyer goodbye on May 28, Eric Forbes-Adam, of the British Delegation, wished the Americans "good luck" in their attempt "to solve the worst riddle" which faced the Peace Conference.[1] President Wilson evidently thought there would be some advantage in the American group going alone. The probability was that it might get "a franker expression of opinion" than a mixed Commission.[2] The President's final word to Dr. King on May 28 was:[3] "Here is God-speed. My thoughts will follow you constantly in the important mission you are undertaking and I am particularly happy to think of the spirit in which you and Mr. Crane are acting in this really critical matter...."

By nine o'clock Thursday evening, May 29, the American Section of the Inter-Allied Commission on Mandates in Turkey left Paris from the Gare de Lyon for Constantinople, via Bucharest, Constanza and the Black Sea.[4] An American Odyssey, of a somewhat peculiar, if not unique, character, had begun.

The French Refusal

The next day, May 30, General Allenby cabled from Cairo to the British Delegation in Paris concerning rumors in Beirut that the International Commission would not come to the Near East, but that a French army would. Allenby considered the situation grave and declared that unless he could assure Prince Feisal that the Commission was coming and would decide the future of the country, it was certain that he would "raise the Arabs against the French and ourselves."[5] When the

---

[1] Lybyer Papers: Forbes-Adam to Lybyer, May 28, 1919. The British were "despatching telegrams around the Near East to tell our people to help you in every way." Forbes-Adam was writing David Hogarth all he could, and knew Hogarth would be "bitterly disappointed in a sense... though the delays had made him less anxious to go. Who knows, though, whether our people may not eventually join you?" Toynbee, however, had had "a baddish breakdown" and could not go in any case. Somewhat earlier Robert de Caix had told Montgomery he could "not get word [with] Clemenceau about trip .... R. S. Baker told King [President] said [Lloyd George and Clemenceau] on bad terms. C. thinks L. G. broke faith about Syria—promised verbally, will not write. [President Wilson] enjoys sitting back and seeing them scrap." Lybyer *Diary*, May 24, 1919.
[2] King Papers: King to Bohn, May 26, 1919.
[3] Woodrow Wilson Papers, IX-A 59. King to Close, May 28, 1919; Wilson to King, May 29, 1919.
[4] Lybyer *Diary*, May 29, 1919. Kerner and others were there. Lybyer quotes Westermann: "Very glad you pushed this through. Never expected to see you off."
[5] *British Documents*, 1919-1939, First Series, IV, 256-57; *PPC*, VI, 136-137. A message from Feisal was included.

Council of Four met on May 31, Prime Minister Lloyd George read the Allenby communication, declared that the time had come to decide whether the Commission was to be sent out, and added his preference "that the Commission should proceed at once", the American Commissioners having already departed, although he did "not wish to send out British Commissioners unless the French also sent Commissioners.... The situation was so serious that he could not postpone action." Premier Clemenceau, however, remarked that his position remained what it had been on May 21,

> namely, that he was willing to send French Commissioners as soon as the relief of British troops by French troops was begun. As long as Syria remained entirely in British military occupation, and Mr. Lloyd George's latest proposals held the field it was useless to send French Commissioners. ... As soon as General Allenby would let him know that the replacement of British troops by French could commence, so that the people of Syria knew that they were not exclusively under British forces he would send Commissioners.

In turn, Prime Minister Lloyd George declared that he would not send Commissioners if the French did not, and he noted the Allenby statement that if French troops went to Syria, "there would be very serious trouble." Lloyd George then read the cable which was to be sent out to General Allenby on May 31 relative to the Commission, authorizing him

> to make it known that the Commission appointed to enquire into the questions dealing with the political future of the inhabitants of Mesopotamia, Syria and Palestine, are due to arrive in the East almost at once. The representatives of America are already on their way. We have been anxious to send our Commission for some time, and it has long since been prepared. Until arrangements have been made for the French to relieve the British troops in Syria, the French Government will not send out their Commissioners. As agreement on this question cannot be reached, French representatives will not proceed. Under such conditions we deem it inadvisable for our representatives to proceed. You are authorised to state to the Americans on their arrival, that the greatest weight and consideration will be given by the British Government to the advice and recommendations made to the Council of the Heads of the Principal Allied States by the American Commissioners. It is the desire of His Majesty's Government that the Commissioners should receive every facility in the execution of their enquiries, and rely upon you to see that this is done. The American, French and Italian Governments have been informed of this decision.
> ... You seem to be under the impression that the future of the different Turkish territories is to be decided by this Commission; but this is not the case. They are not empowered to make any decision. When they have completed their examination of the various problems they will be asked to give their advice to the Council of the Heads of the Principal Allied States, by whom the final decision will be taken.

The situation now appeared clear, and Signor Orlando, of Italy thereupon announced that he would send no Commissioners until the

British and French Governments did so.[1]

THE BEGINNINGS OF AN ADVENTURE

Two months of delay, confusion and obstruction came to an end when the members of the King-Crane Commission left Paris for the Near East. A number of factors had entered into the long controversy concerning the investigation. One lay in the fact that Professor Westermann, Chief of the Division of Western Asia, and his associates in that office, Professor David Magie, Dr. George R. Montgomery and Captain William Yale, were definitely opposed to the sending of an international commission on mandates in Turkey to the Near East. They "felt convinced" that they "had all the necessary data about the desires and wishes of the people of the Ottoman Empire." Nothing therefore would be gained by the sending of such a commission and it might be inadvisable further to stimulate and excite the antagonistic elements in the Near East.[2] These views were shared by men like President Caleb F. Gates, of Robert College, who also felt that the confusion and delay resulting from the sending of a Commission might actually endanger the prospects of relative peace and order in the near future.

On the other hand, Dr. Howard Bliss, the President of the American University of Beirut, a life-long resident of the Near East, as early as the beginning of February had made a distinct plea for the sending of an impartial international commission to go, especially, to Syria and the Lebanon, in order to find out as exactly as possible what the situation was. Bliss was convinced that only an investigation on the ground could yield satisfactory knowledge for the framing of an appropriate policy. He was supported by the Emir Feisal, who, indignant at the French refusal to act, aroused Colonel House and, in turn, President Wilson. In the latter part of April 1919 General Allenby insisted on the sending of a commission. This was likewise true of Rear Admiral Mark Bristol,

---

[1] *PPC*, VI, 132-133; 137. At M. Clemenceau's request Lloyd George altered one passage to make it clear that the French were not willing to send Commissioners until the relief of British forces by French troops had been arranged. See also *British Documents*, 1919-1939, First Series, IV, 259. By June 1 the British learned from Georges Picot that the Commission was "only coming out to keep Feisal in the dark while partition of Syria" was "being arranged", and General Clayton (Syria) was troubled that if Feisal found that the fate of Syria had been decided without his knowledge "and before Commission has made its report he will undoubtedly take hostile action." Clayton (June 8) indicated that opinion in Syria and Palestine was united against any arbitrary division of Arab territories and would regard such action as contrary to (1) the principles of the Covenant of the League, (2) the principle of self-determination, and (3) the declaration of November 1918 to the Arab Notables. See especially *British Documents*, 1919-1939, First Series, IV, 267-272, 272-274.

[2] William Yale to the author, September 28, 1940.

the American High Commissioner in Constantinople. In the end, President Wilson decided that the American Section of the Inter-Allied Commission should be sent to the Near East regardless of what the British and French Governments did. He adopted that attitude because he felt that nothing could really take the place of a direct investigation by a body of intelligent men who were anxious to get at the facts and because of the moral effect which the presence of an American Commission would have in the Near East.

But there were important reasons for the delay in sending out the King-Crane Commission. These involved the appointment of the other sections of the projected Inter-Allied Commission, the British, the French and the Italian. As early as April 10, the British appointed two excellent Commissioners, Sir Henry McMahon and Commander David Hogarth, while Professor Arnold J. Toynbee was to have been secretary of the British group. In appears that the French Commissioners were to have been M. Jean Gout and Senator Augagnard, or perhaps Robert de Caix and M. Maurice Long.[1] From time to time Clemenceau promised to appoint the French Commissioners formally, but he never did so and, despite his statement of May 31 that he would take action when arrangements for the replacement of British by French forces in Syria had been made, it may be doubted that he ever had any real intention of doing so. Doubtless there were various reasons for that failure, but the considerations which governed the French position were distrust of the British, apprehension that both the British and the Americans were definitely opposed to the French claim in Syria in any case and without regard to what an investigation might turn up, and fears as to what an impartial investigation might, in fact, disclose. It was natural, therefore, for the French Government to be reluctant. In the end the French could not be budged. It was clear, as Professor Westermann later remarked:[2]

> The French were opposed to this expedition. Never did they intend that it should go, to judge by their obstructionist policy. Their official policy was to stand absolutely upon the terms of the Sykes-Picot Agreement. After two months of futile conferences of all kinds President Wilson, in exasperation, determined to send out an American commission to ascertain what the Syrians really wanted.

The Italian Commissioners, apparently, were to have been Captain Pallavicini and Signor Galli, but when the French refused to move, the Italians also declined. Moreover, the Italians had certain claims in the

---

[1] Henry Wickham Steed, II, 323-324, states that Long and de Caix were the French Commissioners designate.
[2] W. L. Westermann, "The Armenian Problem and the Disruption of Turkey", in E. M. House and Charles Seymour, *What Really Happened at Paris* (New York, Scribner's, 1921), 198.

Near East which might not bear too close an examination—in the regions around Adalia and Smyrna, especially—which they did not desire to have too intimately investigated. It is true, too, that the Italians were absent from the Conference of Paris during the critical period of April 24 to May 6, and their absence, no doubt, helped to influence and to complicate their decisions, although it would not have prevented the sending of their members had they really desired to do so. Finally, the Zionist Organization did not want to have either an Inter-Allied group or the King-Crane Commission to carry on an investigation in Palestine, and attempted to persuade President Wilson and the American Commission to Negotiate Peace, on several occasions, not to send a Commission there.

But there is no doubt that it was the French failure to act which prevented the Inter-Allied Commission as a whole from being appointed. David Lloyd George, who finally accepted the sending of a Commission, sums up the British position admirably: [1]

> ... The United States, Great Britain and Italy had their delegates already, but it was France who had never appointed their delegates. The agreement to send the Commission had been put into a formal document which had been signed by all of them. The French Government had not carried out their part of the bargain. I did not accuse Clemenceau of not keeping faith, but I said that he certainly had not carried out the bargain.
> The French finally refused to take any part in the Commission. I felt that they regarded our officers as the stimulators of the anti-French feeling. It might provoke further unpleasantness if we were to send out our representatives. President Wilson, however, felt that, being in a more impartial position, he would appoint a purely American delegation to go to Syria to institute an enquiry as to the wishes of the inhabitants. I told the Peace Conference that the British Government was quite willing to agree to a similar investigation into the wishes of the people of Mesopotamia and Palestine. I formally declared at the Conference that "I was quite willing to abide by the decision of the inhabitants as interpreted by the Commission." President Wilson thereupon commented: "That was necessarily his own point of view. He had no other means on which to form judgment. He did not think that these peoples could be left entirely to themselves. They required guidance and some intimate superintendence, but this should be conducted in their interests and not in the interests of the mandatory."

The Allied Powers were not, therefore, to take part in the investigation of one of the world's most ancient and complicated problems. The Inter-Allied Commission on Mandates in Turkey did not materialize. The Americans went alone and worked alone. An American experiment in peace-making was now to begin. Would that experiment succeed in laying sound foundations for peace in the Near East?

---

[1] David Lloyd GEORGE, II, 1077-1078. See also Field Marshal Viscount WAVELL, *Allenby: Soldier and Statesman* (London, Harrap, 1946), 260.

CHAPTER IV

An Inquiry into Zionism: Palestine

Towards the Holy Land

The King-Crane Commission was now on the way to Constantinople, and as the train moved slowly across the plains of Hungary and into Rumanian territory toward Bucharest, something of the wreckage of the war in Central and Southeastern Europe was evident. The American Destroyer *Barnard* awaited the party at Constanza to take it across the Black Sea and into the Bosphorus to Constantinople.

Admiral Bristol was anxiously awaiting the arrival of the group. In a report of June 1, 1919, he declared: [1]

> There are some rumors of disturbances in different parts of Turkey, but I feel that these are probably due to the apprehension of people in the interior who have suffered so much in the past and who naturally exaggerate the present signs of tension. The knowledge that an American Commission is arriving is tending to relieve the situation. I sincerely hope that this Commission will carefully investigate conditions throughout Turkey in order that our country may know the facts so that it can decide for itself from the best evidence available and not be misguided by the selfish and extensive propaganda that is evidently being carried out by countries having political aspirations or a desire to exploit the territories of the Near East for their own benefit without regard to what is best for the sake of humanity.

Admiral Bristol and Consul-General Gabriel Bie Ravndal met the party when it landed about nine o'clock in the morning on Wednesday, June 4. King, Montgomery and Moore were taken to Constantinople Women's College, where they met President Mary Mills Patrick, and remained there for the day. Mr. Crane was already there, and President King conferred with him and Admiral Bristol. The rest of the party, including Lybyer, went to the Pera Palace Hotel, and later Lybyer and Ravndal went over to the American Embassy, where the Embassy hall and three rooms on the second floor had been cleared for the work of the Commission. [2]

Work began almost immediately. Lybyer and Montgomery prepared

---

[1] King Papers, Bristol Despatches: *Report on Operations for Week Ending June 1, 1919* (Senior U. S. Naval Officer, Turkey).
[2] See especially the Lybyer and King *Diaries*, June 4-7, 1919. Lybyer noted seeing Miss Patrick, Professor Hussein Bey and his wife, and Halidé Edib. Dr. Patrick was "anti-Greek, pro-Turk, pro-Bul[garian]. Hopes Crane will be much interested—would name college for him. Told her he seems to think it his first interest." At breakfast on June 6, Crane spoke for one mandatory for the north, with separate areas. He did not believe the Armenians, for the time being, could govern an area. Dr. Tavitian, the Armenian leader, however, believed the Armenians would flock to an area which they themselves governed. See also Gabriel Bie Ravndal's reports of June 4, 7, in American Commission to Negotiate Peace 1918-1919. Cases 181.91 / 165, 168, Vol. 157, The National Archives.

a statement concerning the mission for the Constantinople press. The big question of the moment was whether the group should begin the investigation at Constantinople or go on to Beirut. Admiral Bristol wanted the Commission to remain at the Golden Horn for a while, and Dr. King did have an interview with the Grand Vizier, Damad Ferid Pasha, but at the suggestion of Consul-General Ravndal, it was finally decided to go on to Syria.

The Americans gathered all the necessary preliminary information and then set sail on the *U. S. S. Luce* on June 7.[1] Two days were spent going through the historic Dardanelles and sailing the quiet waters of the eastern Mediterranean. There were conferences on board to decide on a course of action and investigation. Captain Yale was instructed to draw up a plan for the inquiry in Syria. It was decided on June 9 to go to Jaffa rather than Beirut, although one officer and an orderly were to be taken to Beirut to arrange transportation. The decision to go to Jaffa first meant that the Commission would cover the situation in Palestine proper and then journey north to Beirut and Alexandretta.[2]

The Investigation in Palestine Begins

Actual investigation of very specific problems was now about to begin. In Paris there had been one type of general procedure. Now it was to be another. Before leaving the French capital the Commission had become familiar with all the reports and material available to members of the American Delegation and with much other literature bearing upon the problems of the Near East. In Syria and Palestine the Commission was to meet representative individuals and delegations, in order to ascertain as far as possible "the opinions and desires of the whole people." This procedure, inevitably, was "a kind of political education" for those involved, and, in addition, was of value in letting the people know that their wishes were being considered. The Commission was also aware of much pressure and propaganda. It knew that some were prevented from appearing before it and that some petitions presented were questionable and spurious. Nevertheless, the Commission believed that the anomalous elements in the petitions tended to cancel one another when the entire

---

[1] There were conferences with Dr. Barton, of the Near East Relief; the head of the Arab Delegation at Constantinople; Dr. William W. Peet, treasurer of the American Board of Missions at Constantinople. Halidé Edib came to the Embassy on June 7 with four men from Trebizond, all disturbed about the Smyrna situation and about brigandage in their own area.

[2] Lybyer and King *Diaries*, June 8-9, 1919. King spent the last bit of time preparing a statement for the press and for the Turks about their treatment of the Armenians. Crane apparently wanted the work finished as soon as possible, but Yale felt that an effort should be made to go to Mesopotamia. See William Yale, *The Near East: A Modern History*, 336.

country was taken into account, and that, "as in the composite photograph, certain great, common emphases" were "unmistakable." [1]

Preliminaries

Immediately after arrival at the Jerusalem Hotel in Jaffa on June 10, official calls were made on the British military authorities, especially Lt. Col. F. J. M. Postlethwaite, the British Military Governor. The Commission gave to the press a statement clarifying its position in the investigation. The American people, according to the statement, had no political ambitions either in Europe or in the Near East, but did recognize that they could not "altogether avoid responsibility for just settlements among the nations following the war, and under the League of Nations." The American Section of the International Commission, which had been projected by the Council of Four of the Paris Peace Conference, was [2]

> in the Near East simply and solely to get as accurate and definite information as possible concerning the conditions, the relations and the desires of all the peoples and classes concerned; in order that President Wilson and the American people may act with full knowledge of the facts in any policy they may be called upon hereafter to adopt concerning the problems of the Near East—whether in the Peace Conference, or in the later League of Nations.

That afternoon, Dr. King, Mr. Crane and Professor Lybyer went with Col. Postlethwaite to the Tennis Club, where they met "a lot of natives" and talked of coins, agriculture, and the architecture of Palestine, but had "no chance to speak of mandates." Later in the evening, the American Consul, Mr. Glazebrook, and a party arrived from Jerusalem, and Glazebrook went over the information which he had compiled for the use of the Commission. Mr. Glazebrook, moreover, who was both uncomplimentary to the French and opposed to Zionist ambitions, favored the unity of the Ottoman Empire under an American mandate, with the Sultan removed from Constantinople, and each constituent people given an opportunity to develop freely. [3]

Since Captain Yale had been asked to arrange the interviews, immediately on arriving at Jaffa he called upon the leaders of the different religious, racial and economic groups in the city, as well as local officials, explained the purpose and objectives of the Commission, and then drew

---

[1] See text of King-Crane Report in *PPC*, XII, 752-753.

[2] *PPC*, XII, 751-752. The press statement was given out wherever the Commission went in Syria and Palestine. See also the Lybyer and King *Diaries*, June 9, 10, 1919.

[3] Lybyer *Diary*, June 10, 1919. Lt. Col. V. Gabriel, the Assistant Administrator for O. E. T. A., South, Jerusalem, told King "he would be quite contented to see British give up Palestine to the Fr., if that would suit better. Side information that Brit. Gov. told people not to talk of indpdce but discuss the different mandates. Meetg in favor of indpdce broken up by military governmt. c. May 25."

up a schedule of meetings when each group would meet the Commission to present its desires as to the future of Palestine and Syria. With certain variations, this was the procedure followed.[1] Thanks to the changes of plan after leaving Constantinople, the Commission had arrived at Jaffa, when British authorities were not expecting it, so that, in general, the program had to be arranged without their assistance. While an attempt was made to consult every important group, a disproportionate amount of time, seemingly, was given to the Christians because of the number of small Christian groups. In each instance, the Commission read its general statement, and care was taken to make it clear that American policy "in regard to accepting a mandate anywhere was unformed and unpredictable, and that the Commission had no power of decision." It was also hinted that the Commission was not open to social engagements.

To make it more independent in its travel and work, automobiles were procured from the Near East Relief Organization, which had "never mixed their work" with politics, apparently, and was somewhat fearful lest "the high character for freedom from American propaganda ... be injured by their allowing the American Commission to use their cars." Captain Donald Brodie, however, explained that there was no real danger of being "involved in the renting of transportation to the Commission," for it was not "connected in any way with propaganda of any kind." It was, after all, a creation of the Council of Four of the Peace Conference and the two American Commissioners were "in a very real sense the personal representatives of President Wilson."[2] If not particularly comfortable, the transportation was at least highly successful, and somewhat colorful, as described by Captain Brodie:[3]

> On land, the Commission tried out everything except a caravan of camels. Special trains—the best available, though often simply con-

---

[1] William Yale to the author, September 28, 1940. "In Jerusalem, in Damascus, and in Beirut I made it a point of consulting with British, French and Feisal's governments, asking them to let me know what organizations or delegations, or individuals, they would care to have appear before the Commission. However, I also informed them that in the main all individuals and delegations, with the exception of those chosen by them, would be selected by me in behalf of the Commission. Consequently, in most of the large urban centers of Palestine and Syria the delegations which appeared before the Commission were first interviewed by me personally and a time arranged for their appearance before the Commission. However, in the smaller centers it was necessary at times to delegate the authority for selecting delegations to either local authorities or to the British, French and Arabs."

[2] Brodie Papers: Near East Relief to King-Crane Commission, June 12; Brodie reply, June 16, 1919.

[3] Brodie Papers: Unpublished *Brodie Memorandum* on the King-Crane Commission. The King-Crane Commission paid the Near East Relief $1,000 for transportation in Palestine and Syria. See also the Accounts of the Commission in Brodie Papers.

verted box-cars—were provided on the Hejaz, Bagdad, and branch railways, through the cooperation of French and British officials. The greater part of the journey through Syria, however, was made possible by a little fleet of eight "tried and trusty" Fords secured from the American Committee for Relief in the Near East and the British Army. They were sorely "tried" by the journey—as were their occupants sometimes—and while breakdowns did occur, they also qualified as "trusty". The Ford car is not a joke in the Near East. It is the only rival of the camel. By means of them the Commission bumped and jolted over thousands of miles of roads, near-roads, trails, rocks and sand in Syria. Without them the tour of the Commission would have been greatly limited and the value of their report seriously impaired.

The British authorities in Palestine, or O. E. T. S., from General Sir Arthur Money, the Chief Administrator, down, "were courteous, obliging and helpful." Most of them had seen service in India, Egypt or the Sudan and gave the impression of efficiency, ability and genuine interest in the people. General Allenby, the British Commander-in-Chief, had assigned Lt. Col. J. K. Watson, who had served with Lord Kitchener in Egypt, to act as aid to the Commission. Watson's "thoughtfulness, kindness and efficiency" never failed and "the comfort, good health, and success in the investigation of the Commission were largely furthered by him." [1]

The Commission began to receive both oral and written petitions from the citizens of Jaffa on June 11. First came the head of the Protestant Syrian Community, and then a Christian-Moslem Committee, later said to have been hand-picked by the Government. Both favored preservation of Syrian unity with Palestine, under a British mandate, although the Protestants favored France, in the event of British refusal. Still later a Zionist delegation appeared, making a plea for the establishment of the Jewish National Home in accordance with the Balfour Declaration. Professor Lybyer and Captain Brodie interviewed a delegation of Moslem Arabs from Lydda, Ramleh and neighboring towns who wanted a unified, independent Syria or an American mandate. So the story went into the afternoon until there was time for a walk through the old quarters of the city. That evening there was a dinner with Col. Postlethwaite, the Military Governor. Altogether it seemed a rather auspicious beginning for the work of the American Commission. [2]

The interviews continued the next day with the Grand Mufti at Jaffa, Tewfik Dejani Effendi, who was followed by the Archimandrite of the Greek Community, the largest Christian sect in the city, and others. Brigadier General Sir Gilbert Clayton, the Chief Political Officer of the

[1] *PPC*, XII, 772. The Brodie *Memorandum* declares that Watson was of "the utmost service to the Commission."
[2] Lybyer *Diary*, June 11, 1919. See also *Memorandum of Interviews Between Various Delegations and William Yale; Memorandum of Interviews Between Delegation from Ludd, Ramleh, and Neighboring Villages, and AHL and DMB* in The Lybyer Papers.

British Expeditionary Force in Cairo, told the Commission of the difficult situation in Palestine, which had nearly "got out of hand" three weeks before, and had only been quieted by news of the coming of the King-Crane group. Sir Gilbert was sorry, however, that the group had not been given the "full powers" of the "original international Commission." [1]

Some Differences of Opinion and Tentative Conclusions

Before leaving Jaffa certain differences of opinion had arisen between Yale and Montgomery on the one hand and the two Commissioners and Lybyer on the other. [2] These were perfectly natural differences both as to procedure and method, and as to the attitude toward some of the major problems to be solved. Yale was thought to be pro-French in his attitude, as well as pro-Zionist in his approach to the problem of Palestine. He believed the French would not abandon their "vital" interests in the Arab lands, and was aware of the French conviction that many British agents, including Lawrence, had been working deliberately to eliminate France from the Near East. The disagreements were somewhat aggravated when the two Commissioners sent a cablegram to President Wilson from Jaffa on June 12, without consulting any of the advisers. The message warned: [3]

> Possibly at no time has race clan feeling been so tense as just now. People in large bodies, especially armed forces, should move as little as possible, and even then only with great care and on advice of competent officials, in areas affected. The careless descent of the Greeks on Smyrna has produced a distressing reaction all over this coast where there was a profound belief in our own declarations as well as in those of the British and French made November ninth on the rights of people to self-determination.
>
> Here the older inhabitants both Moslem and Christian take a united and most hostile attitude toward any extensive Jewish immigration or toward any effort to establish Jewish sovereignty over them. We doubt if any British or American official here believes that it is possible to carry out the Zionist program except through the support of a large army.

[1] Lybyer Papers: Commission Appointments, June 12, 1919. The program of the Al Muntada al Adabi Society, members of which were interviewed, was based on (1) Anti-Zionism; (2) Unity of Syria and Palestine; and (3) complete independence of Syria and Palestine without a mandate.

[2] Lybyer *Diary*, June 12, 1919. Lybyer talked with King about his "function with Commission, since Yale is managing things. Not clearly defined. Am to read over material and write summary of Jaffa experience."

[3] King Papers: Text of cablegram, dated June 12, 1919. In *PPC*, XII, 748, the cable is dated June 20 from Jerusalem; received June 21. The material on Yale's attitude is from his letter to the author, October 17, 1940.

When Captain Yale learned of the nature of this cable, which he felt misrepresented the situation, he cabled Professor Westermann to discount its more alarming features.

Meanwhile, Professor Lybyer had been asked, in his capacity as General Technical Adviser, to prepare a memorandum of tentative conclusions based on the evidence gathered at Jaffa.[1] He found that the non-Jewish population, about eighty per cent of the whole, appeared to be "unanimously opposed to the Zionist plan." The majority were against further Jewish immigration to Palestine and expressed "full opposition to Jewish political control." The Arabic groups were "opposed to the political separation of 'Palestine' from 'Syria'," maintaining that there was "no racial or national difference among them, on which such a separation" could be based. Many Moslems were not in favor of the Emir Feisal ruling over them. In the more positive sense, the Moslems and a large portion of the Christians, perhaps a few of the Jews, claimed that Syria constituted a nation which was "nearly or entirely capable of full self-government, though needing for a time, in the opinion of many, advice and financial aid." Possibly a majority of the population favored the independence of the entire region between the desert and the sea, Aleppo and Akaba, with more or less decentralized or federal political structure, related to the other Arabic-speaking peoples within a larger federation. The Arabs promised democratic, secular government, with equality for all elements. Some believed a mandate unnecessary, but if the Peace Conference required a mandate, the majority preferred a single mandatory, whose control would be "as light as possible and limited in time." With the exception of the Latins, all elements seemed to favor an American mandate, since the United States had "fewer permanent interests in the country." In the city of Jaffa a majority seemed to prefer Great Britain next, while the Maronites desired a French mandate. But in the district of Jaffa there was an apparent preference for a French mandate over the entire country to a divided mandate, a part of which would go to the British and another to the French. In the one case it was feared that the British "would give Palestine to the control of the Jews, and that France would attempt to gallicize Syria according to her policy in Algeria." In both cases the Arab language, nationalism and religion would be neglected or opposed.

The British authorities had shown "a keen interest in the work of the Commission," and were helping to conduct its work, under the aid of Col. Watson, but Lybyer thought that there were persons who were reporting on their work to the British intelligence service. Nevertheless, the British had not interfered with the Commission, partly because they were surprised by the Commission's coming to Jaffa instead of Beirut,

---

[1] Lybyer Papers: A. H. L., *Tentative Conclusions After Three Days at Jaffa*, June 13, 1919. Lybyer *Diary*, June 13, 1919.

and partly because the Commission had exhibited "an unexpected independence of method". Within limits the British authorities wanted the Americans to have freedom. On the other hand, they were said "to have prepared the way . . . by influencing the selection of the Moslem-Christian Committee, and by giving instructions to certain groups to suppress expressions of desire for independence." Such instructions, however, were only partially heeded. [1] The occupying government appeared to be working along the following lines:

a. Syria and Palestine were not to be independent. b. Palestine was to be under a British mandate, with a small Syria under France. c. These mandates were to have no genuine time limit, but to look to permanent control, hardly distinguishable from ownership. d. Palestine was to be given "in some form" to Zionism, using the least troublesome method of executing the Balfour Declaration. e. All means were to be used to keep the population quiet until the Peace Conference announced its decisions, and the proper dispositions had been made to carry out the decisions.

Lybyer felt that the Zionist representatives tended to assume that their claim had been settled by the Balfour Declaration and President Wilson's statements, and that they needed only to make their plans "for the political and economic management of the country." They took it for granted that the Mandatory Power would hold off the Arabs and allow the small minority of Jews "to control affairs, political and economic, and to introduce Jewish immigration until Jews became a majority." Then a virtually independent Jewish State would exist. The British authorities, trying to keep the country calm, were in a difficult position. The promises made to the Zionists were almost in direct contradiction to those made to the Syrian Arabs. Prior to the advent of the Commission

---

[1] Captain Yale believed that the British had stirred up considerable anti-French feeling. In its *Confidential Appendix Prepared by the Commission for Use of Americans Only* (*PPC*, XII, 848-863), the Commission found that, in each of the areas visited, the policy of the occupying government had an influence on the course of the investigation. At both Jaffa and Jerusalem the British military governors were consulted about the program, though at other places they themselves prepared the program. There was no attempt, however, to hinder any groups from meeting the Commission, although in one or two cases, the Commission requested a British governor to leave the room. There was some evidence of official attempts to influence opinion in favor of a British mandate, as at Jaffa, Jenin and Acre. Some British Palestine officials assumed permanent British control. Brigadier General Sir Ronald Storrs, the Military Governor of Jerusalem, however, denies all this. He notes in *The Memoirs of Sir Ronald Storrs* (New York, Putnam's, 1937), 375-376: "All I can say is that I myself, having been asked by one or two Arabs once or twice what they should say, and having replied that they should tell the truth, refused to receive any more questioners, conveying to them this standard reply through a subordinate; nor do I believe that any officer in General Money's Administration acted otherwise."

there had been no consultation of the peoples, and the Syrians believed that both the British and the French had forgotten what they had promised during the war. The trend at Paris was well known in Syria and had aroused the anger of all the Arabic elements.

The Commission had done well to come to Jaffa first because it had disorganized any possible British plans for close management of the work of the Commission from the beginning, and it gave an introduction to the situation on a small scale before reaching Jerusalem. Moreover, it was desirable to consider all applications for a hearing. Otherwise the Commission could be charged with partiality, and might have failed to obtain some of the information which it desired.

About ten o'clock in the morning of June 13, the Americans left for Jerusalem by car, going by way of Tel Aviv. On the way they stopped at two Jewish schools and took lunch at the Jewish colony at Richon-le-Sion, where they had the pleasure of meeting the principal men from a number of Jewish settlements, as well as members of the central Zionist Commission. The colonies seemed "clearly industrious and prosperous, self-contained." [1]

IN THE REGION OF JERUSALEM

The American Commission arrived at the Grand New Hotel in Jerusalem about eight o'clock that evening, where it remained for a week. The next morning, Saturday, official calls were made on General Sir Arthur Money, the Chief Administrator, O. E. T. A., South, and Brigadier General Sir Ronald Storrs, the Military Governor. A limited amount of "hospitality was accepted in a quiet way from the British and French officials" in and around Jerusalem. [2] Mr. Glazebrook, the American Consul, and Major Reed also called that morning for a conference. Glazebrook insisted that the group should affirm the genuine character of the mission, since some were spreading the rumor that it was "all camouflage." [3]

---

[1] For an indication of attitudes see Lybyer Papers: *Addresses of Welcome. Zionist Colony, Richon, June 13, 1919*. Handwritten. One address of welcome said: "To you, Gentlemen, has been entrusted the sacred task to realize this ideal [of Zionism]. We hope that after you will see all we created in this country, our life, our relations with our native neighbours, you will certainly contribute to the realization of our wish namely the Regeneration of our Nation on our Forefather's land." Another said: "We firmly believe that your visit will give you a clear conception of what the Jewish People have done in this country .... The Civilized World has recognized after this terrible war, that an end must be put to the sufferings of the under-yoked small nations."

[2] *PPC*, XII, 771-772.

[3] Major Reed had come to Jerusalem favorable to Zionism, but was later "very much opposed." He contended that all Americans and British, as well as the "natives", were opposed to Zionism. Mr. W. T. Ellis, the correspondent of The New York *Herald-Tribune*, also called on the Com-

The Zionist Commission

While members of the Commission made some visits around Jerusalem, the real work did not begin until Monday, June 16. The interviews were to prove of exceeding interest, and the first group to be received consisted of a Moslem-Christian Committee, which took a strong anti-Zionist position. Later in the day three Moslem deputies from Constantinople appeared, and finally a Greek Orthodox delegation. Both the latter groups were anti-Zionist. [1]

The real event of the day, however, was the interview and conference with the members of the Zionist Commission in Palestine, which began at eleven o'clock in the morning. The Zionist Commission was composed of a number of prominent Jews, the chairman of which in Palestine was Dr. Harry Friedenwald, of Baltimore, Maryland, a distinguished ophthalmologist of broad, humanitarian interests. Another was Dr. David de Sola Pool, Rabbi of the Spanish and Portuguese Synagogue, Shearith Israel, in New York since 1907, who had also been one of the three Jewish representatives on Herbert Hoover's food conservation staff in 1917. Two other American Jewish representatives were Mr. Robert Szold, Washington, D. C., and Mr. E. W. Lewin-Epstein, of New York. The others were Mr. van Vriesland, of the Netherlands, Mr. Jack Mosseri, of Egypt, and Dr. M. D. Eder, of London. The Zionist Commission in Palestine was the representative of the Zionist Organization, the principal institution through which was expressed the "desire of the Jewish people to reconstitute their National Home in Palestine." It had been sent to Palestine in March 1918 as the first step "in making concrete reality of the promise" of the Balfour Declaration. [2]

---

mission. See also the Lybyer and King *Diaries*, June 14-15, 1919. Lybyer noted a conversation with Mr. and Mrs. Spofford, missionaries, on Sunday: "Believe 80 % of villagers prefer British rule because of prosperity. If Lord intends Jews to return, they will, and people should accept it .... Curious tales of rumors about our Commission. Worried a little about prestige but think will come all right."

[1] Lybyer Papers: *Moslem Memorandum, Jerusalem, 4 p. m., June 16, 1919.* Presented earlier to the Peace Conference at Paris, 8 pp., typed. At dinner that evening General Money told Lybyer that he believed the "Balfour Declaration a mistake."

[2] For the Zionist Commission see Weizmann, Ch. 21. On June 18, Weizmann asked Balfour to forward a message to Friedenwald urging that the Zionist case be presented to the American Commission "with firmness, moderation and dignity," along the lines of his own presentation at the Peace Conference in February. At the same time, in a note to Sir Louis Mallet, Weizmann outlined an ambitious program for the development of the Jewish Homeland, with provision for immigration, settling of Jewish soldiers, and external assistance. Both Weizmann and Sir Herbert Samuel complained of the attitude of the British military authorities. See especially *British Documents*, 1919-1939, First Series, IV, 277, 303-308; Frank E. Manuel, *The Realities of American-Palestine Relations* (Washington, Public Affairs Press, 1949), 246.

In the statement to the King-Crane Commission, the Zionists adopted the same attitude which the Zionist Organization had already presented in Paris. Their demands were: [1]

1. That the League of Nations recognize the historical title of the Jewish people to Palestine and the right of the Jews to reconstitute Palestine as their National Home and there to establish the foundations of a Jewish Commonwealth, the civil and religious rights of non-Jews not to be prejudiced.
2. That the sovereign possession of Palestine should be vested in the League of Nations.
3. That Great Britain should act as Mandatory or Trustee for the above purposes.

The statement described the establishment of some sixty Jewish settlements in Palestine during the past many years, several of which contained more than 1,000 inhabitants each. The right of the Jews to a National Home was "clear". The Zionist Commission contended that there was "ample room in the land for a large increase in the population," for the density of the population in Palestine was only "from 70 to 100 per square mile." Almost ninety per cent of Palestine's ten thousand square miles was uncultivated, although from forty to forty-five per cent was cultivable "by the ordinary methods of agriculture." Expert estimates, based on existing methods of agriculture, indicated that the land could "sustain a population of at least three times the number of present inhabitants." The establishment of a Jewish National Home and the promotion of Jewish immigration was "quite consistent with a strict regard for all the rights of the non-Jewish inhabitants."

The coming of the Jews, it was said, would materially benefit the local inhabitants. It would not injure them in any way, for in the past, relations between the Jews and their non-Jewish neighbors had been very friendly. With the coming of the Zionists, Western culture would be brought to the land of the ancients and transmitted to the Arabs, as in the medieval Christian era the Arabs had transmitted the culture of the ancients to Western Europe. It was in that spirit that the Emir Feisal had written to Professor Frankfurter on March 3, denouncing the "irresponsibles", recognizing the moderation of the Zionists, bidding them welcome, and expressing the hope of agreement through "reciprocal goodwill." [2]

The Zionist Commission accepted Feisal's statement to Frankfurter and declared that it would do everything possible to avoid difficulties

---

[1] Lybyer Papers: *Members of the Zionist Commission in Palestine, June 16, 1919.* Zionist Organization, *Statement to the International Commission on Mandates in Turkey.* American Section. By Zionist Commission in Palestine. June 1919. This document may be compared with *Statement of the Zionist Organization Regarding Palestine.* February 3, 1919. [Strictly Confidential. American Peace Commission. 14 pp. Printed.] See also *PPC*, IV, 161-162.

[2] For text of Feisal's letter to Professor Frankfurter, March 3, 1919, see Weizmann, 245-246.

although it was well aware that the establishment of a Jewish National Home would "indeed involve certain problems," and that "wise, able and strong leadership" would be required. Nevertheless, the problem could be worked out. The Peace Conference could without hesitation provide for the "foundations of the Hebrew Commonwealth"; the definite mandate could be delivered and undertaken. There would be peace then, and progress and harmony in the land. A great and necessary step would have been taken in "the security of a better world." [1]

End of the Work in Jerusalem

The next morning on June 17, a Buick and Ford caravan brought the Americans to Bethlehem. In that old Biblical city all the delegations showed very careful organization. They were in general agreement concerning the unity of Syria and Palestine, wanted complete independence if possible, and were opposed to Zionism and Jewish immigration. Following the hearings at Bethlehem, the King-Crane group drove across desolate country to Hebron, arriving about noon, where eleven delegations were interviewed, and some members of the party went to Beersheba and Gaza for further interviews. [2]

By the middle of June the Commission began to hear consistently about a forthcoming congress at Damascus. For the first time the Arab delegations were sounding the note that the problem of a mandatory power should be left to a conference shortly to assemble in Damascus. Four delegates were to come from Jerusalem itself. The group sponsoring the gathering seemed well organized, and both the British and the French, for a while at least, seemed inclined to encourage it, each hoping to win support from it. Arab Christians were joining in the movement, although they felt the need of a mandatory power. The Moslems asserted that the Arab government to be established would be divorced entirely from religion and placed on a secular basis. [3]

A number of delegations were heard in Jerusalem on June 19, the testimony fitting into a standard pattern, already well established by now. [4] Meanwhile, Mr. Crane had reached the conclusion that through-

---

[1] Mr. Justice Brandeis, who came to Europe and thence to Palestine, at the urgent call of Professor Frankfurter, concluded that British authorities were opposing the Balfour Declaration. He wrote to his wife on July 1 that the problems would be solved "if only the British and we bear constantly in mind, that it is a question not of whether, but of how and when, Palestine shall become in fact the Jewish Homeland; that the irreducible minimum is a Palestine large enough, with the water, land, and ports requisite to a self-supporting and reasonably self-sufficient community." See Mason, *Brandeis: A Free Man's Life*, 456-457.

[2] Lybyer Papers: Hebron, June 17, 1919. The Chief Rabbi called for the restoration of Israel, according to Holy Scriptures.

[3] Lybyer *Diary*, June 18, 1919.

[4] Since M. Georges Picot, the French High Commissioner, was not

out the whole length and breadth of Syria and Palestine one would not find "one single Moslem" who would tolerate "the idea of a French mandate." But there was a very great attraction for the United States: [1]

> We found that there were several things which had given them this great sympathy for America. There was in the first place that wonderful educational institution at Beirut which for fifty years had been sending out thoroughly trained, fine men—Moslems, Maronites, Druses, Christians—all kinds of people. There were the Syrians who had been coming to America from that semi-arid country and who struggled along for years and years. The Syrians, in their tremendous loyalty and appreciation, were different from some of the people who came here. They did not get much out of America; they did not ask a great deal of America; they did not try to run our politics or anything else. But they were intensely loyal. And they had always sent such appreciative word back, or carried it back themselves, which had made the people of Syria and Palestine come to trust America.
>
> Then, curiously, the story of the Philippines had gone up and down there. Everywhere our mission went we got that note. Even the Bedouin of the desert said, "We want America to come here and do for us what she has been doing for the Filipinos."

By this time the Commission had concluded its work in Jerusalem, and on Saturday morning, June 21, at 8:30, the group started out in three cars, with a Reo truck for baggage, for Ramleh and Nablus, where interviews were to be held *en route* to Damascus. At Ramleh there were local delegations and about thirty-five groups from other villages in the region. The Americans then drove over the plain of Sharon to Nablus, where there were interviews in the afternoon, with interesting statements from Protestants and Samaritans, and an Arab delegation stood out in favor of an independent unified Syrian state. [2]

The Americans left for Jenin on June 22, just west of Nablus, passing the scene of a Turkish defeat in 1918. The party passed Samaria, with the two Commissioners stopping for a time, then ascended the ridge of Mt. Carmel, getting a superb view of the long stretch of the coast from north of Jaffa to Carmel point, and finally came down the ridge and rode along the valley and over the small plain to Jenin. Altogether nine delegations were received there, in the upstairs hall of the governor's office. The

---

coming to Jerusalem, the Commission planned to leave for Damascus on June 20. At lunch with Colonel Gabriel, the Assistant Administrator in Jerusalem, Gabriel gave Lybyer a "constitution" for Palestine, with modifications of the Zionist plans. General Money expressed the opinion that the common people of Palestine mostly favored a British mandate. See also, Lybyer Papers for *Petition of Damianos, Patriarch of Jerusalem to the American Section of the International Commission on Mandates in Turkey, Jerusalem, June 6/19, 1919.*

[1] See Crane's unpublished *Memoirs*, 371 ff.
[2] Lybyer Papers: *Petition of Arab Delegations, Nablus.* At dinner that evening the Military Governor proved to be "anti-French, anti-Zionist."

responses to questions were "very regular", since most of the people were Moslem and united on a program.

By late afternoon the group was on the way again, across the plain of Esdraelon and up the hill to Nazareth, a city sacred to all the Christian world. It was Sunday and that evening at eight the party had dinner with the British Military Governor, Colonel B. Romilly and his wife, a sister of Mrs. Winston Churchill. The dinner, which consisted of oatmeal soup, hardboiled eggs with mustard sauce, beefsteak with potatoes, beans and a salad, sponge cake with jam and cream, and apricots and coffee, must have impressed Dr. King. He noted in his *Diary*: "Dinner at 8 o'clock with the Gov[ernor] and staff—ran late. A good deal of liquor." Perhaps the setting of liquor—a good deal of it—on a Sunday evening in old Nazareth was a bit shocking for a Congregational minister!

The next morning twelve delegations from Nazareth, Safed and Tiberias were to be heard in the governor's palace, and still others in the afternoon. With a visit to Haifa and return to Nazareth, the work of the King-Crane Commission in Palestine proper was concluded, for on June 27, at about 7 a.m., Dr. King and his cohorts left Nazareth in a convoy of ten automobiles for Damascus via the road to Tiberias Capernaum, on Lake Tiberias. The party reached Damascus late in the afternoon, seeing the Mosque of the "Night of Power", where about 4,000 people were praying. That evening, also, they met the Emir Feisal, who had preceded the Commission to Syria. Feisal invited the members of the Commission, and Mr. W. T. Ellis, of the New York *Herald-Tribune*, to the platform, which was covered with costly Oriental rugs. After the prayer there was magnificent chanting. There were brief conversations with the people—as a kind of introduction of what was to follow— which indicated their intention to ask for an "American mandate", a position which was "somewhat startling." [1]

The End of the Palestine Journey

Judging from the evidence which had been presented to the Commission during its short visit to Palestine, June 10-25, only the Zionist Jews, about one-tenth of the total population, favored the establishment of a Jewish National home in that country. The rest of the population, Moslem and Christian Arabs alike, desired to preserve the unity of the country with Syria, of which they considered Palestine to be both historically and geographically a part.

Conflicting Views

While we have no summary of the Commission's views immediately on leaving Palestine, with the exception of a memorandum of Dr. Mont-

---

[1] Lybyer *Diary*, June 25, 1919. Lybyer Papers: Suggested Itinerary, June 21-23; Itinerary of Nablus to Acre, June 23, 1919.

gomery, it would seem that the members were not prepared to accept the Zionist views, at least in the extreme form. Captain Yale had been distinctly opposed to Zionism while in Paris, although not because of any anti-Semitic prejudices. He was aware of the growing, intense Arab opposition, and thought that Zionism would be a very dangerous thing for the Jewish people scattered all over the world, a view shared by others. However, under the influence of Dr. Westermann, who presented the realities of the problem, Yale became convinced that opposition to Zionism was futile and impractical because of the commitments which had already been made. Consequently, he endeavored always to present the possibility of a compromise between Arab nationalism and Zionism. His experience within and outside his work with the Commission in Palestine and after the period of the investigation had ended did not alter this attitude.[1]

Dr. Montgomery raised a series of questions concerning Zionism in a communication to Dr. King, shortly after arriving in Syria.[2] He wondered, among other things, whether it might not be worthwhile to try to appreciate Zionist opinion, since in his view, President Wilson, Colonel House and others high in the Conference had seemed favorable to Zionism. He felt, too, that in presenting the views of the Commission there might be a danger of overestimating the advantage of information gained in Palestine and Syria, since Palestine was not the only country concerned with Zionism. Dr. Montgomery, in other words, doubted that Palestine was the place "for one to make up his mind whether to be pro- or anti-Zionist." Distance from the scene might lend a more proper perspective for analysis of all the factors involved in the problem. Were there not also Rumania, Poland, Russia, Great Britain and the United States? Should not the Christians of Europe and America be considered as well as the Arabs and the Jews? Montgomery, in good Benthamite fashion, believed that the "greatest benefit of the greatest number," should be the basis of politics, "rather than the matter of rights." Perhaps the Peace Conference had been impressed with the long history of the Jewish people, and with the fear of the problem of anti-Semitism. Probably the voice of the Jew should be heard in the matter of Zionism. Could it not be said that the Jews regarded Palestine "not only as a refuge from persecution but as a place for trying out an experiment in nationalism"? Moreover, would any report describing Arab opposition to Zionism "be new to the Peace Conference?" Was not opposition, especially "the bitter opposition of the large land holding Arab families" to be expected?

Montgomery also raised questions concerning the attitude of the British military authorities, many of whom were professedly anti-Zionist.

---

[1] Yale to the author, October 17, 1940. See also Manuel, 248-252.
[2] Lybyer Papers: George Montgomery, "Questions on Zionism", July 1, 1919. For Dr. King.

Should not the constructive work which the Jews were likely to accomplish in Palestine be envisaged in the forthcoming report of the Commission, and should it not be remembered, in any event, that the mandatory would "be present to insure justice?" Was it fair to mention as a possible advantage "the placing of a block of non-Arabs between Syria and Egypt as an announcement to the Syrians that their national development must seek growth in other ways and not through union with the Arabs of Egypt?" Was political union with Palestine "essential to the economic development of Syria?" Was Palestine "essential to the growth of a Syrian national feeling?"

The Majority View

But the majority of the King-Crane Commission found it impossible to accept Montgomery's hypotheses. Except for certain official groups, the Commission felt that the people of Palestine were "practically unanimous for the independence of United Syria." Those groups which had been interviewed at Jaffa had taken the position that Syria was capable of "self-government without a mandatory power," although they preferred the United States if there were to be a mandatory at all. At Jerusalem and in all other places as well, the "program of independence was affirmed." In general, the question of a mandate was referred to the Syrian National Congress which was soon to convene in Damascus. While some rejected the idea of a mandate altogether, it became clear later on, when the Damascus Congress approved the idea of an American mandate, that this was to be the program to which the great majority of the Palestine Moslems were committed. The Christian groups, constituting less than ten per cent of the population, were more divided than the Moslems. For example, the Latin Catholics of Tiberias and Haifa, as well as a majority of the Christians at Nazareth, like the Moslems, preferred independence and reference to Damascus. Maronites, Greek Catholics, and usually the Latin Catholics, desired a French mandate. If there were any possibility that the United States would accept a mandate, "most Christians would favor this solution," although it was true that "none asked directly for the United States." The Jews, who constituted only about one-tenth of the population, "were all for Zionism, under a British mandate." But the Moslem and Christian population "was practically unanimous against Zionism, usually expressing themselves with great emphasis." The problem of Zionism was closely integrated with that of Syrian unity under one government.[1]

There were some differences of opinion among the Jews as to the realization of their program. There was agreement that Palestine, "with a fairly large area," should be set aside as a Jewish National Home. It was also agreed that sooner or later the government would be organized

[1] *PPC*, XII, 763-774.

as a "Jewish Commonwealth". Again, there should be free immigration for Jews from all parts of the world, "unrestricted purchase of the land by the Jews," and recognition of Hebrew as an official language. Great Britain was definitely preferred as the mandatory for Palestine. The Great Powers having declared in favor of the scheme, the plan for a Jewish National Home in Palestine only awaited execution. But there was disagreement as to whether the Jewish Commonwealth was to be established soon, or after a considerable period of time, whether the major stress should be placed on a restoration of the ancient life and culture, or upon "economic development in a thoroughly modern fashion." There was a feeling that some kind of special provision, with the appointment of a permanent Commission with supervisory powers, should be made for the Holy Places of Palestine, which were sacred alike to Christianity, Judaism and Islam.[1]

The problems of Palestine, involving British imperial interests at the crossroads of the continents, the conflict of eastern and western cultures, the rising tide of Arab nationalism, and the age-old dream of Zionism, were easier to describe than to solve. Solution would require, no doubt, the legendary wisdom of Solomon. Could the Americans meet the complicated issues involved, no matter how hard they tried?

There were some who considered the King-Crane Commission's visit to Palestine a bad gesture from the beginning, which only harmed those whom it was intended to benefit. According to some students much of the ferment which "marred the Near East" in the post-war era could be traced to such "thoughtless and heedless western methods, and in-

---

[1] *PPC*, XII, 851-852. The Commission was aware of the benefits of Zionism, but pointed out that the Arab inhabitants advanced these considerations: "The land is owned and occupied by them; the Arabs were there before the Jews came; the Jews were immigrants, who treated the former inhabitants with the greatest cruelty, and who remained a comparatively short time; they were unable to maintain control over the whole land or even union among themselves; they were expelled by the Romans and formed permanent residence elsewhere 2,000 years ago; the Arabs conquered the land 1,300 years ago, and have remained ever since; it is their actual home, and not merely a residence of long ago; as Christians and Moslems, they can honor all the holy places, whereas the Jews can honor only their own; the Jews are a religion and not a nation; they will, if given control, forbid the use of the Arabic language, the measure which caused the break between the Young Turks and the Arabs; the Jewish colonies have shown no benevolence to the Arabs in their neighborhood; it is denied that their activities have influenced the Arabs toward progress; the Jews have much money, education and shrewdness, and will soon buy out and manœuvre away the present inhabitants; the Arabs are friendly toward the Jews long resident in the land who use the Arabic language; they will resist to the uttermost the immigration of foreign Jews and the establishment of a Jewish government."

trusion in local affairs."[1] On the other hand, William T. Ellis, of the New York *Herald-Tribune*, who was in Jerusalem and Damascus while the King-Crane Commission was there, wrote of its work in Palestine:[2]

> I saw the Commission at work. They came to Jerusalem while I was there, and again overtook me at Damascus.... I witnessed enough to understand the painstaking impartiality, the tireless diligence and patience, and the American shrewdness and courage of the Commission amidst difficulties.... Every American in the area visited, so far as I could ascertain, was proud of the efficiency, the thoroughness and the fairness of Dr. King and Mr. Crane and their assistants. They succeeded where Paris failed.

[1] De Haas, 491-492; Manuel, 244-246.
[2] Letter to the New *York Times*, December 3, 1922.

CHAPTER V

Some Answers to the Syrian Riddle

The King-Crane Commission was to confront very serious issues in Syria, complicated by an Anglo-French conflict of interests, French political and colonial ambitions, and the tide of nascent Arab nationalism. There was a basic distrust on every hand, and it had been very clear in Paris that Premier Clemenceau and other French political leaders did not want either an Inter-Allied or an American Commission to enter the country for purposes of investigation.

The Emir Feisal had gone back to Damascus from Paris, in advance of the King-Crane Commission, as the French authorities believed, in order to stack the cards against French ambitions in the country. Following a talk with the French Ambassador, M. Cambon, on June 11, Lord Curzon expressed his lack of confidence in the French High Commissioner, M. Georges Picot, and stated that the Syrians would be "greatly surprised to learn that it was to the French," as Picot had declared, "that they must look for their independence." [1] Moreover, General Allenby cabled Lord Curzon on June 12 that he had received a message from Feisal, in Aleppo, asking him to find out from the King-Crane Commission or elsewhere whether the League of Nations was "prepared to put into force recommendations" made by the Commission and whether that body was really authorized to recommend the assignment of the mandate over Syria to any power wanted by the great majority of the people. Unless this were known, the Syrian people would be greatly handicapped in approaching the Commission. They would certainly want independence, it was said, unless Great Britain assumed the mandate. But if Great Britain would not assume the mandate and Syria could not be independent, the people would "ask for America in preference to France." General Allenby had replied that the Commission would advise the Peace Conference concerning the wishes of the people, that the British Government was unwilling to accept a mandate, but would give the fullest weight to the advice of the Commission. While the Emir Feisal understood the British position, he added that the Syrians would be "unanimous" in expressing to the Commission their wish to have Great Britain alone as the mandatory, for reasons which he would set forth before a conference to be held at Damascus. [2]

Georges Picot conferred with Feisal on June 18, when the latter insisted on independence and asked Picot why France had failed to fulfil its promise as to participation in an Inter-Allied Commission. Picot indicated that the United Kingdom was claiming Palestine and an area which included the Hauran and the Jebel Druze area, but that France

---

[1] *British Documents*, 1919-1939, First Series, IV, 274-275.
[2] *Ibid.*, 275-276, 285-286.

was opposing the claim, and Picot was pressing for a greater Syria which would include Diarbekir and Mosul. He professed surprise at the statement of the King-Crane Commission that it represented the Peace Conference, since "the fact was that it had been sent out privately by President Wilson, and that its findings would carry no weight at all with the Conference," an "error" which he intended publicly to correct. Feisal refused to accept the French point of view, and declared his intention to leave the verdict to the Syrian people. Nor would he discuss the matter further "until after the American Mission had come and gone."[1] Despite the French impression that there was some sort of agreement with Clemenceau in Paris, there was little doubt in General Clayton's mind, as reported on June 23, that the Emir Feisal had "in no way changed his attitude of uncompromising opposition to any form of French intervention in Syria." In any event, back in Syria, Feisal had decided to instruct his people "to ask for complete independence for Syria, at the same time expressing the hope that it would be granted to other Arab countries." He hoped, thereby, to reconcile those who were "thinking only of Syria and those who favoured the idea of a great pan-Arab State." At the same time the Emir proposed to tell the King-Crane Commission that he had been forced into this course because of his fear of the French "and that he would at any time accept a British mandate." In view of the importance which Syrians and Palestinians both attached to the King-Crane Commission, General Clayton thought that no decision concerning the future status of Syria and Palestine should be made until the Commission had published its report.[2]

A Visit to Damascus

Having spent about two weeks in Palestine, and visited some thirteen or fourteen towns and villages in which interviews were held, the King-Crane Commission was now ready to spend the period from June 26 to July 21 in the Arab and French-occupied regions of Syria, with a day or so left for Cilicia. Having arrived in Damascus late in the afternoon of June 25, the group settled down to hard work the next morning. Curiously enough, the Commission arrived at just about the time the Treaty of Versailles was ready for signature, for that instrument of peace, the first of the Paris treaties, was signed and sealed in the Hall of Mirrors

---

[1] *Ibid.*, 278-280. Feisal had said the same thing to General Allenby on May 12, and had added that the French could enter Syria only by force of arms.

[2] *Ibid.*, 289-94, 295, 296-297. On June 24, Lord Curzon wired Clayton concerning Feisal's propaganda in Mesopotamia regarding "the complete independence of Arabia," which was causing trouble, and all responsible British officers were instructed to "discourage the movement by all means in their power."

at Versailles on June 28, 1919. Concerning the Commission's work, Dr. King expressed his sentiments in a letter from Damascus: [1]

> We're in the midst of a most interesting week here, with delegations galore. The staff is doing well, and I find Mr. Crane very pleasant to work with. We succeed in getting in some sight-seeing between whiles. Have already covered considerable part of Palestine and Syria. Expect to finish before middle of July.

The Beginnings in Damascus

If Dr. King really expected to complete even the Syrian portion of the work before the middle of July he was to be sadly disappointed, for the Syrian investigation, with "interviews galore", was quite as complicated as the inquest in Palestine. As soon as the Commission arrived in the city it was greeted by a series of demands which had been distributed in the bazaars of Damascus and presented to the Commission as the "demands of the People of the Coast, now found in Damascus:" [2]

1. The complete political independence of Syria with its natural boundaries, the Taurus Mountains in the north, the two rivers of Khabour and Euphrates in the East, the line between Akaba and Rafa in the South, and the Mediterranean Sea in the West.
2. We protest against and refuse Art. 22 of the Covenant of the League of Nations regarding the necessity of a Mandate.
3. With all respect for the French Government we refuse every right she claims in our country, and we protest with all our power against the secret agreements regarding Syria.
4. We refuse the immigration of the Zionists to our country, and the making of Palestine (southern Syria), which is an inseparable part of Syria, a native home for the Jews.
5. After the acknowledgement and the granting to us [of] our complete independence we will take what we need of money and men from any Government we wish, and we prefer this to be America. We refuse the assistance of France under any circumstance.

Immediately after arrival in Damascus, the Commission published its statement in the press, so that the aims and purposes of the American investigators would be clear. Moreover, as agreed in a conference of the staff, the statement embodied the text of Article XXII of the Covenant of the League of Nations regarding mandates in the territories of the former Ottoman Empire. [3] Lybyer had a long talk on Thursday, June 26, with Dr. Shahbender, a distinguished graduate of the American University of Beirut and a leader in the Syrian national movement, about the political situation. In mid-afternoon the Emir Feisal called and a talk of about half an hour ensued, at the close of which Feisal declared that

---

[1] King Papers: King to Bohn, June 28, 1919.
[2] Lybyer Papers: *Demands of People of Coast: Distributed in Bazaars of Damascus at 3:40 P. M., Wednesday, June 25, 1919.*
[3] Lybyer Papers: *Commission's Statement to the Press of Damascus*, June 26, 1919.

the people were asking for independence—they asked "one hundred per cent and expected ninety per cent," and wanted either American or British, not French, assistance. [1]

Later in the afternoon, the Commission met the Mayor of Damascus, the Kadi, the Mufti, and the Ulema, or "Gentlemen of the Pen", at the Damascus Palace Hotel. [2] The latter, apparently, were especially interesting, and made out a strong case for American or British assistance. Vigorous stress was laid on three points: 1) The request for an American mandate; 2) the refusal of a French mandate; and 3) the placing of Palestine under none but an Arab Government, along with the rest of Syria. The group preferred complete independence and considered the people ready for self-government, although for financial and economic reasons, a mandate was considered desirable. It was urged that the United States take the mandate because it cared for humanity, had entered the war in behalf of oppressed nations, would not colonize Syria, and was "very rich", and the group desired to put their destiny in "the hands of a nation not exhausted by the war." But if the United States would not assume the mandate, Great Britain was to be preferred. The American Commissioners were told that the whole country rejected France because French methods and habits were objectionable. To place the people under a French mandate "would be like handing them over as captives from the Turks, with whom, though an Eastern people, they did not get on well, to the French," who were a Western people, "with whom they would get on much less well." The group also objected to the Zionist plans because the Jews were "shrewder and richer than their people." There was fear for the land and fear that the Jews would try to force the Hebrew language on Palestine. The Ulema also rejected the idea of Palestine as an international "park",

> since many millions look to it as a holy place, the Arabs are as servants in the house for all, who will be permitted to visit freely. There are in Palestine places holy to Christians and Moslems and not to Jews, and places holy to Moslems and not to Christians; all places are holy to Moslems; therefore the Moslems should control the land.

---

[1] Lybyer *Diary*, June 26, 1919. King noted in his *Diary*, June 26: "A very good conference of staff at 11:50."

[2] Lybyer Papers: *Interview of Commissioners, Advisers present, with the Kadi, Mufti, and six others of the Ulema at Damascus Palace Hotel, at four o'clock p. m. June 26, 1919.* A. H. L. Also Chicago *Daily News*, August 1, 1919. The *Report* (PPC, XII, 777) says that "the interview of the Commission with the Mufti, Kadi, and Ulema was published with considerable accuracy in the local newspapers (of course by no act or permission of the Commission), and this gave rise to animated discussions on the part of the people and the press. The Commission accepted hospitality from the Emir Feisal on two occasions." In the version printed in the Damascus press, June 27, 1919 [Brodie Papers], the Ulema "absolutely refused" the Zionist program and French assistance, demanded independence under Feisal, and the unity of the country.

The Ulema wanted the Emir Feisal as King or Prince, "because Syria and Irak had agreed to respect this house, and because he rescued them with the help of the Allies." Finally, the Ulema desired "a civil democratic constitution" and promised "thorough safeguarding of the rights of minorities." These very strong views appeared to reflect the sentiments of articulate elements over the country.

In the evening the two Commissioners had dinner with the Emir Feisal and met General Gabriel Haddad Pasha, the Chief of Police and Gendarmerie at Damascus, with whom they also talked the next day. [1] While Gabriel Haddad Pasha was not permitted to discuss the mandate problem, he did indicate the need for guidance, under a mandatory which would not "colonize the country". Catholic, Greek Syrian and Latin Maronite groups also appeared before the Commissioners, and there was a vigorous discussion with the Council of Ten, who wanted independence, after which they would choose financial and technical advisers, who were not, however, to interfere in the internal administration. They would have nothing to do with France. The Greek Orthodox leaders expressed willingness, under certain conditions, to cooperate with Feisal, and desired a British mandate, while the Greek Catholics preferred France as the mandatory. The Grand Rabbi of the Jewish community and other Jewish leaders wanted Palestine separated from Syria, under a mandate. [2]

June 28 proved a very notable date. It was the last day of Ramadan in Damascus, and in Paris the Treaty of Versailles was signed. About eleven o'clock in the morning eighteen "splendid men" of the Druze came to present their case for "complete independence" under either a British or an American mandate, and in the afternoon there were other Arab delegations. [3] That evening the Emir Feisal invited the two Commissioners and the entire staff to an Oriental dinner and *soirée* at his house and garden on the lower slope of the mountains northwest of Damascus. There were about twenty-five European guests all in Arab costumes, as well as the Arabs, and a group of small girls and boys. There were songs of war and independence, wild Arab music and dances. Then came the

---

[1] Lybyer Papers: *Notes on Interview of Commissioners, Advisers present, with General Gabriel Haddad Pasha, Chief of Police and Gendarmerie*, Damascus, 3:30 P. M., June 27, 1919. The Zionist problem was not raised, but General Haddad declared that "native Jews are fully protected in the rights which everybody enjoys." See also The Program of Interviews in Lybyer Papers.

[2] During the day, Dr. Frederick J. Bliss and Mr. James Stewart Crawford, of the American University of Beirut, came to confer with the Commission about Syrian affairs.

[3] Lybyer Papers: A number of Druze statements are available in the collection.

dinner, served on large trays each heaped with a mound of food. There is no doubt of the impression of that evening in Damascus:[1]

> The dinner was a true oriental affair from the first salaam to the last. When the Commission and the French and British officers at Damascus who had also been invited entered the outer court of the royal residence they were given complete Arabian costumes. The transformation from European or American to Arab was soon accomplished. Uniforms and frock coats were covered by the silk robes, headdresses and circulets worn by the wealthier Arab in his numerous hours of leisure. The little group of amateur Arabs was then ushered out into a spacious balcony overlooking one of the lovely gardens of Damascus with the usual palms, and flowers and murmuring fountains. The announcement was made that dinner would shortly be served, but the chances seemed against it as apparently no preparations had been made. There wasn't the slightest thing to suggest even a sandwich or a glass of lemonade. There wasn't a table of any kind on the broad balcony, not even a chair or a stool, just a few rugs and cushions. The Americans had faith however in Prince Feisal.... And presently their faith was vindicated. A single column of liveried servants approached, each holding high a great metal bowl at least three feet in diameter and a foot or so in depth. The bowls were placed at regular intervals on the floor and following His Highness the guests grouped themselves about the mysterious bowls, four to each bowl. There was the dinner, all in one bowl. For economy in housekeeping the Arab was setting another precedent. Think of the dish-washing the Ancient Arab saved! Just a few bowls for a company of fifty, for though this modern party was indulged by being given a large spoon apiece we were informed that the true Arab of the olden days would not have hesitated to use the fingers that Allah had given him to minister to his needs! With these spoons the guests began to explore the contents of the great bowls, and one after another new delicacies were discovered in their depths. Beneath the crust of pastry there was first of all a generous layer of chicken; then a field of delicious rice cooked in an inimitable oriental fashion; underneath the rice a deep "level"—it was a regular mine—of broiled strips of mutton...; next came some vegetables akin to our cucumbers and vegetable marrows; and last of all, at the very bottom of the bowl, one of the rich syrupy desserts so dear to an eastern epicure. Quite a dinner was it not, all in layers, in the same dish! After the feast, two servants came to each guest, the first to spray the hands with toilet water, and the second with towels, for in former times handwashing was a post-prandial rite. And then a little later the spiced coffee of Arabia was served out in the garden where everyone gathered for a program of ancient dances including the famous sword dance, Arabic songs and strange music on queer stringed instruments. For a few hours the Americans had lived in the days of the Sultan Saladin....

A few days later Feisal entertained the Commission at a formal state dinner in the best European style, exemplifying the westernization among

---

[1] Brodie Papers: This account is from Donald M. Brodie's *Memorandum.* See also the Lybyer and King *Diaries,* June 28, 1919, and especially Lybyer's letter to his wife, June 29, 1919 for an excellent account. One song declared: "The land is ours, we will live for it; we will die for it."

the Arabs of the Syrian region, but magnificent though the latter occasion was, it could hardly match the Oriental grandeur of that June evening in the garden of the Emir.

Perhaps it was well that a quiet Sunday followed the banquet, for no doubt the Americans needed something of a rest. There were letters to be written, and it was very hot in the afternoon. Dr. King and Mr. Crane made a formal call on the Emir Feisal and others, and then took a long drive about the city in order to get a good view of Damascus, the gardens and public parks, and "the place of departure of pilgrims for Mecca." At dinner that evening there was considerable discussion with Dr. Bliss and Mr. Crawford, who were anti-French and in favor of an American mandate. Bliss thought the Arabs should not be given independent government immediately. [1]

Another "long day of interviews" followed on Monday, and there was an especially interesting statement from a Protestant group. At 10:30 a.m., the Commission drove to Feisal's palace to see General Allenby, with whom they had a conference for about an hour. [2] That afternoon a delegation of twelve Moslem women, relatives of the martyrs of Jemal Pasha's terrorism, presented an eloquent appeal for absolute independence, with no help whatsoever. They wanted no assistance because of their assumption that it would make their men lazy! It was discovered that there were "two or three very good looking" women, for they all raised their veils in the presence of the Americans! [3]

A Visit to Amman

In the midst of the Damascus visit, the Commission, with the exception of Crane, who was ill, and Yale, who remained to investigate anti-French propaganda in Damascus, took a journey south to Amman and Dera. The city of Amman, where the Emir Abdullah ibn Hussein, brother of Feisal, was to rule under British guidance, traced its lineage almost to

---

[1] Lybyer *Diary*, June 29, 1919. F. J. Bliss was the son of Daniel Bliss, late President of the Syrian Protestant College, later the American University of Beirut, and was well known for his work on *The Religions of Modern Syria and Palestine* (New York, Scribner's, 1912).

[2] King and Lybyer *Diaries*, June 30, 1919. See also General Sir Archibald P. WAVELL, *Allenby: A Study in Greatness* (New York, Oxford, 1941), 386 n, for Allenby's estimate of Feisal. On June 26, following the meeting of the Council of Four in Paris, Balfour advised Allenby that Great Britain would not assume the mandate for Syria. Allenby was to tell the Emir Feisal that he was entirely unjustified in thinking that this refusal constituted "an abandonment either of himself or of the Arab cause." But for reasons with which Feisal was "perfectly well acquainted," Great Britain could not "add to the responsibilities" which it had "undertaken on behalf of the Arab race, the position of Mandatory of Syria." See *PPC*, VI, 676-677; *British Documents, 1919-1939*, First Series, IV, 298-299.

[3] Lybyer *Diary*, June 30, 1919.

the days of Lot, while twenty centuries ago Ptolemy Philadelphus gave the name of Philadelphia to the city.

The Americans left Damascus by train on June 30 and arrived at Amman early the next morning. Now came the "charge of the American Commission upon Rabbath Amman," for the Arabs rode to the station on horseback, and insisted on mounting their guests on the finest steeds for the ride back to the town, a distance of about three miles. It was to be, as Dr. King noted, a "rather exciting" trip, and Captain Brodie recalled it as "by all odds the most memorable bit of travel..., a wild ride with a band of Bedouins on the edge of the Arabian desert near Amman." The hopes for "a quiet, comfortable mount" were "disastrously shattered." Assuming that only the safest, steadiest horses would be offered them, the Americans boldly mounted their steeds, thinking that the Arabs would ride in "an orderly and dignified procession." But "within a few seconds the leaders were off in a wild gallop in which the horses of the Americans absolutely refused to be left behind." Laurence Moore was thrown from his horse, and Lybyer lost his helmet and glasses. Dr. King, "despite his seniority and the fact that he had seldom if ever ridden for thirty years..., put the younger members of the party to shame and actually won the race." They were all somewhat sore as a result of the equestrian experience, and were to return to the station, after a hard day's work, in a carriage. Dr. King wrote later on about the trip to this region east of the Jordan: [1]

> The trip to Amman was especially interesting as we heard delegations from many distant villages, one delegation riding thirty hours to meet the Commission. We had a great time at Amman too, because they met us with riding horses at the station, which is three miles from the village where the sessions were to be held. We found when we got on our horses that they were not tourist hacks but really spirited Arab horses. The one I got on was the sort that does not like to be left behind anybody, and simply rushed ahead of most of the crowd and brought me to the village three or four minutes before the rest of them appeared. I was thankful to be able to stay on and keep alive. One of our group was thrown from his horse and it was a mercy that he and others were not injured. That was an incident that one was not quite prepared for....

In two and one half hours, nineteen delegations, about two hundred persons in all, were heard, the group from Kerak having ridden thirty hours. The Americans declined lunch, paid a hasty call on the British governor, glanced at the ruins of the old Roman theater, left by one o'clock and had lunch on the train. At four in the afternoon they reached the village of Dera, where two hundred sheikhs on horses were lined up to greet them, but fortunately they had the distinct pleasure of walking

---

[1] King Papers: King to Bohn, July 23, 1919; King and Lybyer *Diaries*, July 1, 1919; Brodie's *Memorandum*.

to the town hall. One delegation represented forty villages of the Dera region. Another group of "nine splendid orators" sat with the Americans for an entire hour, while other sheikhs waiting outside "applauded their orators." They were all back at the train ready to leave, after proper farewells from their hosts, at six in the evening.

The general impression received from the journey to Amman and Dera was that all the Moslems were "for complete independence without protection or a mandatory power; but recognizing that they needed financial and economic advice, they proposed after the recognition of independence to ask for advisers from America." Eloquent speakers appealed to the United States as "having freed them, to uphold their independence before the Peace Conference," saying that they held America responsible before God for completing the work so well begun. On the other hand, the few Christians "were in great fear," and desired a strong mandatory power in order to have full protection. They wanted Great Britain as the mandatory and Syrian unity with Palestine. [1]

SOME TENTATIVE IMPRESSIONS OF THE SYRIAN SITUATION

The period immediately following the return from Amman was exceedingly busy, for the Commission heard Iraqi, Circassians and Kurds, not to mention a fake organization known as the "Society of Miserable Syrians," which favored French control of Syria. On July 1, the Damascus journal, *Hermon*, published an open letter welcoming the Commission to Syria, but warning that the period of non-interference in the affairs of Europe and Asia was now at an end. American money and blood had been spent "to attain a noble end," and the United States could not now turn its back on the old continents with the plea that it could not become entangled with their affairs. All Syria looked for a solution of the Syrian problem "in a satisfactory way for all the various sects." The Syrian nation was "ingenious and very intelligent," and was capable of independence, with the temporary assistance of some western power. *Hermon* indicated that Great Britain should be the power assigned to guide Syria along the paths to the freedom which the country sought. [2]

The Yale Impression of Syria

There was now some evidence for a preliminary estimate of the Syrian

---

[1] Among the nine Arab petitions in the King Papers is one from Amman, for example: Nadi el Arabia (Amman). It demands complete independence for Syria, does not recognize any rights of the French in Syria, and requests assistance from the United States or Great Britain. In the Brodie Papers is a statement of the Ajarma tribe demanding: 1) Complete independence; 2) assistance from the United States or Great Britain; and 3) rejection of the French claims. Both King and Brodie were somewhat ill as a result of their Amman experience, while Crane was still unable to carry on his work. See also the several statements from Jebeil, July 2, 1919, mostly from Druze sources, in the Lybyer Papers.

[2] Lybyer *Diary*, July 2, 1919; Editorial in *Hermon*, July 1, 1919.

situation, and both Yale and Lybyer had sketched out their impressions by July 2. Yale was very sceptical of any genuine sentiment of nationalism in Syria, and he was to remain so.[1] From Beersheba in the south to Damascus and Baalbek, he felt

> a distinct note of pan-Arabism and Pan-Islamism. By a clever, well organized and thorough propaganda the Moslems of Palestine and Syria have been united on a program which superficially has every sign of being Syrian nationalism, but which is basically Islamic.

Although the masses had no understanding of western nationalism, they supported the program because they were "ordered to". The effendi class in the cities supported it because they believed it would "maintain their position as land owners and over-lords and their position of superiority to the Christians." The program pleased the Moslem clergy and fanatics because they saw "Moslem supremacy and independence" in it. The few younger men who were experiencing "a vague but acute sense of nationalism" were an exception. Some older Moslems felt that they were being "driven on towards a catastrophe."

The Christians in Palestine had been "driven to throw in their lot with the Moslems," thanks to their fear of Zionism. They had supported the nationalist program "out of fear for the Jews and in concession to the Moslems," feeling certain that a "strong mandate" would be arranged by the Peace Conference. Before and during the war

> there was absolutely no national feeling in Palestine. The evidences of its existence at the present time are, it is true, violent, but the feeling is one born of the circumstances and has no solid foundation and promises little for the future, and should not be given real value as being a national feeling.

Christian support of the program in Syria, likewise, was due to fear, and Christians hoped for a strong, protective mandatory power. A reign of moral terror existed in Syria, and the "ever timid" Christians had been obliged to "fall in with the Moslem scheme." Captain Yale did not have much confidence in the Emir Feisal:

> Emir Feisal is a man of liberal views, large sympathies, and a man who sincerely loves his country. Although he has won the love of many of the Arabs and has a wide prestige among them he is not a strong man. He cannot, I believe, hold the Moslem element for long; the younger chauvinistic Moslem element, the older fanatic element, and the larger over-lords will either bend him to their will or when they are ready, brush him aside. He is used today by these elements, but he does not control them.

---

[1] Lybyer Papers: Captain William YALE, *Strong National Feeling*, about July 1, 1919.

By careful cultivation over a long period of years, Yale believed a genuine "national spirit" might be created in Syria. But with Christian and Moslem forces opposed to each other, and Christian fear of the Jews in Palestine, the real issues involved had been obscured in Christian minds, and thus their support of the "Moslem program of unity" had been won. The character of the struggle was far better understood in Mt. Lebanon, where the Christians were stronger and the vast majority of Christians were not "allowing themselves to be deceived by 'National Propaganda'," which they recognized as "essentially Islamic propaganda." French and British interests had only served to deepen the natural gulf between Moslems and Christians and had divided the Christian community as well. Yale had a "sincere hope to see Syria eventually a united country with a real national spirit," but since he did not believe it then existed he thought that "to have confidence in such a national spirit" was dangerous, and to act on the assumption that it existed "would shipwreck any future hope of the development of Syrian nationalism." He recalled that there were more intelligent and well-meaning elements among the Young Turks in 1908 than among the members of the Arab movement, and he remembered how "the Young Turk movement soon turned into a chauvinistic nationalism and pro-Islamism." It was almost certain that the Arab or Syrian national movement would "turn into fanatical Islamism." Yale was, therefore, afraid that a misjudgment of the Arab movement might "cost the lives of thousands of Christians in Syria, as the misunderstanding of the essential element in the Young Turkish movement cost the lives of over a million Christians in Turkey."

The Lybyer Estimate of the Syrian Situation

But Captain Yale's views were not representative of those of the Commission as a whole, although they were largely shared by Dr. Montgomery. Professor Lybyer summed up his tentative views on July 2.[1] The Moslems, who constituted about four-fifths of the population of Palestine and three-fifths of the population of all Syria, Lybyer pointed out, were almost unanimous on the following program:

a. The unity of Syria, within "historical limits", that is to say between the Mediterranean Sea and the desert, the Taurus Mountains and the boundary of Egypt and the Hejaz (Rafa or El Arish to Akaba). This includes all Palestine and the Lebanon District.

b. The independence of Syria within limits, with the belief that a real nation is there, which is at least as ready for self-government as were the Balkan states when created. The preference grows that the independence of this new state should be immediate and complete.

[1] Lybyer Papers: A. H. LYBYER, *The Apparent Situation in Syria*, July 2, 1919. Copy. King's Notations. 4 pp. The document is dated July 1, but according to Lybyer's *Diary* it was written on July 2, 1919.

c. The assistance of a Great Power in financial and economic respects and through the advice of technical experts is felt to be necessary for a limited time. This assistance is to be arranged by free negotiation after the Peace Conference shall have recognized the independence of Syria. Objection to the plan for a "mandatory", as given in Article 22 of the Covenant of the League of Nations, since the assistance should not involve any interference in administration.

The Moslem element was also in agreement in preferring, as a first choice, the United States as a mandatory, with Great Britain as a second. France was not wanted at all. The Moslems were unanimously opposed to Zionism and against any further immigration of Jews into Palestine. The Emir Feisal was to be the "king or prince of the country".

A constitution was to be drawn up under the guarantee of the League of Nations,

providing for democracy, decentralization of local government (the idea seems to involve a system like our own of four or five states with a federal government), separation of church and state, guaranteed representation of minorities, equal rights for all irrespective of religion.

This was eventually the Damascus program, which Lybyer believed was "associated with a genuine national feeling," in which Arab Christians participated. It was in this respect that he did not accept the Yale thesis.

On the other hand, the Christian Arabs were unanimous only on one point: They feared "immediate complete independence under an Arab Government," and wanted a strong mandatory power. All desired Syrian unity, but some Palestinian Christians preferred separation under Great Britain to Syrian unity under France. Moreover, most of the Greek Orthodox Christians wanted Great Britain as a mandatory, although some adhered to the Moslem program, the United States being a second choice. Most of the Latins and the Maronites were for France. The very few native Protestants preferred the United States, Great Britain or France, in the order named, as a mandatory.

The Jews of Palestine were "apparently unanimous for the Zionist program," involving free immigration for Jews, administration under Great Britain, ultimate building of a "Jewish Commonwealth", all of which they regarded as promised and only awaiting fulfilment. The Jews of Damascus desired autonomy and protection for themselves, and sympathized with Zionism for Palestine.

Lybyer now proceeded to examine the problem of "propaganda", for it was important to find out how the people came to have these desires, "as bearing upon the consideration of the settlement for Syria." In other words, were the feelings of the people genuine or artificial? Lybyer found "practically no evidence of propaganda by the British." Only one British military governor in Palestine "seemed to have tried to influence opinion, and he did not accomplish much." The Greek Orthodox Community had "officially agreed to support [the British] everywhere"; but the charge that this rested on a financial agreement could not "be given weight without evidence." The Druze had been "pro-British for decades." There was also little evidence of propaganda by the French, "other than constant pointing out the extent of French educational work and the use of the French language in Syria." The Latins and Maronites were "in evident agreement everywhere to present an official demand for France." There was a great "active system of propaganda" carried on in behalf of Syrian unity and independence, which had been shaping under the very eyes of the American investigators, and which was somewhat "influenced by a desire to meet the supposed inclinations of the Commission." The nationalist program was supported by "Arab societies whose effort for independence began before the war." Moreover, it was encouraged by the Wilsonian principles and the Anglo-French declaration of November 1918. The Emir Feisal's agents had been "working very hard for it," and both printed and oral propaganda were being used. Again:

> The immense personal popularity of the Emir has first been enhanced by propaganda, and then used to push the rest of the program. It is probable that this program now represents the popular opinion of the majority of the people of the country, as truly as popular opinion can be represented in any western land. Most of the elements are solidly held, whether well based or not.

In the light of the information then available there were five possible schemes for settlement. The first of these was complete independence, which appealed strongly to the American mind, although "the evident fear which the Christians and Jews" felt "toward an Arab government" made "it of doubtful wisdom." Moreover, Article XXII of the Covenant of the League of Nations, and the instructions of the Commission, implied that the Peace Conference did "not favor immediate independence of any detached part of Turkey." A second possibility was "unity under an American mandate." A majority, including many high British officials, appeared to desire the United States "chiefly because of her disinterestedness." The United States was the second choice of those who preferred Great Britain, including, perhaps, the Jews. A third possibility lay in "unity under a British mandate." Druzes, Jews and Greek Orthodox Christians preferred this solution, and it was the second choice "of practically all of the Moslems," who desired the United States first. Probably it was also the personal choice of the Emir Feisal. A fourth alternative was "unity under a French mandate," desired by Latin and Greek Catholics and the Maronites. Other Christians listed it as a third choice, but the Moslems were "practically unanimous against it," and many were "vehement and violent about it." As matters stood, "it could only be enforced by a fierce war, or the overawing presence of 150,000 to 200,000 troops. It would meet the strong opposition of Jews everywhere and of many British." The French had not recently hoped for it "or asked for it." The final possibility was "division of the country." While this solution pleased the Jews and some Christians in Syria, it was

> very strongly opposed by nearly all the Moslems. It is clearly against the will of the population of Syria in large majority. It might not lead to immediate war, but it would involve continual bitterness and friction, and would necessitate an occupying force of perhaps 100,000 men for a considerable time. This solution was contemplated at Paris when we left. The most serious objection is that it cuts one nation into three parts, along geographical lines which tend to become lines of religious separation.

Professor Lybyer summed up his impressions, based upon the mounting evidence, as follows:

> The first proposed solution appears to be unwise at present, though the nations are pledged to give Syria a Government according to the will of the people, looking toward independence when they shall be fitted for it. If they are now fitted for it, it would be logical that they should have it now. The second plan does not seem likely of acceptance at present, but since the people of Syria seem to incline toward it, next after complete independence, and since the British might come to prefer it, and the French may come to consider it the best way out of the difficulty, the American people might be asked to take it up, and might accept the responsibility—it may possibly become the one reasonable solution. The third plan would destroy the understanding between England and France, and upset the balance of the world. It would be in many ways good for the country. The fourth plan involves too much force, is too obviously against all the declarations about taking the wishes of the people into consideration, and would meet effective opposition in Paris on the part of the Jews and English. Nor is it good for the country morally. The fifth plan also involves too much force and too little regard for the wishes of the people. If it be put through, it will be one of the bad compromises which will receive the disapproval of future generations.

Dr. King was in general agreement with Professor Lybyer and made a notation indicating his belief in Arab political ability "as shown in constructing the Damascus program." Moreover, he pointed out that the extreme Zionist program could be "established and maintained only by force," which was also true of an extensive French mandate in Syria.

The General Syrian Congress, July 2-3, 1919

From the very moment the King-Crane Commission had reached Jaffa early in June, much had been heard about the forthcoming Syrian Congress which was to meet during July 2-3, 1919. The idea of holding such a Congress, in part, went back to the Emir Feisal, who, on his return from Paris late in April 1919, had found considerable anxiety concerning the future of Syria.[1] Subjected to much soliciting on the part of various political organizations, he had been very cautious, publicly laying stress on the coming of the Inter-Allied Commission to investigate conditions in Syria. Feisal had, however, been much disappointed when he understood that only an American Commission was coming to Syria, and had sent a telegram to David Lloyd George on June 25 "complaining of a breach of faith that the Commission was not an Allied Commission."[2] The Emir's caution led to some suspicions on the part of the more extreme Syrian patriots. Leaders of the new Arab Independence Party (*Hizb al-Istiqlal al-'Arabi*), which, evidently, was only the Young Arab Society (*al-Fatat*) under another name, took the initiative in proposing a national assembly in Damascus. Feisal supported them and tried to canalize their activities along orderly lines. Believing that the Inter-Allied Commission was soon to arrive in Syria, hasty elections to the Congress, in which the ordinary procedures were not always observed, were held all over the country, although some of the delegates from the French-occupied portions of Syria were not permitted to go to Damascus. The result was that, while eighty-five delegates were chosen from Syria and Palestine, including more than a proportionate number of Christians, only sixty-nine finally arrived in Damascus.[3]

The Syrian Congress and the King-Crane Commission

A delegation of fifteen was selected by the Syrian Congress to present its resolutions to the American Commission at about two o'clock in the afternoon of July 3.[4] The resolutions demanded recognition of the

---

[1] See, for example, Stephen Hemsley LONGRIGG, *Syria and Lebanon Under French Mandate* (London, Oxford, 1958), 83-93; A. K. HOURANI, *Syria and Lebanon: A Political Essay* (London, Oxford, 1946), 41-52; Elie KEDOURIE, *England and the Middle East: The Vital Years, 1914-1921* (London, Bowes and Bowes, 1956), Ch. 6.

[2] See *Miller Diary*, XVI, 461; *PPC*, VI, 676-677, XII, 765; *British Documents, 1919-1939*, First Series, IV, 298-299. On June 26, Feisal was advised that Great Britain, "in no circumstances" would take the Syrian mandate. British authorities indicated (June 26) that fear of a French mandate and knowledge of French propaganda had led Feisal to adopt the program of "complete Arab independence." There appeared to be little anti-British sentiment in Syria at the time, and the British denied that anti-French agitation derived from British officers.

[3] George Antonius, 292-293, considered the Congress representative and its deliberations as reflecting the sentiments of the vast majority of the population. This was also the view of the King-Crane Commission (*PPC*, XII, 779-781).

[4] Lybyer Papers: Statement of Syrian Conference, Damascus, July 3, 1919; *PPC*, XII, 780-781. The Commission had already conferred with Dr. Shahbandar and Michel Lotfallah, of the Syrian Independence Party, who wanted independence for all Syria and Cilicia. See Lybyer Papers for Lotfallah's communication to Premier Clemenceau (undated),

"complete political independence" of Syria, including Palestine, with the Emir Feisal as king, under a "democratic, civil, constitutional monarchy," based on the federal principle. The independence of Iraq was also to be recognized. Both the Sykes-Picot Agreement and the Balfour Declaration were denounced. The idea of a Jewish Commonwealth in Palestine was repudiated, although Jewish citizens would enjoy "common rights and assume the common responsibilities." Article XXII of the Covenant of the League of Nations, with its provision for a mandate system, was rejected, but American or British assistance which did not infringe on national independence or the unity of the country was acceptable. Finally, the Congress denounced "any right claimed by the French Government in any part whatever" of Syria and rejected French assistance "under any circumstances and in any place." With the exception of the provision concerning foreign assistance, the resolutions were adopted unanimously.

While the members of the King-Crane Commission could make no promises concerning the resolutions, they were much impressed and considered the program "the most substantial document presented to the Commission." Not only did it deserve "great respect"; it afforded a basis on which the Syrians could get together and constituted as "firm a foundation for a Syrian national organization" as could be obtained. The mandatory power over Syria, in the Commission's view, would now have a commitment "to liberal government" which would "be very valuable in starting the new state in the right direction." [1]

Passed with "an impressive display of patriotic fervour," there appeared little question that the resolutions did, in fact, represent the general sentiments of the country as a whole. There were mass demonstrations in towns and cities in those parts of Syria not occupied by the French forces, and large delegations came to Damascus to cheer both the Congress and the Emir Feisal. [2]

Shortly after the appearance of the delegation from the Syrian Congress, the Emir Feisal came to address the Commission for about one and a half hours. He told of his conversations with M. Clemenceau, seemed to respond to questions frankly and truthfully, supported the Damascus program, and explained his preference for Great Britain. He

embodying principles of unity, independence, democratic federalism, guarantee of minority rights. About fifty representatives of the trades of Damascus also appeared. In the Brodie Papers see the Petition of the Al-Ahi Party, signed and sealed by one Reshid, (undated), giving a history of the nationalist movement, and calling for a similar program of unity and independence.

[1] *PPC*, XII, 781.
[2] Antonius, 294.

declared that if worst came to worst, he would rather be "imprisoned with the rest of the Arabs" than have freedom merely for himself.[1]

Feisal's statement was very similar to the one which he had made in Paris on February 26 at the Peace Conference. He was gratified to speak with the Commission on behalf of the Syrians, "being authorized to represent them by official documents containing over three hundred thousand signatures." He had assumed responsibility for the Arab uprising, which he had successfully led against the Turks. He felt that Syrian sentiments, which varied "according to the degree of feeling, level of education, and attachment to the nationality and solidarity," could be summed up in their "fear of colonization and division of their country" and their desire "for liberty and independence." The boundaries prescribed for Syria were identical with those outlined by the Syrian Congress. Feisal pointed out that the country was inhabited by a homogeneous people, Semitic in origin, and "Arabic in culture, language, traditions, and customs, united by common bonds of geographical and historical nature." The people were related to those of Iraq and the Hejaz and the rest of the peninsula. There could be no existence in the future "without the national unity" which was "the center of their aspirations." The Syrians did not want "to have their country partitioned or divided into zones of influence among the Powers to the advantage of colonization and the promotion of unpatriotic interests; or to have barriers raised between them and their brothers, the inhabitants of the other areas." They wanted the Commission to mediate with the Peace Conference and the League of Nations to obtain recognition of Syrian independence, without such restrictions or conditions as would "reduce them to dependence or enslavement."

These demands for independence were not recent, but dated from the Nineteenth Century.[2] The Syrians were opposed to Article XXII of the Covenant of the League of Nations because of its "restrictions on their freedom." But they did not reject American or British assistance which did not "impair their independence." The Syrians asked for the formation of an Arab Government in Iraq, with no customs duties or "strict boundary considerations" between Iraq and Syria. They also wanted the same educational system "in order to prepare the Arab people for unity as soon as possible."

The majority of Syrians were "sorely grieved" at French actions in western Syria and were opposed to separating this region from the rest

---

[1] For the Statement of the Emir Feisal, July 3, 1919, see Lybyer Papers. According to the Lybyer *Diary*, July 3, 1919, the Feisal statement appears to have been composed about July 1, 1919. See also *British Documents*, 1919-1939, First Series, IV, 311-313.

[2] But see Zeine N. ZEINE, *Arab-Turkish Relations and the Emergence of Arab Nationalism*, cited.

of the country, which would deprive the other districts of ports connecting them "with the civilized world." At home and abroad, Syrians were "agreed and determined on Syrian unity." The "great tumult" from the French zone, with the purpose of "severing Lebanon from Syria politically and economically," was "inconsistent with the common welfare." The Lebanese desired freedom and unity no less than other Syrian Arabs, regardless of religious faith. The Lebanese separatist movement was an unnatural development inspired by the French and supported by a section of the clergy, but rejected "by the broadminded and intellectuals." All Syrians respected the privileges of the Lebanon, dating from 1864, and wished to retain the *status quo ante*, provided it did "not impair the general unity." The privileges would be guaranteed by the mandatory under the League of Nations. Indeed, the Syrians wanted "to establish a democratic government on the decentralization principle, safeguarding the rights of minorities and maintaining local traditions." They had always shown themselves to be moderate in their attitudes and actions.

There were many reasons why the Syrians did not want the French as the mandatory power, and the Emir Feisal, in his capacity as "political representative and defender of the rights of Syria," felt compelled to explain those reasons, which were not a result of "whims and prejudices or instigations," but arose from economic, social and political factors. In the first place, the Syrians had come to believe that French "commercial exclusiveness" would injure the economic life of their country. Industrial stagnation in the French colonies was taken as proof of what might happen to Syria economically. But there was also the feeling that France, unlike other colonial powers, applied its own system to countries brought under its supervision, and disregarded national feeling, a prospect which "would mean certain death to Syrians as a distinctive people." In other words, the Syrians thought "the French Government oppressive to the country under her rule." France had interfered in Syria to such an extent as deliberately to promote internal discord, "thus leading the clergy to meddle in administrative affairs," especially in Lebanon. Those who were opposed to the French political views were persecuted officially, while those who adhered were favored.

Long since aware of French ambitions in the country, Syrians were all the more shocked by the Sykes-Picot agreement of 1916. Although the Arabs knew that the agreement between Great Britain and France was based on presumed fundamental interests, they were fearful of the possible division of Syria and Iraq into future zones of influence. As a result of Anglo-French political and economic rivalry, "the position of the Arabs between these two great nations exceeding four hundred millions, would be untenable and exposed to great perils." Were both France and Great Britain to undertake the education of the Arabs, their sentiment of unity would be weakened.

Feisal closed his address with the blessing of the Almighty on the work of the Americans. The next day he requested the President of the Peace Conference at Paris "to postpone the deliberations on the question of Syria" until his arrival at Paris, for he was in possession "of all the important information regarding it." No doubt he was anxious to present the situation as he saw it following the meeting of the General Syrian Congress. [1]

End of the Investigation in Damascus

The King-Crane Commission had now spent its last full day in old Damascus and left the Arab occupied region early in the morning of July 4. It is well, therefore, to note the general impression which the Commission obtained as to the wishes of the people. There was a general feeling that the sentiments in O. E. T. A. East "were much nearer to unanimity than in the South or the West." Most of the oral and written statements were in general conformity with the resolutions of the Syrian Congress. That program had been achieved "in the presence of a general feeling that it was overwhelmingly important for reasons of national safety to reach unity of expression." While there was pressure on the part of the government and the various political parties, on the whole there seemed to be no doubt "that the main elements of this program" represented "the popular will" as nearly as it could be expressed "in any country." Almost unanimously the people favored a United Syria and complete independence. They were opposed, fundamentally, to the French and against the Zionist program. The Moslem element was practically unanimous in favor of American assistance. The Druze were in favor of an Arab government under a British mandate, while the Jew

---

[1] S-H Bulletin No. 476. I. July 4, 1919. Secretary-General of Hejaz Delegation transmits request of Feisal to Peace Conference. On July 1 a "Very Secret" letter anonymously written by a gentleman who had appeared before the Commission on June 30 was received. The letter, in the Lybyer Papers, pointed to the lack of unity in Syria and the fears of the Christians as to the consequences of Moslem rule. The writer doubted the practical success of Feisal's liberal principles. A strong mandatory, having the following functions, was urged: 1) Preservation of public security and order, with full command of the army and police; 2) minute inspection of all government departments; 3) sanction of all laws promulgated in the name of the Emir; 4) reports and instructions of foreign inspectors appointed by the mandatory to be executed immediately by the local authorities; 5) deficit in the budget to be supplied by the mandatory; 6) encouragement of the development of the agricultural and other resources of the country; 7) the execution of laws and regulations to be guaranteed by the League of Nations; 8) when the League of Nations decides the Syrians are able to stand alone, "the Mandatory Power would withdraw from the country." Great Britain and America were preferred as the Mandatory, with France a third choice. The complete unity of the country, including Damascus, Palestine, Beirut, Lebanon, Aleppo and Adana, was urged.

wanted autonomy for themselves, and "the Zionist scheme for their brethren in Palestine." The Christians, however, were divided, partly geographically and partly by sect. The few Christians in the south, including even the Latin Catholics, were in favor of a British mandate, with the United States as a second choice. This was also true of the Damascus Greek Orthodox community, and a part of the Greek Orthodox group farther north. The various Protestant groups desired either Great Britain or the United States as a mandatory, while the Orthodox Syrian community favored the United States. On the other hand, "all the Catholics (except at Amman and Dera) and the Maronites were for France." Nearly all the Christians desired a strong mandatory control. [1]

The Americans were aware that there was considerable governmental pressure in support of the Damascus Program both on the more articulate groups, and in the back country where more primitive methods were sometimes employed. Feisal had concluded agreements with the Greek Orthodox Christians and Druzes to support his program in return for local autonomy and proper treatment. There was some evidence that the Emir Feisal had tried, before the arrival of the Commission in Damascus, to secure the support of certain groups for a British mandate and had failed. While Feisal had declared equally for an American or British mandate, it was thought that because of the "benefits" he was receiving from Great Britain and the prospects of a "speedy larger Arab union" if Syria and Mesopotamia and other regions were under one mandatory control, he really preferred a British mandate.

The Commission found that the higher Arab officials included "a number of men of dignity, ability, intelligence, and apparent honesty and patriotism." Most of the lower officials in the region, like those in the other occupied areas, had been continued from the Ottoman regime, with all the virtues and faults of the former Empire. The Arabs made every effort to honor the Commission and "execute its wishes." But

[1] *PPC*, XII, 850. Note the general similarity of views with those expressed in the Lybyer statement of July 2, 1919. See also Woodrow Wilson Papers VI-A Folder 40, Box 5; American Consul Gotlieb, Damascus, to Secretary of State, July 5, 1919. "American Commission on Mandates left Damascus for Baalbek and Beirut yesterday morning. Commission makes no report but it would appear to me, after my journey through the interior from Constantinople, majority of the population would prefer complete independence with the exception of Christian element failing which they desire that the United States accept the mandate, if not, then Great Britain. France apparently not wanted except by those educated in French schools. Both countries carry on strong propaganda in which British are in ascendency with military occupation and Emir Feisal favoring. It would seem both Turkish Anatolia and Syrian desires are as above indicated. France seems unalterably set on the Lebanon, more if possible, Britain seemingly working for a large Arabic state controlled by her. Copy sent to Paris. Signed Young." Gotlieb.

"sometimes ostentatious attempts were made to give the impression of absolute non-interference with freedom of access to an expression before the Commission." [1]

THE FRENCH OCCUPIED REGION (O. E. T. A. WEST)

The American Commissioners and their staff left Damascus early Friday morning, July 4, for Baalbek. [2] The mechanized caravan rode out along Abana-Barada road and up the pass, through green gardens and orchards, up and over the first ridge, with splendid red coloring of the hills, along the north side of Mount Hermon, then went down and up again over the Anti-Lebanon, and finally moved into Hollow Syria—the Bekaa—a "wonderful long trough", the mountains opposite still showing streaks of snow. The last few miles to Baalbek, however, were through a rather barren region. They arrived at Baalbek about noon, had lunch in "an old quarry", and spent the day interviewing various groups. Here was "encountered first the struggle for and against annexing 'Hollow Syria' " to the Greater Lebanon.

Some Lebanese Testimony

The next day the Commission heard delegations, from about nine o'clock until noon. Those questioned favored the government position, with the Latin Catholics and the Maronites especially desiring a French mandate. The French authorities, apparently, had been offering low taxes and military exemption as an inducement. After lunch, the Commission proceeded over the mountains toward Beirut, stopping on the way at Shtora to see the pro-British Selim Bey Tabbit, who thought, in any case, that Great Britain and France would prevent an American mandate. Dr. King admitted that he believed in Syrian unity and saw it possible only with an American mandate. After tea, the Americans

---

[1] *PPC*, XII, 778. Some officials, like General Haddad Pasha, chief of police and gendarmerie, and Daud Pasha Zoucair, financial adviser, were trained under the British administration in Egypt; others, like Col. Yussef Bey, aide-de-camp of Feisal, General Jaafar Pasha, Military Governor of Aleppo, were educated in the Ottoman service.

[2] Lybyer and King *Diaries*, July 4, 1919. After the Commission left Damascus Feisal cabled President Wilson expressing the fear that he had "incurred as a matter of course the risk of a terrible strong current against us" and asked that he not be left "between the paws of the devourers." The French were stirring up people against Feisal. Gotlieb cabled Washington on July 25: "Rumors and local newspapers would indicate influencing result of such [French] propaganda before the American Commission . . . at both Beirut [and] Tripoli . . . French militarism apparently set on Lebanon which is seemingly biggest bone of contention and Emir claims French create religious antagonism there that may result in serious consequences. His Royal Highness requests the President's intervention as in the case of Fiume if necessary." See Feisal to Wilson, July 9, 1919; Gotlieb to Secretary of State, July 22, 1919; Woodrow Wilson Papers VI-A Folder 40, Box 5.

left, beginning the ascent of the Lebanon mountains, and arrived at last at Aley, just above Beirut, about 6:30 in the evening, where they stayed at the Hotel d'Orient.[1]

The days spent in the vicinity of Beirut, July 6-12, were full of interviews and all sorts of activity, beginning with the initial meeting shortly after nine o'clock, on Monday, July 7, on the third floor of the Hotel Royal, which had a fine view westward over the town and out toward the sea, with the Commission sitting on the balcony.[2] The Moslem Ulema, Mufti and Kadi favored the Damascus program. There was a long "intelligent discussion" with a Christian group which favored a French mandate and the political and administrative independence of the Greater Lebanon. Later in the afternoon a delegation of Greek Catholics and a group of Maronites appeared, although one member of the latter committee did most of the talking "both morning and afternoon" in behalf of a French mandate. Already there were evidences of French pressure, indications of a strong Maronite attitude favorable to France, and a serious difference of opinion within the Greek Orthodox Community. Delegations began to arrive early the next morning—Protestants, Jews, Syrian Catholics, Jesuits, Druzes, Latins and other delegates from the Greater Lebanon.

After lunch, at which M. Picot, the French High Commissioner, entertained Dr. King, Mr. Crane and Captain Yale, the afternoon was featured by the appearance of Moslem women before the Commission. The Commission visited the Moslem Trade School, an institution established in 1916 by some wealthy Moslem women, which was on the highest point in Beirut. While there the Commission received a rug, to be given to the Peace Conference, "patterned so as to show the area claimed by Syrian Nationalists for United Syria." On the way back the Commission stopped at a women's club and heard a delegation of Moslem women, headed by Ibtihaje Kaddourah.[3] They made an excellent impression, and expressed their desire not merely for independence, but the right and

[1] King and Lybyer *Diaries*, July 6, 1919.

[2] Lybyer *Diary*, July 6, 1919. Dr. Nickolay, of the American University of Beirut, told Lybyer that "No American in Beirut is for French mandate, or Arabic independence without mandate." The municipal council demanded Syrian integrity with independence under Feisal and an American mandate, with Great Britain as second choice. The Committee of Christian nationalities represented some 18,000 citizens. See Chicago Daily *News*, August 1, 1919, quoting the Beirut correspondent of *Le Temps*.

[3] See Lybyer and King *Diaries*, July 8, 1919. Lybyer Papers: Address of Moslem Women of Beirut to Commission, signed by Ibtihaje Kaddourah, July 8, 1919; The Desiderata of the Societies of Moslem Women in Beirut Submitted to the Honorable American Section of the Commission on Mandates for Turkey; Credentials of Delegates making this statement.

opportunity of development, which would assure a place for Syria "among the responsible nations of the world." A critical moment had come which might send them "either backward or forward". Hence they had for the first time disregarded oriental customs barring women from taking part in public affairs, "in the hope of achieving that liberty and independence" on which they had set their hearts. In general the women supported the Damascus Program of unity and independence, and desired American assistance to help them along that road.

Some Christian Views

The Apostolic Delegate of Syria, Msg. J. F. Gioranimous Archer, also testified on July 8.[1] He pointed out that the questions which were "agitating the whole country" were not, in general, "the fruit of conscious and well-grounded political aspirations, in a true sense of the word." The development of a "national conscience" had been prevented as "much by religious divisions as by the Turkish regime." The only sentiment which was unanimously shared by the people was that "of indomitable hatred against the odious Turkish domination, from which both Moslems and Christians desired to be liberated by anybody," whether by the Central Powers or the Allies. The Apostolic Delegate also insisted that if the Allied Powers, especially France and Great Britain, had come to Syria with a well-defined program, both Christians and Moslems "would have accepted quite willingly the political arrangement which they thought proper to offer them."

Unfortunately, however, certain "local agents" had presented the spectacle of Anglo-French jealousy and rivalry, and then trouble had begun. More deplorable was the appearance of Sherifism, which led to "the rejuvenation of Moslem fanaticism." Nevertheless, Msg. Archer believed that the country would be pacified as soon as "an authoritative decision" intervened in the uncertainty and confusion in Syria. The only reasonable decision to be adopted, in view of the inability of the country to bring about order itself, while excluding the theocratic dreams of Sherifism, whose place was "in the Hejaz and not at all in Syria," would be to assure to all, Moslem and Christian alike, as well as others, the benefits of a regime worthy of a generally civilized people. Msg. Archer charged that the Moslems had hidden behind "the screen of Jewish Zionism, in order to exclude the other Powers from the Holy Places of Palestine," and urged the establishment of a French protectorate over the country, with full protection of the rights of the Lebanon. In closing,

[1] King Papers: J. F. Gioranimous ARCHER, Délégué Apostolique de Syrie, *A la Commission Américaine d'enquête pour la Syrie, Beyrouth, July 5, 1919. Ci-joint un Mémoire sur les questions syriennes, serait en Novembre 1918.* Paul Knabenshue, the American Consul, later American Minister in Baghdad (1941), gave a reception to the American Commission in the evening of July 8.

he asked and prayed that "God would clarify the minds of the Delegates of the victorious nations, assembled in the Congress of Paris," and hoped that they would recognize the "justice of his modest observations."

While these sentiments were echoed by representatives of the Chaldean Christian Community and the National Association of Syrian Youth, they were fundamentally at variance with Moslem ideas and differed basically from the views of the Native Protestant Church at Beirut, [1] which asked for the unity of Syria, including Palestine, on the basis of federalism. Each state of Syria would be "absolutely autonomous in the management of its internal affairs." Mt. Lebanon would retain its ancient privileges within this federal structure. [2] The Syrian state, under either an American or British mandate, would "have no political connection whatever with the Kingdom of the Hejaz."

In the morning of July 9, the Commission visited the St. Joseph University at Beirut, a Jesuit institution established in 1875, and Professor Lybyer was shown some rare manuscripts and books. The Anti-French Orthodox Archbishop told him that his congregation was divided concerning the future of Syria, and that he had very nearly sided with one portion, but could not publicly express his ideas, because of fierce attacks in the French-controlled press. King and Lybyer ran into a "small demonstration" the next day at Sidon, but at Tyre the French governor "had everything thoroughly arranged." Nevertheless, the Shiite Ulema "spoke out strongly for the Damascus Program," which was supported by other delegations. When they motored back to Sidon, they met Yale and Montgomery, who were with the French governor. The latter had not been able to hold the people in line—they were mostly favorable to the Damascus Program of independence and union. Some Christian ladies, however, spoke for France, and a few Jews expressed their fears as to the future. A rapid ride brought the party back to Beirut, and still later

[1] In the Lybyer Papers see *Statement of the Chaldean Catholic Community of Beirut, July 8, 1919*; *Statement of Association Nationale de la Jeunesse Syrienne, July 8, 1919*; *Statement of Ali Ashi Saadi, Sheikh of the Alieh Sadieh Sect*; *Statement of Abdul Rahman Kraitun and six others*. The Statement of The Native Protestant Church of Beirut, June 1919. In the Brodie Papers there is a paper from "*The Society of Laborers [of the Greater Lebanon]*," in Arabic, calling for a French mandate. Another, from "the representatives of the Catholics, Greek Orthodox, Armenians, Protestants and Moslems . . . assembled at the Literary Society," called for unity of Syria under a mandatory. A third listed the crimes of the French and called for "blood and revolution rather than France." But a fourth insisted that "We have no life except with France . . . . No life, no rest, no security, no peace except under the shadow of France. Long Live France."

[2] Ovhannes Pasha Gouyoumdjian, former Under-Secretary in the Ottoman Foreign Office and Governor-General of the Lebanon at the outbreak of the war in 1914, who appeared before the Commission in Constantinople on August 11, preferred an autonomous Lebanon.

King, Yale, Montgomery, Moore and Haddad went north to hear delegations separately. [1]

The staff were all busy at work the next morning, too. Montgomery and Yale went to Zahleh and Muallaka, while King and Lybyer journeyed to Ainab to meet the Druzes, who dominated the program, and generally favored a British mandate, except for a small delegation of pro-French Druzes, which left before their time to speak. [2] As the Americans arrived at the hall high on the hill, there were shouts for "America and Wilson". There were magnificent groups of the Druze Ulema and sheikhs, all of whom favored the Damascus program, except that they preferred a British to an American mandate. The Druzes, incidentally, asked to be cut out of the Lebanon, if the mandate were to be assigned to the French. Down at Baabda, Lybyer and King found a French governor who was very pleasant, but the delegations all appeared to be handicapped, and Lybyer "nearly threw out" one presumed spy.

A Report to President Wilson and The Peace Conference

Meanwhile, it was time for another report to President Wilson. Dr. King, Mr. Crane and Professor Lybyer had prepared a cable on Sunday, July 6, which was now ready for transmission, but when it was shown to Dr. Montgomery and Captain Yale, the latter were "displeased with portions" of it. Yale, therefore, wrote a letter to Professor Westermann, a copy of which he showed to Dr. King, and which together with communications from Mr. Crane to President Wilson, and from Captain Brodie to Mr. Grew, was given to William T. Bliss, on July 10, who was leaving for Paris. [3]

---

[1] Lybyer *Diary*, July 10; King *Diary*, July 10, 1919. There were twenty delegations at Sidon. King noted on July 11 that at Baabda "there was spying and general evidence of pressure and silencing on all sides."

[2] Lybyer Papers: Various Druze statements from this district. See also Lybyer *Diary*, July 11, 1919.

[3] See Lybyer *Diary*, July 6, 1919. Lybyer Papers: William Yale to W. L. Westermann, describing conditions in Syria and Palestine, Beirut, July 8, 1919; Receipt from William T. Bliss to Donald M. Brodie, for letters (Brodie Papers), July 10, 1919; Crane to Wilson, Brodie to Grew, Yale to Westermann. In the communication from Brodie to Grew, Beirut, July 10, 1919, were included: 1) Copy of partial report of Commission cabled in code, July 10th; 2) Statement of Emir Feisal to American Commission; 3) Statement of Syrian National Congress, Damascus, July 3, 1919; 4) Résumé of Syrian Situation by Dr. A. H. Lybyer. The copies in The Woodrow Wilson Papers II-B are marked in President Wilson's handwriting: "Syrian Congress."

Captain Yale's Views of the Problem

Captain Yale wrote that after nearly a month in Palestine and Syria he had reached certain conclusions which took into consideration "not only the forces at work here but also those at Paris; namely the force of the Zionist Movement and the promises made to the Jews, and also the tenacity of the French in Syria." His conclusions were similar to the decisions reached at Paris, which he believed fundamentally sound. Yale thought that "Palestine should be under the British who should be allowed to work out the Zionist Question according to their lights and along reasonable lines." With guarantees for the Palestinian Holy Places, the Zionists "should be given their opportunity to work out a Jewish Commonwealth." A commission ought to be appointed to study the matter of the eastern and northern boundaries for Palestine, as well as the advisability of separating Syria from the Hejaz. But "because of the Christian minorities east of the Jordan," there were reasons for including "Ajlun and Trans-Jordania in Palestine."

The Greater Mt. Lebanon should be separated politically from Moslem Syria, and Hollow Syria and the valley of the Orontes south of the Lake of Homs "should be included in the Greater Mount Lebanon." The exact boundaries would have to be determined by an expert commission. While the northern boundaries, too, required further study, Tripoli should be left in Syria because of its Moslem character and its possibilities as a port with connections with the East. Mt. Lebanon should be under French protection, with guarantees for the Druzes, Moslems and non-Catholic Christians "as well as the American College." Feisal should be brought "to some arrangement with the French so that Syria could be brought into close contact with Mt. Lebanon." Protection of minorities would be impossible under a regime of complete independence. Yale did not believe Syria ready for union. The Lebanese did not want it and were determined not to have it. Syria wanted it because the Moslem element desired "to dominate Christian Mt. Lebanon."

Nevertheless, Yale confessed that, "except in Lebanon," there was a strong expression for the unity of Syria. In Palestine, it seemed that both Christians and Moslems, because of their fear of Zionism, demanded "a union that they never thought of before." In addition the Moslems wished "to dominate in Palestine and be free of European control." In Syria, they desired union because they wanted an "independent Moslem country and because Palestine" was "still to them the battle ground taken from the Christians by Saladin." There was a small educated Moslem element who had "a sincere desire to develop a national Syrian state, but a Moslem one." The Christians, too, wanted union because they had to agree and concede to the Moslems, although they wanted and expected "a strong mandatory Power." In Mt. Lebanon, where the situation was somewhat different from that in the other districts, the Druzes and the Greek Orthodox desired union because they were afraid of Maronite domination and also feared France. But so also did the Protestants and some other Christians, who sincerely believed in Syrian nationalism and did "not rightly gauge the forces working in the interior." Finally, the Moslems of Mt. Lebanon, like those of Syria proper, desired union.

According to Yale the Syrian national sentiment had been more or less artificially created by propaganda and by the fears outlined above. Added to these were the ideas of Syrians in the United States and Egypt, who had lived for such a long time away from "Moslem oppression" that they were no longer afraid of it or even understood the danger to the Christian minorities in the Arab national movement.

The expression of National feeling which is in so much evidence at the present time has been organized by Emir Feisal and his entourage, mostly Moslem; money, influence, power, religion and thorough organization, and perhaps the British, have accomplished astounding results. The organization and the entire Movement has much in it that resembles the Young Turkish Movement and many Christians have been taken in for the reasons enumerated above. Among the great mass of the population there is nothing really sound in this national feeling and it is a sentiment upon which it would be entirely unsound to try to build a state. Syria as a whole is not ready for union.
By this I do not mean that eventual union should not be an aim; it should be, but until Moslem fanaticism and Christian fanaticism are abated by education it would be dangerous and unstatesmanlike to try to bind together unreconcilable elements. Mount Lebanon is profoundly Christian and Syria profoundly Moslem; until these two civilizations can be brought closer together it would be folly to try to bind them together by artificial bonds. Such an experiment would possibly prove disastrous for the minority.

If not politically unified, however, Syria, Palestine and Mt. Lebanon, Yale thought, should be bound together "by a close economic union," with similar commercial regulations and monetary systems.

Yale did not consider the Emir Feisal a very strong personality. He was not "all powerful even in Syria," but was controlled by various forces "in the Syrian Moslem world." Outside Syria, Feisal had "no authority in Arabia, the Yemen or the Idrissi, while Ibn Saud and Ibn Raschid stood apart." In Mesopotamia there was a large Shiite element which might not support the Emir, while the Indian Moslems would have to be weaned away from the Ottoman Sultan, the Caliph of Islam. In Syria proper, Feisal had a following of some two million people, a smaller following in Mesopotamia, and a waning group of adherents in the Hejaz. Perhaps Feisal could be won over if France made liberal overtures to him, but "if he wished to go counter to such a decision," the dangers were not to be over-estimated. Yale continued:

As to the sentiment of the country—the Moslems are overwhelmingly in favor of complete independence as is quite natural; and if they needs must have aid they want it from America or Great Britain; France they refuse absolutely. The Christians all want a strong Mandatory Power and, outside of the Lebanon, and the Catholics in Palestine and Syria, they want America or Britain. The Catholics, Maronites and Greek Catholics of the Lebanon have as a body declared for France, but I firmly believe they want America, at least the great majority, but they distinctly do not want England.

An American mandate for Syria was left entirely out of the question. Yale felt that the United States had "made very definite promises to the Jews," the implementation of which would cause "untold difficulties with the Moslems and political complications at home." France was determined to remain at least in Mt. Lebanon, and it would be impossible to give this up peacefully. "The development of a Syrian National State" by the United States would meet with constant resistance "from the British Empire, which would act through Mecca, Bagdad, India, Cairo and probably Constantinople." Again, Yale referred to the alleged "impossibility of reconciling the Jewish, the Christian, and the Moslem civilizations we would have to try to unite." Finally, there were greater American obligations in Constantinople, Anatolia and Armenia.

In conclusion, Yale reiterated that the Moslems "could with care be reconciled" to French control, even though "there would undoubtedly be some trouble" in the beginning, especially if more French troops were not to be brought to Syria immediately. The "feeling against France" was of long standing and went back to the French policy of protecting Christians in the Syrian region. Hatred of France had been encouraged not only by the Germans and the Turks, but Feisal and the British had conducted "a thoroughly well organized anti-French propaganda" during the past five months. The British denied these charges, but Yale warned Westermann to be on

> the lookout for a move on the British part to force us to take Syria. That is their game here and they have locally played it most successfully. As an indication, Feisal has been tipped off by the British to ask Howard Bliss to be in Paris in August. Feisal intends to go there and so does Picot....

The French had been maladroit in their repressive measures "to prevent an expression of pro-American feeling in Lebanon," and they viewed American efforts along all lines with suspicion. Yale did not share British apprehensions concerning the Zionist program, for "properly and discreetly handled" it could be "carried on." A strong army of occupation would be required, however. With such a force, trouble could be localized. Great Britain knew how to handle the problem, but "certainly no one else could." In closing, the letter admonished that "the dangers of the Arabs running amuck if Zionism be carried out, and if France be given control of Syria," were being "greatly exaggerated by the British."

Communications to the President

William Bliss carried a brief letter of July 10 from Mr. Crane to President Wilson, providing a somewhat different analysis. Mr. Crane advised the President that the mission of investigation had been "very worthwhile" and that there was raw material in the Near East "for a much more promising state" than the United States had in the Philippines. The common people were "sober, industrious and intelligent," and there was a great deal of national feeling which had been revealed whenever the region had "come under great strain or menace." There were, indeed, three special elements of nationality "extending over a wide area," including "the rich and beautiful Arabic language," "both Christian and Moslem faiths," and "the ancient and interesting culture." The people had been touching in their confidence in the Commission. It would have been difficult for an Inter-Allied Commission "to have been given so much self-revelation, even in a very long time." [1] Crane hoped that if Howard Bliss were still in the United States, President Wilson would ask him to look over the papers to see if their conclusions and observations, based on so "brief an experience," tallied with his own.

On July 11, at the end of their visit in Beirut, the two Commissioners and Professor Lybyer sent a cable to President Wilson summarizing their views of the situation in Syria. [2] The Commission had now "covered strategic points from Beersheba to Baalbek and from the Mediterranean to Amman," and the various military governors had given every facility to the Americans, although there had been "some steering." It had been "heartily welcomed everywhere," and there was no doubt of the great popular interest. The three men felt that the program was developing in range and definiteness, "showing considerable political insight." There was much to indicate that the inquiry was greatly worthwhile, and there

---

[1] See also the Crane *Memoirs*, 374: "Not in any American State could things have been more orderly, clear or definite. The groups were always in hand, knew what they wanted, and knew how to express themselves. All the various races, religions, professions, social and economic classes were represented .... The trust in the American delegation was most touching."

[2] See *PPC*, XII, 749-750, in which this cable is dated July 10 (received July 12), 6:30 a. m. In the Lybyer Papers it is dated, however, as of July 11. See also Lybyer *Diary*, July 6, 1919. It appears to have been sent on July 15 and arrived in Paris on July 17. See also Woodrow Wilson Papers II-A State Department, Box 73, in which it is indicated that the delay was "due to badly garbled condition" and the cable was "laid aside because of more urgent and important messages."

had been "freer expression of opinion" to the American Section than could have been possible before an Inter-Allied Commission. Certain points were "unmistakable." There was an "intense desire for unity of all Syria and Palestine and for as early independence as possible." There were "unexpectedly strong expressions of national feeling" and "singularly determined repulsion to becoming a mere colony of any power, and against any kind of French mandate." Proclamation of a French mandate for all Syria "would precipitate warfare between Arabs and French," and force Great Britain to a "dangerous alternative."

The United States was "genuinely" the first choice of most people for a mandatory because it had "no territorial ambitions." There was also a general demand that fundamentally the solution "should be the same for Iraq as for Syria." Both British and French officers were said to share the conviction that the unity of Syria and Palestine was most desirable for the peace and security of the region. But there was little evidence that either Great Britain or France was willing "entirely to withdraw." The experience of the Commission had only confirmed its earlier cable from Jaffa on June 12 regarding the dangers of the extreme Zionist position.

A section of the cable written by Professor Lybyer summed up the demands of the Syrian National Congress at Damascus, and pointed out that the Near Eastern situation involved "elements of world-wide importance." The solution proposed in Paris of placing Syria under a French mandate would produce Anglo-French enmity, and the Arabs would resist "by every means." While the Moslem world might reluctantly accept the reduction of the Ottoman Empire, Moslem hostility would certainly follow refusal to establish an Arab state. The Emir Feisal, despite his limitations, had become a "unique outstanding figure capable of rendering greatest service for world peace." Given "proper sympathy and surroundings," there was no danger of his getting adrift or taking any big step "without Anglo-Saxon approval." Every policy concerning Syria should take this "into consideration." [1]

---

[1] By July 19, Col. French (Cairo) had received a report concerning these conclusions and sent it on to London. Among other things, he noted that (1) the Syrians would not accept a French mandate; 2) the Zionist program could only be implemented by force; 3) the Arab national movement under Anglo-Saxon aegis was worthy of encouragement; 4) the general wish of the peoples was for a United Syria. He also noted the Commission's high opinion of British officials. See *British Documents, 1919-1939*, First Series, IV, 315-316.

The Commission Leaves Beirut

General Allenby placed his private yacht, the *Maid of Honor*, at the disposal of the Commission for the brief journey from Beirut to Tripoli, Alexandretta and Latakia on July 12. Delegations were thus heard from every part of O. E. T. A. West. With French cooperation, arrangements were made both for the hearings and for the comfort and well-being of the American investigators.

Incident at Tripoli

The *Maid of Honor* landed at Tripoli about 2:45 in the afternoon, after a journey of about four hours. A military launch came out to greet the Commission with French and British officers and an American missionary. While Crane was somewhat ill and remained aboard, the other members of the group went on to the government house in Tripoli for the interviews, where they heard fifteen delegations, including the city Ulema. The French authorities had everything carefully arranged, soldiers with fixed bayonets being at the gates and in the streets. The Moslems approved the Damascus program, the Greek Orthodox Community was divided, while the carefully selected delegations of Maronites and Latins favored an independent Greater Lebanon and United Syria.[1] On their way back to the ship there was a "near riot," and altogether Dr. King could not help recording that they had witnessed "the most barefaced suppression of opinion anywhere seen...."[2]

---

[1] Lybyer Papers: See especially: 1) *Moslem Petitions* supporting the Damascus Program, (a) Moslems, Sheikhs and Arab Tribes in Husun el Akrad, (b) Kaza Akar, Notables and Landowners, (c) Kalmun District, (d) Judges of the Court of the First Instance, (e) Credentials of Ulema, Presented Damas Program, July 12, 1919, (f) Merchants of Tripoli, (g) Grocer's petition; 2) *The Greek Orthodox Community*, La Communauté Grecque Orthodoxe de Tripoli de Syrie, signed by Gabriel Nahas, urging a French mandate; 3) Jewish-Christian Society, July 12, 1919, demanding French mandate, complete independence of Lebanon, under French mandate; 4) Society of Syrian Youth, July 12, 1919, demanding a French mandate, unity of "Syria, Palestine and Cilicia."

[2] Lybyer Papers: I. *Protest from Tripoli*, handed in at Homs, July 4, 1919. Representatives of societies, landowners, merchants, etc., of Tripoli indicate they were "stopped, arrested and forbidden" to appear before the Commission when in Tripoli. II. *Petition from Mohammedans and Christians of Kaza Husun el Akrad* protests against "the non-democratic spirit" exhibited in Tripoli and upholds the Damascus program, refusing "French mandatory interference and every right that is pretended by France in our Country." III. *A Statement Presented by the Beneficial Societies of Tripoli to the Hon. American Commission*, protesting against the illegal nature of the French select-Municipal Council. IV. *To the British Base Commandant of Tripoli*, from the Kura district, protesting against interference of French troops, claiming they were arresting "all those in favor of having England or America as the protecting power for Syria.... The government is

Alexandretta and Latakia

When the Americans arrived the next morning at Alexandretta, the French Governor and his staff, together with some British officers, came on board to greet them. Yale went ashore to make arrangements, and the others followed, and were taken to a "large private house looking north" for the conferences. In Alexandretta there was a "fairly free expression of opinion," although the work of the French officials, particularly with delegations from Antioch, appeared to have been thoroughly done, with memorized formulae about "Great France, the Mother of Civilization" and others.[1] Nevertheless, a Greek Orthodox group asked for either a British or American mandate, and one Greek priest told of the French methods in the region. Three Turkish groups from Antioch described Ottoman administration before the war, Arab control immediately after the armistice, and the French officials who then dominated the country. In general, the Turks, the largest single element in the Alexandretta vicinity, wanted union with Constantinople, and a "sane mandate." Altogether the Americans heard some twenty-one delegations in the morning at Alexandretta, had lunch with the French staff, and were back on their yacht by 3 P.M., although it was midnight before the boat sailed back to Latakia.

The crowds had gathered early on Monday morning, July 14, when the American Commission arrived at Latakia, and there were crowds lining the shore. The French governor and the former Kaimakam of Latakia paid a visit to the ship, although the latter had resigned the day before in order to be free to express himself. The French had not been able to manage or control the situation very well, and there was "evidence of great political excitement." The Nuseiriyeh group was divided in sentiment. The Greek Orthodox delegation desired a French mandate, along with the few Catholics and Maronites of the region. After lunch

---

taking all unjust measures to oppress the people and to make the people vote in favor of France." See *PPC*, XII, 775, 849-850; Lybyer and King *Diaries*, July 12, 1919.

[1] Lybyer Papers: The Commission received a telegram from representatives of the "Districts of Antioch, Harim, Alexandretta, Jisr, and Eshouge, the number of whom exceeds 200,000," indicating their desire to "inform you about our political desires and to direct your attention to what we are suffering from oppression and intimidations of the French Governors of our district in the way of imprisonment, deportations and ill treatment to the extent that freedom of thought and speech is considered an unpardonable crime. And in that this treatment is going to stand in the way of our getting the benefit from the noble rules which the American justice has proclaimed through President Wilson, the great, we ask you in the name of humanity and justice to pay attention to us and grant us our usurped freedom."

the Americans left Latakia about 2 P.M., for the return trip to Tripoli, arriving there late at night after sailing a "decidedly rough sea."[1]

Homs and Aleppo

The King-Krane Commission did not linger in Tripoli. By 9 A. M., on July 15 it left by car for Homs, over a very bad road, while Crane and Brodie went on to Beirut. Some papers were given to Dr. King at Tripoli, and about twelve miles from the city, near Tel el-Hais, the Americans were stopped by a large gathering of several hundred people who were protesting the French behavior of two days before. About one hundred horsemen—an Arab guard of honor!—rode ahead of the American caravan, "in magnificent clothes, spears and swords". The group stopped at Tel Kale Husn, where there were brief speeches, and later had lunch under the fig trees at the village of Habib. A ride over the plain brought the Commission to Homs, which was reached in mid-afternoon. The next morning the Commission heard fifteen delegations, arranged by Major Goldenstedt, at the home of the commandant. The sessions, which had been well managed, ran from nine o'clock until noon. For the most part the delegations favored "the straight Damascus program" and protested against the French behavior on the coast. The Circassians, unhappy with the Arab government, expressed hope for a British mandate.

After lunch the Americans were on their way once more, driving through picturesque villages with white conical houses. After a very hot two-hour ride, just outside the city of Hama, they were met by another group of Arab horsemen, who galloped ahead, holding their guns high. Immediately the Americans called on the governor, but in order to avoid the appearance of official influence, they were taken to a private house, where they heard seventeen delegations that afternoon. Anxious, apparently, to get on with their work, the Commission did not remain overnight in Hama, but left by train—which was four hours late— about 11 P. M., arriving in Aleppo before dawn.[2]

On hand to greet the Commission were the American Consul, Mr. J. B. Jackson, the Mayor of the city and other notables. Mr. Jackson had already made arrangements for the Commission to see prominent people, and had sent an employee of the Consulate to meet the Commission in

---

[1] Lybyer and King *Diaries*, July 15, 1919. A note was sent to General Allenby on July 15 thanking him for his kindness and courtesies and congratulating him on "the devotion and high character of your aides everywhere we have been.... All of your aides, both aboard and ashore, and especially Colonel Watson and Captain James, have taken the best care of us and smoothed the journey in every possible way." Brodie Papers.

[2] See the King and Lybyer *Diaries*, July 15-16, 1919. Dr. King noted that on the way they met "two stirring delegations... with many horsemen."

Hama. During the day there were the usual calls from General Jaafar Pasha, the Military Governor, and Brigadier-General Clarke, the temporary commander of the Fifth Cavalry Division. After a rest, the Americans visited the bazaars, despite a very hot sun, and in the afternoon Professor Lybyer and Dr. Montgomery visited a British-supported Armenian camp, with some 5,000 to 6,000, mostly women and children, "an unprepossessing lot". There was also a boys' camp, the boys marching in groups with flags on the drill-ground. In the evening, Mr. Jackson, who was not pleased with the British and hoped for an American mandate, entertained the group at dinner in the Consulate. [1]

The Commission, which stayed at Baron's Hotel, began to receive delegations on Friday, July 18, when members of the Ulema, Greek and Armenian Catholics appeared. In the afternoon delegations of Jews, Syrians, Chaldeans and some Moslem women were received. But the delegations came in so slowly that about one-third of the time was wasted in waiting. There was an appearance of "great freedom, but every evidence of both Arab and French influence." Those who supported France favored "a Greater Syria under France", and the Commission heard groups of Catholics more than half the time that day. The Moslem ladies lifted their veils, but did not prove to be "very beautiful". The spokeswoman for the group, however, was quite "emphatic and energetic". In general, the pro-French groups claimed that the "great majority would be for France except for governmental pressure."

Early next morning members of the Municipal Council were received, along with various notables, agriculturalists, and tribal chiefs. The Mayor, Ihsan Jabri, who had been trained in the Turkish law, and served under the Sultan for twenty years, seemed "very intelligent", arguing that the "presence of France would make continual trouble." In the afternoon Jaafar Pasha brought in a group of Iraqis who demanded independence for Mesopotamia, including Diarbekir, Deir-es-Zor, Mosul, Baghdad and Muhammerah. Jaafar Pasha's group urged that the government should be a constitutional civil monarchy, and the king a son of King Hussein of the Hejaz, either Abdullah or Zeid. The group protested against Article XXII of the Covenant of the League of Nations, and wanted no external interference with the country, although, after the recognition of Iraqi independence, it was willing to have technical and financial assistance, especially from the United States. Objection was raised to all immigration, particularly to that of Hindus and Jews. The Iraqis also asked for the complete independence of Syria, and protested against any interference in Syria on the part of France. [2] That evening, when

---

[1] Lybyer *Diary*, July 17, 1919.

[2] Lybyer *Diary*, July 19, 1919. *PPC*, XII, 782: "It was impossible for the Commission to visit Mesopotamia at this time. Earnest requests

Lybyer and Yale had dinner in Aleppo, it was agreed that the country needed good government and good education, "especially for the women", and Yale argued for Syrian nationalism as opposed to the pan-Arab program.

Following their interviews of July 18-19, the Commission had really completed its work in Aleppo and left the next morning for an examination of the problem of Cilicia. In a despatch to Washington on July 21, the day after the departure of the visitors, Mr. Jackson summed up his impressions of the investigation as well as of the situation as he saw it. [1] He had been

> reliably informed that complete independence was desired and the United States was clearly indicated by a large majority, composed of Mohammedans (Arabs, Turks and Circassians), and the Greek Orthodox as having the preference as a mandatory power, and that these same categories expressed the earnest desire that if the United States did not accept, they would be satisfied with Great Britain instead, but were unalterably opposed to France.

On the other hand, Mr. Jackson had understood that "the Catholics of all denominations made flat demands for France," as did "the leading sheikhs of the Aneza tribe of Arabs," which lived principally in Mesopotamia, only a small portion being within Syria proper. However, Mr. Jackson had heard a report on July 21 that a number of the tribal sheikhs had been caught by local Arabs, "possibly through British influence," and forced to sign a petition demanding independence, with the United States or Great Britain as the temporary mandatory. The American Consul had also learned that many prominent Iraqis had requested that the delegation visit Mesopotamia, as there was a strong feeling

to make such a visit were presented at Damascus and Aleppo, accompanied by complaints that the British occupying forces are restricting freedom of speech, movement, and political action, and that they show signs of an intention to allow extensive immigration from India, to the great detriment of the rights and interests of the inhabitants." See also King Papers: G. R. MONTGOMERY, *Southern Kurdistan* (carbon), which indicates that while the Commission was at Damascus on July 2, Montgomery saw Said Ahmed, who claimed he was sent from the "Republic of Kurdistan," as a delegate to Paris. Montgomery told Said Ahmed and others the Commission would try to meet them at Aleppo. Jaafar Pasha, who presented the Iraqis to the Commission at Aleppo, later distinguished himself as Prime Minister of Iraq, and was assassinated on October 29, 1936. There is an interesting Pan-Arab document in the Lybyer Papers, July 19, 1919, handwritten, calling for Pan-Arab unity under King Hussein.

[1] Lybyer Papers: Consul J. B. Jackson, Report to Department on Commission's visit. Aleppo, Syria, July 21, 1919. Arrival of American Delegation of International Commission on Mandates in Turkey.

against Great Britain and "an ardent desire for help from the United States." Since there had been "strong evidence" of possible trouble on the part of the population, the local government was induced to maintain good order.

A Day in Old Cilicia

A four-car special train brought the King-Crane Commission from Aleppo to Adana on Sunday evening at 6 P. M. It passed through fertile fields, and the stations and other buildings along the Baghdad Railway were "magnificent stone with tile roofs, artistically designed." There were excellent tunnels, good grades, stone ballast, although the rails were rather light and not "aligned with absolute perfection." On the west of Amanus the fields were greener and more wooded, and there were superb spillways for mountain torrents, with a gradual descent to the plain, only part of which was cultivated. Everybody was tired, it was very hot during the middle of the day. Dr. King read a number of articles and Rex Beach's *The Ne'er Do Well*.[1]

At Adana the Americans were met by the French governor, a British general, and Mr. W. N. Chambers, of the Near East Relief. While the group had planned to remain on the train, Dr. King and Mr. Crane "put up" with the Chambers, and had a "hot day and night" and only a "fair sleep", while the rest went to the hospital for the night. After dinner they all had a talk with Dr. Chambers, who was very hopeful for the Armenians, and "very distrustful" of the Turks, while he thought French rule had "accomplished very little." There were some 20-25,000 Armenians back in Adana—and "very faithful mosquitoes". Lybyer thought well of the members of the Near East Relief, but the Armenians were "cocky and difficult."

After breakfast the next morning the Commission prepared for the Adana interviews, which Montgomery and the French governor had arranged. Some of the Turks were "uneasy of appearance" and looked "sheepish". They asked for the preservation of the Empire, and were willing to leave the question of guidance in Constantinople to others. The Vali and most of the Turkish officials were still in office. The Armenian Catholics desired the annexation of Cilicia to Armenia, the whole to be placed under an American mandate, but the Greek Orthodox delegation wanted a French mandate.

Following an excellent luncheon at the hospital, the Americans took Dr. Chambers along to Mersina with them. At Tarsus, all the Americans of the city, the French governor, and others came on the train, and at

---

[1] Montgomery had already gone ahead to make arrangements, and Crane had joined the party again at Aleppo, only the day before leaving. He had been ill and living mainly "on youghourt for two weeks." See Lybyer and King *Diaries*, July 20, 1919.

Mersina, French and British officials received the American group. They went to the home of the British colonel for tea and had a long talk with Major Anfic, the French governor, who had had colonial experience in Algeria, and whose "smooth-talking" wife was much interested in schools and in improvement of the port. The major was convinced that all the people were friendly to France, although a delegation of Turks asked the Commission for an American mandate.[1]

Although the Cilician visit was extremely brief, the findings of the Commission were not without interest. Professor Lybyer pointed out[2] that Cilicia had been included in the Syrian claim for unity, as formulated everywhere, since the Taurus mountains lay to the north of it. But few had been found to argue strongly that it belonged historically and economically with Syria. Even at Aleppo there had been no disposition to insist more than that Alexandretta should be united with Syria, rather than with Cilicia. Syria was abundantly supplied with ports, but the region northeast of the Gulf of Iskanderum needed the Cilicia outlet. Dr. Montgomery, in a somewhat longer memorandum,[3] gave a general description of the Cilician problem, generally involving "the unity of the Turkish part of the Empire, the joining of Cilicia to Syria, the joining of Transcaucasian Armenia to a possible Armenia, the choice of a mandatory, [and] the form of the future government."

The American Commission reached the end of its Syrian venture at Mersina. At 7:30 P. M., on July 21, Dr. King, Mr. Crane and their staff boarded the *U. S. S. Hazelwood*, the American destroyer which had come a week before to pick up the group, and sailed toward Constantinople. Soon the Americans would be back on the Golden Horn—soon, perhaps, home!

---

[1] Lybyer *Diary*, July 21, 1919. Lybyer Papers: *Document on the Province of Adana.* Prepared by the Turks, three parts. Part I. The Vilayet of Adana, an Historical Summary, 15 pp.; Part II. The History of the Movement of Population in the Province of Adana, 16 pp.; Part III, Footnotes, 8 pp. August 5, 1919. The documents claim Cilicia as Turkish, the historical analysis going back to about 900 B. C., and assert that "there is no place and no corner within this province that does not bear witness to the existence of the Turkish communities, and there is scarcely a province of Turkey that has preserved the essential features and the original character of the Turkish race so faithfully as has done Adana." Some 341,000 out of a total population of 371,000 were Turks, or about 77%, the Moslem population being 22%. The memorandum insisted that the French occupation was illegal, and declared the province of Adana, with its port of Mersina, was indispensable to the economic life of Turkey.

[2] Lybyer Papers: A. H. LYBYER, *Brief Memorandum on Cilicia.*

[3] Lybyer Papers: G. R. MONTGOMERY, *Adana* (about July 25, 1919). General Mudge felt that French administration had been good, and that the French were going ahead as though they expected to remain, with the aim of creating a *fait accompli*, if the United States "did not take the mandate for Armenia."

The End of the Syrian Journey

The journey to Syria and Palestine had, indeed, been eventful. During forty-two days from June 10 to July 21, from the landing at Jaffa to the embarkation at Mersina, the Commission had visited some thirty-six of the more important towns, scattered throughout the four military districts under British, French and Arab administration, and had heard delegations from many other significant centers of population. Moreover, while the Commission did not and could not visit every place, altogether delegations from about 1,520 villages were heard.[1]

The Petitions

The Commission had not only heard delegations, but had received 1,863 petitions from all over Syria and Palestine.[2] There were some qualifications to the general accuracy of these reflections of popular sentiment. In the first place, the number of petitions from the various sections of Syria was not proportional to their respective populations. Palestine, with thirteen cities in which delegations were received, was represented by only 260 petitions, while 1,157 came from O. E. T. A. East, which was under Arab military control, and included Syria east of the Jordan line and the Lebanon boundary, only eight of whose cities were visited. As the Commission journeyed north there were more petitions, doubtless because of the knowledge that the Americans were coming, which allowed more time for the preparation of written documents, as well as "for the activities of propaganda agents, and for the natural crystallization of public opinion." Secondly, "the number of petitions from the different religious organizations" was "not proportional to the numerical strength of the religious faiths." In Palestine, thanks to the number of Christian sects, fifty-three delegations of Christians were interviewed, but only eighteen Moslem delegations, although the Moslem element was eight times as large as the Christian. But this disparity did not "hold for the total number of petitions from Moslem villages" which were presented to the Commission at Aleppo and other northern centers. Thirdly, many petitions betrayed "the influence of organized propaganda," as sometimes indicated by verbal similarities or identical wording, sometimes by printed forms, and finally by the use of models. There were also external evidences of pressure and propaganda, as when "the same

---

[1] *PPC*, XII, 752-755. These towns included Jaffa, Tel-Aviv, Richon-le-Sion, Jerusalem, Bethlehem, Hebron, Beersheba, Ramleh, Nablus, Jenin, Nazareth, Haifa, Acre, Damascus, Amman, Dera, Baalbek, Beirut, Jebeil, Batrum, Bkerke, Sidon, Tyre, Ainab, Baabda, Zahle, Tripoli, Alexandretta, Latakia, Homs, Moalaka, Hama, Aleppo, Adana, Tarsus, Mersina.

[2] These summaries are based on Captain Brodie's figures in *PPC*, XII, 758-762. The reader should also consult the tables which Mr. Brodie prepared as Secretary to the King-Crane Commission.

Arab agent was observed in four cities of Palestine, assisting in the preparation of petitions. Similar activities on the part of French sympathizers were evident in Beirut. In the fourth place, there was evidence of outright fraud, including two instances of signatures in the same handwriting, and three repeated signatures. Fraudulent seals were discovered, as in the case of the socalled Trade Unions of Beirut. They had been ordered "by the same propaganda agent a few days before the arrival of the Commission." Finally, the value of the individual petitions varied with the number of signatures, although mere numbers could not be taken as the sole criterion. Despite these reservations the petitions appeared to present "a fairly accurate analysis" of Syrian political opinion. Coming as they did from a wide range of political, economic, social and religious classes and organizations, it was felt that they were representative. Even where the authorities had sought to exert control over the delegations, "without exception the opposition parties found opportunities to present their ideas to the Commission, if not always orally, at least in writing."

The petitions had "clearly revealed" six distinct programs, and, indeed, 1,364 of the 1,863 petitions were exact copies of some of the programs, while others closely resembled them. First was the *independence program*, the dominant note in Palestine, calling for opposition to Zionism and complete independence for Syria. [1] Second was the *Damascus program* of the Syrian General Congress, embodying the principle of independence, modified with a request for an American or British mandate. Third were the programs for The Lebanon, which included a demand for the French *independent Greater Lebanon*, involving complete independence and separation of the Greater Lebanon from Syria, with the Bekaa and in some instances the city of Tripoli, under a French mandate. With almost identical wording, 139 out of 146 petitions from French-occupied Syria contained that program. The *Independent Lebanon Program*, supported by 33 out of 36 petitions, asked for independence and separation from Syria, without a French mandate. But forty-nine petitions supported the so-called *Autonomous Lebanon Program*, which demanded an autonomous Lebanon united with the Syrian state, without mention of a mandate. A fourth program embodied the *Zionist Plan*, calling for a Jewish Homeland in Palestine and extensive Jewish immigration. There were eleven petitions with different phraseology which favored the Zionist Program, all from Jewish delegations. Eight others expressed approval of Zionist colonies in Palestine, but without endorsing the complete Zionist scheme. Four of the latter were statements by Arab peasants who were "on good terms with the Jewish colonies." From Syria as a whole only .32 % of the petitions favored a separate Palestine, while 1,500, or 80.4 % called for a United Syria, with 73.5 % calling for independence of Syria as well.

---

[1] *PPC*, XII, 763-770, for summary analysis.

Captain Brodie's summaries concerning the "geography of the claims" are also of significance. He noted, for example:

> The largest percentage for any one request is that of 1,500 petitions (80.4 per cent) for United Syria, including Cilicia, the Syrian Desert, and Palestine. The boundaries of this area are usually defined as "the Taurus Mountains on the north; the Euphrates and Khabur Rivers, and the line extending east of the Abu Kamal to the east of Al Juf on the east; Rafa and the line running from Al Juf to the south of Akaba on the south; and the Mediterranean Sea on the west." In addition to being the first plank of the Damascus program, a United Syria received strong support from many Christians in all the O. E. T. A.'s., as the number of petitions indicates.

Nevertheless, there was some opposition to Syrian unity. For instance, six of nineteen Zionist petitions asked for a separate Palestine, and two Palestinian Christian groups favored a separate Palestine under a British mandate, while twenty-four, mainly from Christians in Palestine, asked for an autonomous Palestine within a United Syria. Moreover, opposition to a United Syria was reflected in 203 petitions (10.9 per cent) demanding an independent Greater Lebanon. But "the request for a United Syria" was rendered "even more emphatic by the 1,062 protests against an Independent Greater Lebanon."

The largest number of petitions (1,500, or 80.4 per cent) called for a United Syria. The second largest group of petitions called for "absolute independence." There were 1,370 (73.5 per cent) favoring this portion of the Damascus Program, which was "supported generally by all Moslem delegations." But "independence" was seldom employed in the sense of "an entire freedom from any foreign guidance," such as that of a mandatory, since the request was often associated with a choice of mandate or a request for some kind of assistance. A few of the Young Arab clubs "defined a mandate to mean only economic and technical assistance, because of a widespread fear that the mandatory arrangement would be used to cloak colonial annexation." Independence for Mesopotamia was demanded by 1,278 petitions (68.5 per cent), although with the addition of similar petitions the figure totaled 1,371.

It is especially interesting to note the form of government desired. 1,107 (59.3 per cent) petitions supported the establishment of a "democratic, non-centralized, constitutional" kingdom in accordance with the Damascus Program. Many considered a large degree of local autonomy "as implicit in the general idea of a democratic, non-centralized government."

There were differences of view as to the choice of a mandate. Only sixty-six (3.5 per cent) of the petitions, of which forty-eight were from Palestine, gave first choice to Great Britain as the mandatory, and thirteen of these were from Greek Orthodox delegations and four from the Druze. But Great Britain was the second choice in 1,075 petitions (57.5

per cent), thanks "to the 1,032 requests for British 'assistance'," if the United States declined, "in accordance with the Damascus Program." France, it is noteworthy, was the first choice of 274 (14.48 per cent), although all but fifty-nine of these petitions came from the Greater Lebanon, with a majority of Christians, and under French control. Significant was the fact that the second choice total was only three. There were 1,064 requests for the assistance of the United States, as embodied in the Damascus Program, with fifty-seven selections of the United States, and eight more if it were necessary to have a mandatory. This brought the total of first choices for the United States to 1,129 (60.5 per cent). A few left the choice of a mandatory to the Syrian Congress, which would have increased the American first and the British second choice total.

The third largest number of petitions on any one point were the 1,350 (72.3 per cent) against the Zionist program. This group represented

a more widespread general opinion among both Moslems and Christians than any other. The anti-Zionist note was especially strong in Palestine, where 222 (85.3 %) of the 260 petitions declared against the Zionist program. This is the largest percentage in the district for any one point.

A final classification had to do with "protests and criticisms," involving general statements of criticism of national claims, character or policies; specific criticisms concerning mismanagement, corruption, etc.; protests against interference on the part of military authorities trying to prevent access to the Commission. While only three general anti-British statements were presented to the Commission, there were 1,129 (60.5 per cent) petitions professing anti-French attitudes, largely because such a protest was included in the Damascus Program. But there were also twenty-four specific criticisms of French administration. There was some Christian criticism of the Arab government, and fear of the fate of Christians under an independent Arab Moslem state. Included in 1,033 petitions was the protest of the Damascus Program against the application of Article XXII of the Covenant of the League of Nations to Syria, perhaps because of a misapprehension of the nature of the mandate system, or because of fears as to how it might be implemented. This protest appeared only after the text had been published in the statement given by the Commissioners to the Damascus press. There was another specific protest, for 988 (52.9 per cent) petitions opposed the "secret treaties dividing Syria without the consent of the Syrians." It was usually understood that the Sykes-Picot agreement and the Balfour Declaration were especially in mind, although they were not mentioned.

Some Observations on the Syrian Problem

Professor Lybyer summed up his observations, especially in O. E. T. A. West, under French occupation, the day after the arrival at Constantinople, on July 24.[1] He pointed out that, while the French were in control of O. E. T. A. West, a strip of land along the coast from Alexandretta to Tyre, part of it was under "the former Turco-Arab local government modified by the French," and the rest consisted "of the Lebanon district, as set off in 1860 and administered since then under French guidance, except during the late war." In all that region the French had "worked to obtain the reality or at least the appearance of a desire for a French mandate."

> Their propaganda, some of which they have carried on directly, and some through native officials and agents, has taken many forms. We have ourselves observed inspired articles in newspapers, demonstrations organized to cry "Vive la France", attempts at browbeating and espionage in our presence, the hindrance by French soldiers of the attempts of individuals and groups to reach us, and the ushering in before us of officials, manifestly unsuited to their position, freshly appointed in the room of others who had been removed because they declined to support a French mandate. We have been told by persons interested and disinterested, and of various nationalities, native and European, of threats and bribes and even imprisonment and banishment for the same purpose. The management of the sessions at Tyre, Baabda, and Tripoli was so bad as to be insulting to the intelligence and almost to the dignity of the Commission, and was saved from this at other places only by the greater intelligence and natural politeness of some French officers who kept their methods out of sight.

Agents of Prince Feisal had worked to a limited extent, in support of the Damascus Program in the French-occupied region.

The action of the French officials "made it difficult to reach anything like certainty in ascertaining the wishes of the people," since all who did not declare for the French were against them, and one could never be sure that "those who declared for the French spoke their real minds." Nevertheless, the situation was in accord with that in Palestine and the region of Damascus. In general, the Moslems were for either American or British assistance under the Damascus Program, the Druze favored a British mandate, the Catholic and Maronite elements supported France, the Greek Orthodox Community was divided, the Ismailians were generally pro-French, and the Nusairiyeh were divided. Even those who were pro-French differed concerning "the place and relationship of Lebanon in Syria." From Tyre to Tripoli generally they favored a "rigid formula," calling for a Greater Lebanon, "absolutely independent of the rest of Syria and under France: the supporters of this view showed no response to the idea of Syrian national unity, and apparently wish to

[1] Lybyer Papers: A. H. LYBYER, *Additional Observations on Syria Situation*, Constantinople, July 24, 1919. A portion, or the general outlines, may have been written *en route* to Constantinople. See Lybyer *Diary*, July 24, 1919. See also *PPC*, XII, 848-863, for Confidential Appendix to the King-Crane Report, since portions of these "additional observations" became a part of it.

become French citizens at an early moment." But others desired unity under the mandate of France, and an enlarged Lebanon district, with a "high degree of autonomy."

Perhaps the majority of the Lebanese were sincerely pro-French. Although the Commission "could not inquire" whether the pro-French elements might accept an American mandate, there were some emphatic indications that this was the case. In any event, if the mandate for the Lebanon were to be assigned to France, the Druze asked "emphatically to be left out." In Tyre, Sidon, "Hollow Syria", and Tripoli, a distinct majority seemed "strongly averse to French rule," including practically all the Sunni Moslems, most of the Shiites, part of the Greek Orthodox community, and the few Protestants. Most of the latter favored either the United States or Great Britain. But in the region north of the proposed Greater Lebanon in O. E. T. A. West,

> the majority is probably against a French mandate in any circumstances. A considerable proportion of the remainder are wholly averse to separation from the interior of the country, and place the unity of Syria above their preference for France. It is worthy of note that whereas the Syrian nationalists everywhere distinctly and by name rejected the assistance of France, no one who supported France declared a specific rejection of England or America. In a number of instances, however, the fear was expressed by Christians that England, if made the Mandatory Power, would show more favor to Moslems than to Christians.

Professor Lybyer offered many objections to the French plan in the Lebanon, which called for the area from Tyre to Tripoli inland to the crest of the Anti-Lebanon, to be assigned to France, if the rest of Syria were attributed to another mandatory. Such a scheme was contrary to the wishes of a majority of the people. The Syrians outside the area were "so opposed to the plan as to be inclined to make war rather than accept it." If put into effect by overwhelming force, "a state of settled equilibrium could never be attained...." The land was too small for satisfactory division. The separation of the Greater Lebanon from Syria, if accompanied by the separation of Palestine, would intensify religious differences, which it was "most desirable to diminish in favor of the growth of national feeling. The tendency would be for Christian Syrians to concentrate in the Lebanon, Jews in Palestine, and Moslem Syrians in the remainder of the country." In each region the government would probably conduct intrigues in the others, with the result that the "three areas would be implicitly hostile," with all that this would mean in the way of armaments. Finally, the mandatory powers themselves would be in danger of hostility. But

> a plan which would add to the Greater Lebanon the remainder of O. E. T. A. West, extending from Tripoli to Alexandretta, and give the whole to France, and at the same time the interior to Britain,

would intensify all the above difficulties, and would besides cut off Aleppo and western Mesopotamia from access to the sea.

In the region of Homs, Hama, and Aleppo, Lybyer concluded that the Moslem population was "practically solid" for the Damascus Program. The Christians were divided, since the Catholics and Maronites, few in number, as well as the Greek Orthodox, were pro-French by majority. Moreover, the obstacles which the French authorities interposed in the path of some delegations which desired to appear before the Commission, especially at Tripoli, "aroused sharp comment and protest," and almost added another point to the Damascus Program. Finally the people at Aleppo did not strongly demand the inclusion of Cilicia with Syria, but were much concerned to have Alexandretta as their natural port, and Aintab, as the source of their water supply.

Bases of the Position Relative to France

Parts of Lybyer's analysis went into his later historical sketch of the investigation in Syria and ultimately found their way into the "Confidential Appendix" to the King-Crane Report,[1] outlining in some detail the situation not only in Palestine proper, but in Syria and Cilicia as well. Considerable evidence has already been given concerning the Arab attitude toward France, but the "Confidential Appendix" declared that the strength, persistence and universality of that feeling "came as a distinct surprise." Nor did the Americans find the sentiment to be entirely artificial, stimulated either by the British or the Germans, as the French had charged, and as Captain Yale, to a certain extent, thought—for the sentiment did "seem to be deep-rooted in a large proportion of the Syrian population." In general it appeared to be based on the view that the French were "enemies of religion." The Syrians disapproved of the French attitude toward women, and felt that the French educational system did not build character like the Anglo-Saxon system. Moreover, the French had not treated the Algerians or the Tunisians as equals, and in Syria they had a tendency to favor the Catholics especially, a policy which stimulated religious divisions in the country, endangering "the possibility of Syrian nationalism on a non-religious basis." The French were more inclined toward a policy of colonization than toward one of a genuine mandate. Again, the French had lost so many men and suffered so much financially and economically during the war that the Syrians wondered

---

[1] King and Lybyer Papers: A. H. LYBYER, *Brief Historical Sketch of the Visit to Syria, Palestine and Cilicia of the American Section of the International Commission on Mandates in Turkey.* Constantinople, Turkey, August 1, 1919. Annotated and revised by Dr. King. Lybyer noted in his *Diary*, August 9: "After decision to prepare a report which could be seen by French and British, Dr. King cut out about one-half, and I had to patch it together. P. M. I put in a 'Confidential Appendix', for Americans only." For Confidential Appendix see *PPC*, XII, 848-863.

whether the French could perform the tasks of a mandate adequately, without financial exploitation. France was also partly blamed for what had happened to the Arabs under Jemal Pasha, since certain correspondence during the war had fallen into Ottoman hands. Whether these charges were true or false was not so important as the fact that a majority of Syrians believed them, and were therefore "very strongly against French control of the country."

The Possibilities

There appeared to be four possibilities for the adherents of a United Syria: independence, or a mandate under the United States, Great Britain or France. Only those who favored Zionism or a separate Lebanon were opposed to a United Syria, and only the Jews really supported Zionism. Support for the Lebanon lay primarily among the Maronites and Catholics, sincerely devoted to France, while outside the Lebanon only a few supported France. Aside from the Druzes, a surprising few declared for a British mandatory, although in general Great Britain and the United States could be classed together. Practically all the Moslems were for the United States as the first choice. The Commission did not doubt the genuine feeling with reference to the United States, which rested on confidence in President Wilson, gratitude to the Near East Relief Organization, and the American reasons for entering the Great War. Moreover, there was the knowledge that the United States was not primarily a colonizing power—"the examples of Cuba and the Philippines were frequently cited." There was also a confidence that the United States would get out when the job had been well done. There was a genuine approval of American education, with the example of the American University of Beirut, a trust in the American sense of justice, and confidence in the trained men and women who could be sent out to serve under an American mandate.

Many British officials, including General Allenby, thought that the best solution was "an American mandate over the whole of Syria," and that France could not really desire a mandate for the entire country, "when so much of it" was "utterly averse" to France. It was quite evident that the French resented the British failure to play "a fair game in the Syrian area." There was the Sykes-Picot agreement, although France was now threatened with the loss of all its sphere, while Great Britain was keeping its gains and expanding its influence "toward the rest." The United States, thanks to its interest in Armenia and the despatch of the Commission to Syria, seemed "to be an accomplice of England in despoiling France." The French also resented the monthly British subsidy to the Emir Feisal, British influence with the Arabs, and held the British responsible for "the undeniably strong anti-French feeling shown by practically all the Moslem and non-Catholic Christian elements of Syria." The British could not resist "the desire to connect Egypt with

Mesopotamia under one control as a bulwark of India and as a new field for profitable commercial exploitation." While the Commission believed that some of these contentions were difficult to refute and that the British record would be better if the British got out of Syria, nevertheless, the popular aversion to France was "so great and deep-seated" that Great Britain could not leave Syria to France "without seeming to abandon her friends to their enemies." There was good reason, therefore, for the position of many British officials who were "strongly desirous that America should take the whole situation off their hands," including the French and Arab entanglements and the promises to Zionism.

The denial of French "rights", embodied in the Damascus Program, led to an inquiry into the validity of the French claim. For centuries there had been French Catholic missionaries, and there were many French schools. France had a special interest in the Maronites and had landed troops in the Lebanon to protect them in 1860. But none of these facts had established a right "to claim territory or mandatory control." On the other hand, there was "no reason why any tie that France" had had "with Syria in the past should be severed or even weakened under the control of another mandatory power, or in an independent Syria." The most recent French policy in the Lebanon included control of the coastal region from Tyre to Tripoli, as far inland as the Anti-Lebanon, if the rest of Syria were to be assigned to another mandatory. This was objectionable because it was contrary to the wishes of the people, who were "inclined to make war rather than accept it." But, in any case, Syria was simply too small to be divided satisfactorily, especially when religious differences would be intensified and the road to national unity made more difficult.

Feisal and Independence

Unless Syria were to be considered as a conquered country, or as a republic, it seemed obvious to the King-Crane Commission that the Emir Feisal should head the state. [1] While the loyalty and attachment of the people varied in different places, some Christians fearing Feisal's Moslem faith, most Moslems favored him, although the Palestinian Moslems had made almost no declaration in his behalf. Feisal desired the friendly co-operation of all faiths, and seemed "kindly, gentle and wise." Although some thought he was weak, he seemed able "to maintain his leadership" and promised to build up a constitutional monarchy. Were he to become the head of the Syrian state, however, he was to renounce all rights of

[1] The British were paying Feisal about £ 150,000 ($ 750,000) per month, of which $200,000 went for personal expenses, staff, propaganda, etc., with the balance going to administration, the army and gendarmerie. It was estimated that under normal conditions Feisal could get along with $125,000 per month.

inheriting the crown of the Hejaz, for "otherwise serious complications might arise in the future."

In view of the Christian fear of Moslem domination, the Commission carefully investigated the means proposed to investigate the problem of the protection of minorities, as embodied in the Damascus Program. Ordinarily the minorities were promised constitutional guarantees. At Damascus there was a proposal "to grant Moslems one-half of the seats in the future legislative assembly while the other half would be distributed among the rest of the population," although the method of distribution of seats among Druzes, Maronites, Shiites, Nusairiyeh, Ismailians, Turks, Jews, Orthodox and Catholic Greeks, was not discussed. Feisal had promised the Greek Orthodox to rule without despotism in the fear of God, to establish constitutional government, to respect all religions with equal rights for all, to guarantee public security, to place education on a basis of equality, and to consider only fitness and merit, not family, for public office. The Commission believed that the majority was ready to implement the protection of minorities. But the Moslem and Druze minority in the Lebanon also needed protection, and in the event of a Jewish Home in Palestine, "Moslems and Christians would need protection there."

The Syrian aspiration for complete independence deserved special attention because the opposition to Article XXII of the Covenant of the League of Nations was definitely related to this demand. Bedouins and villagers of the southeast, as well as the Young Arabs, supported this position. The Syrian Union Party asked the League of Nations to guarantee the constitution and independence of Syria. A large number of the older and wiser Moslems recognized that some sort of supervision was necessary, while the Christian and other non-Moslem elements unanimously urged a strong mandate, because they did not have "confidence in an Arab government, which in a country four-fifths Moslem might be too favorable to the majority." In any event, the Commission saw no reason for modifying the original recommendation of the Paris Conference for a Syrian mandate. Moreover, the fourth article of the Damascus Program provided for the possibility of a mandate, defining it as equivalent to such economic or technical assistance as did not prejudice "complete independence." The Commission, however, believed that the mandatory "should have a real control over the administration so as to eliminate as far as possible corruption, waste, inertia, serious error of judgment, etc." Either Great Britain or the United States could be allowed a basic control, since the demand for complete independence was largely motivated by "the fear of a French mandate, and in part by apprehension of the conversion of mandatory control into permanent possession." In time, a true and lasting independence could be awarded by the League of Nations.

The programs presented by Moslems and about two-thirds of the Syrian Christians were nationalistic, calling for an independent United Syria, under democratic monarchy, without religious distinction. The Moslems expressed no desire for political union with the Hejaz, although most Moslems felt that the Caliphate should be at Mecca and held by King Hussein. All affirmed, nevertheless, that King Hussein was "in no sense their political head, but only their religious head." Some Christians contended that Syrian nationalism was feeble and new and warned against false impressions, but the Commission as a whole did not share that view. Pan-Arabism "would unite under one independent government the Arab-speaking portions of the former Turkish Empire," but the Commission could see no special danger in that possibility. In a larger sense, Pan-Arabism "would wish to add also the Arab-speaking belt across North Africa."

In the narrow sense, Pan-Islamism would establish a Moslem government within the framework of the former Ottoman Empire by agreement between the Turks and Arabs. But the Commission

> found no sign of a desire for the re-establishment of the rule of Turkey over the Arabs .... If there is any thought of a federation of Arabs with Turks, or of a political union of any sort, the Commission saw no trace of it. Still less was there any sign of movement toward the realization of a larger Pan-Islamic idea.

The Commission discerned no trace of an attempt to restore the Saracen Empire, with all its alleged dangers, nor was it "practically conceivable under present world conditions." Indeed, the development of Near Eastern Nationalism would seem to preclude such an eventuality, as the post-war world amply demonstrated. The Moslem world, whatever the bond of religious sympathy, was traveling the road traced out in the Christian world.

The American Commission took the sensible attitude that the basic question was whether Christians and Moslems were to cooperate in a friendly manner. The Moslems of Syria had offered their hands to their non-Moslem fellow citizens "with the promise of putting religious separation out of sight." Were they to be taken at their word? "Or shall they be told: We do not believe what you say; we do not trust you; we think it best to break our word with you, so that you may not have the opportunity to break your word with us?" The Commission could not accept this negative attitude:

> The western world is already committed to the attempt to live in peace and friendship with the Moslem peoples, and to manage governments in such a way as to separate politics from religion. Syria offers an excellent opportunity to establish a state where members of the three great monotheistic religions can live together in harmony; because it is a country of one language which has long had freedom of movement and of business relations through being unified under the Turkish rule. Since now the majority declare for nationalism, independent of religion,

it is necessary only to hold them to this view through mandatory control until they have established the method and practice of it. Dangers may readily arise from unwise and unfaithful dealings with this people, but there is great hope of peace and progress if they be handled frankly and loyally.

Syrian Journey's End

When the members of the King-Crane Commission were piped aboard the *U.S.S. Hazelwood* at Mersina the Syrian portions of their Near Eastern venture were at an end. Shortly after the ship had entered the now untroubled waters of the Dardanelles, not far distant from the minarets of Constantinople, Dr. King wrote his own impressions of what he had seen and what, perhaps, the Commission had accomplished.[1] The brief sea journey had been "very refreshing" as compared with some of the recent noisy, hot nights, and soon the group would be busy preparing the *Report* for President Wilson. Dr. King portrayed in brief and interesting detail something of the highlights of the trip:

> We began our work in Syria..., June 10 at Jaffa, and we have kept steadily at it ever since .... At Damascus I saw a good deal of the Emir Feisal who is expected to be the head of the new Syrian State if that is formed. He is a son of the King of the Hedjaz Kingdom and seems in many ways very well fitted for the responsibility that probably awaits him. He gave us the impression of being a broad and openminded man, though he has not had the training of the schools. He gave us a garden party there at which Bedouin costumes were furnished for the guests, and he had us take these costumes with us when we left.
> From Damascus we went to Baalbek, a very old city where there are some remarkable ruins of classic times. We then went to Beirut and spent a number of days in that vicinity, where the French are in immediate charge. I am sorry to find that there was much more evidence of coercion and suppression of opinion there than anywhere else in Syria. Among the places which we visited in that vicinity were Tyre and Sidon, both of which we visited in one day and where we heard more than 40 delegations. We also went considerably farther north, to Tripoli, Ladikiyeh and Alexandretta. General Allenby let us have his yacht, the "Maid of Honor", for this trip. This made these places much more accessible than they could have been otherwise, though we did have a half a day of misery when the sea was pretty rough. The boat brought us back to Tripoli.... We visited Homs, Hama, and Aleppo. We found Aleppo very interesting, and I liked its bazaars much better than those of Damascus. At Aleppo we took to the railroad and made a fourteen hour trip to Adana (in the province of Cilicia) where we met a number of delegations, chiefly to get light on the feelings of the people in this province, which is claimed both by Syria and the Turkish-speaking portion of the Empire. We made a brief stop at Tarsus, Paul's birthplace, and then went down to Mersina where the destroyer was waiting for us, leaving Monday (July 21). Our plan is to put in about one week at Constantinople in summing up the results of our Syrian trip and prepare our report and recommendations. We

[1] King Papers: King to Bohn, July 23, 1919.

expect then to begin our study of the Asia Minor problem (Aug. 1) unless we find that word has been sent us from the Peace Conference calling us back for consultation there. I shall not feel myself as if we had quite finished our survey as it should be finished unless we finally get to Mesopotamia, but it would be very unwise, undoubtedly, to try to go there until fall when the excessive heat has passed. It is hard to tell you what time we can expect to finish. It is possible that we may be able to see so many delegations at Constantinople that we can avoid much traveling through that part of the Empire and finish up our work sooner on that account. On the other hand it would not surprise me if it took a month or six weeks to finish the Asia Minor part of our survey (Sept. 15), saying nothing about Mesopotamia. I think our trip has been very worth while, and that we have gotten results that could not possibly have been gotten without such a commission. The people will certainly feel that they have been consulted and cannot help having a somewhat different attitude on that account.

It was clear that Dr. King and his staff rather expected to make the long journey into Mesopotamia before they completed their work. Moreover, it was apparent that there were possibilities of remaining in the Near East for another two months before returning to Paris and the United States. Dr. King hoped the Oberlin Commencement exercises had gone off well, and was very glad to have received "a little circular about the theological buildings," which he had shown to Mr. Crane, though he had not "taken up the matter with him at all." Crane had been a "most congenial associate" and both had "looked at things in . . . much the same way". King did not know when he would be back in Oberlin, but a few days in Constantinople would tell the story.

CHAPTER VI

The Problem of the Turkish Homelands: Mandate or Independence

THE TURKISH QUESTION AT PARIS

Some Views of the Situation in Turkey: Admiral Bristol's Reports

The Paris Peace Conference was not relieved of the troublesome Turkish problem when the King-Crane Commission left for the Near East toward the end of May 1919. Neither was the American Commission to Negotiate Peace, for Admiral Mark Bristol kept reporting on the difficult situation which was developing within the Ottoman lands. In a despatch of June 22, 1919,[1] the Senior United States Naval Officer at Constantinople pointed out that up to the time of the Greek occupation of Smyrna, it was "believed that ... the Near East was as peaceful a part of the world's battlegrounds as any part of Europe or Asia." The Smyrna incident had disturbed the relative calm and "destroyed the confidence that the Turks had in the Allied and Associated Governments," and now arguments for self-control had been met with counter-statements that they did not trust the Allied Powers. Bristol had no special sympathy for Turkish acts during the Great War but he could find no excuse whatsoever "for granting the Greeks any consideration as against the Turks."[2] He did not believe that

> the Turks should be allowed to govern themselves at the present time. At the same time I do not think that any of the other races now in Turkey are at the present time, able to govern themselves. I most decidedly feel that the Greeks are not the proper people to be placed over any of the different races that now inhabit Turkey. They are notable [in their inability] to govern other people. The occurrences in Smyrna have borne out the statements that I have heard from so many different sources in this part of the country regarding the Greeks. Likewise, I have had Greeks who are Ottoman subjects tell me frankly that they do not think Greece should be given any part of Turkey.

Bristol added that the pot had begun to boil throughout the Moslem Near East. Of that there could be no question, as the world was soon to see in the Turkish nationalist movement. But the Admiral concluded with emphasis:

> The big point of view in any question like this Near Eastern situation should always be kept in view. The peace of the world is the big point of view. The peace of the world depends upon making the world safe for democracy. Democracy is not possible without education of the

---

[1] King Papers: Admiral Mark BRISTOL, *Report of Operations for Two Weeks Ending 22 June 1919*. Senior U. S. Naval Officer, Turkey, Part Four.

[2] President Wilson was much disturbed by the situation in Smyrna, as indicated by his comments on May 30. See *PPC*, VI, 116, 134, 370.

masses. Likewise, self-determination is not possible without education. The different races now living in Turkey are not at the present time educated so as to permit democracy and self-determination. It is absolutely impossible to draw any boundary line in Turkey according to races or nationality. It is the belief of many who have made a study of conditions in this region, that the different races that live in Turkey are so intermingled because it is a natural way for them to live and any arbitrary separation of the races would be artificial.

Bristol, therefore, strongly recommended that the entire Ottoman Empire "be placed under one mandatory" to educate all for democracy and self-government. Such a development would constitute "the greatest balance to all the other small nationalities" which had been created in the Near East in the past. Moreover, it might even set an example to the Balkan peoples and encourage them to form a federation along similar lines.

Admiral Bristol was not averse to American assumption of definite mandatory responsibilities, although he declared that if the United States were to assume a mandate, it should be for "the whole or nothing." But to sum up:

> The whole of Turkey should be maintained as one country and placed under one mandatory. If the United States desires to fulfil all the obligations for which she went into this war, she would never give up fighting for Turkey being maintained as one country and under one mandatory; and still further if it be necessary to obtain this result, the United States should accept the mandatory for the sake of the peace of the world.

When he reported at the end of June,[1] Admiral Bristol declared that the Greeks had behaved in a way which was neither creditable to themselves nor to that of "troops of a civilized country." Events were moving rapidly in Turkey. Before the Smyrna incident the conservative Turks had held the upper hand. Since that time the "progressive element," the hot-heads, had taken hold. The one thing which would break up the influence of the "progressives", in the Bristol view, would be to remove the Greeks from Smyrna. At the same time, he thought, the Italians should be cleared out of the places they had occupied. Once more, Bristol urged that Turkey be organized with one mandatory, "and not be divided up until such time as good government" had been established and the people educated so they could determine what nations should be developed in the Near East.

The Turkish Issue at Paris

Meanwhile, on June 17, while the King-Crane Commission was in the midst of the Syrian-Palestine investigation, His Highness Damad Ferid Pasha, the head of the Ottoman Delegation to the Paris Peace

---

[1] King Papers: Report of Operations for Week Ending 29 June 1919. Senior U. S. Naval Officer, Parts Three and Four.

Conference, was permitted to read a statement before the Council of Ten.[1] While Damad Ferid did not condone the crimes of the Empire, he insisted on a Wilsonian peace, based substantially on the *status quo ante bellum*. In Thrace he called for a defensive line northwest of Constantinople and Andrianople, and in Asia Minor a line from the Black Sea to the Tigris river and the Turco-Persian frontiers, including the vilayets of Mosul and Diarbekir, and a portion of Aleppo to the Mediterranean Sea. The islands near the coast should also remain under Ottoman sovereignty for the protection of the Asiatic mainland. The Ottoman Delegation, on the other hand, was willing to discuss the Armenian frontiers, and not unwilling to grant autonomy to Syria, Palestine, Hejaz, Assyr, Yemen and Iraq, which, however, would continue technically under Ottoman sovereignty. The Ottoman people would never accept "the dismemberment of the empire or its division under separate mandates," and Damad Ferid warned that "a fresh parcelling out of the Ottoman Empire would entirely upset the balance in the East."

Damad Ferid indicated that the Ottoman Delegation was preparing a memorandum summarizing its views, and the Council, which was not at all pleased with his statement, decided to await the written communication before making a reply. The Ottoman memorandum, which summarized the views already presented orally, was despatched on June 23, but as early as June 21, Mr. Balfour had prepared a draft reply which had been written at the request of the Council of Ten, at a short, unrecorded meeting after the hearing on June 17.[2] The reply was unanimously approved, subject to a few drafting changes, President Wilson subscribing to it with "great satisfaction." Balfour indicated that there were some, however, especially Mr. Montagu, who did not share the views expressed. Montagu "was strongly opposed to the removal of the Turks from Constantinople," although this was not mentioned in the note. On June 23,

[1] *PPC*, IV, 509-512; *Miller Diary*, XVI, 419-421. See also Howard, 236-237.

[2] *PPC*, VI, 576, 577-580, 617, 688-691; Ottoman memorandum, 691-694. See also S-H Bulletin, No. 405, June 26, 1919. Confidential Note from the Turkish Delegation, June 23, transmitting a Memorandum on the new Organization of the Turkish Empire. *S-H Records*, Vol. 7. British Translation, Paris, June 27, 1919 follows, 5 pp. For an objective account of the reforms and changes in the Ottoman Empire see the excellent account in Bernard LEWIS, *The Emergence of Modern Turkey* (London, Oxford [The Royal Institute of International Affairs], 1961), 495 pp.

Meanwhile, the Zionist Organization was especially active in Paris although Chaim Weizmann wrote to Forbes-Adam on July 23 that little could be done until the mandate for Palestine had been granted, even if he were anxious to get immigrants there. He felt that Sir Gilbert Clayton was not in sympathy with British Zionist policy, and suggested his friend, Col. Richard Menertzhagen, as political officer. See *British Documents*, 1919-1939, First Series, IV, 330-335; Weizmann, 250-251, 254.

David Lloyd George fully approved the Balfour draft, subject to two slight alterations to show that (1) when referring to Ottomans, the letter applied only to Ottoman Turks, and (2) the Conference was "not committed in any way to removing the Turks from Constantinople." That the Ottoman demands were impossible was clear and, perhaps the Clemenceau letter, dated June 25, was understandable, if far from accurate historically:

> ... There is no case to be found either in Europe or Asia or Africa, in which the establishment of Turkish rule in any country has not been followed by a diminution of material prosperity, and a fall in the level of culture, nor is there any case to be found in which the withdrawal of Turkish rule has not been followed by a growth in material prosperity and a rise in the level of culture. Neither among the Christians of Europe nor among the Moslems of Syria, Arabia and Africa, has the Turk done other than destroy whatever he has won by war. Not in this direction do his talents run.

Granted the prevailing attitude, it is difficult to see how there could be serious question of an equitable settlement of the problems at issue.

In view of President Wilson's impending departure, Lloyd George raised the Turkish problem once more on June 25,[1] outlining the future frontiers, but leaving the final disposition of the territories until the American attitude on the acceptance of a mandate was definitely known. Wilson agreed that the final solution ought not to be left for the next two months, while Clemenceau pointed out that the question of Constantinople was involved. President Wilson asserted that the amputations would involve Mesopotamia, Syria and Armenia. Allied troops would remain to preserve order. Lloyd George was concerned about the Americans and Clemenceau had the Italians in mind, their actions being entirely unauthorized by the Conference. President Wilson's proposal was to "cut off all that Turkey was to give up; and to oblige Turkey to accept any conditions with regard to over-sight or direction which the Allied and Associated Governments might agree to." He thought a mandate over Turkey would be a mistake, but "some Power ought to have a firm hand." "Constantinople and the Straits should be left as a neutral strip for the present," and it was already under Allied occupation. Wilson "would make the Sultan and his Government move out of Constantinople and he would say what was ceded to the Allied and Associated Powers," although this was not final. Wilson considered that question "decided". He had "studied the question of the Turks in Europe for a long time, and every year confirmed his opinion that they ought to be cleared out."

The next day, on June 26, the Council of Four again considered the problem.[2] President Wilson agreed to present the plan for an American

---

[1] *PPC*, VI, 675-677; *British Documents*, 1919-1939, IV, 643-651.
[2] *PPC*, VI, 711-713.

mandate for Constantinople and the Straits to the United States Senate, and he noted, among other things, that "Constantinople was not a Turkish city; other races were in the majority." The difficulties relative to a settlement arose, he said, from the Italian attitude. M. Clemenceau was "inclined to refuse discussion of Asiatic questions with the Italians for the present," and Lloyd George was afraid that Italian intervention would "cause unrest among the Mohammedan population of the world." Wilson was so exasperated that he thought the Italians "should be asked clearly to state whether they remained in the Entente or not." If so, Italy must take its part with the Allies, "and do nothing independently." Lloyd George insisted that Italy had gone beyond even the grants of the agreement of St. Jean de Maurienne. On June 27 it was agreed that further consideration of the treaty of peace with the Ottoman Empire should be suspended until "such time as the Government of the United States of America could state whether" it was "able to accept a mandate for a portion of the territory of the former Turkish Empire."[1] The United States, Great Britain and France warned Rome that the action of the Italian Government, unless curbed, would mean "the loss of all claim to further assistance or aid from those who were once proud" to be its associates.[2]

On June 28 the Treaty of Versailles with Germany was signed, and a few days later, President Wilson and the American Delegation as a whole went home, although a few remained to work in one capacity or another on the treaties which were yet to be concluded. But the Turkish problem proved so complicated that even a provisional settlement was delayed until 1920. Of special significance was the problem of the Straits. As David Lloyd George remarks:[3]

> It was impossible to contemplate any peace settlement which would leave so vital an international waterway to be dominated by the guns of a country that had taken so disastrous an advantage of its command of an indispensable way of communication between great nations. A peace which would not secure the world against this menace would not be a peace to which any responsible or even sane statesman could append his signature. The Allies, therefore, soon after the war commenced, came to the conclusion that the freedom of the Narrows from

---

[1] *PPC*, VI, 729; *British Documents*, 1919-1939, First Series, IV, 652-653.

[2] *PPC*, VI, 741, 755, 757, 760-762; Howard, 238. See also René ALBRECHT-CARRIE, "New Light on Italian Problems in 1919," *Journal of Modern History*, Vol. XIII, No. 4 (December 1941), 493-516; "Documents: Italy and Her Allies, June 1919," *American Historical Review*, Vol. XLVI, No. 4 (July 1941), 837-843.

[3] David Lloyd George, II, 1252-1260. See also The Russian Political Conference (Lvov, Sazonov, Chaikovsky, Maklakov), *Memorandum Presented to the President of the Conference of Peace, Paris, July 5, 1919* (Paris, 1919); *British Documents*, 1919-1939, First Series, IV, 653-654.

the Bosphorus to the Dardanelles must be secured, not by paper guarantees above a Turkish signature, but by entrusting the keys of this channel to hands that could be relied upon to maintain free access along its waters to all nations that kept the rules of the Covenant of Peace . . . .

It was obvious, therefore, that the Straits no longer could be "left in the hands of a weak and venal Power like Turkey" with "no special interest in securing freedom of access to any ports beyond her own." An American mandate had been proposed, and President Wilson was not unopposed to an American mandate over either Constantinople or Armenia or both, but "it was obvious that neither France, Britain nor Italy could undertake the task . . . ." Russia, however, "would have been the most fitting choice for a mandatory in Armenia and the Straits," had not the Bolshevik revolution intervened in November 1917. On the other hand, the Straits might have been assigned to Greece, with much "historical and ethnical justification." The other alternative, implying the establishment of an international commission with Great Britain, France, the United States and Italy as members, was also one of the suggested proposals. It seemed clear to Lloyd George

> that the best solution would be the choice of a mandatory Power not involved in the jealousies and rivalries of European states; one whose remoteness from these age-long contentions would have been a guarantee of impartiality and whose power and position in the world would have given authority to its decisions. The same principle applied to the Armenian problem . . . . When the delegates of the Great Powers assembled at the Conference examined the difficulties, it became clear that America was the only mandatory who would have been acceptable to all alike . . . . Had the President displayed any reluctance to entertain the idea, we would have been forced to contemplate the next best arrangement. In my judgment that would have been the placing of the Greeks in control of the Straits . . . .

Further Reflections on the Turkish Problem

With the departure of President Wilson, the Council of Heads of Delegations, on June 30, decided to postpone further discussion of the treaty of peace with the Ottoman Government until the United States was in a position to state whether it would be able to undertake a mandate for a portion of Turkish territory. At a meeting of the American Commissioners Plenipotentiary on July 1 the question of an American mandate over Armenia and Constantinople was discussed briefly, with Mr. Herbert Hoover "very averse" to the United States becoming the mandatory over Armenia alone, since it was "the poorhouse of Europe" and would require an army of from 50,000 to 100,000 men. In the Hoover view it would be "a terrific burden and a public act of charity for the United States to take a mandate" over the Constantinople area, since Constantinople would no longer be more than "a coaling station" and "a home for pilots." Because of the associations which it "would undoubtedly have with Russia," France would be the logical mandatory.[1] As the discussions continued, on July 18, Mr. Henry White, the Acting Head of the United States Delegation, informed the Council of a cable from President Wilson, stating that there would be a very considerable delay in the Turkish treaty if the Council were to await the American views as to the assumption of a mandate before proceeding with the matter, and, meanwhile, the President desired to know what attitude the Powers were taking toward the Turkish problem. M. Clemenceau indicated that he could not wait indefinitely for the American views and stated that, when other work had been accomplished, the Council would do its best to settle Turkish affairs. But the Council could take note of President Wilson's views: [2]

> He wished to obtain a mandate for Armenia and an American Commissioner had been appointed. He asked for part of Cilicia, and was favorably disposed towards accepting a mandate for Constantinople. The question of Constantinople was one of the greatest importance for Europe. It had caused wars in the past, and required the closest study.

There were also brief discussions of the problem in late July and August, especially as related to the plan for an international "State of Constantinople," but the questions were too complicated for easy or ready solution.[3]

The Inquiry at Constantinople

The members of the King-Crane Commission arrived in Constantinople about six o'clock in the evening of Wednesday, July 23, after a pleasant trip from Mersina. Three tasks awaited them. Almost immediately they began to prepare their report. They also initiated a series of interviews and conferences dealing with the problem of the Turkish homelands, which involved the fate of Turkish Anatolia as well as the specific questions of Constantinople and the Straits, the Greeks and Bulgarians in Thrace, and the troublesome and difficult issue of Armenia, which, in turn, was tied up with the fate of the Turks and the entire Caucasus region, not to mention Kurdistan. Finally, there was a possibility that the Commission might go to Mesopotamia, unless the American Delegation at Paris ordered it to report back to the Peace Conference. In the end the journey to Mesopotamia was not taken.[4]

---

[1] *PPC*, XI, 261-262. See also *British Documents, 1919-1939*, First Series, IV, 670-678.
[2] *PPC*, VII, 14, 193, 194-198, 200-201; *British Documents, 1919-1939*, I, 131-136. See also Herbert Hoover, *The Ordeal of Woodrow Wilson* (New York, McGraw-Hill, 1960), 222-229.
[3] *PPC*, VII, 234-235, 242-248, 353, 355, 434-442; XI, 342-344; *British Documents, 1919-1939*, First Series, I, 161-163, 258-266.
[4] Lybyer *Diary*, July 22-23, 1919. Dr. Haddad had been brought along to help prepare the Syrian Report. Lybyer had heard on July 22 that Col. W. N. Haskell had been appointed High Commissioner for Armenia by the Allied Powers.

After dinner at the Pera Palace Hotel, Dr. King and Mr. Crane, followed later by Professor Lybyer, moved out to Constantinople Women's College. There were conferences the next day with Admiral Bristol, Dr. Peet of the American Board of Missions, and the American Consul-General, Gabriel Bie Ravndal, who had much material on the situation in Smyrna and was very strong for an American mandate. Lybyer was now very busily writing his summary of the trip to French-occupied Syria, while Yale was preparing his own memorandum on Syria for the Commission. Yale was "very pessimistic", condemned British diplomacy as "wholly false—untrustworthy", and thought there was "no chance whatever" that the United States would accept a Near Eastern mandate. But it was not until July 26 that the Commission really got down to work on its *Report*, partly because some rest was a necessity and Dr. King seemed to have "had a touch of malaria" shortly after returning to the Ottoman capital.[1]

By this time, however, it was necessary to make some kind of report to President Wilson, who had returned to Washington immediately after the signature of the Treaty of Versailles. Mr. Crane, who was very much concerned with developments in European Turkey and the Balkans, cabled the President on July 29 complaining that "for one reason or another," Paris was not consulting "the wisest people" in the Near East about a settlement. He warned that if the Macedonian Bulgars were not allowed to join Bulgaria, or Macedonia given autonomy, provision would have to be made for the thousands of Bulgarians under Greece, Serbia and Rumania, whose lives were "intolerable". On the other hand, there were many thousands of Moslems in Thrace who could not "possibly live under Greece," especially after the shocking "brutality of Greek soldiers at Smyrna," although these Moslems (Pomaks) might get along well in Bulgaria. But if Bulgaria were to be saddled with a large indemnity, it would have to be given access to the Aegean Sea. Venizelos, under the assumption of moderation, was pushing a vast scheme of national and personal ambition in Greece. Professor Lybyer, who wrote the latter part of the message, warned that the Greek Prime Minister would "utterly spoil" the "possibility of decent settlement" in both the Balkans and Asia Minor, if allowed to have his way. The Greeks could not maintain themselves unassisted either in Bulgarian Thrace or in Western Asia Minor, and the League of Nations should not be burdened with enforcing and maintaining "unjust and unnatural arrangements."[2]

[1] King and Lybyer *Diaries*, July 24-28, 1919. On Monday, July 28, King and Crane called on General Franchey d'Esperey, and in the afternoon the Commissioners, with Montgomery and Yale, interviewed the Grand Vizier.
[2] Lybyer Papers: Charles R. Crane to Woodrow Wilson, Constantinople, July 29, 1919. There was, of course, great difficulty in making any headway on the Thracian issue. See for example, *PPC*, XI, 609-611, 634-635, 670-673.

The Turkish Interviews

By July 29 the members of the King-Crane Commission had "ceased to think of going to Mesopotamia," were already hard at work preparing their report, and two days later were immersed in a series of long interviews with Turkish leaders in Constantinople.[1] In Palestine and Syria it had been possible to make investigations on the ground and to travel over the countryside in order to obtain the desired information. This was not possible in the case of Anatolia, as Captain Brodie wrote sometime later:[2]

In northern Turkey limitation of time forbade such an extensive tour of the country as had been possible in Palestine and Syria. The Americans were forced to adopt the oriental policy of having the mountain come to Mohammed. Delegations representing all sections of Anatolia and Armenia appeared before the Commission at Constantinople, and the results were virtually the same. All shades and varieties of opinion in the Turkish Empire were presented to the Americans from all classes and conditions of mankind.

There were other reasons for the type of investigation conducted in Constantinople. Since Syria and Palestine were already virtually separated from the Ottoman Empire, it seemed feasible to "go from community to community to seek the desires of the peoples concerning a mandate." But these conditions did not apply to Asia Minor. In the case of the projected state of Armenia, the territory had not been set off and the boundaries were not determined. The wishes of the Armenians as to a mandatory were not known. Moreover, the desires of other peoples could not be taken "primarily into account," since the establishment of an Armenian State would be a kind of punishment for the Turks, to be "accepted only as a necessity." If a new Constantinopolitan State were to be created, similar difficulties would be confronted, because the primary concern in such a state was a worldwide, not a local interest. But even in those portions of Asia Minor which were to remain Turkish, an investigation like the one in Syria was not practical because the Peace Conference had not yet decided whether Turkey was to be placed under a mandatory. It was, therefore, largely within the choice of Turkey whether it would "have a mandatory at all." In any event, Turkey had long been an independent country—as the Ottoman Empire—and a mandate would have to be modified accordingly. But even if such an investigation concerning the choice of a mandatory were practical, it would have been difficult to get "trustworthy results," because Constantinople was "not free to express itself," thanks to political pressure and censorship of the press.[3] Since it was not clear whether the United

---

[1] Lybyer *Diary*, July 29, 1919.
[2] Brodie Papers: This is from an unpublished *Memorandum on the King-Crane Commission*, 31 pp., prepared by Captain Donald M. Brodie late in 1919 or early in 1920.
[3] For instance, an American Intelligence Report in the Bristol

States would assume a mandate, there was fear of punishment from some other Power which might do so. In view of conditions in Anatolia little might be gained from further inquiry in other parts of the Empire, "in addition to the frequent reports by various investigators" to which the Commission already had access. The Commissioners, therefore, accelerated their report, because the essential facts seemed to be readily at hand. The method chosen was as follows:[1]

> To build, first of all, on our two months' study in Paris of the Turkish problems in the course of which we used the reports and other material of the Western Asia division of the American experts, and had many conferences with experts there, and with able authorities coming direct from Turkey; to take full advantage of all the general work done in the survey of Syria, as part of the former Turkish Empire, with its fundamentally similar problems and its incidental sidelights; especially to see as many representative groups and individuals as possible in Constantinople, and so to get reports on all phases of our inquiry, and from all parts of Asia Minor; to supplement the information so received with reports, for recent months, of the American Embassy and Consular Offices (through the kind co-operation of Admiral Bristol and Commissioner Ravndal); and to supplement still further with reports of personal investigations by American Missionaries, knowing the country thoroughly, and by representatives of the American Commission on Relief in the Near East, and of American business corporations.... To test our conclusions, expert advice at all possible points was also sought from American and other leaders—many of them personally known by members of the Commission. The report of the Commissioners is based on the whole of the resulting evidence.

Some Turkish Views of the Armenian Problem

Among the first to be interviewed were representative Turkish leaders and groups, beginning on July 31. Dr. King and Mr. Crane startled them all with a discussion of the Armenian question, and Dr. King read the instructions "about severing Armenia completely from Turkey."[2] Earliest to appear were Jami Bey and Kemal Bey, who represented the *National Liberal Party (Milli Ahrar)* and the *Committee for the Protection of Smyrna*. In contrast to the program of the Unionists, Jami Bey and Kemal Bey explained that their program involved a minimalist plan "in the direction of nationalism." They did not believe that Turkey could recover alone, and had, therefore, accepted the principle of "foreign assistance"

Despatches (King Papers), Confidential 3459-19, May 27, 1919, declared that "the censorship of newspapers in the capital of Turkey is severe, arbitrary and partisan.... There is no representative of this command on the Allied board of censors.... The writer has been told... that certain members of the censorship board had declared that they 'would refuse to publish the American news service *as a matter of principle.*' ... The opposition to American propaganda is believed to be exercised chiefly by French representatives...."

[1] *PPC*, XII, 803-804; King *Diary*, July 31, 1919.
[2] The text of interviews in Lybyer Papers. The interviews began at 10 a.m. in the morning in the American Embassy and did not end until 5 p.m.

even before the arrival of the Commission. They did not wish to preserve the traditional Ottoman Empire, but did insist on preserving the national existence of Turkey according to Wilsonian principles in the regions where the Turkish people were in the majority. Socially, they desired "renovation according to Anglo-Saxon culture and education" and they wanted "assurance of non-separation of blocks of territory" under a mandate. But they had no program concerning the Armenians, except that they recognized the rights of nationalities and had accepted the establishment of Armenia in principle, to be applied where the Armenians were in a majority. But "the government of the majority by a minority would never insure peace in the Near East," and, if the Armenians were given all they asked, no Turkish state would be left. The Turks declared that if the decision to establish an Armenian mandate had already been made, there was no need for discussion, but they pointed out that the people were mixed in with a Turkish majority, and would be "happier if kept together." Jami Bey desired to find a disinterested power which would assist in reform, prevent foreign intrigues, and form a new Turkish government. Dr. King pointed out that Armenia would then be placed under the Turks and that this was not allowable after all that had happened —a definite program was needed for restoring land and property to the Armenians. The Turkish group replied that those who had been guilty of the massacres should be punished, although in some instances, at least, the Armenians were "just as guilty as the Turks in the wrongs that were done." In the Turkish view, there were places in Van and part of Bitlis, with an Armenian majority, which might be added to Russian Armenia. The Turkish Government, however, was not in a position to restore the Armenians, because the Turkish people were also dying of hunger. The *Milli Ahrar* did not defend what the Government had done or not done, but had accepted the independence of every nationality where it was in a majority. In conclusion, Mr. Crane declared that it was very important for the Turks themselves "that an area should be set aside" into which the Armenians could drift. Dr. King pointed out that the Commissioners could not conscientiously urge the American people to accept a mandate unless they could say that the Turkish people were "now ready to treat the Armenians justly."

The former Minister of the Interior, Mustapha Arif Bey, of the *Peace and Safety Party*, accepted the Wilsonian principle of self-determination, although he could think of no place within Ottoman territory where the Armenians were in a majority. He welcomed any solution which would "guarantee the rights of all," but could not accept "a solution which would guarantee the rights of Turks and Kurds under an Armenian minority." Mustapha Arif Bey urged a plebiscite in the eastern vilayets, since his party could not decide the question. Ahmed Emin Bey [Yalman], the Editor-in-Chief of *Vakit*, who had studied for the Doctorate of Philosophy at Columbia University, told the Commission that the atrocities which had been committed against the Armenians had come from the military and coercive type of government in the Ottoman Empire, and he did not consider it reasonable for the Armenians to remain Turkish subjects. The Armenians, in his view, should be given territory proportionate to their pre-war numbers, although it would be unwise "to give them so much territory containing Turkish and Kurdish majorities" that they could not "govern at all," for that "would condemn them to extermination". Populations could be exchanged with the Greeks, but the Turks should keep enough land "to live up to a minimum standard." The Peace Conference, according to Ahmed Emin, had displayed no recognition of the Turks who were tolerant, and the plea of the Indian Moslems in behalf of the Turks had been unfortunate and might lead to intrigues.[1]

Late in the morning, Zeinel Abeddin Irfani Bey, Safadin, former Governor of Scutari, and Dr. Essad Halil, representing the *Entente Libérale*, expressed their hope that the Wilsonian principles would be applied justly to the Turkish situation. But they were not prepared to talk about the Armenian problem, even if their program called for "a good understanding between the different nationalities." Dr. King declared that it was not the idea of the Commission

> to set apart an area in which a minority of Armenians shall rule a majority of Turks. All other problems of the Turkish Empire are obscured by this, which must be cleared up. The most practical things for the Turks to do now are to restore property and land, and women and children . . . .

The group had been opposed to the Committee of Union and Progress, were now opposed to the government, and had "profound confidence in the friendship and sincerity of the American people and the Commission."

Similarly, Ali Kemal Bey, a journalist, spoke of the danger of establishing an Armenian state because of the Moslem majorities, and urged establishment of a single mandatory control. He noted that many Armenians accepted the idea of a single mandate and pointed out that the Turks and Armenians had lived together so long that they were now complementary, and "to separate them would be like separating the nail from the flesh." Given economic improvement there would never be another massacre: "It should be remembered that aside from the massacres, ill-treatment by the Turkish Government was the same to the Armenians and the Turks."

When Ahmed Riza Bey, President, and Mahmud Pasha, Nabi Bey and Reshid Saadi Bey, of the *Ottoman League of National Unity*, appeared,

---

[1] Dr. Ahmed Emin Bey [Yalman] appeared again on August 13. He was the author of *The Development of Modern Turkey, as Measured by Its Press* (New York, Columbia, 1914) and later was to write *Turkey in The World War* (New Haven, Yale, 1931), 310 pp.

Mr. Crane stressed the two problems of Armenia and the Straits, emphasizing that they were "more important for Turkey than for the Commission." Like the other groups, the Ottoman League of National Unity proclaimed its support for the Wilsonian principles, and Ahmed Riza Bey contended that establishment of a separate Armenia would contravene them, and asked for an American mandate. Moreover, he believed that the United States should not leave Turkey until it was certain there would be no recurrence of massacres, and asked for the genuine application of Wilson's Twelfth Point to Turkey.[1]

Representatives of the *Milli* [*National*] *Congress* protested strongly against the accusation that "the Turkish administration was the same which oppressed and persecuted subject races," and declared that the world had not yet learned the truth about the Armenian massacres. It was true, they said, that there had been massacres, but they "were all in the nature of reprisals, and more Turkish lives than Armenians were sacrificed in this feud." The Committee of Union and Progress, not the Turkish nation, had been responsible for the Armenian deportations. Mr. Crane thought it better to have a region to which the Armenians could go, but was told:

> We certainly want the Armenian question to disappear from our lives, but what you suggest is not a fair solution: that we sacrifice a part of our country to be given over to the Armenians. In the six Armenian vilayets the Armenians have not been in the majority since Selim conquered them, more than 600 years ago. We are willing to make a sacrifice of territory on the border of our state to be added to Russian Armenia. The six vilayets are much more Turkish than Alsace-Lorraine is French. They were our very flesh. The Armenians are already enjoying facilities of development and have enjoyed it throughout every century. Do you mean . . . that the Armenians in the rest of the Empire should be removed to the next area or not? If the Armenians in the rest of the Empire are to go to the new State, very well; otherwise the scheme is not practicable. If they cannot live with the Turks then they should be completely separated.

The *Milli* delegation thanked the Commission for coming to Constantinople in order "to find an impartial solution" for difficult problems, for it had not "found an impartial feeling among any Europeans."

The Plea for Turkish Unity

Halidé Edib Hanum,[2] the distinguished Turkish writer, who had already contributed much to her country, served as the interpreter for the

[1] Lybyer *Diary*, July 31, 1919. Ahmed Riza's group was interviewed again on August 13.
[2] Halidé Edib was the first Moslem woman graduate of the Constantinople Women's College. In the *King Papers* there is a letter of the Thracian Committee, signed by Faik Bey, M. Jelal, and H. Tahsin Kassim, asking for "the creation of a buffer state out of Thrace, extending to the river Struma." Nedim Bey, Suleiman Nazif Bey, Ismail Hakki and Sakim Bey represented the Committee for the Protection of the Six Oriental Vilayets.

next two groups which came to consult with the Americans. The first of these was the *Committee for the Protection of Thrace*, represented by Faik Bey, the former deputy for Adrianople, who asked for the restoration of Thrace to Turkey. If the Peace Conference refused, the Committee wanted an independent Thracian area, "within its historical boundaries." Under no condition did the Committee accept either Greek or Bulgarian domination, although it was confident that the Greeks and Bulgarians would be happy if the region were restored to Turkey. Mme. Edib also served as interpreter for the *Committee for the Protection of the Six Oriental Vilayets*, which was anxious for a settlement of the Armenian problem, and noted the ethnic admixture in that area. A British or American mandate offered the possibility of a solution, but what would be "the good of a mandatory except that it should solve the problem of race hatred?"

Halidé Edib, who had met Mr. Crane when he attended the Commencement exercises at Constantinople Women's College in the spring of 1919, has described her own appearance before the Commission:[1]

> ... The Thracian representatives asked me to take them to the Commission and interpret for them. It was not pleasant. I felt as if everything had come to an end as I walked up the stairs of the American Embassy. Anatolia had some chance, now that the movement was becoming stronger; but these peoples, thrown amid hostile races and cut off from the mother country, were absolutely helpless.
>
> There it was—the Commission: where we used to take our social tea with friendly Mrs. Bristol. There they sat. Any man sitting at a big table with a green cover is imposing, and there were five of them, all looking ominous. It made me feel bewildered and hurt to be obliged to defend national rights before an embassy.

After translating for the Thracian group, Halidé Edib acted in that capacity for Suleiman Nazif, who

> stated the case, which of course was self-evident—namely that as the Turks were in an incontestable majority in Eastern Anatolia, it was impossible to establish an Armenia there. Things went smoothly until one member of the Commission mentioned the word "massacres". This immediately set Suleiman Nazif Bey on the high horse. He poured forth an eloquent and just view of the case—how the massacre was two-sided, and if they would condemn the Turks they must also condemn the Armenians. It sounded almost like what President Wilson said on September 27, 1918, in New York: "The impartial justice meted out must involve no discrimination between those to whom we wish to be just. It must be a justice that knows no favorites and knows no standards but equal rights of the several peoples concerned."

---

[1] Halidé EDIB, *The Turkish Ordeal* (New York, Century, 1928), 58-61. Suleiman Nazif Bey, son of Said Pasha of Diarbekir, with his father and whole family, held a high place in Turkish literature. He was a first cousin of Ziya Gökalp, but his own place in Turkish thought and literature was probably as great. In March 1920 he was deported to the island of Malta by the British. See especially Edmond SAUSSEY, *Prosateurs turcs contemporains. Extraits choisis* (Paris, Boccard, 1935), 85-95.

MANDATE OR INDEPENDENCE

The interview was extremely painful to me. I was very much aware of the somewhat unsympathetic attitude of the Commission at my left, sitting at an enormous table, and of the four Turks in black on my right with fixed and tragic faces, while in the middle of the room on a single chair I sat like an interpreter (and perhaps like a lawyer too) defending the case of Eastern Anatolia.... As we walked out of the room it seemed to me that Suleiman Nazif Bey's face was ashy pale. He smiled at my inquiring face and said, "If it had not been for the Moslem-like understanding and benevolence of that old man's face in the middle, I could not have borne it." "The Moslem-like understanding face" belonged to Mr. Crane. I was rather subdued by the pathetic sorrow of Suleiman Nazif Bey's face: he is accustomed to express his passions very forcibly. We separated at the door....

In his unofficial capacity, Mr. Crane was very friendly to the Turks, while "Mr. King seemed a very cool-headed man with an impartial view." Above all, however, "the presence of Professor Albert H. Lybyer was a very fortunate thing for future historians. For Professor Albert H. Lybyer and Professor Arnold J. Toynbee are the two most dependable and fairminded writers on the impossibly difficult tangle of the Near East." Later on, Mme. Edib became well acquainted with the members of the Commission.[1]

On August 1 two interesting petitions were submitted to the Americans, the first from some Turkish women [2] asking for a "constructive power" which would bring a lasting peace to the Near East—the United States of America. The petition asked for preservation of "the unity of the Turkish lands and the evacuation of Smyrna, Adana and Konia" and protested against "the separation of Constantinople from Turkish lands," because that city was "the heart and the brain of the Turkish nation." The women were sure that an Armenian state would never bring tranquillity and prosperity either for the Armenians or the Turks, but would be "the cause of many troubles." Hope centered on the United States, a humanitarian nation which respected the ideals of other peoples and could put out the "perpetual fire" in the Near East.

According to a second memorandum, of similar import, the Turkish people accepted the "material and moral assistance" of a foreign power as a necessity, but insisted that the assistance should be "exercised over

---

[1] See the King and Lybyer *Diaries*, August 9, 1919. Mme. Edib took Dr. King and Mr. Crane to the Old Seraglio on August 9. In his *Memorandum* Brodie notes among the luncheons and receptions, "an evening reception given by a Turkish lady which was quite a departure from the traditional seclusion of Turkish women. The lady was Halidé Hanum, that brilliant and talented leader whose writings and speeches are exceedingly influential in Turkey today."

[2] King Papers: This is the original and translation of the document: *Petition of Turkish Women to Commission.* There is no indication as to authorship. See also S. B. Sureyar to A. H. Lybyer, August 1, 1919 (Lybyer Papers), asking for an interview, and Lybyer reply on August 5, 1919.

the whole Turkish Empire" and should endure not less than fifteen or more than twenty-five years. It should be confined to the administrative and economic fields. Otherwise the Turkish state was to be independent both in internal and foreign policy and to have the right of diplomatic representation. The Ottoman Constitution of 1876 was to remain in force. Specialists appointed by the assisting nation were to occupy high positions in the administration according to their specialty, and their decisions were to be "absolutely and fully executory." To assure unity in the administration as well as the supremacy of "foreign competence in every matter," no Minister was to interfere, "but only to sanction *pro forma* the decision of the expert." The rights of the Sultan as Caliph and Sovereign were to be fully maintained. The liberty of the press was not to be "restricted under any pretext whatsoever." In case the assisting Power infringed on the letter or spirit of the convention, the Sublime Porte was to have the "right of recourse to the League of Nations." During the period of assistance Turkey was "to be placed under the régime of neutrality." In view of the close bonds and interests between the Turkish and Arabic vilayets, "the same form of assistance by the same Power" should be extended to the latter. Finally, the memorandum urged guarantees for the minorities within Turkey similar to those which had been adopted in the case of the Turks in Bulgaria and Greece and of the Jews of Poland and Rumania.[1]

The long statement of *The Ottoman Press Association*, presented on August 3 by Velid Eleuzzia, greeted the American inquiry with satisfaction.[2] In view of the censorship and other difficulties, the Press Association gladly seized the opportunity "to submit some of its views on national problems to the attention of the Peace Conference." It was in agreement with the Wilsonian principles, and recognized "the right of every population, both victorious and defeated, to decide its own destinies." Ottoman history was

> full of striking examples of religious and racial tolerance. With the exception, to some extent, of the Romans in the pre-Christian period, the Turks, as well as the Arabs, are the first people in history who not only tolerated foreign religions, but also granted the adherents of these religions a full chance of development and the right of autonomous community organization.

---

[1] Lybyer Papers: Turkish Statement, August 1, 1919. There is a remarkable similarity with the principles of the Ottoman League of National Unity discussed above. This document was apparently accepted "by all the political parties in Constantinople" and later communicated to Mustapha Kemal. See Mustapha KEMAL, *Speech*, October 15-20, 1927. Official translation. (Leipzig, K. F. Koehler, 1929), 87-88.

[2] King Papers: *Memorandum Presented to the American Commission of Inquiry by the Ottoman Press Association* (Original), 7 pp. Presented on August 3, the Memorandum is dated from Constantinople, July 28, 1919.

That tolerance in Europe had been known "only during the last century." Foreign intrigue had brought about the change in racial relations, primarily between Turks and Armenians. The Turks accepted international guarantees of minority rights, provided Turkish independence and territory were recognized in accordance with the Wilsonian principles. Outside the Arabic-speaking parts of the country, however, there was no Turkish district where the Turks were not in an absolute majority. Nowhere could Greeks or Armenians "claim a majority which might justify a separate administration for the district involved." And the Greek occupation of Smyrna and Aidin, with its attendant murder, pillage, burning of towns and villages, and the attacking of women, was a distinct violation of Turkish rights. It was hoped that the United States and the world would not permit the Greeks to retain territory under a spurious application of Wilson's principles. The Press Association begged the Commission "to do everything possible" to put "a speedy end to the Greek horrors."

The Press Association could not overlook the occupation of essentially Turkish territory like Adana, Adalia and Thrace, and declared that the Turks would actively oppose such infractions of their territorial rights. A partition of the Arab lands would also be contrary to the principles which the American people had "made the basis of a better future." The Press Association maintained, too, that "any division of Turkey into spheres of influence would constitute the beginning of an annexation" and hoped that the United States would "prevent such an injustice" which would not be acceptable in Turkey. While it opposed any exceptional measures for non-Turkish elements, it favored protection of minorities. The Turkish capacity for education and good government was emphasized. Despite intrigues and obstacles "which would have crushed many a nation," the Turks had succeeded not only in maintaining their existence, but had demonstrated a capacity for adaptation "to the new ways of doing things." With assistance, with "friendly guidance and help, instead of paralyzing intrigues," the Turks could once more prove their constructive qualities.

Within the next several days Greek, Armenian and other delegations appeared, and on August 6, the Turkish Social Democratic Party, founded on Wilsonian principles and representing some eight to ten thousand people, in full harmony "with the democratic principles of all Islam," presented a statement. The party had taken no thought of the Armenian problem, since the idea of Turkish sovereignty over Turkish lands seemed "to cover the question." But the Armenian problem did offer difficulties, and while the party was willing to accept an independent Armenia, it wished the Peace Conference "to consider whether a large Armenia might not become so strong as to be a danger to Turkey."[1]

[1] The Social Democratic Party was represented by a lawyer, Isaac Mouammu, and a commission agent, Zeki Bey. Lybyer noted in his *Diary*

Some Representatives of the Eastern Vilayets

The interviews with Moslem or Turkish delegations were essentially closed by August 13. Among the last to appear were representatives of the Kurdish Democratic Party [1] who called for the establishment of a Kurdish government in those districts where the Kurds were in a "great majority," although curiously enough, these were substantially the very regions in which the Armenians claimed a majority, while the actual majority appears to have been Turkish. The Kurdish group claimed Harput, Diarbekir, Van, Bitlis, a part of Erzerum (Bayazid), and all of Mosul, together with an outlet on the sea. In general the party followed the program of General Sherif Pasha. The Assyrians, it was said, were not entitled to a separate territory because they were "nowhere in the majority." On the other hand the Kurds themselves desired autonomy "under a British mandate as part of Iraq." They did not want any political relations with the Arabs, although they were all Moslems, because they considered themselves "more tied to the south than to the west." Neither did they wish to be connected with the Turks. Kurdistan was their own homeland. They were ready to recognize Armenia outside their own Kurdish territory, but not elsewhere. They were willing to exchange the Armenians in Kurdistan for the Kurds in Armenia, and wanted the restoration of the Kurdish refugees, since "the Turks only tried to make Turks out of them." Moreover, the Kurdish representatives denied the charges against their people relative to the Armenian massacres.

On August 12 the Commission heard Jemal Pasha, the Prefect of Constantinople, who pointed out the need either for a British or an American mandate and favored a decentralized administrative system to meet local conditions. Shefik Bey of Bayazid and Riza Bey, the former governor of Erzerum, testified concerning the problems of the Eastern vilayets, and told the Commission that, out of a pre-war population of 125,000 in Bayazid only 13,000 were Armenians, and of some 500 villages, only 40 were Armenian. Most of the Armenians, they said, were in the Erivan region, while only 30,000, out of a population of 370,000 in the vilayet of Van, were Armenians. If this territory were added to Armenia, the Turkish population would have to be evacuated. Both Armenians and

---

on August 6 that Crane was "averse to further travel—wishes to go to Paris soon. King no longer talks of going to Mesopotamia—doubtful about interior of Asia Minor." There was talk of returning to Paris, but the American Commissioners in Paris noted on August 6: "In view of the fact that this mission had been appointed by the President for a particular purpose, the Commissioners [Polk, White, Bliss] considered that it was inadvisable to instruct them to return, and that they should be permitted to complete their work" (*PPC*, XI, 358).

[1] These were Nejmuddin Bey, Hussein Bey, and Aziz Baban Bey. Their expressed desire for a British mandate and to be part of Iraq is interesting in view of the British claims to the Kurdish regions. See HOWARD, *The Partition of Turkey*, Chs. VIII-IX.

Turks had been responsible for massacres in the past, and the two Turkish spokesmen, who noted the opposition of the Erzerum Congress of July 23 to separation of the Eastern Vilayets, spoke on behalf of a British or American mandate, and recommended that the Commission investigate the problem.[1]

A former deputy of Van, Munir Effendi, and Teha Effendi, from Hakkiari, explained that before the war there were some 150,000 people in Hakkiari, 90 per cent Moslem, but the ethnic mixture was so general and thorough that it was difficult to distinguish among Turks, Arabs and Kurds. In Van they estimated the population from 130,000 to 150,000, about 30 per cent being Armenians. The people were said to want educational, administrative and financial assistance, but not separation from Turkey. The former governor of Bitlis, Mazhar Bey, an Albanian who had been in Bitlis during 1913-1914, estimated the population of the district at about 450,000 to 500,000, of whom 75,000 to 100,000 were Armenians. The rest were Kurds, except the Turks in the city of Bitlis, the Kaza of Achlat, and the city of Mush. The city of Sert was Arabic, while the Kaza of Samsun contained many Turkified Arabs. There was general agreement with these views among others present, and a feeling that the United States should assume a mandate, despite some skepticism that under an arrangement of this kind, independence would be lost.

Sheikh Riza Effendi, of Kirkuk, and Baban Zadeh Hikimet, of Suleimania, from the Kurdish-Turkish districts near the vilayet of Mosul, declared that the people in those areas desired to be attached to the Ottoman Empire and that establishment of an Armenian state would prove disastrous, since the Armenians did not constitute more than 15 per cent of the population. Professor Shemseddin Bey, of the University of Constantinople, who spoke on behalf of the Eastern Vilayets, since he was from Harput, was primarily interested in the problem of independence or mandate. He insisted that "the divergencies of races and the dissension" had been "the result of European intervention." While no one would refuse "reform and such assistance as would mean the living together of different races in peace," the Turks wanted only American assistance.

Mustapha Zia, a former deputy in the Ottoman Parliament from Sivas, also discussed the situation in the eastern vilayets, declared that the Christians constituted only about 20 per cent of the population, and asserted that the Turks had always lived on friendly terms with the Armenians, although external influences had disturbed these relations during the past twenty-five years. He favored a mandate only if it did not infringe upon Turkish independence, and declared that the people

---

[1] Mr. Crane must have been impressed with the general tenor of this testimony, for he sent Mr. Louis Edgar Browne, of *The Chicago Daily News*, to Sivas to study the Anatolian point of view. See Browne's despatches in *The Chicago Daily News*, August 8, 11, 1919.

of Sivas would be shocked if President Wilson's Twelfth Point were not to be applied, and "if a majority should be put under a minority." Jelal Bey, former governor-general of Erzerum (1908-1910), regarded the Armenian problem as most important, but did not believe Turkish and Armenian interests necessarily antagonistic. He urged that the United States assume a mandate for the entire country, and was convinced that all the people could live there in peace.[1]

Closure of the Turkish Case

Ahmed Riza Bey, President of the Ottoman League of National Unity, and Ahmed Emin Bey [Yalman] appeared once more on August 13 to close the case of the Turks.[2] Ahmed Riza Bey presented three documents to the Commission, the first of which affirmed the desire of the League for the "happiness, prosperity and the free development of the Armenians," but held that the aggrandizement of Armenia, in view of the Turkish minorities, was impossible. Moreover, if a great Armenia were created, "with the assistance of a powerful army," bloody struggles would occur and lead "fatally to the complete ruin of the country." Only an integral application of the Wilsonian principles could solve either the Armenian or the Turkish problem. Again, the partition of Turkey under different mandates or zones of influence would be "a flagrant injustice in regard to the sovereign rights and the existence of the Turks." If such an imperialistic policy were to be pursued "it would create in Asia Minor a new Macedonia and peace and tranquillity would be compromised." Therefore the League demanded the abrogation of the secret treaties relative to the Ottoman Empire and the application of the Wilson ideals. Moreover,

> if the United States of America would decide to assist and guide us in the application of reforms in Asiatic Turkey, including Constantinople and Thrace, within the conditions laid down in our second

---

[1] In his *Diary*, Lybyer noted a talk with Raouf, editor of *Istiklal*, on August 11, and Lutfi Bey, former first chamberlain. Both men wanted an American mandate, and spoke of British and French intrigues against the idea. Raouf's paper had been stopped recently, supposedly for supporting an American mandate. Lybyer talked with Crane on August 12 about going into the interior. He noted that the representatives from the eastern vilayets were "good arguers". Montgomery was opposed to "going to interior without King or Crane. Crane doesn't want to go." A communiqué received on August 12 spoke of General Harbord coming to Armenia.

[2] See Lybyer *Diary*, August 13, 1919. Ahmed Riza Bey, Ahmed Emin, and the city prefect appeared, the first two asking directly for "an American mandate over Turkey; the last indicated that help is needed." The three documents presented by Ahmed Riza Bey included: 1) A statement on the Armenian Problem; 2) Memorandum on Problem of the Mandate; and 3) List of members of the League for Unity. The Memoranda are in the Lybyer and Brodie Papers.

memorandum and for a limited period, public opinion both in America and in Europe could rest at ease concerning the fate of the Armenians.

From the point of view of the League the most logical and practical solution of the Armenian problem was the following:

> Aggrandizement of the Republic of Armenia, already formed in the Caucasus, in the direction of Ardahan and Kars. The Moslem populations of these territories could, within a reasonable period, move to provinces under Ottoman sovereignty. The Armenians, inhabitants of Turkish vilayets who emigrated to the Caucasus or other countries, could be settled on the territories which had been abandoned by the Moslems. If the Republic of Armenia thus increased were not sufficient for settlement of the Armenian émigrés a portion of the territory could be accorded under the form of a frontier rectification to the Republic of Armenia, provided this cession were accepted by the Ottoman Parliament. The Port of Batum could be transformed into a free port so that all the Republics constituted in the Caucasus could make use of it.

But what of the solution for the problem of the future Turkish state? The second memorandum declared that the successive occupations of Ottoman territory, and the sad events in Smyrna had proved that the Entente Powers were merely pursuing old ambitions under the cover of Wilson idealism. Under the mandate principle, they were proceeding toward the partition of the Ottoman Empire. The Turkish nation, on the other hand, could only take its stand on the basis of "the integral application of the principles of Mr. Wilson" which had been "unanimously recognized" as the basis for the conclusion of peace.[1] The memorandum concluded that the application of these principles would safeguard the Turkish nation:

> But we must not dissimulate that our administrative machinery needs a great transformation. In order to realize and to assure our free development, and at the same time, peace among the different elements, we need a guide. After serious reflection we have concluded that the assistance of the United States of America will have happy results for our future. We now solicit this assistance, for a limited period and under the following conditions, for the entire Ottoman Empire:
>
> 1. The integral application in all Turkey of the Wilsonian principles, unanimously recognized by the belligerent powers.
> 2. The complete evacuation of the Ottoman territories, occupied contrary to Article XII of the Wilsonian principles, and their reinstatement under the direct administration of Turkey.
> 3. The maintenance of the constitutional regime and the conservation of the sovereign rights of His Majesty the Sultan.
> 4. Free exercise of religion and instruction.

---

[1] Although it accepted the Wilson principles, the British Government did not consider itself legally bound to do so in the Near East.

5. The preparation of a project of reforms and reparations, taking note of local necessities and proceeding everywhere and without favoritism to their application.
6. The right to keep diplomatic and consular representation.
7. Abrogation of the secret treaties relative to Turkey and the non-application, under any form whatsoever, of the capitulations.

We hope that the United States of America which has participated in the general war, with a purely humanitarian aim, will grant our request and will thus render new services to humanity in assuring the peace in the Near East.

The third memorandum was that of Ahmed Emin Bey [Yalman], whose views were essentially similar to those of the Ottoman League of National Unity.[1] Ahmed Emin insisted that "any radical settlement of the Near Eastern question" would have to take account of a number of fundamentals. First, any artificial settlement, not founded on the Wilson principles or the ethical aims of the League of Nations, would merely lead to a new conflict and the "continuation of the old chaos in a new form." Second, the Near East was "sick of agitators and intrigues"—the primary desire of the people was for good and honest government. They had, however, intellectual groups which did not

> take a good and honest government to mean only justice, good roads, and better economical opportunities, as some of the colonial powers would think to be the highest standard of good government for an alien population. The idea of good government must include a good preparation for citizenship in the form of universal education, good sanitary conditions, a struggle for social betterment and a rising standard of living.

Third, the Turkish people were "the helpless victims of bad conditions and circumstances," and the settlement ought to improve their lot. But fourth, the Near Eastern peoples were

> under pressure of a large social and economic deficit, of mutual religious and racial hatred, of a deficient general equipment for the modern life, and all sorts of foreign intrigues. Left to themselves, they would not be able, although no fair-minded man can contest their capacity and educability, to produce modern government and the best type of leaders. The product of the existing conditions will always be a militaristic and aggressive government and a survival of the unfit.

Finally, good government in Turkey could not be based on solid foundations unless minority rights in the Balkan States, especially in Macedonia, were fully secured.

---

[1] King Papers: Ahmed Emin Bey [Yalman], Memorandum Presented to the American Section of the International Commission for Mandates in the Near East. Typed. 7 pp. See also Ahmed Emin YALMAN, *Turkey in My Time* (Norman, University of Oklahoma Press, 1956), *passim*.

Ahmed Emin believed that if there were a genuine League of Nations, its first duty would be "to establish the principle of universal education for all nations." Every nation which did not fulfil certain minimum requirements "would have to submit itself to some outside help and training." Unfortunately, however, there was no present possibility of applying the principle of universal education in an unprejudiced manner:

> Under these circumstances a mandate of the League of Nations could not have any sincere meaning, as far as Turkey is concerned. As a matter of fact, the question of a single mandate for Turkey for the good of the population itself, has not even been raised at Paris. There is only a talk of several mandates, which would only serve to disguise the annexations of imperialistic powers and would mean a partition and exploitation for the benefit of aliens. In both cases the principle of mandate is not acceptable for the people of Turkey.

Nevertheless, the Turks needed some assistance and were ready to submit to "regular schooling, instead of making new hazardous experiments with new ignorant leaders." Such leaders "would make ignorant attempts under the pretence of saving the country and would, in reality, waste energy, create conflicts, and exterminate people with a critical mind."

There was no unanimity among Turkish groups regarding the future. The large majority realized that the choice was between an American mandate and chaos, "coupled with foreign occupation and the loss of national unity." A minority desired a British solution, but it was largely composed of elements which did not enjoy popular respect and who hoped that a British mandate "would give them opportunity to fish in troubled waters." Another group wanted no settlement implying a "theoretical restriction of the sovereignty." One of the chief supporters of an American mandate was the socalled National [Milli] Congress, formed in Constantinople by the delegations of fifty-three different Turkish organizations. Since "all the Turkish intellectual" groups were represented in the Congress, it could be considered as typical of the educated classes. The Ottoman League of National Unity, with about forty most respected statesmen and a majority of the Ottoman Senate, was similarly disposed. But many other statesmen and diplomats, who did not belong officially to the League, also approved an American mandate, as did, in general, the Anatolian Nationalists, university professors and "most of the lawyers, teachers, technicians and merchants," leaving aside the press. [1]

---

[1] Ahmed Emin listed *Tasviri Efkiar, Vakit, Istiklal, Zeman, Aksham, Serveti-Funoun*, as "insistently for the American mandate." *Ifham, Ileri, Tirmindji, Asr, Memleket* and *Yeni Gazetta* took the same view, with reservations regarding independence. *Sabah, Ikdam* and *Peyam* were neutral, although the editor of the latter was a founder of the Wilsonian League. Only the *Alemdar* and *Turkdje Stamboul*, which had no circulation and made a "living on blackmail", were openly supporting a British mandate.

This situation was somewhat strange in view of the intimidation, bribery and pressure and the lack of American propaganda. In the press, for example, there was "perfect freedom to speak for England, though every discussion of the American side" was restricted. Those who wanted an American mandate were insisting on it as "the only means to secure good government and a good chance of development for the people, and a real and lasting peace for the Near East."

But what of the difficulties in American acceptance of a mandate?
... The Americans would not have so much difficulty.... A military occupation will hardly be necessary. A native gendarmerie and police under American management would be sufficient to secure public order. A body of experts with executive power for every department of state, including those to be created to perform new functions of State, with a small body of leaders to guide the whole work of reform, would be sufficient to reorganize, reform and run things. Good leadership is all that Turkey needs. The Americans would find here very brave, attentive, and capable pupils, and a very fertile field of action to work on. As soon as they are there, foreign intrigues would lose every importance. The strifes and conflicts among the different elements of population would cease. There is no opposition in the country against new ways of doing things. The opposition shown sometimes against so-called innovations was a very sane one, because these innovations were only imitations of external forms of European life, initiated by half educated men, at the expense of the social cohesion in the country.

The genuine success of the mandate, however, would depend on a radical solution of the ethnic problem. Enough territory would have to be given to the Armenian Republic to take in the refugees from the eastern Turkish provinces who now lived in the United States, and Turks living in the Armenian territories would have to be exchanged. Likewise, the Armenian Patriarchate in Constantinople would have to be transferred to Armenia. On the other hand, the Armenians living in Turkey would have the rights of equal citizenship if they chose to remain Turkish citizens. If they became citizens of Armenia, they would have all the rights accorded to foreigners. In any event, they could make a free choice of allegiance, for citizenship in the Near East at last should be given "a real and loyal meaning." The Arabs, too, "should be given opportunity to run their own affairs autonomously." The only effective solution "would be to extend to them the supervision of the same mandatory power." The Kurds, as well, should be trained for self-government in the regions in which they lived. On the other hand, the only workable solution for the Greeks on the coast was to exchange them "against the large Turkish population in Macedonia." [1] In conclusion, Ahmed Emin once more urged an American mandate:

[1] This was substantially the solution adopted at Lausanne in 1923. Ahmed Emin Bey states that "the basis of such an exchange was already reached in 1914 between the Turkish government and Mr. Venizelos, who was prime minister at that time. The deliberations in this respect had already resulted in a perfect agreement, and was partly carried out

If America assumes the responsibility of a mandate there will be a peaceful Turkey, interested in her own affairs. Such a Turkey would be a very important factor of peace and prosperity in the world. She would be able to bridge over the differences between two different worlds, prejudiced in a high degree against each other. If Americans do not assume the role of the mandatory, there would be eternal chaos and unrest in the Near East. The idea of a League of Nations would not make any progress. Turkey would be a dangerous source and field of agitation and intrigue for the pan-Islamistic and Asiatic idea. The Turks who have a very high degree of national consciousness would become in case of a partition or a division into zones of influence a very dangerous ally of all destructive tendencies which are sure to go on in the world in this or that form. Owing to the geographical, religious and racial factors, it is even in the interest of the imperialistic powers not to be shortsighted and not to give such a bad turn to the destinies of the Turks.

The Greek Interviews

Almost from the beginning of the Peace Conference, under the political leadership of Venizelos, Greece had advanced grandiose ambitions concerning the disposition of the Ottoman estate, with pretentions to Smyrna, Thrace, and even the city of Constantinople itself. The King-Crane Commission was fully aware of these dreams before arriving in the capital city of the old empire. Mr. King had had one interesting communication from the so-called American Association of the Greek Community of Chicago, an organization composed of American citizens of Hellenic descent,[1] which had heard that Constantinople might remain as the Ottoman capital and wrote that Greece was "the only logical claimant for Constantinople," since it was a Greek city. Under Greek control, it was asserted, "Constantinople would develop free speech, religious freedom, and guarantee life, liberty and property rights, irrespective of nationality or other affiliations." Moreover, Constantinople would become a free port and assure the neutrality of the Dardanelles.

The Greek population in Constantinople was very large and it was natural that distinguished representatives should state the Greek case before the King-Crane Commission. The first appeared on August 1, among them the Greek Patriarch of Constantinople, with Casanova, the

on both sides. This proves that Mr. Venizelos considered an exchange as the only possible radical settlement at the time, when he had not so vast imperialistic dreams." For a Jewish statement of Grand Rabbi Haim Nahoum Effendi expressing general sympathy for the Palestine Homeland and a desire for an independent Turkish Republic under an American or British mandate, or autonomy under Turkey, see *Chicago Daily News*, August 16, 1919.

[1] King Papers: Paul Demos, President, American Association of the Greek Community of Chicago, to President (Rev.) Henry Churchill King (Oberlin, Ohio), July 3, 1919.

Metropolitan of Kayseri (Caesarea), Caratheodoridi, the Metropolitan of Enos, and M. Haralambidis.[1] They declared that the first desire of the Greeks was that the Ottoman Greeks should be "once for all delivered from the Turkish yoke." All Greeks wanted to be united with the Kingdom of Greece, and if this were not possible, they desired "autonomy," and, if a Greek mandate proved out of the question, an American mandate was preferred. They neither claimed land where the Greeks were not in a majority, nor territory in the interior. Greeks and Turks, it was stated, had never got along well together even where the Greeks were no longer in a majority in such Byzantine centers as Konia, Ankara and Kayseri. Moreover, the Greeks had been deported from Thrace and the coastal region of Asia Minor during the war, and had died of "white massacres" in great numbers. The archbishop declared that one half of his diocese had been destroyed by the Bulgarians and the other by the Turks. Those who had survived lived "only with the hope of being united to Greece." The Greeks, he asserted, would take no part in the elections to the Turkish Parliament, and the whole coast was "truly Greek." If placed under a mandate, however, the people would always long to be united with Greece.

The Greek Smyrna Committee, with Metropolitan Erenaos at its head, adopted the Greek official position with regard to recent developments in that area, including the landing of Greek forces. Similarly, the Greek Thracian Commission presented the Greek claim for the retention of Thrace, which both the Turks and the Bulgarians also claimed, and asserted that the Turks had deported some 220,000 Greeks from that area. The Committee of the Pontus, from the Black Sea region, representing essentially "the old Empire of Pontus or Trebizond," asserted that, before the massacres, "there were only 50 to 60,000 Armenians, 840,000 Greeks, and 839,000 Mohammedans" in that area, and claimed that there were some 2,000,000 to 2,500,000 Greeks in Asia Minor as a whole, and about 8,000,000 Moslems, "by no means all Turks." While the other ethnic elements hated the Turks, the Greeks were "willing to forget everything and live peacefully *as rulers of the Turks*."

Other Greek delegations appeared on August 11 and 12. One, from Smyrna, explained the "chaotic" situation which had prevailed in that area, but indicated that the Greeks would need an army of 200,000 to hold the zone. A Greek lawyer from Constantinople, Mr. Bambahas, urged the removal of the Sultan from Constantinople, in accordance with the Allied and the American "point of view." All that was necessary to remove the Sultan was "to send Allied troops" to Constantinople. Mr. Bambahas declared that the United States "had saved the Occident"

---

[1] These interviews are from the Lybyer Papers. See also the King and Lybyer *Diaries*, August 1, 1919.

during the war, and it should "save the Orient by removing intrigues" from Constantinople.[1]

SOME OTHER CHRISTIAN GROUPS

The Greeks were not the only non-Turkish group to claim Thrace, for on August 11, a Bulgarian Commission, headed by Dr. Nicolov, the Archbishop of Veles, appeared before the American investigators.[2] The Bulgarians declared that their people desired for themselves and others the right to educational and religious privileges, in accord with President Wilson's principles, and added that there were then 6,000 Bulgarians living in Constantinople and some 12,000 in Thrace. If there had been no expulsions, however, there would now be more than 300,000 Bulgarians in Thrace, and it was asserted that the Bulgarian element was still in the majority in Macedonia.

From the internal and even eastern regions of Anatolia there were other groups. On August 11, some Georgian representatives came to describe conditions in the new Georgian Republic, whose independence had been declared on May 26, 1918, some time after the Bolshevik revolution. Among other things, the Georgians pointed out that they had inaugurated a confederation with the Russian Armenians, but the Turks "began to come up along with the Germans and the Azerbaijanis and caused the break-up of the confederation." All Christians, with few exceptions, the 200,000 to 300,000 Georgians needed financial and economic assistance, and hoped that the Great Powers would allow them to remain separate from Russia, since their customs and manners were different.

As early as August 6 the Chaldean Patriarch explained that the Assyro-Chaldean people were scattered in Turkey, Iran and the Caucasus, and had played a significant rôle against the Turks during the war, when some 250,000 had been killed. There were now some 600,000 in the Mosul vilayet, Diarbekir and Deir-ez-Zor, 100,000 in Iran, and about 650,000 in India. The Assyro-Chaldeans wanted to remain a separate nation, under the mandate of the Great Powers.[3]

---

[1] Mr. Bambahas presented a document which he had written to the British Secretary of State for India, Mr. Montague, on the subject of the unity of Turkey.
[2] These interviews are in the *Lybyer Papers*. See also the King and Lybyer *Diaries*, August 11, 1919.
[3] Brodie Papers: Conseil National Assyrien, Constantinople, August 20, 1919. To Hon. Charles R. Crane, Chairman, American Commission for Turkey, Constantinople. It was claimed that there were 2,000,000 Assyrians, one half of whom were in India. 350,000, it was said, were Maronites, living in Mt. Lebanon and Beirut. Of the remaining 650,000 there were 50,000 in Syria, Palestine, Egypt and North and South America, while 600,000 lived in compact masses in Asia Minor. Other Assyrian representatives appeared on August 12 and August 20.

The Armenian Problem

Among the Christian groups within the Ottoman Empire none was more persistent in its claims to independence than the Armenians, who were interviewed on August 1.[1] Prominent among these were the Gregorian Patriarch, Professor Besjian (the Protestant Vekil), Dr. Tavitian, and Mgr. Augustine Seyeghian (Armenian Catholic). Mr. Crane wondered whether the Armenians would "drift" into the territory which the Armenians desired, and the Patriarch expressed the belief that they would go to the new state, although Dr. Tavitian felt that they would not do so if the new state were only a makeshift. Dr. Tavitian added that the Armenians had lived so long under the Ottoman yoke that they could not be placed "in charge of a state at once" — a mandate would be necessary to train the people in the art of government. The Patriarch declared that the Turks had overstressed the problem of majorities, while Dr. King thought the mandatory control should continue until there was practically an Armenian majority. Professor Lybyer, however, reminded the Armenians that the Turks had been in the Armenian areas during no less than 850 years. While Dr. Tavitian estimated that there were about 550,000 Armenians in Turkey, including those who had accepted Islam, Mr. Besjian thought that in calculating the numbers, the 1,500,000 Armenians in Russian Armenia should be considered, along with those who had been massacred.[2]

The Basic Armenian Position

Mr. Tahtadjian, who represented the Armenian Republic in the Caucasus, declared that political relations with the Georgians and Tartars were difficult and the latter had carried out an attack recently in the Shusha region. The Russian Armenians, he said, had no idea of returning to Russia, but wanted "an integral reunion with Turkish Armenia in one state." A representative of Admiral Kolchak had promised that a reconstituted Russia would not claim Armenia through any resultant irredentism. A representative of the *Tashnakists*, or *Armenian Federation Party*, then in power in Russian Armenia, which claimed to represent

---

[1] These interviews are in the Lybyer Papers.

[2] Lybyer Papers: The Association of the Armenian Alumni and Former Students of Robert College had presented a Study on Kizilbasch-Kurds to Colonel W. N. Haskell, U. S. A., consisting of ten pages, which made a plea for Armenian independence and related the Kurds to the Armenians in a peculiar sense. Sir Mark Sykes was cited as having remarked in December 1918 at Aleppo that the Kurds were "Kizil-Bash", that consequently it was impossible to convert them to Christianity. The whole trend of the document was to prove that the Kurds could be included in the new Armenian State. Far from convincing, the document is signed by David Hovaanessian. See also Louis Edgar Browne's despatch in *The Chicago Daily News*, August 26, 1919.

about three-fourths of the people, favored a program of gradual socialization of land and industry. The Social Democratic Government in Georgia, on the other hand, favored immediate nationalization, and demanded the territory in Turkey claimed by the Armenians, and asserted that there were more than 600,000 Turks in the six eastern vilayets. Because of political conditions, a customs union among Armenia, Georgia and Azerbaijan was not an immediate possibility.[1] The *Armenian Democratic Party*, represented by MM. Shahnazar, Hagopian and Rapazian, rejected the class struggle and nationalization, and stood for a "free and independent united Armenia with ports on the Mediterranean and Black Seas." It hoped for "the speedy setting up of an organized government" and saw little difficulty in the claims to Turkish territory. Arrangements between Turkish and Russian Armenia, it felt, could be left to a mandatory power.

There were two different groups, with somewhat opposing views, in the old *Armenian Hunchakist Party*.[2] Both desired independence, but the older group kept closely to some socialistic principles, while the newer one, which called itself the National Liberals, wished to work on national principles for the Armenian people. In general, the Hunchakists believed that the only way to prevent more bloodshed was by military occupation and that, if some Power would add a few troops to those the Armenians had, the Armenians could occupy the entire country.

A few days later, on August 6, the Commission received a number of Armenian leaders from the eastern vilayets of Kayseri, Sivas, Van, Bitlis, Harput, Erzerum, Diarbekir and Yozgat. The primary inquiries covered the number of Armenians in the various districts and the attitude of the Turkish people toward the Armenians as distinguished from that of the Ottoman government. In general, all were agreed on an Armenian mandate as the best solution of the problem, although the responses varied somewhat concerning the attitude of the Turkish people toward Armenians. While there were some Turks, it was said, who had been "friendly", basically, all Turks were "against Christians and especially against Armenians."

Another witness in behalf of the Armenians was Miss Mary Graffam, an American missionary in Sivas, one of those "brave American women" who had remained at her post in the interior of Anatolia during the war and given help to "the distressed people and the refugees."[3] Miss Graffam, who knew the country well, told the Commission of the massacres during the war, but noted that out of the 80,000 Armenians from

[1] In general see Firuz KAZEMZADEH, *The Struggle for Transcaucasia* (1917-1921), Ch. XII.
[2] MM. Zeitundjian and Nersessian represented the older group and MM, Yezijian and Sharunian the new.
[3] Caleb F. GATES, *Not to Me Only*, 230.

the Sivas region, 10,000 to 20,000 had drifted back. Despite the massacres, Miss Graffam saw "some arguments on the side of keeping Turkey together," but, since the Armenians had "had too much done against them," she felt it "impossible for the Turks and Armenians to live together," a matter in which she disagreed with Admiral Bristol and President Gates. The only solution lay in establishing some kind of Armenian state. Otherwise the Armenians would drift into brigandage, for it was "past human imagination" to leave the Turks and Armenians together.

Dr. Tavitian returned to the Commission with more information on August 11, particularly about the Armenian Church, which, he explained, had been definitely national, but usually tolerant, although religion had "preserved the entity of the Armenian race." While the new government would be Christian, it would not prefer Christianity over other religions. Dr. Tavitian, who agreed to the entire separation of Church and State, saw no reason for continuing the old Ottoman *millet* system, under which the various religio-national groups had lived under their special ecclesiastical regimes. He considered the existing limits in the Caucasus maximum for Russian Armenia except in the Karadagh region. Although the Armenians should have an outlet on the sea, he did not believe they wanted to create a large territory. Nor did he believe there was any real distinction between Turkish and Russian Armenians, since they were one race and "one in hopes and aspirations." Armenia would need protection "for a long time," and the plan should be "to give sufficient economic life and strength" so that it "could exist in the midst of the Moslems." Despite some opposition on the part of the French Armenia Committee, the great majority of the people desired an American mandate, and "all would be patient in waiting for complete independence," if they had security. Nevertheless, there was "great need for speed and decision" because Turkish agents in both Russian and Turkish Armenia were "working to surround and crush Armenia."

The last Armenians to testify on August 11 were Besjian Effendi, the Armenian Protestant Vekil, and Arakel Effendi Geuzubuyukian, both of whom stressed conditions in the vicinity of Aintab, where there were "only Turks and Armenians." Both considered it wiser to "have a single mandate over all Armenia with some autonomy in the different provinces." Arakel Effendi felt that "the power in Armenia should be absolutely in the hands of a mandatory for at least twenty years," although he was not certain whether the Russian Armenians agreed.

End of the Armenian Case

Professor K. K. Krikorian called for the immediate formation of a large Armenia. [1] Dr. Krikorian pointed out, first, that the geographical

[1] Lybyer Papers: The Krikorian letter to Dr. G. R. Montgomery

situation of Armenia was such that Armenia was "surrounded on all sides by Moslem peoples," and was, therefore, "the only important oasis in the Moslem desert, and in the future struggle of western civilization with the Moslem militarism," Armenia would hold a very important strategic position, which ought to be put on a firm foundation. Moreover, by creating a large Armenia, Europe would "save another portion of this country from Turkish and Moslem misrule." Professor Krikorian advanced as a further argument "the mentality of the Turk," who was a fatalist and understood only material force.

Dr. Krikorian believed that Armenia could be separated from Turkey proper by dividing the area into two zones, with Erivan and its vicinity constituting a state, and the rest "managed directly from the center as the Armenian territories." On the other hand, there were dangers of failure in such an arrangement—the Turks might take advantage of the situation, the Russian Armenians might obtain an "unnecessary superiority," and there might be trouble with the future Russia. The best solution appeared to be to "put the whole Armenia under one mandatory and let it govern it all dictatorially." With the boundary lines finally drawn, the mandatory could then occupy the Armenian territories, the Erivan Republic should be abolished and the country divided into provinces. Gradually the mandatory should allow the people to participate in the administration.

In a longer memorandum, Dr. Krikorian filled in the details of his scheme for an independent and united Armenia, [1] although he admitted that the majority of the people in the Six Provinces and Cilicia were non-Armenian and that the number of Armenians was "insignificant now." But he considered the only solution to be establishment of an Armenian state under a separate American mandate. The real trouble was not caused by the assertion of Armenian independence, but by Allied hesitancy and lenience in dealing with the Turks.

THE AMERICAN WITNESSES

The American Commissioners were anxious to obtain the expert testimony of Americans and other foreigners long resident in the Ottoman Empire as well as *ex parte* statements of interested native groups with a

---

is dated Bible House, August 8, 1919, although his memorandum is dated August 10 [?], 1919.

[1] See Lybyer Papers: *Memorandum of the Association Patriotique Arménienne*, Pera, August 6, 1919; Dr. K. K. Krikorian, *The Mandate for Armenia* (Constantinople, 1919), 18 pp. See also Kazemzadeh, Ch. XIV. The Armenians did not make too favorable an impression on the Commission. In his *Memorandum*, Brodie recorded that the Armenian was "not quite such a worthy fellow after all .... But probably the chief cause of whatever anti-Armenian reaction there may be is the unfortunate personality of some Armenians, the obtrusion of some of his unpleasant

cause to plead. Almost from the day of the return to Constantinople on July 23, King, Crane and the staff were in constant touch with Admiral Bristol, the American High Commissioner in Constantinople. There were conferences with people like Dr. Peet, of the Bible House, and Dr. Barton, of the Near East Relief, who knew the situation very well, along with Mr. Gabriel Bie Ravndal, the American Consul-General at Constantinople, and others.

In a two hour conference with Peet and Barton on August 3, the Commissioners were urged to visit the interior of Anatolia, especially Ulukishlu, Kayseri, Sivas and Marsovan. Both Peet and Barton believed in a "minimum Armenia" which, in fact, appeared to embody the major Armenian claims. The Reverend Robert Frew and Sir Edwin Pears, the distinguished British journalist, appeared on August 4. A few days later, on August 7, at a party on the *U.S.S. Scorpion*, given by Admiral Bristol, there was considerable discussion of the Turkish and Armenian problem, and Admiral Bristol expressed his firm inclination toward preserving the unity of Anatolia, with Syria and Mesopotamia, and his dislike of both the British and the Armenians.[1]

But there were other matters. While Dr. King and Professor Lybyer were now very busy writing the Report of the Commission, Mr. Crane was going "to town a great deal." Interestingly enough, Miss Eleanor I. Burns, whom President Mary Mills Patrick had left in charge of Constantinople Women's College, was instructed "to do everything possible to please Mr. Crane," who was president of the board of trustees and was going to support eight or ten Albanian girls at the school. Apparently, too, Mr. Crane was getting the *wanderlust* again, for on August 16 he slipped away to Brusa to see Sheikh Ahmed of the Senussi. During their interview on August 17, Mr. Crane told Sheikh Ahmed about the Commission, only to find the old Moslem scholar thoroughly informed about the Wilson Fourteen Points, for "he had translated everything the President said" and wanted "very much to have his doctrines taught at his capital, Kufra."[2]

---

personal qualities which hide many of his better and more important traits of character.... With all his thrift and industry he has not always made himself genuinely likeable ...." See also in the Brodie Papers an original document signed by about 250 Armenian merchants of Constantinople, August 10, 1919, expressing hope for an independent Armenia. Note Lybyer *Diary*, August 3, 1919.

[1] Lybyer *Diary*, August 7, 1919. Miss Burns, Mr. Ravndal and Col. W. N. Haskell, soon to be the Entente High Commissioner in Armenia, were also present.

[2] The Crane *Memoirs*, 378-380. Dean Reed of International College at Smyrna came to lunch on August 8, and on August 13, Lybyer and Admiral Bristol tried to reach "common ground" in their attitudes toward the problems at hand.

Some American Views

Meanwhile, Dr. George E. White, President of Anatolia College at Marsovan (Merzifon), strongly supported the case for an independent Armenia before the Commission on August 15 and summed up his views in writing the next day.[1] White insisted that

> not a shred of independence should be left to the Turkish Government. Under its administration there is no real security for the life of a man, the honor of a woman, the welfare of a child, the property of a citizen or the rights of a father. The Turks have nothing constructive to their credit except the Seljukian architecture and the Ottomans eclipsed the Seljuks five hundred years ago. Many of their common people are hopeful human material for whom and with whom we like and want to work. But their public institutions are hopeless. Take from their hand the bloody sword, strip off their uniforms and let the rapacious officials work for their daily bread. In the interest of the Turks themselves, place the whole nation under the governance of a firm, friendly mandatory power without fail.

The Armenians, on the other hand, "should receive the opportunity of independent, national development." Unlike Dr. Gates, White thought that "full independence should be assured" without delay under an American mandatory. The rest of the Ottoman Empire, with a capital at Constantinople, including the region of the Straits and all Anatolia, should be preserved. Constantinople always had been the city to which people looked "for political and religious as well as cultural and economic guidance and instruction" and it deserved "an adequate territory and population." A reasonably decentralized administration could provide for local needs. The United States should "accept the Mandatory for Armenia and if possible also for Constantinople and Anatolia." In Dr. White's view, the United States had a duty to perform in the Near East, and, "if taken firmly in hand the task should not be really very difficult, not really very costly in men, money or American enterprise." The United States was "first choice of all Armenians, most Turks, and everybody else." The second choice would be "Great Britain and no other." But it was very important to act promptly, since the whole country was falling into chaos. Robbery and semi-political brigandage were rife and increasing.

> The pulse of the Central Government beats more feebly. Mustapha Kemal was recently in the region, where I met him personally, inflaming all the Turks to a campaign of bloodshed, spoliation and warfare with all Christians beginning first with those nearest at hand,

---

[1] King Papers: George E. White to the International Commission on Mandates in Turkey, American Embassy, Constantinople, August 16, 1919. Anatolia College, a small American missionary institution at Merzifon, was founded in 1866. "After thirty-five years of splendid service in Turkey, preparing men for moral and intellectual leadership in all walks of life," it moved to Salonica, Greece to serve its "old constituency, exiles in a new environment."

namely, the Armenians and the Greeks. The prospect for next winter is awful if the settlement is deferred beyond Autumn.

President Caleb F. Gates, of Robert College, was in the United States while the American Commission was in Constantinople, and was not expected back before Christmas at the earliest, but he had already made known his views in Paris during May 1919, and just before the Commission returned to Constantinople, his position on the question of an independent Armenia was made public.[1] It was a product not only of Dr. Gates' long experience in various parts of the Ottoman Empire, but especially of a journey which he had made through Asia Minor for the purpose of studying the various factors involved in the Turkish and Armenian problem. He agreed with Dr. White only as to the necessity of an American mandate.

Dr. Gates felt that the Armenian issue was "both a Turkish question and an international question." The fate of the Armenians was "bound up with that of the Turks," and could not be separated from it. Nor could the question be settled "by an independent Armenia with the Turks left to govern themselves." The problems of government for the Turks and the Armenians would have to be settled simultaneously. The long delay in reaching a settlement had rendered what would have seemed a comparatively easy problem "much more difficult," because Turkish nationalism had now been inflamed and very much, indeed, had happened. Gates felt that a "fatal mistake" had been made in putting Armenian soldiers into Cilicia and "entrusting police duties to them," for that had created the impression among the Turks "that the Armenians were to be armed against them." But another serious error had been made when the Armenian delegation at Paris published a pamphlet claiming "territory reaching from Sivas to Persia, and from Georgia to the Mediterranean, including more than one half of Turkey in Asia." One consequence was that the Turks, aware of the extravagant nature of the Armenian claims, believed that their co-nationals living in that region were to be placed under the control of the Armenians from whom they could expect no mercy. As a result, the Turkish population of Asia Minor was determined to resist any efforts which might be made "to create an independent Armenia." Even though the Ottoman Government had demonstrated its desire to assist the relief commissions and to preserve order throughout the country, its authority was not absolute, and an antagonistic spirit had developed which left little hope.

Under these conditions it seems possible that if an attempt be made to create an independent Armenia, it would be a signal for disorders

---

[1] See Louis Edgar Browne, Special Correspondent, *The Chicago Daily News,* Constantinople, July 15, 1919: "Turks and Armenians Want Aid of America."

to break out all over the country, in which the remnant of the Armenian nation would probably be destroyed. The entente forces in Asia Minor are hardly adequate for their protection. They are in the most cases posted in the outskirts of cities, while the Armenians live within the cities alongside the Turks.

In view of all these circumstances, I believe that the wisest policy would be to establish a protectorate for the whole of the Turkish Empire, which should administer the government wisely and justly and with impartiality. This government should encourage the schools, develop agriculture, trade and manufacture, and insure prosperity for the whole country. Prosperity is the best medicine for national discontent.

Armenian refugees then living in camps and waiting to return to their homes, ought to be directed to the eastern vilayets, helped to take up land, build houses, and be furnished with tools, seed, oxen and other items needed for their trades and industries. Gates thought, too, that Armenians living in other portions of the old Empire could be attracted to the eastern vilayets and that "gradually a homogeneous Armenian population would be established there." Since the Armenians were capable and industrious, they "would soon become a strong and prosperous people. Home rule should be accorded to them" as soon as they were capable of it. Moreover,

> in this way an Armenian state can be built up gradually, through natural economic and educational forces. Such a solution is the only one that will give hope of being permanent. An arbitrary enactment creating a state cannot give it stability, while it possesses only a small population, of whom 60 per cent or more are widows and orphans, and who are living scattered all over the empire, surrounded by hostile Moslem peoples, more numerous and better armed.

The Armenians should be freed from Turkish rule, but the question was: How and when should "a separate government be devised" for them? The educator had left the Caucasus Armenians out of consideration because he was not personally acquainted with them. He had read various reports, however, and did not believe that the Armenian government in the Caucasus represented "the best elements of the Armenian population" or furnished a "hopeful foundation on which to build an Armenian state." In conclusion, Gates was convinced that the Turks could be reconciled to such a program as he had outlined, granted that their fears were allayed and good government guaranteed. The Turks, like the other national groups, had suffered under Ottoman misrule, and a majority of the Turkish people would welcome foreign assistance if they were sure that "it would deal justly with them." Dr. Gates was

> astonished at the ardor and unanimity with which the people of Asia Minor, both Turks and Christians, expressed their desire for an American protectorate, and I have come to believe that the proclamation of such a protectorate would do more than any other measure to diminish the tension of feeling, and to induce the Turks to wait quietly for the solution of their difficulties. I realize that the United States is not

so well prepared for such a task as some other countries, but this strong and universal desire for American protection is certainly an asset which should not be undervalued.

Essentially Dr. Gates was in agreement with another distinguished American educator who had come out to the Ottoman Empire at about the same time—Dr. Mary Mills Patrick, President of Constantinople [Istanbul] Women's College.[1] Miss Patrick had been in Paris and had conferred with many members of the American delegation at the Peace Conference. Like Dr. Gates, she favored an American mandate for Turkey, and in a memorandum[2] outlined her position for a general American mandate. Peace in the Near East, she declared, could not be brought about by force, but must come from within. "All the people of the Near East would welcome an American mandate," and

> the Turks would prefer an American Mandatory to one from any other country for two reasons. They think that other nations would never resign a mandatory once undertaken, but that America having taught the people how to govern themselves would retire and leave them their independence. They also prefer Americans to deal with, because they are more democratic.

While the Moslems predominated in the Empire, numbering from 14,000,000 to 15,000,000, there was the problem of some 2,000,000 Greeks, most of whom would prefer a Greek government, but would welcome an American mandatory. The Armenians, who numbered "approximately one and half millions," would naturally desire an American mandate, whatever the arrangments for "an independent Armenia," for there would always be many Armenians in all parts of Turkey. A fifth consideration lay in the problem of religion and politics, the secularization of the state, a matter of grave importance in the Near East. The removal of political control from all religious organizations would tend to promote peaceful relations beween the different nationalities, while at the same time both Moslems and Christians would be protected in the free exercise of their religion. An American mandate would introduce American educational methods and ideals, and the influence of the English language as a means of communication among the polyglot peoples of the Empire would be excellent. Likewise, "an American Empire," with the possible exception of Mesopotamia and Southern Palestine, "would insure the same coinage, the same railway system and the same custom house regulations for the whole Empire."

---

[1] Miss Patrick went to Turkey in 1871, Dr. Gates in 1881. See her autobiography: *Under Five Sultans* (New York, Century, 1929), 347 pp.; *A Bosphorus Adventure: A Short History of Istanbul Women's College* (Stanford University Press, 1934).
[2] King Papers: Mary Mills PATRICK, "Fourteen Reasons for an American Mandatory for Turkey," 2 pp.

It was also true that under an American mandate all the nationalities would have "security of life and an unmolested opportunity of autonomous development." Again, modern agricultural methods "would make a veritable paradise of Asia Minor," and in view of the great mineral wealth of the country, American commercial methods "would make it a great commercial center." Miss Patrick also stressed that under an American mandate "the Dardanelles would be permanently opened as a free passage to the ships and commerce of all nations." Close commercial relations between the United States and Turkey would assist the latter in developing its own wealth, while both countries would profit from mutual exchange. Finally, the United States, in Miss Patrick's view, should assume its "share of the burden in the new order of things" in accordance with the principles of President Wilson.

Gabriel Bie Ravndal, the American Consul-General, held somewhat different views as to the future of Turkey, formulated over a long period of time, and he appears to have been considerably influenced by the writings of M. André Mandelstam, long the Chief Dragoman of the Imperial Russian Embassy in Constantinople. [1] Ravndal's general thesis was that

---

[1] Ravndal, who had talked with Montgomery on August 5 and with Lybyer on August 15, had returned to Constantinople on March 5, 1919, at about the same time that Consuls Chesbrough, Morris and George Young were ordered to Constantinople. His duties were to be concerned with commerce, not politics, as Heck was to be in charge "of political matters in Constantinople." Jackson had been ordered to Aleppo at the same time, and Glazebrook to Jerusalem. On May 3, Ravndal was to assume the functions of Commissioner, succeeding Heck. See *U. S. Foreign Relations* (1919), II, Polk to Ravndal, March 5, May 3, 1919, pp. 811-812. For the conversation with Montgomery see King Papers: George R. MONTGOMERY, "Memorandum on Interview with Commissioner Ravndal," 2 pp.; and Lybyer *Diary*, August 15, 1919. See also Lybyer Papers: Résumé of Letter to State Department from G. B. Ravndal, October 1, 1918, No. 91, transmitting extracts from Mandelstam Report, and extracts of an address of Mandelstam on "The Soul of the Turk." Mandelstam is known for his work on *Le sort de l'Empire Ottoman* (Paris, 1917) and *La Société des Nations et les puissances devant le problème arménien* (Paris, 1926). In his address on "The Soul of the Turk," Mandelstam repeats many things concerning the despotic rule of Abdul Hamid II, and then discusses the Ottoman regime under German war influence, with the partial realization of the so-called Pan-Turkish ideals through the destruction of non-Turkish elements such as Armenians, Greeks, Nestorians, Arabs and Jews. Mandelstam repeated the usual clichés concerning the Turks, held that they had no "national genius", and declared that they had "done nothing from the point of view of civilization to legitimate" their "existence", and it was therefore "just and right that the non-Turks should be liberated and that the Ottoman Empire should be expelled from Europe." While the "regeneration of the Turkish race" was possible, a "new Turkish state" would have to be created for that purpose. See also G. B. RAVNDAL, *Turkey—A Commercial and Industrial*

the Turks were unable to rule either themselves or other groups, partly because of European diplomacy and intrigue and the European attitude of superiority, and partly because of the British failure to direct Turkish destinies after 1908 in opposition to German influence and turn the Committee of Union and Progress into genuinely constructive channels. Mr. Ravndal was willing to accept a general American mandate and was convinced that a "benevolent but firm foreign" control would be necessary for many years. International control might be feasible for the Straits and Constantinople, but it would be dangerous for Turkey proper, including Anatolia. In his view, an American mandate over the region would be desirable, because the Allies seemed to prefer the United States to any other nation, and because the United States ought to accept "some significant mandate in Europe." Moreover, the Turks also preferred the United States because of the American record in Cuba and the Philippines and their belief in the political disinterestedness of the United States and American opposition to "unjust concessions." There were also elements in the general Near Eastern situation which appeared favorable to a successful American mandate. The Turks were accustomed to foreign administrative control, and a mandate would be for an indefinite period to be determined by the degree of progress, although a protectorate would not be necessary. It would be a Turkish regime under American advisers. Furthermore, the Turks were a chastened people, worthy of redemption, and the government had already "accepted the idea of separating law from religion."

In general, Ravndal set off three distinct zones: Constantinople and the Straits, Anatolia and Armenia. There were good reasons, he thought, for the internationalization of Constantinople and the region of the Straits. The people of that area, for instance, "should have an opportunity for development under good government," although it was "unfair to compel non-Moslem peoples to live under minority Moslem rule." It was unsafe, too, "to leave Turks at such a strategic point" as Constantinople and the Straits. But to carry out the program for internationalization, it would be necessary to have a clear definition of the district to be involved. Mr. Ravndal would exclude Adrianople and a part of Thrace intended for Bulgaria, and would not necessarily include Brusa in the area of Constantinople and the Straits. This would leave Samsun and Adalia as ports for the new Turkish state in Anatolia, and possibly Smyrna, if it were not given to Greece. Secondly, the region of Constantinople and the Straits should have a constitution granted by the Peace Conference, establishing a Commission of Three representing three disinterested powers such as the United States, Switzerland and Norway, and

Handbook. Trade Promotion Series, No. 28. Department of Commerce (Washington, 1926). For a different view see Bernard LEWIS, *passim.*

a legislative council chosen by the people. The powers could have consular, but not diplomatic, agents in the region.[1]

Ravndal also favored an autonomous Armenia including the "ancient kingdom." The boundaries embraced the Taurus and Anti-Taurus ranges in the west, Sivas east to Batum on the north, Batum to a point fifty miles east of Van on the east, and a point fifteen miles west of Koi to Diarbekir, Aintab and the Gulf of Alexandretta on the south. Armenia would have the ports of Mersina on the Mediterranean and Batum on the Black Sea. Additional territory in the Caucasus might be added to the state. Foreign guidance, preferably American, should be given. Under these conditions of independence with guidance, Ravndal thought that the Armenians would migrate to the new state and the Kurds would drift elsewhere or a separate Kurdish province within the state could be created in the neighborhood of Mardin.

One of the most interesting interviews concerning the future of Turkey was that which Lybyer had on August 19 with Mr. Heathcote Smith, an intelligence officer with the British High Commission, on the balcony of Hamlin Hall at Robert College. Heathcote Smith, who thought the British Foreign Office incompetent, favored an American mandate in Armenia and Constantinople and joint Anglo-American control of Anatolia. He would give the Turks a port on the Marmara, and Constantinople could be retained as the seat of the Caliphate—the latter point to meet the objection of the Indian Moslems. Smith was very depressed about the Near Eastern situation and wished to leave Turkey for good. He wrongly believed that Mustapha Kemal was working with the Young Turks and that the government in Constantinople was secretly in agreement with the Nationalist movement. But he agreed that it was a great mistake to let the Greeks go into Smyrna, although it would be very difficult to get them out. He hoped that the United States would become involved there, "so as to help carry the burden of the world."[2]

---

[1] Ravndal did not believe that the "relatively large" Ottoman Public Debt should either be cancelled or placed entirely on the shoulders of the small Turkish state. See also Lybyer *Diary*, August 16, 17, for conversations with Mr. Beury, of the Near East Relief, Admiral Bristol, and Ahmed Emin Bey [Yalman]. Ahmed Emin stoutly maintained that the Nationalist Movement in Anatolia was patriotic, had no connection with the Committee of Union and Progress, and contemplated no violence to the Armenians. He favored a limited Armenian territory, and believed that a great majority of intelligent Turks favored an American mandate. Bristol now approved a "small Armenia", and would even give up Syria, but held out for the Turks in Constantinople.

[2] Lybyer *Diary*, August 19, 1919. Smith had gone along with a Turk to serve notice of the dismissal of Mustapha Kemal from the Ottoman military service. He remarked confidentially that he had recommended in December that one British officer be sent to different towns to gather the evidence concerning those who had killed Armenians, and had made

On the last day in Constantinople, the Commission received a communication from Mr. H. E. Pears. Curiously enough, Pears was the only witness, aside from the Greeks themselves, who supported the Greek claims in Asia Minor. He wanted to have "a few words respecting the question of giving to Greece a part of Asia Minor," *i.e.*, the Smyrna vilayet, a project which could be carried out either through the creation of an autonomous Greek community, or, preferably, through the establishment of a more or less independent Greek state. While "not very fond of the Turks," Pears was not sympathetic, either, with the British, Greeks, Italians, French or others in Smyrna, who had "always been the opponents of development in the interior of the Vilayet of Smyrna by objecting and intriguing against the establishment of industries ... in the towns along the railway lines." The sooner the Turks became "a governed race" or even "extinct as a race the better," and the best means to do it was to set up Christian states in Anatolia. In any event, it was "perfectly well recognized" that the Turks were dying out "at an exceedingly rapid rate," while the Greeks were always increasing. Mr. Pears, therefore, ventured to suggest that "in the interest of humanity (a crusade if you like)," the sooner the Greeks were established in Asia Minor "as part of Greece, or as an autonomous state," the sooner the Turks would become extinct. The Greeks would be safe, with security of life and property. They would then go ahead and in a short time would gradually penetrate everywhere in Anatolia, "accomplishing a conquest by peaceful penetration." But, fortunately, such ideas appeared too fantastic for the consideration of the King-Crane Commission. [1]

a list of 400 names. Lybyer told Smith that Americans could not trust some British diplomats and that Americans were not very well acquainted with the Near East. Mahmud Bey, uncle of Hussein Bey, of Robert College, defended the Turks, and declared that three-fourths of the people wanted an American mandate, although an Armenian state must be set off.

[1] H. E. Pears to G. R. Montgomery, August 21, 1919 (King Papers). Pears, son of Sir Edwin Pears, had been associated for many years with the Smyrna-Aidin Railway, and was very familiar with the situation in that region, despite his very obvious prejudices.

CHAPTER VII

Project for an American Policy:
The King-Crane Report and Recommendations

We have seen that, on its return to Constantinople, the King-Crane Commission had the two essential tasks of investigating further the Turkish problem and preparing the Report for President Wilson and the American Delegation at the Peace Conference in Paris. The latter task fell mainly on President King and Professor Lybyer, ably assisted by Captain Brodie. On July 24 Lybyer prepared an extended summary concerning Syria.[1] Dr. King spent the time quietly at the Constantinople Women's College, "trying to shape up points" for the Report, although a touch of malaria was interfering with his work. Dr. King, as usual, was somewhat enthusiastic concerning early completion, hoping that it might be finished within two or three days.[2]

THE MONTGOMERY AND YALE MEMORANDA

It was on Saturday, July 26, that Captain Yale and Dr. Montgomery, who were living in the Pera Palace Hotel, turned in their own recommendations regarding Syria for the consideration of Dr. King and Mr. Crane. Both advisers had had their differences with the Commissioners concerning the nature of the solutions to be set forth, and Yale seemed quite pessimistic. He did not believe the United States would assume any mandate in the Near East and was distrustful of British diplomacy.[3]

The Montgomery Report

Dr. Montgomery, who, in general, shared the opinions of Captain Yale as to Syria, prepared a report,[4] in which he made clear his belief that Syrian unity had not existed in the past and that it would be a mistake to force such unity now. Lebanon had always gone its own way and Palestine had been separately administered. Dr. Montgomery saw little evidence of a "Syrian national character" and felt that the economic benefits of unity could be obtained through agreements. He advocated almost complete autonomy for Lebanon as a better way of "leading up to a confederation later." If union proved to be advantageous, the benefits would be visible to all. But Montgomery firmly believed in political decentralization as the solution for the present. Religious hatreds

---

[1] Lybyer Papers: A. H. Lybyer, Additional Observations on Syrian Situation, Constantinople, July 24, 1919. This memorandum has already been examined in connection with the Syrian investigation.

[2] King and Lybyer *Diaries*, July 25, 26, 1919. See also King Papers: King to Bonn, July 29, 1919.

[3] Lybyer *Diary*, July 25, 1919.

[4] Lybyer Papers: George R. Montgomery, Report on Syria, 9 pp. Original typewritten copy. Annotated by Dr. H. C. King. Undated, the Report appears to have been given to the Commissioners on July 26.

ran very deep in the Near East, and if union were imposed before Lebanon felt a need for it, and at a time when only the Moslems desired it, perhaps because of the greater power they would gain, the reactions would lead toward disruption. Montgomery thought it would be wiser not to force Christians and Moslems together under a single government.[1]

Montgomery had little expectation that a Moslem Arab Government in Syria could develop any importance. He asserted that Moslem empires "grew and prospered only as long as there was loot to be looted and divided"! Islam, to him, contained "no nucleus of unselfishness" which held any hope of a Moslem reformation, since it was vigorous only as it conquered, not as it served, and would not meet "the needs of a modern society."[2] Montgomery anticipated that most of the efforts of the Moslem Arabs would be spent "in a fight against Christians and Christianity." He admitted that this was a pessimistic view, but felt that religious antagonisms were uppermost, a fact difficult for those who had not lived in the Near East to understand.

The dominant issue in Palestine clearly was Zionism, which must be considered not from the point of view of Palestine alone, but from "the standpoint of history, of racial achievements, of Jewish persecution and of anti-semitism." There should be no narrow interpretation of the idea of rights, but "the greatest benefit to the greatest number must be considered." Among the Arabs there were naturally the elements of jealousy and rivalry and the apprehensions of the large private land holders.[3] Montgomery believed that Zionism would bring great economic advantages, for the Jews had already accomplished much in Palestine. There was little ground for fearing Zionist treatment of the Christian and Moslem Holy Places,[4] and there would be some advantage in having a non-Moslem *bloc* between Asia and Africa. It would show the Arabs of Syria that they could not expand in the direction of Egypt.

---

[1] Dr. King commented on the margin, quoting from Sir William Ramsay: "The attempt to sort out religions and settle them in different localities is wrong and will prove fatal. The progress of history depends upon diversity of population in each district." King and Crane, at least, read the report very carefully.

[2] Montgomery felt that "one should not be misled by the ancient importance in arts and sciences of an Arab nation. As despotisms the Moslem governments provided for brief periods the tranquillity and prosperity in which the arts and sciences could grow. No such despotism is possible to a Moslem government under the new system. Islam, on the one hand, will be fighting for its existence and the Christians on the other will be backed by a part at least of western Christianity. The presence of even a small minority of Christians will tend to put Mohammedanism on the defensive so that it will not become reactionary."

[3] Dr. King noted at this point that Montgomery's reasoning was "certain to arouse Arabs."

[4] King felt that this statement was "much under the point."

Considering the problem of Alexandretta, Dr. Montgomery felt that obviously Cilicia belonged with the north rather than with Syria, an opinion shared, evidently, by others serving with the Commission. The problem of the exact boundary did not arise and the economic significance of Alexandretta had to be considered. In the period of caravans it was the port for the whole northeastern hinterland, and the construction of the Adana-Mersina railway brought Mersina into prominence, and emphasized Alexandretta's connection with the northeast. Not only Aleppo, but Marash, Aintab, Harput, and even Bitlis, "all Armenian towns", found Alexandretta the most convenient port.

The choice of a mandatory for Syria, in Montgomery's view, depended upon the advantages which the different religious groups hoped to gain. France had loudly proclaimed itself as the champion of the Christians in Syria, but the Protestant sects considered France as "pro-Roman Catholic". With the exception of the Armenian Catholics of Adana, the Catholic groups favored France. The Moslems regarded France [1] indiscriminately as pro-Christian, and with the exception of a few Shiites in the Bekaa, the Ismailiye and some of the Annusariye, they preferred the United States or Great Britain if they had to choose a mandatory. The Greek Orthodox groups would have chosen Russia, if that country had been a possible candidate. As it was, the priestly element, and in most cases, the laity, considered the antagonism to Roman Catholicism "more important than the danger from Islam and so they opted against France, namely for the United States or Great Britain." In some cases, where the ecclesiastical influence was less pronounced, the Greek Orthodox preferred France. There was no doubt that the Christians feared Moslem domination, and, indeed, much evidence existed that "among the Moslems the words Islam and Arab meant one and the same thing." In view of the American record in Cuba and the Philippines and the British in Egypt, the preference for the United States "was to be expected" and did not seem to be as enthusiastic as might have been assumed.

Were there any possiblity of the United States accepting a mandate for the whole or a part of Syria, Montgomery would have recommended it "heartily", but the United States, if it assumed any mandate at all, was committed to Armenia, and if it took any additional responsibility, that should be in mandates over Kurdistan or Anatolia, which would contribute "to the success of the Armenian experiment". [2] There seemed

---

[1] King raised questions concerning the identification of the Moslem faith with Arab national feeling and regarding the lack of enthusiasm for a possible American mandate in Syria.

[2] So far as any of the papers of the King-Crane Commission reveal, Dr. Montgomery appears to have been the only member of the staff who could be said genuinely to have favored the Armenian state under

to be no probability that Europe would "consent at one and the same time to such mandates and also to a mandate over Syria." Therefore, Montgomery left the United States out of the proposed settlement and made three definite recommendations:

1 . . . that Palestine be autonomously administered with Great Britain as the Mandatory; that the immigration of the Jews be encouraged for the benefit which it will bring to the country; that proper reservation be made for the safeguarding of the Christian and Moslem Holy Places; that the boundaries of Palestine extend to the Litany river on the north, and on the east include Es Salt and the Kerak, running along the heights south of Kerak to the Hejaz east of Akaba.

2 . . . that the Lebanon be autonomously administered with France as the mandatory; that no restriction be put upon schools or universities with respect to language or religion; that the boundaries of Lebanon be enlarged to include the northern part of the Litany basin, but not to include Tripoli.

3 . . . that Syria be administered with Prince Feisal as emir under a joint mandate to France and Great Britain;[1] that the boundaries of Syria on the north be a line drawn from somewhere in the vicinity of the mouth of the Orontes, following as well as possible the language line to just south of Birajik on the Euphrates river; that the boundary on the east be the Euphrates river to some point like Abn Kemal and then the boundary line should run south to the Jof and west to Palestine.

The Yale Recommendations Concerning Syria

Like Dr. Montgomery, Captain Yale appeared more interested in the problem of Syria and Palestine, and his memorandum of July 26 is much more detailed, thorough and to the point.[2] Yale began with an analysis of the desires of the people of Palestine. The Moslems, who made up about three-fourths of the entire population, mainly tillers of the soil and tenders of flocks, with some large landed proprietors, office holders, religious leaders, shop keepers and artisans, were mostly illiterate. In such centers as Hebron, Nablus and Jenin, Yale found them "profoundly fanatical, anti-Jewish, anti-Christian, anti-European," although the village fellaheen were mostly "docile and easily managed."

The Moslems as a body demand complete independence, union with Syria under Emir Feisal, prevention of Jewish immigration. They

mandate *per se*. Later on Montgomery was to represent the America-Armenia Society at the Lausanne Conference favoring an Armenian National Home north of Alexandretta.

[1] Montgomery was the only one to recommend a Joint Anglo-French mandate for Syria, although he realized that "the idea of a joint mandate may suggest rivalry between France and Great Britain."

[2] Lybyer Papers: Captain William YALE, *A Report on Syria, Palestine, Mount Lebanon for the American Commissioners, Prepared by Captain William Yale, Technical Adviser to the American Section of the International Commission on Mandates in Turkey.* July 26, 1919. Constantinople, 34 pp. Original in Lybyer Papers; carbon copy at the Hoover Library, Stanford University, with a note indicating that Professor A. C. Coolidge, of Harvard, considered it more accurate than the King-Crane Report.

protest against Palestine being made a National Home for the Jews, and want no European interference in their affairs. Some of the better educated and more enlightened Moslems appreciate the need of a strong Mandatory Power and would prefer to have the United States or Great Britain.

With the exception of the Catholics, who preferred France, the Christians, comprising less than one-tenth of the people, wanted the United States or Great Britain as the mandatory. Opinion of the Christian Arabs as to union with Syria was divided. Those who had commercial relations with Great Britain desired a separate Palestine,[1] while others wanted unity with Syria whether France or Great Britain were to be the mandatory. Practically all Catholic Arabs desired unity with France. All objected to the establishment of a Jewish National Home in Palestine and the majority protested "against Jewish immigration". The Jews, about 100,000, undoubtedly a high estimate, who made up only one-eighth of the population, 15,000 of whom were farmers living in modern Jewish colonies, were united in demanding a separate Palestine, a British mandate and the establishment of a Jewish National Home.

Yale then proceeded to analyze what he considered to be the specific desires of the Palestinians. Prior to and even during the war, he declared, there "existed in Palestine no national feeling and no sense of national or political union with Syria"—the Palestinians thought only of deliverance from the Ottoman yoke and asked nothing better than British or French protection. "Even up until November 1918 there was but little thought of union with Syria or of independence." The Moslems had only recently expressed a desire for union with Syria, prompted by fear of the Jews and a longing for independence. As Yale saw it:[2]

> Such sense of political unity with Syria, which is so much in evidence in Palestine at the present time, is a *creation of the last eight or ten months caused in a large part by a fear of Zionism among both Christians and Moslems and by a desire for independence under a Moslem government among the Moslems.* It must not be forgotten that during the years from 1908 to 1918 when the Syrian Movement and Young Arab Movement were at work in Mount Lebanon, Syria and Mesopotamia, first for decentralization and later for separation from the Ottoman Empire, there was no response from Palestine and no evidence of a national feeling. It is in

---

[1] Lybyer noted that "very few expressed these views," and indicated that practically all the Christian Arabs protested against Jewish immigration.

[2] Dr. King raised fundamental doubts about the Yale premises concerning Arab nationalism, and Dr. Lybyer did not agree at all. Captain Yale may have neglected the various "artificial" factors which may have entered historically into the development of modern nationalism in western as well as eastern Europe from the sixteenth to the nineteenth and twentieth centuries. See George ANTONIUS, *The Arab Awakening, passim*, and Zeine N. ZEINE, *Arab-Turkish Relations and the Emergence of Arab Nationalism*, Ch. V.

this light that the present vociferous claims for the political union of Syria and Palestine must be judged.

Opinions differed in Syria, too. In the region from Deraa south to Ma'an, including the Hauran, Ajlun, Jebel Hauran, and the region of Es Salt, Madeba and Kerak, the Moslems expressed a desire for union with Syria and complete independence. As a mandatory they would prefer the United States or Great Britain. Some, dissatisfied with the Young Arab Administration, preferred union with a British-administered Palestine, although Arab propaganda had had some effect. The Druzes had come to agreement with the Young Arabs as to a genuine local autonomy in the Jebel Hauran, were opposed to a French mandate, and favored the United States. The Christians, terrified that under the Young Arab regime their lives were in danger, wanted a strong mandatory power, probably the United States.

In the vicinity of Damascus, with a population of from 250,000 to 300,000, eighty to ninety per cent of whom were Moslem, the great mass of Moslems demanded "a united and independent Syria under Emir Feisal." They wanted no European interference of any sort, were very anti-French, and opposed to Article XXII of the Covenant of the League of Nations. Feisal and the more moderate groups, however, wanted mandatory assistance and favored the United States. Yale wondered whether the opposition to a mandate was born out of fear that the mandatory would never leave the country, or indicated the desire for Moslem domination, with no real hope "for the development of Syria along national lines wherein Moslem and Christian would be on an equal footing." Did it give evidence "of a profound anti-western feeling, the next development of which would be oppression of the native Christians and a suppression of their rights"?[1] Fundamentally the Moslem opposition to France seemed to be due to the fact that France had been for centuries the "bulwark of Christianity in Syria." In the valley of the Bekaa and the Baalbek region, it was impossible to judge accurately the sentiments of the people from the delegations which appeared before the Commission. In reality, Yale thought, the valley marked the dividing line between Moslem Syria and Christian Mount Lebanon. "Here the intensity of feeling between Moslems and Christians, between the Young Arab and the Greater Lebanon Party" was at its height. Nevertheless, it was "very probable" that most of the Moslems were in favor of the Young Arab program, while most of the Christians desired annexation

---

[1] Lybyer felt that it was simply the "desire for independence, not to mention the declaration of France and Britain in November 1918 which produced a not unnatural fear of a mandate under Article XXII of the Covenant." King and Lybyer questioned most of the basic assumptions of Yale in his discussion of the Damascus region.

to Greater Mount Lebanon under French protection, and would favor Syria's being under French control. Some Protestant elements proposed the United States or Great Britain as a mandatory. The vital point was whether the country was to be "Christian or Moslem; here the thought of Syrian Unity or Syrian Nationalism" fell to "zero". [1]

The three cities of Homs, Hama and Aleppo were overwhelmingly Moslem and enthusiastically devoted to the Young Arab program. But, as usual, Catholic sects favored France, and seemed opposed to the leadership of Emir Feisal. The Christians had had little contact with the west except through France, and all their education had been French in character. Moreover, the Christians feared the Moslems. Yale scarcely found even the "shadow of Syrian nationalism," a position with which the Commissioners and Professor Lybyer thoroughly disagreed. In the vicinity of Tripoli, the Moslems, in Yale's view, all supported the Young Arab program, opposed a Greater Mount Lebanon, and were violently anti-French—"for which the Moslems appeared to have ample reason," but the Catholic sects were united in favor of a French Syrian mandate, with autonomy for Greater Lebanon under French protection. About the same situation appeared to prevail in Latakia. In the Alexandretta region, however, Yale, like the others, noted "a rather large Turkish population" which "almost unanimously" asked to be joined to Anatolia under Ottoman sovereignty. A very small group had seized power, however, and were "in favor of being included in a United Syria." The Moslem Arabs desired to be under Syria, the Catholic Christians favored a French mandate, and the Greek Orthodox elements were divided, some favoring the United States or Great Britain, some France.

Mount Lebanon presented a somewhat different problem from that of the rest of Syria, since the pre-war population was about 79 per cent Christian, about 84 per cent of which was Catholic, and 21 per cent non-Christian. In Beirut, Tyre and Sidon the Moslems were opposed to a separate Greater Lebanon and endorsed the Young Arab Program of independence under Feisal. [2] The Druzes approved the same program. The Mt. Lebanon Catholic sects asked for independence or autonomy under a French mandate for Syria. Yale found some evidence of French suppression of anti-French sentiments, although he doubted that the expression of opinion was much affected by French pressure. The key to the whole situation lay in the fact that

> Mount Lebanon is distinctly a Christian country, and it is quite natural that the Christians have no desire to fall under the Moslem domination

---

[1] Lybyer noted that he "did not get such an impression at Baalbek."
[2] Lybyer noted that France was also a great Moslem power, and indicated that at Tyre the Sunni Moslems appeared to favor France, but he noted that only about 66 per cent of the population of Mt. Lebanon were Catholic, of which about 36 per cent were from Beirut.

of the interior. The Christians of Mount Lebanon numbered approximately before the war 345,000, and of Greater Mount Lebanon 518,000. If the total population of "Syria" is put at 2,500,000 then nearly 1/5 of this number demand that Greater Lebanon should be constituted as a separate state with no political relations with the interior. The Christians of this region have suffered a great deal from Moslem oppression and because of the conditions imposed upon them between 300,000 and 400,000 have emigrated during the last half century to North and South America. These emigrants take an intense interest in their Mountain and in the welfare of the Christian brethren there.

As elsewhere, the Christians did not intend to fall under Moslem rule. Nevertheless, those few Christians who opposed a Greater Mount Lebanon, did so because they feared Catholic supremacy, and thought that in a United Syria, under a strong mandatory, they would not suffer from Moslem oppression.

In an interesting section devoted to British policy, Yale noted that the Syrian problem was closely connected with that of Mesopotamia, Arabia and Egypt, and the general Moslem situation. In British opinion, Haifa, Tripoli and Alexandretta would become "the gates to Mesopotamia, Persia and the East." The British did not want the French in these regions and had been trying, especially since 1917, to keep them out. They were supporting the Young Arab movement.[1] If the British themselves could not get the mandate—they had already announced that they would not take it—they would like to have the Americans assume it, although they intended, if possible, to keep Palestine, and to control Syria, and did not want the French even in Mount Lebanon.

But on the other hand, since the beginning of the war, the French had considered Syria part of their booty after the close of hostilities, in view of long-standing French traditions and interests. Unable to win the people by friendship, they were resorting to a policy of coercion, and their administration was "a most unpleasant spectacle to contemplate." Yale thought both British and French policy in Syria had been "a curse to the country."

---

[1] "Since 1917 the British have been working to keep the French out of Syria, and have tried to create a situation such that it would be impossible for the French to occupy the country. The present Arab Government is their creation, and it can only exist through the large subsidy that they give to it. For the past five or six months the Young Arab Government has carried on an aggressive propaganda against France, this with the knowledge of the British and with money supplied by them to the Young Arab Government. The Young Arabs have been encouraged by British officers in their dislike of France." T. E. Lawrence pointed out the danger of allowing France to dominate Syria, with Alexandretta, in a letter of March 18, 1915 to D. G. Hogarth. Alexandretta was the only place from which a fleet could operate against Egypt. See GARNETT, *The Letters of T. E. Lawrence*, 193-194.

In general, Yale felt that Arab policy differed basically from that of the Emir Feisal. Feisal wanted a mandatory power, hoped that the United States would assume the responsibility, and wished "honestly and sincerely to build up a United Syria for the benefit of all the Syrians." Feisal was liberal and open minded, and wanted "to see Christians, Druses and Moslems working together for the best interests of the State." He believed that a French mandate would ruin "all hope for the development of Syria" and wanted "to eliminate the chance of France holding any part of Syria." In order to attain these ends, Feisal had "fallen in with the Young Arab Party" and with British policy. But the Young Arab Party itself, like the Turkish Committee of Union and Progress, was not really nationalist and aimed not at the building "of a Syrian state in which the Christians and Moslems would be on terms of equality," but desired "the resurrection of a Moslem Arab State and eventually a Moslem Arab Empire somewhat along the lines of the empires of the Ommayads and the Abbasids." There had been clever propaganda over the country, but it was easy to see through the "cloak of nationalism."

There was a very feeble liberal movement among the Arabs, but even with the blessing of the moderate Emir Feisal it would have little weight among Moslems "without the support of a liberal western power." Yale did not have a very high opinion of Feisal's possibilities as a ruler:

> [Feisal's] power is due to several causes. In the first place he is the son of the King of the Hedjaz and of the family of Mohammed; in the second place he, as the leader of Arab forces which helped in the liberation of Syria from the Turks, has a certain temporary popularity; in the third place he has won the affection of many by his charming personality and sincerity; in the fourth place he is a useful instrument of the Young Arab Party in aiding them to secure their aims; and finally, as the head of an organized government, with a princely income from the British, he is the dispenser of favors and lucrative posts....
> Feisal's prestige as a military leader is but temporary and already has lost much of its *éclat*. His influence won by his personality is not a powerful one, he is loved but not feared, he is courted but not obeyed. Should the Emir fail to satisfy the Young Arab Party they would dispense with him. And finally, under a just and equitable government the Emir would no longer be able to win supporters by lavishly bestowing honors and appointments. In fact, Emir Feisal is not a strong personality, he has not enough power and influence in the country to make his ideas prevail without the support of a foreign power.

There were only a very few educated Moslems, mostly young men with little influence, who supported the liberal policy of the Emir, according to Yale's findings. The majority of the educated Moslems were "profoundly fanatical, profoundly Islamic." This was the group which constituted the basis of the Young Arab Party, in whose hands the real power lay, and these men had "as their ideal a Moslem, Arab State, not a liberal Syrian State." Since over 90 per cent of the Syrian Moslems were ignorant, they could be swayed by their religious leaders, land owners and tribal chiefs and were distinctly anti-Christian and anti-foreign. While the Syrians had disclaimed any connection with the Kingdom of the Hejaz, the son of whose sovereign, Hussein, they were anxious to enthrone in Damascus, nevertheless, Yale could hardly imagine Hussein as being "satisfied with Syria as a secular state over which Emir Feisal ruled as a nominal Prince."

In an analysis of "Syria as a Unit," Yale pointed out that, economically and commercially, Syria, Palestine and Lebanon were "dependent upon one another, and no economic barrier should be allowed to exist between them." Palestine depended on the Kerak and Madeba region and the Hauran for wheat, while Mt. Lebanon and the coastal region to Alexandretta also looked to the interior for their grains. The back country got its oranges and grapes from Palestine and the coast. Palestine and Mt. Lebanon could not live without the products of the interior. Economically Syria could not be separated from Palestine and Mt. Lebanon, but politically the three regions did not form a unit. Although three-fourths of its people were Moslems, Palestine was a land apart because it was the Holy Land of three great faiths. Mt. Lebanon was overwhelmingly Christian, and its civilization and ideals were profoundly different from those of the interior. Politically it was not a part of Syria and even should it be united with Syria, it would require a different political regime. Religiously, Syria was a crazy-quilt of intolerant and fanatical religions, while the racial mixture was not conducive to unity. A further complication was the great social diversity ranging from nomad to fellaheen and from landowner to poor and rich merchant in the city. One found in Syria co-existent tribal life, feudal life, and the beginnings of modern industrial social life. It was true that "economically and commercially," "linguistically and geographically" Syria was a unit, but in no other way. Other than these factors there was nothing which bound the people of Syria together "but the exigencies of the present crisis and the propaganda of the Young Arabs." One should not, therefore, be deceived by the expression of Syrian nationalism, for neither nationalism nor unity existed—these were simply words which Syrians did not understand.

> A national spirit and feeling may in time be developed, but it can never be done by commencing with the hypothesis that it already exists. To develop Syrian nationalism will need many years of constant and thorough teaching and it cannot be accomplished unless there exists in the minds of those who take the task in hand an appreciation of the profound differences which separate the different groups and have for centuries made the development of a national spirit an impossibility.

The fact that the Syrian National Congress had met on July 2 in Damascus and formulated a program of unity and independence proved nothing to Yale's skeptical mind. In the past United Syria had "never been a country by itself"; moreover, the Syrians had "no national history, no national traditions and no national sentiment." The present crisis had stimulated something of a national feeling, but it appeared weak and largely superficial. Captain Yale closed this part of his report:

> There does exist in Syria a sense of unity of Syria, a feeling that Syria cannot be separated without causing economic disadvantages, and onerous restrictions in regard to communications, and travel. The Christians in various parts of "United Syria" are related by family ties and connections, the same being true to a lesser degree of Syria as a commercial and economic unit but not as a political unit. There is no sense of Syrian nationalism, no desire for union in the political sense among the peoples of Syria.

Yale made a number of recommendations regarding Palestine and Syria. He urged that Palestine "be separated from Syria and constituted as a National Home for the Jewish People under the Mandate of Great Britain acting as the custodian of the Holy Land in the Name of the League of Nations." Because this recommendation was "entirely contrary to the wishes of the people of Palestine and those of most of the inhabitants of Syria," Yale naturally felt impelled to present an extended discussion in support of his proposal. He admitted that if Syria were "a nation, with a national history, with national traditions and with strong national feelings, such a solution would be unjust and unwise," but he thought this was not the case, and although injustice might be done "to the individuals who inhabit Palestine" an injustice was "not being done to a nation." Moreover, Yale considered that the wishes of 14,000,000 Jews over the world, who had "a national history, national traditions, and a strong national feeling must be taken into consideration"—and he was not unmindful of the promises which had been made to the Jews, even if, perhaps, he appeared to minimize those which had been implied in the case of the Arabs. The promises to the Jews had to be "fulfilled and the Jews must be given their chance to found in Palestine a Jewish Commonwealth." There was no question but that the Jews would bring all the benefits of western science and civilization to Palestine, and, as an American, Yale stressed that a Jewish state would fall under the control of American Jews who would develop a veritable outpost of Americanism in the Near East. Many difficulties would have to be worked out, especially the great bitterness among the Arabs of Palestine and Syria toward the Jews and the "determined opposition to the establishment of a Jewish National Home." In some Palestinian towns the feeling was so intense that it was "not safe for a Jew to pass the night there." Arabs would resist Jewish immigration, and it would be "necessary to protect the interests and rights of the Christians and Moslems of Palestine." The Holy Places would have to be safeguarded for Christians, Jews, and Moslems. Great Britain, not unnaturally, was recommended as the mandatory,

> not only because the Jews all desire the British but because Great Britain is for many reasons more fitted for the task than any other power. As Great Britain has a very large number of Moslem subjects she will be obliged to see that the Moslems of Palestine are rightly treated by the Jews. The Jewish population of the British Isles is very small and the Jewish question will not play any part in her internal politics, and Great Britain is not a Catholic country, so will not have the world-wide forces of Catholicism reacting upon her to put stumbling blocks in the way of Zionists. Finally the British are primarily responsible for the promises given to the Jews and it was British armies which delivered Palestine from the Turks.

Great Britain was also better prepared and able to assist in executing "the Zionist program than any other country."

Before recommending with regard to Syria and Mt. Lebanon, Yale thought it necessary to examine the various alternatives. The two should be considered as a political unit, placed under one political system and given one mandate only in the case of a unified development along similar lines. Over a period of years this spirit of unity might be developed through a system of education. Such a development could not be expected under a British mandate, for, among other reasons, a British United Syria "would tend inevitably to gravitate towards an Arab Moslem confederacy," a solution which would be unjust to the Christian Lebanese. In all probability, too, such unity could not be achieved under France. With obligations to the Christian populations, France could not enter into agreement with the Young Arabs without causing continual trouble between Moslems and Christians. On the other hand, the United States, if it accepted a mandate over Syria and Mt. Lebanon, could in all probability hold a neutral position among the different religious groups, and might develop a better feeling among them. But whether the United States would succeed in creating a genuine nationalism in United Syria, and in separating the Moslem Arabs of Syria from those of Arabia and Mesopotamia was another question. The Syrian Moslems were interested in an Arab Moslem Confederation, and the Young Arabs were not really concerned with a national state. Moreover, there were hidden European forces which might frustrate any American efforts looking toward national unity. Finally, "a strong nationalistic Syria would not be welcomed in the Moslem world unless it was a Moslem Syrian state; nor would it be welcomed by the British in Mesopotamia and in Egypt." To attempt to develop Syria and Mt. Lebanon as a

> united and secular state, unless the rest of the Arab provinces of the former Ottoman Empire were under our control, would be a dangerous, troublesome and uncertain experiment for the United States. America should not accept a mandate over United Syria or any part thereof

unless she could accept at the same time a mandate over Mesopotamia and could assume the responsibility for the supervision of Arabia.

In view of these convictions, Yale felt obliged to reject "the possibility of an American mandate" altogether.

Having ruled out a British, French, or American mandate over a united Syria, Yale recommended that Mt. Lebanon should be constituted "as a separate political unit, with its boundaries enlarged to include roughly what is termed Greater Mount Lebanon, and placed under the Mandate of France." Tripoli, on the other hand, should be set aside as a Syrian port and not included in Mt. Lebanon. Beirut should be incorporated in Mt. Lebanon, with Syrian rights and privileges guaranteed. This solution would be approved by a majority of Mt. Lebanon citizens, Yale thought, and by more than one-fifth of the total population of United Syria. Moreover, it would give the Christians "an opportunity to develop without let or hindrance from the Moslems." It would preclude the possibility of a continual Moslem-Christian struggle for domination. While it was dangerous to prophesy, the creation of a separate, autonomous Mt. Lebanon State might have a beneficial influence throughout both Syria and the Lebanon, for a self-governing Christian Arab community might have a civilizing influence on the Moslems "which they would be reluctant to accept from Europeans or foreigners." The Christians would become more self-respecting and the Moslems would cease to despise them as inferior. Yale also thought that if the forces which did tend to unify the Syrians had potential strength, the establishment of an autonomous Lebanese state might actually do more to bring these two elements together than a compulsory union which was both "unnatural and abhorrent" to the Christians.

Yale also recommended that Damascus, Homs, Hama, Tripoli, Aleppo and Latakia be constituted as an Arab state under the Emir Feisal, a proposition in which he was in substantially complete agreement with the rest of the Commission. In order to aid this community to develop and to protect the minorities, foreigners and foreign interests, it was to be placed under the League of Nations, which was to name the mandatory. But too close relations among Syria, Palestine and Mt. Lebanon made the choice of a mandatory difficult. Most of the inhabitants had flatly rejected French assistance. Even France as the mandatory of the Christian Mt. Lebanon "would find many difficulties in trying to assist a Moslem Arab State in the interior and such an arrangement would not prove very satisfactory." On the whole Great Britain would be acceptable to the Syrians, although Great Britain as the mandatory for a Jewish National Home in Palestine would meet trouble in attempting "to supervise the government of Syria." Not unlike Dr. Montgomery, Yale thought that either Great Britain or France or both together should be named as the tutor of the new Arab state. There was much to be said, he thought, in behalf of a joint mandatory, especially since Palestine and Mt. Lebanon were geographically and commercially an integral part of Syria, and their commercial development was intimately associated with that of Syria. Moreover, the powers which held the Palestinian and Lebanese mandates would necessarily exert a certain influence over the government of Syria. Yale did not include Alexandretta in the Arab state because it was the port of Aleppo and of Cilicia, Armenia, Kurdistan and the Mosul vilayet as well. Moreover, its population was not purely Arab, but contained a considerable Turkish and Armenian group. Such an important port ought not to be included in the Arab state.

In a few concluding sentences, Captain Yale ended his recommendations:

> Commercially and economically Syria, Palestine and Mount Lebanon should be considered as a unit with similar monetary systems, similar custom duties and trade regulations. No trade restrictions or barriers of any nature should be allowed to exist between these areas.
> The solutions herein proposed are not ideal solutions. There is no ideal solution of the so-called Syrian question. The solutions recommended are, as far as is possible, in accordance with the desires of the peoples concerned. The Jews of the world are accorded what they desire and what they have been promised. The Moslem Arabs are granted self-government and a State in which they can work out their destinies. The Lebanese are granted their political independence under French protection and an enlargment of their territory. The desires of the people are thus more than half way met. In view of conflicting desires and wishes of the different groups it would be impossible to do more. Both French and British interests have also been taken into consideration.
> Unless the United States should take the mandate of Syria, which she would be unwise to accept unless the other Arab provinces of Turkey were under her control, there is no other practical or workable solution of the Syrian question which would meet as completely the desires of the various peoples of Syria and be as beneficial to them.

Both the Montgomery and Yale memoranda and recommendations received full consideration on the part of President King and Professor Lybyer, for the margins were carefully annotated. The Yale memorandum especially illustrated the many instances, from the beginning to the end of the investigation, of basic disagreement concerning methods of the inquiry and the conclusions reached. But the differences went much deeper than that. King and Crane rightly felt that they were appointed by President Wilson and were, therefore, under the compulsion of implementing the Wilsonian ideals, regardless of any commitments to the contrary on the part of the Allied Powers. Yale, a military intelligence officer, did not feel bound specifically by the Wilsonian idealism, but did feel obliged to consider actual political commitments made by the United States and those of the Allied Powers to one another. He, therefore, attempted to find solutions through compromise and concession which, he thought, might prove acceptable to all the conflicting parties. In view of the disagreement, the actual preparation of the official, and only, Report of the King-Crane Commission, fell to President King, Mr. Crane, Professor Lybyer and Captain Donald M. Brodie.[1]

The Preparation of the King-Crane Report

On July 26, the day that Captain Yale and Dr. Montgomery turned in their memoranda, Professor Lybyer finished his summary description of the visit to Syria. Two days later he began the preparation of his historical account of the trip, which, after revision, was embodied in the Commission's *Report*.[2]

---

[1] Later, something of a controversy, of which Yale knew nothing, arose as to the nature of the memoranda of Dr. Montgomery and Captain Yale. Professor W. L. Westermann, Chief of the Western Asia Division at the Paris Peace Conference, and Professors Dana C. Munro and A. C. Coolidge, considered Yale's memorandum a "minority report." It is well to keep in mind, however, that both Montgomery and Yale, like Lybyer, who was General Technical Adviser, were advisers to the Commissioners. It should be recalled, too, that on April 24, 1919, the American Commission to Negotiate Peace advised Dr. King and Mr. Crane that they "should themselves take the responsibility for the persons whom they might desire to take with them." Memoranda of members of the technical staff could not, in the strict sense of the term, be considered as "minority reports." Professor Yale wrote the author on September 27, 1940: "The disagreement had become so serious by the time the Commissioners arrived at Constantinople that neither Montgomery nor Yale was consulted about the report which was being drawn up by the Commissioners and Dr. Lybyer. In fact, I never saw the Commission's report until it was completed, nor was I in any way consulted in regard to the conclusions arrived at. As I recall, neither was Dr. Montgomery. Montgomery and Yale, both being in disagreement with the Commissioners and Lybyer, each drew up a statement of his own conclusions. Montgomery's report dealt with the Turkish parts of the Ottoman Empire and Yale's report dealt with the Arab parts of the Empire. It was these two separate reports of the two technical advisers which I take it you refer to as the minority report." There is nothing in either the King or Lybyer *Diaries* to indicate serious difficulty, and Dr. King wrote to Lybyer on January 18, 1923 that "of course their reports were prepared for the Commissioners, at our own request, and our entire report was made in the light of the statements of all the Advisers." Lybyer noted in his *Diary* on August 12, 1919 that he had lunched with Montgomery and Yale and that Yale wanted "more discussion in report of possible division of Syria," although he had no note of Yale talking with the two Commissioners urging them to modify the report in that direction. Neither did Dr. King.

[2] Lybyer Papers: Begun on July 28, the sketch was completed on August 1, 1919. See A. H. LYBYER, *Brief Historical Sketch of the Visit to Syria, Palestine and Cilicia of the American Section of the International Commission on Mandates in Turkey*. Annotated and revised by Dr. H. C. King. Constantinople, August 1, 1919. Lybyer recorded on July 28: "Work on

8

The Lybyer Views

Professor Lybyer's tentative recommendations concerning Syria ran fundamentally counter to those of Captain Yale.[1] He firmly believed in the political and economic unity of Syria, "her most valuable inheritance from Turkey," and felt that a single mandatory under the League of Nations, should be assigned to Syria. A large measure of local autonomy should be established, however, in certain carefully delimited areas such as the Greater Mt. Lebanon. Lybyer felt that religious rivalries and antagonisms should be discouraged:

> The general attitude should be, not a hostility of Christianity toward Islam, but an earnest effort to find and maintain friendly *modus vivendi* between them. Religious minorities must be thoroughly protected, but they should not be recognized as possessing such rights as will impair the political unity of the country.

Moreover, "the feeling of Syrian nationalism should be cultivated, to replace religious particularism, and to strengthen the new state." Education should be put on an inclusive secular, national foundation as rapidly as possible, and the economic life of the country should be developed without too close association with the affairs of the mandatory power. While the established privileges of foreigners, such as the maintenance of schools and commercial concessions, should be preserved, such rights should be subject to modification under the mandatory. Lybyer believed that in Palestine the Zionist problem should be solved peacefully and guarantees given "against rude disturbance of the delicate world-wide religious balance" which centered there. Provision should be made for the Lebanon which would not destroy the popular sense of security, or "impair the political and economic unity of Syria." As to the mandatory—should it be the United States, Switzerland, or Great Britain, or, perhaps, "Great Britain with an adjusted relationship providing for the participation of France, particularly in the Lebanon"?

---

notes, preparing after reading them all over, to write historical account of trip to be a part of the Commission's report on Syria."

[1] Lybyer Papers: A. H. LYBYER, *Tentative Recommendations as to Syria, including Palestine,* July 29, 1919. In a penciled outline in Dr. King's handwriting dealing with the Syrian situation, King stated the pros and cons of a French or Swiss mandate for Syria. "*As to France*: *Pro*—Long connection with Syria; Education, language, etc; in protectorate—long continued; Lebanon desires; French Feeling; *Con*—Arab feeling a[gainst]; see reason for feeling ag. Fr. *Swiss Mandate*: *Pro*—Thoroughly democratic; no imperialistic bearing...; used to a difficult and intricate situation; experienced...; a large body of trained administrators, gov't and provincial. *Con*—danger of Ger...; no sufficient Power to hold from aggre.; not asked by people, asked for strong Power; need more financial assistance, situation too difficult for a small Power; Peace Conference have had large Power in mind; Need reason for passing Italy by; Better be held for Albania."

Lybyer pointed out, in conclusion, that only the British were "capable of carrying out satisfactorily the 'desirable general conditions'."

The work on the Syrian portion of the Report moved somewhat slowly and required many hours and days of serious effort. The analysis of the problem of Mesopotamia was somewhat easier, since it was generally agreed that Great Britain should have the mandate there, and the two Reports were completed by August 13.[1] The Commissioners now concentrated on the question of Asia Minor, or Turkey and Armenia. Basically there were three essential problems yet to be settled, those of Armenia, the projected Constantinopolitan State and its boundaries, and Anatolia. Lybyer prepared brief memoranda on all three problems, the essence of which found their way into the final Report of the King-Crane Commission.

Views on the Armenian Problem

The first of the memoranda dealt with the Armenian problem. As Lybyer remarked:[2]

> Having read most of the documentary material on hand, and the time being short, I found myself ready to express opinions which have been forming for some time. I completed statistical work on estimating the Armenian population in 1914, 1920, and 1925, and wrote a draft of reasons why the smaller Armenia, substantially what the Russians held in 1917, had a chance for existence which the larger scheme could not have. My draft pleased Mr. Crane and King greatly, and I was asked to do the same for the Constantinople state and other areas in doubt.

The analysis began with the proposition that the Armenians should be given a definite territory, taken from both Russia and Turkey, and organized into a self-governing, independent state as soon as practicable. Otherwise the Armenians might remain a center of world-disturbance. They were entitled to an amount of land which took into account their

---

[1] See King Papers: II. *The Southern or Arab Area*. Marked "Entirely Personal", 8 pp. A discussion of the problems of Syria and Mesopotamia. The Commission also had at its disposal a document prepared by Howard Crosby BUTLER, *Report on the Proposals for an Independent Arab State or States*, 42 pp., which gives a rather detailed study of the geography, political divisions, recent history, peoples and languages of the Arabic lands. Butler outlines a number of possible alternative solutions for the Arab peoples, including unity under King Hussein, and a proposal to establish a number of small independent states on the Arabian peninsula. A final proposal involved a federation of the small Arab states, but Butler thought this would face "many of the problems involved in the proposal for a united Arabia...." Butler gathered from personal experience and reading that the Arabs had "no real national consciousness." Race consciousness, on the other hand, was strongly developed and sometimes was mistaken for national consciousness.

[2] Lybyer *Diary*, August 19, 1919. King Papers: A. H. LYBYER, *Reflections as to Armenia*, August 19, 1919. Original.

losses in the massacres of 1894-1896, 1908-1909, and 1915-1916, estimated at 1,000,000 altogether. But they "should not be given an excessive amount of Turkish territory," if their community were to prove viable. There was a danger, in Lybyer's view, of leaving Turks, Kurds and others with just grievances against the Armenians. Moreover, the Armenians were not yet ready for self-government and should not be permitted to rule over other peoples now or later. The League of Nations or a mandatory power should not be asked "to hold down and perhaps squeeze out a large majority" merely to give a small minority time "to multiply and fill the land." If the Armenians were given too large a territory, they would "never be able to occupy and hold it." Neither could they properly serve as a buffer state between the Moslem areas held by the Turks and the Arabs.

Dr. Lybyer rejected as impossible the proposed large Armenia which extended from the Black Sea to the Mediterranean, for within that area both in 1914 and before 1894 the Armenians were only a small minority, "probably never exceeding twenty-five per cent." Even if all the losses were included, the Armenians would not amount to more than one-third of the population as a whole. It would be a violation of the Wilson principles to place them in control over the region. Besides, "there never was an Armenia which ruled all this territory." The real Armenia, a highland country, at one time reached the Caspian Sea, but did not approach the Euxine, and never came near the Mediterranean. The demand for the Black Sea littoral or Cilicia was "an imperialistic claim, based historically upon an overstrained interpretation of the facts." In 1919 the Armenians constituted only about 10 per cent of the population of the large area. Since no European power would assume the difficult task of the mandate, it would have to fall to the United States to supervise the state. But the chances were considerable

> that the large Armenia would never become an Armenian state at all, but a mixed state, composed of minorities of Armenians, Turks, Kurds, etc., which could not maintain internal order or security against external aggression without the perpetual support of a strong mandatory power.

On the other hand, a state limited to the Armenian highlands in both Turkey and Russia, with an outlet on the eastern shores of the Black Sea, would have "a good chance of establishment and continuance." Turkish and Russian Armenia would constitute this smaller, limited area. The Turks and Kurds could not justly complain, because this would be "historical Armenia", and if the 1,000,000 dead could be restored, "the Armenians would have about one-half the population", a proportion which they might reach anyway, by natural increase, within a few years. For the smaller area the term of the mandate could be shortened, the burden lessened, and the probability of a durable Armenian state would be increased, since the minorities would be smaller and the land defensible. The economic opportunities within the land would be ample, too, since the basic foods, fuels and shelter could be obtained locally, and surpluses produced. In both Turkish and Russian Armenia the people had been able to live, and often to prosper. The region, moreover, was crossed by important ancient commercial routes, notably through Erzinjan and Erzerum between Anatolia, Persia and Transcaucasia. Lybyer concluded:[1]

> All this is argued with the best interests of the Armenians in mind. I have always been friendly to them, and am now concerned with giving them a real and not an illusory opportunity. They are in genuine danger of grasping at too much and losing all. There is no reason why, if they establish themselves securely in this area, and if Anatolia fails to develop as a well knit and successful state, the question should not be resumed later of connecting Cilicia with Armenia.

A Constantinopolitan State

In his memorandum on the Constantinopolitan state, Lybyer pointed out that[2]

> the primary reason for the setting up of a separate area at Constantinople, to be forever under a special regime controlled by the League of Nations, is that the Straits between the Black Sea and the Mediterranean, being the concern of many nations, who cannot remain satisfied with the ownership of any one power, should be permanently and freely open.

Since the Sea of Marmara was small and substantially a part of the Straits, a minimum boundary would have to include "not only the whole of both sides of the Bosphorus and the Dardanelles, but also the entire shore of the Sea of Marmara," in agreement with the American experts on international law at Paris who had declared that serious complications might develop if "an independent state should reach these waters at any point." Constantinople was also the place where the railways crossed between Europe and Western Asia—the gateway to three continents. Since the population was already mixed, there was "no need to adjust the boundary to social racial groups." On the European side, it was better to leave with Constantinople the present remnant of European Turkey substantially to the Enos-Midia line, with some minor alterations, and Turkish Thrace. Thrace had been ceded to the Balkan Allies early in 1913, and had been assigned to Bulgaria, but was regained by the Turks after the Second Balkan War. If Bulgaria were kept "out of her rightful lands in Macedonia," it was felt that it would have ground for

---

[1] Lybyer Papers; See also David MAGIE, *Proposed Boundaries of Turkey and Armenia.*
[2] Lybyer Papers: A. H. LYBYER, *Re: Boundaries of the Constantinople State.* See also the Lybyer *Diary*, August 20, 1919.

claiming Turkish Thrace as a region for refugee settlement. However, there had been a considerable population exchange since 1915, so that few Bulgarians remained, while the number of Turks had increased. The Greeks wanted the territory and their claim had been admitted by the Peace Conference without adequate investigation or real justification, for in 1914 the Greek population was barely 25 per cent of the total. On the basis of population, "Turkish Thrace was really Turkish in 1914, the population reaching at least 60%." There was no present prospect that, without violent changes, a non-Turkish element would become a majority for a considerable time. But if a change did take place in ethnic composition, boundary alteration could be effected by the League of Nations by transferring "a portion of Thrace out of the Constantinople area." On the Asiatic side the frontier, beginning on the Black Sea at the mouth of the Sakaria river, might extend to near Lefke, then ascend to the ridge at the north, and proceed west along the heights south of Isnik, Mudania, and Panderma, as far as the boundary of the Sanjak of Begha, which it might follow to the sea south of Mt. Ida. Another line between the Black Sea and Ismid would run east of the Sakaria, including the land mass near the mouth of the river, so as to facilitate the solution of drainage problems. Brusa should be left to the Turks

> because it has no relation to the defense of the Straits, because the local population is predominantly Turkish, and because the Turks are sentimentally attached to this as the first Ottoman capital. To take from them all three capitals, Constantinople, Adrianople, and Brusa, would be very severe.

On the other hand, the region of Troy, although predominantly Turkish, because of its position, should go with the Straits. The population of the entire area in the beginning would be about 2,000,000, of whom about 60 per cent would be Turkish, 25 per cent Greek, and 10 per cent Armenian. In time the Turkish portion would probably decrease, in relation to Greeks and western Europeans, "especially in Constantinople and the smaller cities of the area."

The Disposition of Anatolia

The disposition of Anatolia was a complicated problem.[1] After setting off all the Arabic-speaking areas, Armenia, and Constantinople, there remained a large mass of territory, in which there was a predominantly Turkish element for which provision would have to be made. The seriousness of the problem was accentuated by the demands of the Kurds, Greeks, Syrians, and even the Italians, for portions of the territory.

The Kurds claimed a very large area in which they were greatly mixed with Armenians, Turks, and others, and were themselves divided into

---

[1] Lybyer Papers: A. H. LYBYER, *Anatolia: Draft of Opinion.*

Kizilbash Shiites and Sunnis. But it seemed best to confine them to the natural geographical region "between the proposed Armenia on the north and Mesopotamia on the south, with the divide between the Euphrates and the Tigris as the western boundary, and the Persian frontier as the eastern boundary." Under close mandatory rule, a measure of autonomy could be permitted, with the object of preparing them for independence or federation with their neighbors "in a larger self-governing union." By shifting both Turks and Armenians from this region through a voluntary population exchange, a group of about 1,500,000 Kurds could be obtained, although full security would have to be provided for the minority Syrian, Chaldean and Nestorian Christian populations. Since the area contemplated for the Kurds looked to the south rather than the west and was wholly around the upper waters of the Tigris and its tributaries, it seemed better to place it under the mandatory for Mesopotamia, rather than to connect it with Armenia or Anatolia.

Kurdistan seemed about the only case to be handled separately. One half of the area demanded by the Greeks of the "Pontus" should go to the Armenian state, in order to give it access to the sea and the other half was "needed by Anatolia for the same reason." There were only about 200,000 Greeks in each of these portions when the war began in 1914, and this was too small a minority "in both Armenia and Anatolia to be erected into an autonomous province." The rights of the Greeks could be protected by general laws enforced by the mandatory power.

Cilicia, which both the Armenians and Syrians were claiming, was in a similar position, for in neither case did the minority involved exceed 25 per cent in 1914. It should not be given to the Armenians, and it was not important for Syria as an outlet, since Syria had many ports. It was, however, vital "to the areas both at the northeast and the north." Cilicia should not be separated economically from Anatolia, and if given to the Armenians, provision would have to be made for the interior regions of Anatolia to have free use of its ports. The region between Cilicia and Armenia, which included Albistan, Malatia, and Harput, although claimed by the Armenians, "should also be left with Anatolia." That area contained a mixture of Turks, Kizilbash, Armenians, Sunni Kurds and others. Because of all the difficulties involved, a strong mandatory would be necessary.

Like most observers, Dr. Lybyer could not justify the Italian claim to Adalia at all, for

> Italy's claim to the southwest of Asia Minor rests upon nothing that is compatible with the principles of the Commission's instructions. There are no Italians native to the country, and no evidence exists that the population desires Italy as a mandatory over them. In this region the Moslems are to the Greek Orthodox Christians as ten to one. None of this area should be separated from Anatolia.

The section devoted to the Greek claim in Smyrna and the west was almost equally severe. The problem was difficult not because of the "intrinsic situation, but because of the persistency of the Greek Government in demanding an area there," and of the fact that a Greek army, ruthless in its methods, was in occupation. The Greeks were not in a majority in the region except perhaps directly in the Sanjak of Smyrna itself. It could be doubted whether modern Greece had reached such a degree of development that it could be "entrusted with mandatory rule over a people of different faith and hostile feeling." The Greek army should be withdrawn from the area. Until the Greeks had substantially conquered Anatolia or been "wholly removed," there would be neither peace nor order. There was no justification for establishment of an area in western Asia Minor as a special Greek preserve. The character of the country provided no natural boundaries except in the high hills, but the population of that district would contain three Moslems to one Greek, and if a more or less arbitrary line were drawn farther west, it would not be a barrier for defense, but might constitute an economic barrier cutting off Smyrna and other coastal towns from the hinterland. Finally, both Greeks and Turks in western Asia Minor would assume that it was "the intention of the League of Nations to permit Greece later to annex the territory set off." The maximum which Lybyer advised was a single, strong mandatory power for all Anatolia which "should take special pains to protect Greeks and Turks alike and preserve order in the west." The problem of a future Greek area could then be left in abeyance, to be brought up again if circumstances justified it.

Many Turks, especially in Constantinople, had suggested a mandate over Anatolia, and some had urged that the United States assume the task. As Lybyer reasoned:

> The need for supervision over finance, public works, education, internal order, and all the processes of government is hardly less for the Turks, despite their centuries of political experience, than for the Armenians, Syrians, and Mesopotamians. It is in fact impossible to discern any other method of settling Western Asia in order. The Turks if left to themselves in a condition of poverty, ignorance, and general exhaustion, with a feeling that they had been unjustly treated and then abandoned by all the world, could not fail to be a source of trouble and disturbance until another crisis, with perhaps another great war, would necessitate some such solution as is now suggested, but under conditions less favorable to success.

The Desirability of a Single Mandatory

The desirability of a single mandatory for Armenia, Anatolia, and Constantinople was next to be discussed. Mr. Crane really favored it, Dr. Gates had urged the necessity for unity, and Admiral Bristol had sent many telegrams and despatches urging such a solution. Moreover, many Turks in their testimony before the Commission in Constantinople had pled for it. Professor Lybyer argued that while it was desirable that Armenia, Anatolia, and Constantinople be placed under separate mandates, and governed by separate administrations, it was preferable that "the three mandates should be held by one great power." These areas had been held together for centuries under Ottoman rule, and they had numerous close ties, "the delicate adjustment" of which could best be accomplished under a single power. In addition, the "unity of economic control," with similar commercial regulations, coinage, weights, measures, language, was "advantageous to all concerned." Problems of repatriation and population exchange could be facilitated under a single mandatory. Likewise, the question of the public debt could be more satisfactorily adjusted. Moreover, the construction of railways and roads could be more easily arranged, and police control and repression of brigandage could be simplified. Unity had been urged by many well-informed foreigners. Some had favored not merely a single mandatory, but a single mandate, for virtually all the benefits of the first plan could be obtained under the second, and a number of serious difficulties could be avoided —such as persecution of the Armenians, interference with navigation, and complications of intrigue. There would be relatively little friction under one mandatory. Finally, the transition would be more acceptable to the Turkish people, especially if the mandatory established central control in Constantinople.

Completion of the Commission's Work

August 20 was the last full day of work at Constantinople, for the King-Crane Commission had instructions to leave for Paris the next day. That evening at dinner the work was pleasantly summed up when Lybyer remarked: "Dr. King contributes the morality, and I the territoriality of the report." Dr. King added quickly: "And Mr. Crane the geniality."[1]

The members of the Commission left their comfortable quarters at the Constantinople Women's College, donating the remaining supplies of coffee, sugar, cocoa, jam and other products to the College, and departed on the *U. S. S. Dupont* in the afternoon of August 21. The King-Crane Report was essentially completed by the time the Commission left the Golden Horn, although there was a little final work to do on the ship, and even after arriving in Paris. Following the trip up the Adriatic

[1] Lybyer *Diary*, August 20, 1919. The Commission received instructions on August 17 through Ravndal, noting the Commission's intention to complete work by the end of August. The Commissioners Plenipotentiary at Paris had stated: "This is in accordance with the desire of Department and Ammission which have adopted a general policy of withdrawing field missions. Ammission expects therefore that you will leave with all personnel not later than September first." See also *PPC*, XI, 358, 389-390.

and a two-day stop in Venice, visiting churches and other places of interest, the Americans left by train for Paris on August 26, reaching the French capital, ready to present their report, the next day.

Dr. King and Mr. Crane, in an hour and a half interview on August 28, presented an outline of their recommendations to Frank L. Polk, Henry White, and General Tasker H. Bliss, of the American Commission to Negotiate Peace, who listened very sympathetically. Lybyer was already preparing maps of Armenia and the Constantinopolitan state and having discussions with various people.

While the King-Crane Report was being put into final form, Mr. Crane, in behalf of the Commission, sent a cable to President Wilson, on August 30, giving a telegraphic summary of the final conclusions.[1] Crane indicated that the situation in Turkey was so serious that the Commission had decided to report to the President "as soon as it had covered essentials." The Report was well founded on vital human facts "not in harmony with many things" the Allies were "doing or planning to do." Crane believed it would help Wilson's campaign in behalf of the League of Nations to have the Report published and indicated that Dr. King, who was sailing soon for the United States, might take part in the campaign with the President. He then added:

> Outside of Armenia and Constantinople the former Turkish state must be kept in trust for the Moslem world or there will be no peace there nor in any other part of the world. The flouting of the doctrine of no annexations will horrify millions of people whose only trust now is in America and in you. It is not fair to the Turks to add to the strain already caused by the Greek landing and killing at Smyrna where one hundred thousand troops have demoralized a country kept well in hand by twelve British officers.

Then followed the specific proposals embodied in the Crane cable to the President:

> We are recommending for Syria first that whatever administration go in be a true mandatory under League of Nations; second that Syria including Palestine and Lebanon be kept a unity according to desires of great majority; third that Syria be under a single mandate; fourth that Emir Feisal be King of the new Syrian State; fifth that extreme Zionist program be seriously modified; sixth that America be asked to take the single mandate for Syria; seventh that if for any reason America does not take mandate then it be given to Great Britain.

The Commission proposed Great Britain as the mandatory for Mesopotamia, "in strict fulfilment of spirit of Anglo-French Declaration" of November 1918. As to the rest of the territory:

---

[1] King Papers: Charles R. Crane to President Wilson, Cable, Paris, August 30, 1919.

We are recommending for Turkey: first separate Armenian state under mandate limited in area for their own sakes; second separate international Constantinopolitan State under League of Nations administered through mandatory; third mandatory for continued Turkish state according to their own desire; fourth that no independent territory be set off for Greeks for present; fifth appointment of Commission on precise boundaries; sixth a general single but composite mandate for non-Arabic speaking portions of Turkish Empire to include subordinate mandates as indicated with governors and governor-general; seventh that America be asked to take the whole if reasonable conditions can be fulfilled; not to take any part if not the whole.

While neither the full Report nor Mr. Crane's cable was published, the work of the Commission was not to be hidden, like the ancient light, under a bushel. Shortly after their return to Paris from the Near East, Mr. Crane and Dr. King gave an interview to the press.[1] Neither divulged any details, although both believed that the United States should take a mandate not only for Armenia and Constantinople, but for all parts of the Ottoman Empire, including Palestine and Syria. President Wilson, in his address at Boston on February 24, had given the impression that only Armenia had been involved, as American opinion had understood. To the press, however, it seemed that "Messrs. Crane and King would include the whole Empire," thus placing under American administration regions concerning the control of which Great Britain and France were then "in sharp disagreement." Mr. Crane remarked:

> We found the opinion of the best Turks themselves in favor of an American mandate..., as the wisest solution of their own troubles, although, of course, there is a powerful sentiment among the Turks, the extent of which cannot be accurately gauged, for the continuance of their complete independence. But among the subject peoples of the Turkish Empire the desire is almost unanimous for the Americans to come as administrators. In certain parts of Palestine the first choice is for England as the mandatory power, and in certain Catholic regions, like Lebanon, the first choice is for France; but for far the greater part of the whole Empire the first choice is for America.

The people of the Near East, according to Mr. Crane, knew all about the United States. They knew the American record in Cuba and the Philippines. The reception of the American Commission had been very cordial because the people thought the Commission "brought them hope and assurances of American rule." It was necessary in every case, therefore, "to warn them against hoping too much," since it was "doubtful" that the United States would assume a mandatory burden.

But for us to take a mandate for all Turkey would do far more for the peace of the world than for us not to take it, and for it to be cut

---

[1] New York *Times*, August 31, 1919; Chicago *Daily News*, September 1, 1919. See also favorable editorials in The New York *Tribune* (September 25, 1919) and New York *Evening Post*, November 15, 1919.

up among the various other powers. We could do work in our own American way with a far smaller military force than any other power would think necessary.

It was clear that the people of the Near East wanted the Americans to assist them in reconstruction, for "they told us everywhere that we had assumed responsibilities which we should not evade, but would evade by not coming to Turkey."

It was true that there had been secret treaties which disposed of the various territories of the Near East, especially among Great Britain, France and Italy. But Mr. Crane thought that it would be good for the world "if some little attention could be paid to the sacredness of open agreements." He referred to the Anglo-French Declaration of November 1918, putting both powers on record "in favor of the independence, the exercise of free will and the honest, unfettered development of the native populations of Turkey." That statement had been spread broadcast throughout the Ottoman Empire and the people had taken it seriously "as the promise of the great things they might expect after the war." Although the United States was not a signatory, the people of the Ottoman Empire believed that Great Britain and France could "best fulfil that agreement by letting America come in with a mandate or mandates for the whole country."

Meanwhile, the King-Crane Report was to go to the American Peace Commission and to President Wilson and it was to be made available unofficially to the Peace Conference, if the British, French and Italian delegations desired to learn of its recommendations. [1]

THE KING-CRANE REPORT [2]

The King-Crane Report was a most interesting and significant document, which fell into three broad, natural divisions: Data, General Considerations, and Recommendations. Basically it was written by President King and Professor Lybyer, while Captain Brodie, the Secretary of the Commission, prepared the data furnished by the inquiry. Since we have already considered the materials which the Commission used in the formulation of its attitudes, policies and conclusions, we may be content at this point in studying especially its various recommendations as to the different portions of the Ottoman Empire.

[1] An editorial in a Paris newspaper, *"Revenant de Syrie"*, August 31, 1919, after casting slurs on the work of the King-Crane Commission, noted that the Americans were under the leadership of Mr. Crane, "a rich American who provided Mr. Wilson with his campaign funds in 1916."

[2] *PPC*, XII, 751-863. See also "First Publication of King-Crane Report on the Near East: A Suppressed Official Document of the United States Government," *Editor and Publisher*, Vol. 55, No. 27 (December 2, 1922), ii-xxvii. Carbons of original copy in King Papers. The Report

Syria and Palestine [1]

In its analysis of the problems of Syria and Palestine, the King-Crane Commission based its position on the resolution of the Council of Four on January 30, 1919 and the Anglo-French Declaration of November 1918. But it also noted M. Pichon's declaration before the French Chamber of Deputies on December 29, 1918, in which he admitted the complete freedom of the Peace Conference to deal with the Near Eastern problem. The sincerity of these intentions would now be tested in their application, and the Commission believed that there was probably no region in which the Allies were freer to pursue their course according to their professed principles.

Syria presented grave and complicated problems. This ancient land was the birthplace of three great religions—Judaism, Christianity and Islam—and Palestine specifically contained holy places sacred to adherents of all three religions. No solution involving considerations for only a single people could be offered.

> As a portion of the bridge-land uniting Europe, Asia, and Africa, too —where in a peculiar degree the East and the West meet—Syria has a place of such strategic importance, politically and commercially, and from the point of view of world civilization, as also to make it imperative that the settlement here brought about should be so just as to give promise of permanently good results for the whole cause of the development of a righteous civilization in the world. Every part of the former Turkish Empire must be given a new life and opportunity under thoroughly changed political conditions. [2]

The break-up of the Ottoman Empire provided a new opportunity to develop in Syria a Near Eastern community resting on the modern foundation of complete religious freedom, especially protecting the rights of minorities. It was a matter of elementary justice to the Arabs that a modern Arab state should be formed. Despite difficulties, the conditions were as favorable as could be expected at that time. The mixed populations had lived together under the Ottoman Empire, and should "do far better under a state on modern lines and with an enlightened mandatory." Thanks to the presence of a modern mandatory there seemed little danger of the Arabs falling into the errors of the Young Turks. There was confidence in the leadership and intelligence of the Emir Feisal, who was to become king of liberated and united Syria. If the policy failed, the

---

was not officially published until 1947 when Volume XII of *Papers Relating to the Foreign Relations of the United States, The Paris Peace Conference 1919,* appeared.

[1] *PCC*, XII, 751-799.

[2] See also Sir Halford J. MACKINDER, *Democratic Ideals and Reality: A Study in The Politics of Reconstruction* (London, Constable, 1919), 112-21, on significance of the Near East.

country could be partitioned later on. Any program for Syria should consider as far as possible "its natural geographic and economic unity." This was in line with the policy of the Peace Conference and the desires of the people. It was pointed out, too, that both British and French officers in Syria seemed to favor the unity of Syria under one mandatory, and that there would be danger of friction if both the British and the French remained. There were obstacles to the unity of Syria, however:

> The apparent unwillingness of either the British or the French to withdraw from Syria—the British from Palestine, or the French from Beirut and the Lebanon; the intense opposition of the Arabs and the Christians to the Zionist program; the common Lebanese demand for complete separate independence; the strong feeling of the Arabs of the East against any French control; the fear on the part of many Christians of Moslem domination; and the lack of as vigorous a Syrian national feeling as could be desired.

In the light of these general considerations the King-Crane Commission made its recommendations concerning Syria and Palestine. Let us turn, first, to Syria. Whatever the foreign administration over Syria, the King-Crane Commission proposed, first, that it be strictly a mandatory under the League of Nations, with the definite understanding that "the well-being and development" of the Syrian people constituted a "sacred trust." The Mandatory should have a limited period to be determined by the progress of the country, and the administration sufficient time and authority, "to ensure the success of the new state," especially in matters economic and educational. Indeed, it was thought that education should be stressed in view of its imperative necessity for democratic citizenship and for "the development of a sound national spirit." This was essential in a country like Syria, which had "only recently come to self-consciousness." The mandatory also should strive to train the Syrian people to independent self-government as rapidly as possible through the establishment of democratic institutions and increased popular participation in government. It was also the duty to guarantee religious liberty, both in theory and practice, and to see that all minority rights were protected, for nothing was "more vital ... for the enduring success of the new Arab State." A dangerous amount of indebtedness should be avoided as well as any financial entanglements with the affairs of the mandatory. Nevertheless, there was no objection to preserving established foreign educational and commercial establishments, but the mandatory power should not use its position to encourage monopolistic control to the detriment of Syria or other nations. It should strive toward developing economic along with political independence. Whatever else was done, the Commission felt that these elementary principles and suggestions were basic to the welfare of Syria. Moreover, the Damascus Congress had betrayed in many ways the intense fear of the Syrians that their country "would become, though under some other name, simply a colonial possession of some other Power. That fear must be completely allayed."

The second fundamental recommendation was that the unity of Syria must be preserved, in accordance with the desires of the vast majority of the people. There were many reasons to support this proposal. The territory was too limited, the population too small, and "the economic, geographic, racial and language unity too manifest" to justify partition of the country. In language, culture, traditions and customs Syria was basically Arabic. A unified Syria was consonant both with the aspirations of the people and the principles of the League of Nations. The precise boundaries of the state could be determined by a commission, after the Syrian territory had been allotted. The Commissioners stressed their dissent from the Damascus Program for the inclusion of Cilicia within Syria, which they did not consider "justified, either historically or by commercial or language relations." Cilicia should be allocated to Asia Minor, rather than to Syria. Syria had no need of more seacoast, as did the large interior sections of Anatolia. While proposing the unity of Syria, a large measure of local autonomy was suggested for the Lebanon, which had had considerable prosperity and autonomy within the Ottoman Empire, and should be even more happy under a modern Syrian national state. But the Lebanon "would be better off if she were a constituent member of the State, rather than entirely independent of it." The argument was well presented:

> As a predominantly Christian country, too, Lebanon naturally fears Moslem domination in a unified Syria. But against such domination she would have a four-fold safeguard: her own autonomy; the presence of a strong mandatory for the considerable period in which the constitution and practice of the new State would be forming; the oversight of the League of Nations, with its insistence upon religious liberty and the rights of minorities; and the certainty that the Arab Government would feel the necessity of such a state, if it were to commend itself to the League of Nations. Moreover, there would be less danger of a reactionary Moslem attitude, if Christians were present in the state in considerable numbers, rather than largely segregated outside the state, as experience of the relations of different religious faiths in India suggests.
>
> As a predominantly Christian country, it is also to be noted that Lebanon would be in a position to exert a stronger and more helpful influence if she were within the Syrian state, feeling its problems and needs, and sharing all its life, instead of outside it, absorbed simply in her own narrow concerns. For the sake of the larger interests, both of Lebanon and of Syria, then, the unity of Syria is to be urged. It is certain that many of the more thoughtful Lebanese themselves hold this view. A similar statement might be made for Palestine; though, as "the Holy Land" for Jews and Christians and Moslems alike, its situation is unique, and might more readily justify unique treatment, if such treatment were justified anywhere....

Thirdly, Syria should be placed under one mandatory, as the natural way to secure genuine and efficient unity. Despite difficulties, the Syrian people were "forced to get on together in some fashion." Granted a reasonable local autonomy, a single mandatory ought increasingly to promote unity. Many Syrians had testified that while there were troubles among various groups, these had many times been caused by the Ottoman government itself. Decent relations could be assured under a just government, and "for the largest future good of all groups," Syria should be placed under a single mandate.

In the fourth place, it was suggested that the Emir Feisal be made the head of the new state, not only because the Damascus Congress had asked for him in the name of the Syrian people and a democratic, constitutional monarchy seemed suited to the Arab people, but because Feisal had come naturally to his position and there was no one else to replace him. Although Captain Yale disagreed, the Commissioners were well impressed with Feisal and recognized his outstanding qualities:

> He had the great advantage of being the son of the Sherif of Mecca, and as such honored throughout the Moslem world. He was one of the prominent Arab leaders who assumed responsibility for the Arab uprising against the Turks, and so shared in the complete deliverance of the Arab-speaking portions of the Turkish Empire. He was consequently hailed by the "Damascus Congress" as having "merited their full confidence and entire reliance." He was taken up and supported by the British as the most promising candidate for the headship of the new Arab State—an Arab of the Arabs, but with a position of wide appeal through his Sherifian connection, and through his broad sympathies with the best in the Occident. His relations with the Arabs to the east of Syria are friendly, and his kingdom would not be threatened from that side. He undoubtedly does not make so strong an appeal to the Christians of the West Coast, as to the Arabs of the East; but no man can be named who would have a stronger general appeal. He is tolerant and wise, skillful in dealing with men, winning in manner, a man of sincerity, insight and power. Whether he has the full strength needed for his difficult task it is too early to say; but certainly no other Arab leader combines so many elements of power as he, and he will have invaluable help throughout the mandatory period.
>
> The Peace Conference may take genuine satisfaction in the fact that an Arab of such qualities is available for the headship of this new state in the Near East.

In the fifth place, the Commissioners advised "serious modification of the extreme Zionist program" of unlimited immigration of Jews, looking finally toward the constitution of a distinctly Jewish state in Palestine. When one has followed the evidence which came before the Commission, this counsel is not surprising and seems justified and supported by the facts. The Commissioners had begun their investigations with a predisposition toward Zionism, but the facts in Palestine, coupled with the principles which the Allies had proclaimed, forced them to take a somewhat different position. They had, of course, come into contact with the Zionist Commission, had studied Zionist literature and propaganda, and had seen something of the outstanding accomplishments of the Jews in Palestine. The Commissioners were familiar with the general encouragement which the Allies had given to the Zionists, especially the famous Balfour Declaration of November 1917. But if the "strict terms" of the Balfour Declaration were to be followed, it could hardly be doubted "that the extreme Zionist Program must be greatly modified." A National Home for the Jews and a Jewish National State, apparently, were not one and the same thing.

The Wilson principle of "free acceptance" of the settlement by the peoples involved was called to mind, and the Commissioners declared that if that principle were to prevail in Palestine, then it should be remembered that "the non-Jewish population of Palestine"—about nine-tenths of the people—were "emphatically against the entire Zionist program." There was nothing on which the population of Palestine was more united. "To subject a people so minded to unlimited Jewish immigration, and to steady financial and social pressure to surrender the land, would be a gross violation of the principle just quoted, and of the people's rights, though it kept within the forms of law."

In the whole of Syria, it was pointed out, 72 per cent, or 1,350 of the petitions presented were against Zionism, and the only two propositions which received a larger support were those demanding an independent and united Syria. The Peace Conference, it was urged, should not be blind to the fact that "the anti-Zionist feeling in Palestine and Syria" was "intense and not lightly to be flouted." British officers estimated that some 50,000 soldiers would be required to carry out the Zionist program, evidence itself of the popular resentment and the feelings of those competent to judge. The Commissioners could not take seriously the claim that the Zionist had "a 'right' to Palestine, based on an occupation of 2,000 years ago." Finally, the fact that Palestine was sacred to Christians, Moslems and Jews alike was an argument against converting it into a National Home for the small Jewish minority, 10 per cent of the population, for the simple reason that neither Christians nor Moslems seemed likely to trust the Zionists with the impartial guardianship of all the holy places.

> In view of these considerations, and with a deep sense of sympathy for the Jewish cause, the Commissioners feel bound to recommend that only a greatly reduced Zionist program be attempted by the Peace Conference, and even that, only very gradually initiated. This would have to mean that Jewish immigration should be definitely limited, and that the project for making Palestine distinctly a Jewish Commonwealth should be given up.
> There would be no reason why Palestine could not be included in a united Syrian State, just as other portions of the country, the holy

places being cared for by an International and Inter-religious Commission, somewhat as at present, under the oversight and approval of the Mandatory and of the League of Nations. The Jews, of course, would have representation upon this Commission.

But who was to be the mandatory? The power ideally to be chosen for this task should be one desired by the people, willing heartily to take the mandate, democratic in spirit, one with sympathy and patience and with the necessary experience "in dealing with less developed peoples, and abundant resources in men and money." While no single power possessed all the necessary qualities, the survey left no doubt as to the choice of the majority of the Syrian people. The returns demonstrated that the United States was "the first choice of 1,152 of the petitions presented—more than 60 per cent—while no other Power had as much as 15 per cent for first choice." Although less experienced than Great Britain, the Commissioners felt confident of American ability to administer the mandate, and certainly there was the great qualification "of fervent belief in the new mandatory system of the League of Nations." The fact that the great majority of the Syrian people favored the United States over any other power, itself rendered the task easier and Great Britain and France would be less reluctant to yield to the United States than to each other. No power would be more welcome to the British in Egypt, Arabia or Mesopotamia, to the French with their interests in Beirut and the Lebanon, or to the Arabs and Syrians. [1]

But there were objections to a single American mandate for all Syria. There was no certainty of American acceptance, and it was not known that either Great Britain or France would withdraw. Again, the vague promises to the Zionists might prove embarrassing to an American administration. But most serious was the feeling

> that if America were to take any mandate at all, and were to take but one mandate, it is probable that an Asia Minor Mandate would be more natural and important. For there is a task there of such peculiar and worldwide significance as to appeal to the best in America, and demand the utmost from her, and as certainly to justify her in breaking with her established policy concerning mixing in the affairs of the Eastern hemisphere. The Commissioners believe, moreover, that no other Power could come into Asia Minor, with hands so free to give impartial justice to all the peoples concerned.

These objections, however, were not insuperable, and they did not relieve the Commissioners from the duty of advising that the United States take the single mandate for Syria. If the United States refused, then, in harmony with the wishes of the Syrian people, the Commissioners urged that the mandate be given to Great Britain, since more than 60 per cent of the Syrian Arabs were "directly and strongly" opposed to France.

[1] *PPC*, XII, 795-796.

There was even grave fear that an attempt to enforce a French mandate on the unwilling Arabs would lead to a Franco-Arabic struggle, "and force upon Great Britain a dangerous alternative." However favorably disposed toward France because of its long historic relations with Syria, the Commissioners had reluctantly come to this conclusion. Therefore:

> The Commissioners recommend... that if America cannot take the mandate for all Syria . . ., it be given to Great Britain because of the choice of the people concerned; because she is already on the ground and with much of the necessary work in hand; because of her long and generally successful experience in dealing with less developed peoples; and because she has so many of the qualifications needed in a Mandatory Power . . . .

The Commissioners frankly confessed their misgivings with regard to a British mandate, however, for they pointed to the honest fear of many that Great Britain might become a colonizing power "of the old kind"; that it would provide too expensive government for a poor people; that Syria's interests might be subordinated to those of the British Empire; that there might be exploitation; that it "would never be ready to withdraw and give the country real independence"; that it would not make adequate provision for education; and that it already had too many possessions for either its own or anybody else's good. It was these misgivings which explained the Syrian demand for absolute independence and the opposition to Article XII of the Covenant of the League of Nations.

In conclusion, the Commissioners emphasized that the interests of all nations were to be protected under the mandate, so that French ties with Syria need not be injured. There remained a final possibility. If France felt so intensely concerning its claims in Syria "as to threaten all cordial relations among the Allies," it might be given a mandate over the Lebanon, separate from Syria, as some groups in that region had requested, although the Commissioners frankly could not recommend such a course as a wise solution.

The Report on Mesopotamia [1]

Since Syria and Mesopotamia had been classed together as Arab countries in the Anglo-French Declaration of November 1918 and in the Resolution of the Council of Four on January 30, 1919, the Commissioners believed that Mesopotamia should receive similar treatment to that given Syria. They, therefore, advised that the mandate for Mesopotamia be considered as a sacred trust leading toward independence. Secondly, they urged that the unity of Mesopotamia be maintained, and that it should "probably include at least the Vilayets of Basra, Bagdad, and Mosul." The Southern Kurds and Assyrians might also be linked

[1] *PPC*, XII, 799-802.

with Mesopotamia. Thirdly, Mesopotamia should be placed under one mandatory, as the best means to secure unity. Again, in view of the past traditions and the desires of the people, the establishment of a constitutional monarchy was advised, and it was suggested that the Arabs of Mesopotamia be given a chance to make their choice of king, which was to be "reviewed and confirmed by the League of Nations." There had been indications already that the choice was likely to fall on one of the sons of King Hussein, although the Commissioners could hardly have guessed that it would have been the Emir Feisal, whom they had "picked" as the king of Syria, but whom the French would never allow to assume that throne.

Since there had been no visit to or investigation in Mesopotamia, there had been no sampling of opinion in the Land of the Two Rivers as to the choice of a mandatory. However, "the Mesopotamia program" had expressed "its choice of America" as the mandatory, with no second preference, since there had been considerable feeling against Great Britain. There was also a great deal of opinion favorable to Great Britain, the Commissioners believed, and the choice, after the United States, would certainly be Great Britain. Moreover, it appeared clear that if the United States did take a mandate for Syria and Asia Minor, it almost certainly would not take one for Mesopotamia. Therefore, the Commissioners advised that Great Britain assume the Mesopotamian mandate

> because of the general reasons already given for recommending her as mandatory in Syria, if America does not go in there; because she is probably best of all fitted for the particular task involved, in view of her long relations with the Arabs; in recognition of the sacrifices made by her in delivering Mesopotamia from the Turks, though with no acknowledgement of right of conquest, as her own statements expressly disclaim; because of the special interests she naturally has in Mesopotamia on account of its nearness to India and its close connections with Arabia; and because of work already done in the territory.

Although the Commissioners were reluctant to add more territory to the British Empire, it was felt that the best interests of the Arabs of Mesopotamia, despite their fear of Indian immigration, would be served under a British mandate, even granted the further dangers of British exploitation of the vast oil resources of the country.

The Non-Arabic-Speaking Portions of the Former Ottoman Empire [1]

In elaborating recommendations for the non-Arabic-speaking portions of the Ottoman Empire, the Commissioners expressed their belief that the ideas embodied in their instructions formed a sound basis "for the

---

[1] *PPC*, XII, 802-804, 804-819. Compare this section with the memorandum of May 1, 1919, sent to President Wilson, and signed by the Commissioners and the staff: "The Dangers to the Allies from a Selfish Exploitation of the Turkish Empire."

policy to be adopted in Asia Minor." Nor was this merely a sentimental program—it was both just and considerate. If the Conference proceeded to deal with the Ottoman Empire "honestly and strongly," and consistently to build on these foundations, "essential justice" would be done to all the peoples, basic wrongs would be righted, and the Allied purposes would be "just so far vindicated." The Conference needed vindication, for set against it were the policies of the old diplomacy exemplified in the secret treaties and understandings of 1915-1917. It was already to be feared that some of the highest ideals of the Allies had been blurred. The Peace Conference would have to decide the policies to be implemented, but after summarizing the background of pertinent action previously taken, the Commissioners warned of the dangers of a selfish exploitation and division of the Ottoman Empire. There had been unavoidable confusion, and under the "pressure of immediate necessity for some kind of action," many steps had been taken in the wrong direction. But whatever the explanation, there need be no mistake about the dangers involved. Constantinople once more was "a nest of selfish, suspicious, hateful intrigue, reaching out over the whole Empire, if not the world." In attempting to find a correct and just solution of the Ottoman problem, then,

> the Allies should bear clearly in mind that their fidelity to their announced aims in the war is here peculiarly to be tested; and that, in the proportion in which the division of the Turkish Empire by the Allies is made a division of spoils by the victors, and is primarily determined by the selfish national and corporate interests of the Allies, in just that proportion will grave dangers arise.

Any action against the interests of the people would have to be imposed upon them, as illustrated by the Greek seizure of Smyrna and all its disastrous consequences. A large number of troops would naturally provoke retaliation, as the Smyrna incident had amply demonstrated. A selfish exploitation would not only arouse American resentment, but would "alienate the best sentiment among all the Allies," threatening their moral unity, thereby contributing to the spread of mutual dissension, and entailing very serious world consequences. Finally, such exploitation would convince men of independent judgment everywhere that the aims of the Allies had been as selfish as those of the Germans. That conviction "would carry with it its own fateful consequences."

There was now an opportunity to provide some righteous settlement for the Ottoman Empire, to build on solid and just foundations:

> No namby-pamby, sickly sentimental treatment is called for here. There are great and lasting wrongs in Turkey which must be set right. And there are world relations and interests honestly to be recognized and permanently to be satisfied. For the sake of justice to Turkey herself and to all her subject peoples; for the sake of the honor of the

Allies and the renewed confidence of men in them; for the stemming of the tide of cynicism and selfish strife; for a fresh and powerful demonstration of moral soundness in the race; the Allies should recognize the grave danger of all selfish exploitation of Turkey and turn their backs on every last vestige of it.

While the Ottoman Empire should not be subject to imperialistic partition, nevertheless it was necessary to make some division on a proper and just basis because of "the hideous misgovernment and massacres of the Turkish rule" and because of "Turkey's utter inadequacy to the strategic position" in which it was placed. There could be no doubt of the age-old misgovernment of the Ottoman Empire even for Turkish citizens, despite the fine, personal qualities of the Turks, their "indolent tolerance" of other people, and the type of unity which the Ottoman Empire, with all its faults, had given to the Near East. It was recognized, too, that the intrigues of the great European Powers had contributed to the demoralization. Nevertheless, the government of the Ottoman Empire had been "for the most part a wretched failure, in spite of generally good laws," characterized as it was by "incessant corruption, plunder, and bribery." But the treatment of other peoples, as attested by the Bryce Report and many witnesses, was much worse, for they were secure neither in life nor in property. Hence, the Peace Conference had been justified in its policy of dividing up the Ottoman Empire, and especially in its attitude toward establishment of a separate Armenia.[1] The Armenian massacres themselves furnished the greatest justification of the policy, although it could be asked if some other solution might not be found. The only alternative was a general single mandate for all Asia Minor, insuring "equal rights to all elements of the population—to all races, and to all religions."

The reasons for a partition of the Ottoman Empire, however, rested on even more fundamental bases than "historical misgovernment." There was also the problem of the strategic position of Turkey. The very fact of age-long Turkish misrule, coupled with Ottoman occupation of territory of critical significance to the world, constituted a "menace to the freedom and security of all nations," and made restrictions imperative for the good of the world as well as the subjects of the Empire. The Turks had not been capable of turning the gifts of nature into use, and the evil influence of the Ottoman blight was greatly enhanced because of the strategic position occupied by the Ottoman Empire astride the routes to three great continents. A proper solution would be to change the Eastern problem from one of selfish exploitation and competition

---

[1] *PPC*, XII, 813-814. The formation of an independent Armenia was almost taken for granted in view of the appointment of Colonel Haskell as High Commissioner in Armenia and of the Harbord Mission to Armenia in August 1919.

among the Great Powers to one "of recognizing here a great and distinctly international or world interest," in keeping with the new conception of the League of Nations. Because of its position as a great continental "bridgeland", the Ottoman Empire naturally became a "debatable land" between the Occident and Orient, but it should now constitute a *mediating* land between the East and the West.

Thanks to that position, the Commissioners arrived at their conception of the control of Constantinople and the Straits in a spirit of genuine internationalism. The problem was an enthralling one for

> no situation in the world demands so compellingly international rule —not only to put an end here to the selfish scramble and perpetual intrigue of the nations, but also, above all, to rise to the possibilities of this strategic opportunity, for the benefit of all the race.

The obvious solution called for a Constantinopolitan State, under the League of Nations, with a single mandatory responsible to and removable by that body.

But if one turned from the immediate issue of Asia Minor to that of the former Ottoman Empire as a whole, there were other evident reasons for a "righteous division." One of these was the possible danger of a revival of the Ottoman Empire, to which some had pointed. Another was the lack of any real unity among the peoples of the old Empire, especially between the Arabic and non-Arabic peoples. It was this disunity, in particular, which had led the Peace Conference to resolve that Syria, Palestine, Mesopotamia, and Arabia should be "completely severed from the Turkish Empire."

The Problem of an Independent Armenia [1]

In order to avoid misunderstandings, it was considered necessary to describe the exact nature of the projected Armenian state. It was not proposed, for example, to establish the rule of an Armenian minority over "a majority of other peoples." On the other hand, an independent Armenia should have a definite territory to which the Armenians might go. A strong mandatory would be required because the state could not start without assistance. The mandatory, moreover, would have to remain to organize a modern government "until the Armenians constituted an actual majority of the entire population, or at least until the Turks were fewer than the Armenians." Only when the Armenians constituted an actual majority could they be safely entrusted with independent government. An American mandate seemed universally desired, not only by the Armenians, but by the Turks as well. The Commissioners could not advise the larger state which many Armenians had been claiming, because of the dangers which the overwhelming majority of non-Armenian

[1] *PPC*, XII, 819-828.

elements would present—difficulties which Professor Lybyer had well pointed out on August 19.

Constantinople and the Straits [1]

In facing the problem of a Constantinopolitan State it was necessary, first, to have a clear understanding of the nature of the proposed state, which should be directly under the League of Nations, and be administered under a permanent mandatory, removable only for cause. Moreover, the mandatory should be a "trustee for international interests, not a power using its position to advance its own national interests." Therefore, the supervising power should be disinterested both territorially and strategically. While the Constantinopolitan State could be administered through a body similar to the International Commission of the Danube, it was thought that a single mandatory could serve better.

Such a State should include Constantinople, and have charge of its own administration. This is the more demanded, for Constantinople is a markedly cosmopolitan city, where the Turks are probably not even in the majority. This State should also have a reasonable territory on either side of the Straits. All fortifications should be abolished. This international territory would of course be open to all people for any legitimate purposes. Like the District of Columbia in America, it would be a natural place for great international and religious foundations, so that Moslem institutions could remain and be further built up. The Turkish population, equally of course, would be free to stay. But Constantinople would not longer be the capital of Turkey. In the administration of the State, however, all possible consideration should be given to Moslem sentiment, and reasonable practical adjustments arranged. The Sultan might even conceivably continue to reside at Constantinople if that were desired under the conditions named.

A number of factors dictated this solution. It was necessary to insure the permanent freedom of the Dardanelles and to remove the intrigue of plot and counter-plot on the Golden Horn. There was also the opportunity to make the heavy responsibility for this world center *international*, rather than to leave it to a single power. Creation of a separate Constantinopolitan community would assist Turkey in developing a proper, democratic form of government in the Anatolian homelands, not only through the power of example, but by relieving it of the responsibility of the control of the Straits. At the same time, the Turks within the region of the Straits would doubtless have the best government they had ever had. The establishment of an international state would avoid future difficulties between rival powers, because otherwise there would be "endless intrigues on the part of various Powers to possess or control the Straits." It was suggested that the new state should include the city of Constantinople, Turkish Thrace and a strip of Asiatic Turkey, with the

[1] *PPC*, XII, 828-833; see also HOWARD, *The Partition of Turkey* 231-242.

shores of the Bosphorus, the Sea of Marmara and the Dardanelles. The solution was not intended to humiliate Turkey or the Moslem faith. The purpose was to safeguard the peace of Turkey and the world, although such a readjustment would involve both disturbance and sacrifice. In the end, however, the whole world would "gain from a permanent solution of this vexing world-question."

The Turkish Homelands [1]

Since an independent Armenia and an international Constantinopolitan state were recommended, the Turks would have to surrender their sovereignty over certain small parts of Asia Minor, but they would not be handled as their own conquerors had "treated territories won in war." The principle of self-determination was to be applied equally to the Turkish people. Anatolia, the Turkish homeland, with outlets to the sea, was to be left for the Turkish state, although under conditions which would "sacredly guard the rights of all minorities, whether racial or religious." The Turks would thus have a territory larger than France, with a population of about 10,000,000, about 8,000,000 of whom would be either Turks or Moslem. Some groups, however, might have to be allowed to transfer to Syria or Mesopotamia, or allowed local autonomy.

A mandate was also recommended for the Turks, a solution which seemed desirable from "every point of view" and which had commended itself to many intelligent, informed and patriotic Turks. It seemed impossible at the time to expect desirable governmental changes through any other method. Had the Turks not suggested a mandatory, the Peace Conference might have found it necessary to impose one. A mandate was required

> to secure genuinely good government, without oppression, bribery, or corruption, for the Turks themselves; to guarantee the rights of all minorities—racial or religious; to deliver Turkey from the demoralization of incessant intrigue from outside; to secure, without selfish exploitation by the Mandatory, or any other outside Power, Turkey's economic development and economic independence, for there is not the slightest doubt that she has been living far below her material possibilities; in line with the Allied settlement with Germany, to disband the most of the Turkish Army, and do away with all military conscription, depending upon a well organized gendarmerie for the larger police duties of the State,—all this for the better good of the common people and to break the power of intriguing imperialists over them; to put beneath all Turkish life a national system of universal education that should lift her entire people; to train the various peoples of the State steadily into self-government; in a word, to make Turkey a state of a high order on a modern basis of equal rights to all before the law, and of full religious liberty. This would inevitably result in a state not purely (though predominantly) Turkish in race and in

[1] *PPC*, XII, 833-840.

control, a cosmopolitan state in which various racial stocks were contained and in whose government all representatively shared.

The Commissioners felt that the Turks themselves really desired an American mandate, and Ahmed Emin and Velid Eleuzzia, two leading Turkish journalists, were especially cited in support of their belief. Moreover, the delegations which appeared before the Commission generally seemed to favor an American mandate. There were other evidences:

> The general judgment of the most trustworthy observers whom the Commission were able to consult confirmed these results. The delegates of a Congress held a few months ago at Smyrna, and representing 1,800,000 people, have declared for an American mandate. The Congress at Sivas held on the 20th of August, probably the most representative gathering of the Turkish people, is expected by those in closest touch with the movement for which it stands, to declare for an American Mandate. On the whole, it is highly probable that a large majority of the Turkish people, wishing a mandate at all, would favor an American Mandate.

While many Turks did favor American assistance in some form, the Commissioners were wrong about the Sivas and Erzerum Congresses, which did not approve a mandate. Mustapha Kemal was definitely opposed to any mandatory control, although it is true that some of the Nationalists who came into touch with the Commission in Constantinople desired an American mandate.

The Problem of the Greeks [1]

It seemed necessary to devote a little more attention to the problem of the Greeks, for their situation was not the same as that of the Armenians, although they, too, had been involved in some deportations, if in no extensive massacres. The Greeks already had a country, some adjacent islands, and had recently acquired some territory providing opportunity for settlement. Nevertheless, the results of the occupation of Smyrna did not seem to justify giving the Ottoman Greeks either rule over others or their own full independence. It was not so much the ability of the Greeks which was in question, nor their enthusiasm for education, but the wisdom of setting them off completely from Turkey. It was felt that the apparent purpose of the Turks themselves in asking for a mandate, and of the Peace Conference in sanctioning it, gave promise of a new Turkey in which Greek rights would be fully guaranteed. Before complete independence should be sought, a trial should be made of life within the Turkish state under new conditions. Therefore, to the American Commissioners, it seemed best for the moment not to establish an independent Greek territory, in the belief that both Greeks and Turks would benefit from "their union in one cosmopolitan state."

---

[1] *PPC*, XII, 840-841.

The Recommendations [1]

The final portion of the "public" King-Crane Report dealt with its proposals for the future of the Near East. After careful consideration, the Commission decided to make a series of "positive" recommendations, always considering, however, the various alternatives involved.

In summary, the Commissioners advised an independent Armenian state under the administration of a mandatory, but objected to the separation of Cilicia from Anatolia for the time being, and urged that an International Constantinopolitan State be formed under a mandatory. The appointment of a mandatory for the Turkish state in Anatolia was recommended, with no independent Greek territory cut off, although local autonomy under the general mandate might be granted to that portion of the sanjak of Smyrna which had a decided Greek majority. A boundary commission should be appointed to define the states within the first three recommendations and the limits of a possible autonomous Smyrna region. The sixth and seventh proposals were especially significant:

> A general single mandate for the whole of Asia Minor (not assigned to Mesopotamia or Syria) to include under it the mandate for Armenia, the mandate for the continued Turkish State, each with a governor of its own to insure full attention to its particular interests, besides a governor-general over the whole. The various inter-relations and common concerns of the constituent states would thus be studied and cared for, as well as their individual needs....
> That the United States of America be asked to take this general mandate, together with its inclusive mandates for the Armenian State, the Constantinopolitan State, and the continued Turkish State.

A number of considerations dictated the choice of the United States as

> the most natural Power to take the mandate for the International Constantinopolitan State, as well as for Armenia; for the simple reason that she is the only Great Power territorially and strategically disinterested. The mandatory for this international state should be herself strong, to discourage any further intrigue for control of the Straits; disinterested, to command the confidence of all the nations concerned; and in unmistakably earnest sympathy with the aim of such a state, and with those international means by which this aim is to be achieved, —the League of Nations and its mandatory system. These needed qualifications are best met by America. Now the full fruits of such an international state cannot be secured, unless the rest of Asia Minor is made a fit environment for such a state, practically embodying the same great principles.

Furthermore, there was the general recognition among the Near Eastern peoples of the high ideals and national convictions animating the American people. The Syrian and Turkish peoples trusted the idealistic international faith of the United States and its belief in the League of Nations. The American record in Cuba and the Philippines, the achievements

[1] *PPC*, XII, 841-848.

of such American institutions as Robert College and the American University of Beirut, as well as the Near East Relief, had made a fundamental impression on the people. Finally, the United States was peculiarly fitted to be the single mandatory power for all Asia Minor, "not only because of her national convictions, her international faith, and her record, but also because the course of duty for her would seem to lie in this direction."

Could the obligation to Turkey and the Near East be denied? The United States had

> believed perhaps more than any other people, in the high possibilities of the League of Nations; but if the League of Nations is not to be a sham and a delusion, all nations must be willing to bear their share in the resulting responsibilities. America, certainly, cannot be an exception.
>
> She came into the war, too, with the ardent faith and hope that a more democratic world might result. Is she willing to carry those war purposes through to the end? Here in Turkey is an unrivaled opportunity to try these purposes out, for the good not only of a single people, but of the entire world; for here in Turkey has been through centuries a center of intrigue and strife that has engulfed all nations in its consequences. Moreover, America's intervention in the war went far to determine the war's issue. Was that intervention justified? America must still do her utmost to complete the proof.

Only the American example of faith in the future could destroy the "cynicism and disillusionment" which already were rampant. It was doubtful if the United States could perform a more significant task than that of "taking on the general mandate for Turkey" and that for Syria, if the Peace Conference approved. American acceptance would "make a reality of the League of Nations," the mandate system, and "set a new standard in international relations." Men's faith would be renewed, and the United States itself might be saved "from a disastrous reaction" from its "genuinely high aims in the war." On the other hand, it should be borne in mind that the costs of the Near Eastern mandates would be heavy, and there could be no "expectation of large financial profits." But even so:

> America might well spend millions to insure relations of peace and good will among nations, rather than the billions required for another war, sure to come if the present cynical selfishness and lack of good will are not checked.

More cogent, prophetic words, in the light of the postwar era and its own aftermath, could hardly have been written concerning American responsibilities.

While some might suggest that such a large mandate was itself indicative of a grasping American imperialism, it was clear that this was not the case and that the United States did not want the mandate in principle, although it might meet its "fair share of responsibility in the world today" and might be persuaded by a campaign of education to assume the burden. But it ought not to take the responsibility at all unless the following conditions were met:

> That she is really wanted by the Turkish people; that Turkey should give evidence that she is ready to do justice to the Armenians, not only by the allotment of the territory within her borders, recommended for the Armenian State, but also by encouraging the repatriation of Armenians, and by seeing that all possible just reparation is made to them as they return to their homes; that Turkey should also give evidence that she is ready to become a modern constitutional state, and to abolish military conscription; that Russia should be ready to renounce all claims upon Russian Armenia; that the Allies should cordially welcome America's help in the difficult situation in Turkey; and especially that all plans for cutting up Turkey, for the benefit of outside peoples, into spheres of influence and exploitation areas should be abandoned.

These were the requirements, and only on condition that they were fulfilled would the Commissioners recommend an American mandate for Asia Minor. [1]

---

[1] There was also a "Confidential Appendix Prepared by the Commission for Use of Americans Only," written by Professor Lybyer as a part of the historical sketch. Use has already been made of these materials in the discussion of the investigation in Palestine and Syria. See *PPC*, XII, 848-863.

CHAPTER VIII

Towards an American Policy in the Near East

THE AMERICAN GOVERNMENT AND THE NEAR EAST

The despatch of the King-Crane Commission to the Ottoman Empire in the spring of 1919 was certainly clear indication at the time of a significant American interest in the development and welfare of the Near Eastern peoples and nations. While the Commission carried on its investigations at Constantinople, however, and while almost all those who appeared before the Commission, whatever their differences, were urging some kind of American assistance to the Near Eastern peoples, the Government of Washington became increasingly hesitant as to what to do about all the complex issues. Admiral Mark Bristol, the American High Commissioner in Constantinople, was in constant touch with the American authorities, whether in Washington or in Paris.[1] Moreover, the United States Government had encouraged and facilitated the work of the American Committee for Armenian and Syrian Relief, or the Near East Relief,[2] but formulation of a policy was quite evidently another matter.

The Bristol Despatches

Admiral Bristol declared on June 11 that the Moslems of eastern Anatolia were organizing for resistance. The movement had been aggravated and encouraged by Greek intrigues in Trebizond with an influx of Greeks from the Crimea. Moreover, the presence of Enver Pasha in the Caucasus had been reported, and he was thought to be organizing that region. Bristol felt that if British troops were withdrawn from eastern Anatolia serious disturbances might develop, particularly because of German and Bolshevik influences. He further protested against the Greek occupation of Smyrna, which had only served to fan the flames of revolt throughout the country.[3]

While Bristol was certainly concerned with the fate of the Armenians, he was opposed to any scheme for their repatriation from the Caucasus to Turkey under cover of military force, lest such a move precipitate outbreaks throughout the country against the Christian peoples. He had worked with the Turkish authorities to bring about some sort of arrangement, but he advised that Armenian politicians were scheming for their

---

[1] For Lansing's instructions concerning Bristol, August 12, 1919, see U. S. Foreign Relations, 1919, II, 812-813.
[2] Ibid., 821-823. The Near East Relief, up to November 1919, spent $ 30,000,000 of voluntary contributions.
[3] Bristol Papers: Bristol to Benson, June 11, 1919. He noted: "There were no disorders nor threatened disorders Smyrna district to warrant occupation and now regular fighting in some places going on between Turks and Greeks, hence nobody can understand the occupation and especially the continued advance of Greeks into interior...."

repatriation in order to extend their claim for Armenia in Turkey. The American admiral thought that every effort should be made immediately to care for the Turkish Armenians where they were until the question of a mandate was settled or until the whole of Turkey could be occupied by military forces. He opposed "in the strongest manner possible" any measures similar to the Greek occupation of Smyrna.[1] After an inspection trip along the Black Sea regions of Baku, Tiflis, Batum, Trebizond, Kerasun, Samsun and Zonguldak, Bristol was convinced that there was increasing evidence of the anarchical effects of the Greek action, and he felt that conditions in the Near East and the Caucasus were now entering a critical stage "requiring most careful consideration" by the Peace Conference.

Back in the United States, a distinguished committee of Americans, headed by Mr. Charles Evans Hughes, urged "the restoration of the independence of Armenia."[2] This committee suggested as a first step that "either the Allies or America or both" should at once send food, munitions and supplies for 50,000 men to Armenia to enable the Armenians to occupy the country within the boundaries of "integral Armenia." In response to the Hughes committee, Mr. Herbert Hoover and Mr. Henry Morgenthau, the Ambassador to Turkey, prepared a memorandum,[3] pointing out that there were approximately 2,000,000 surviving Armenians in Russia and Turkey, of whom about 750,000 were refugees from their homes in Turkey and these refugees were largely centered in Russian Armenia. While much had been done to relieve the suffering of the Armenians, the need was desperate. But

> aside from sheer support to refugees it is necessary to repatriate them, to reestablish their ability to support themselves, and incidentally to dispossess and repatriate the Turkish intruders. Until this is done the entire displaced population must depend on charity.... The area proposed to be assigned to the new state of Armenia in order to include all Armenian settlements will contain a population of approximately 5,000,000 so that the large majority will consist of Turks, Kurds and other non-Christian populations. The state as outlined will in large part be a mountainous area and expensive for railway transportation and

[1] *Ibid.*, Same to same, June 25, 1919 (two cables).
[2] The Acting Secretary of State (Phillips) to the Commission to Negotiate Peace, June 28, 1919, with message of June 22, 1919; *U. S. Foreign Relations*, II, 1919, 825.
[3] The Commission to Negotiate Peace to the Acting Secretary of State, Paris, July 3, 1919; *U. S. Foreign Relations*, 1919, II, 825-826. See also Mr. Hoover's remarks on July 1, 1919, at the meeting of the Commissioners Plenipotentiary, in which he suggested that the British be told that the United States "would be glad" to take the Armenian mandate, if it also took that for Mesopotamia, or that, if Great Britain wished to assume the mandate for Mesopotamia, it should take that for Armenia. He had no doubt that Great Britain would take both rather than lose Mesopotamia. *PPC*, XI, 261.

traffic in general with limited resources beyond primitive agriculture. It is agreed that an Armenian gendarmerie could be built up after some years with sufficient sprinkling of foreign instructors but it is not believed that it could be built up to sufficient strength to dominate the major and antagonistic population that will necessarily be included in the Armenian State and it is generally considered that it will not only require an initial force of at least 50,000 foreign troops to even secure repatriation but to [sic] a continued force of at least one half this number in occupation over a number of years to maintain and support any government that may be created.... To secure the establishment and protection and undertake the economic development of the state until it becomes self supporting such a mandatory must provide not less than $300,000,000. This would have to be looked upon largely as a sheer effort to ease humanity....

In any case, "exhaustive investigation should be undertaken by impartial experts on the ground" before anything other than support to refugees were undertaken. On his own responsibility, Hoover added that he considered this the only practicable method by which a government in the region could be made economically self-supporting. It would be necessary to include Mesopotamia within the same mandated area, where there were

very large possibilities of economic development, where there would be an outlet for the commercial abilities of the Armenians, and with such an enlarged area it could be hoped in a few years to build up a state self-supporting although the intervention of some dominant foreign race must be continued until the entire population could be educated to a different basis of moral relations and that consequently whatever state is assigned the mandate for Mesopotamia should at the same time take up the burden of Armenia.

Meanwhile, as a result of the Hoover recommendations, Colonel W. N. Haskell, who had served as chief of the American Relief Mission to Rumania, under the United States Food Administration, was appointed Allied High Commissioner, with full charge of all relief measures in Armenia,[1] and agent of the Department of State. The American Commission at Paris also suggested that "a mission should immediately be sent to Armenia headed by General Harbord," who was to choose his own staff, to investigate the general political and economic problems involved "in setting up the new state of Armenia." It was believed that Harbord would accept, and that an investigation was necessary before even the repatriation of refugees could be initiated. By August 1 President Wilson had fully approved these recommendations and a commission under General Harbord was appointed.[2]

---

[1] Same to Same, July 5, 11, 1919; *U. S. Foreign Relations*, 1919, II, 826-827.
[2] Lansing to the American Commission, August 1, 1919; *ibid.*, 828. For discussions of the Commissioners Plenipotentiary see *PPC*, XI, 270, 374, 377, 386.

Meanwhile, on July 14, Admiral Bristol reported a "strong Turkish sentiment" for an American mandate under certain reasonable conditions, with the British as second choice. Leading Turkish military and civil officials had convinced him that they "would render every assistance." Bristol indicated, however, that the Turkish situation was on "edge" and that the Greek occupation of Smyrna, together with atrocities, had "done incalculable harm." The Greeks had continued to advance and were devastating the hinterland, with the apparent object of colonization, after driving out more than 100,000 "peaceable Turkish peasants" who were then "half starving" in the mountains between Smyrna and Brusa and required immediate help.[1] Two days later, Admiral Bristol reported the increasingly serious situation in the east, where for the third time the Georgian government had stopped all traffic relief to Armenia, with the Georgians consistently refusing to come to any terms. Both Georgia and Azerbaijan were hostile to the Allies and had formed an alliance against the Russian volunteer army, the embargo on traffic relief being used as pressure to force Armenia into that grouping, which the latter was unwilling to join. British troops were barely able to cope with the situation and the Admiral suggested that the "Georgian delegates in Paris be given *hell*" and instructed to warn their government to permit free and unobstructed passage of relief supplies for Armenia.[2] By the end of July Bristol was convinced that the source of the trouble was within the Caucasus region and northern Persia, not in Turkey. There was also the serious problem of the delay in deciding the whole question of the Near East, and Bristol advised taking up the entire problem on the broad lines of the "greatest good to the greatest number" and disregarding the special or selfish claims of individuals and European countries.[3]

But the difficulties continued into August and there seemed to be no immediate solution of any of the problems. Bristol reported on August 2 that the Turkish Entente Liberale Party was framing a petition requesting a British mandate for all Turkey, thanks partly at least to the success of a careful and widespread British propaganda. The party, however, was losing prestige in face of a strong insurrectionary nationalist movement

[1] Bristol Papers: Bristol to Alusna, Rome, July 14, 1919.
[2] *Ibid.*, Bristol to Ammission, Paris, July 16, 1919. He reported on July 31 that the Tartars in the three Caucasian Republics did not want a mandatory power, least of all the Italians, who were anxious to exploit the oil lands. Bristol noted, too, that he was "personally exceedingly disappointed Armenians whom I as most Americans English in Caucasus found selfish unpleasing untrustworthy but realize through trip need competent American relief work many months."
[3] *Ibid.* Bristol to American Mission, Paris, July 31, 1919.
Bristol, at the same time, advised that Haskell had been designated High Commissioner for Armenia.

under Mustapha Kemal in Eastern Anatolia, although it did control the Government in Constantinople. While orders had been issued for the arrest of Mustapha Kemal, it seemed that they would not be implemented because of the partisanship of all officials in the territory in which he claimed to have held elections.[1]

On August 4 Bristol advised the American Mission in Paris that for some time the press had seemed inspired to force the United States to take a hasty step regarding Turkish mandates. The reports all tended to influence the United States to take the Armenian mandate and the news items were inaccurate or exaggerated the local conditions in Armenia and the threat of Turkish agitation in Asia Minor, while no mention was made of the Greek occupation of Smyrna, the primary, direct cause of the trouble. Greek and Armenian political interests desired an American mandate for Armenia because it would help Greek claims in Asia Minor and Thrace and also promote the political aspirations of Armenian leaders. Moreover, European desires for Turkish spheres of influence would have better chances of satisfaction if the United States recognized the partition of the Ottoman Empire by accepting the mandate for Armenia. The British were very much disturbed by a suggestion including Mesopotamia and Palestine with the remainder of Turkey under one mandate, and could not restrain their eagerness for immediate American action in Russian Armenia and assumption of a mandate for Armenia.[2] The British were also evidently against the Turkish nationalist movement in Anatolia, but Bristol was confident that they were exaggerating its danger. He had learned that the Armenians had been the aggressors in a recent disturbance near Kars. What Admiral Bristol preferred to see was the preservation of the unity of the region, since no single people was capable of solving the problem. He therefore suggested

> that if Greeks are withdrawn from Asia Minor and Thrace is not given to Greece and the whole of Turkey is placed under one mandate there will be no danger of any but minor disturbances in Turkey, constructive relief for every one can proceed at once and reconstruction and establishment [of] good government [can] proceed with minimum military force and expense....

Whereas the Armenians of the entire world represented only about 4,000,000 people, there were 25,000,000 other people in the Ottoman Empire, "suffering from bad government, lack of education and the benefits of modern civilization." If the United States considered a mandate only for a small portion of Turkey and agreed to the claims of Greece, Bristol thought that unconsciously, but none the less surely, Americans would be participating "in the continuation of the past crimes of the Near East."

[1] *Ibid.* Bristol to American Mission, Paris, August 4, 1919.
[2] *Ibid.* Same to same, August 5, 1919.

Gabriel Bie Ravndal, the American Consul-General at Constantinople, shared Bristol's concern about the situation in Eastern Anatolia, which he considered serious from almost every point of view.[1] His report of August 7 included a telegraphic summary of Ralph Chesbrough, the American Consul at Constantinople, who had just returned from Batum and Trebizond. Chesbrough had picked up some interesting reports on the Turkish Nationalist movement and the Congress at Erzerum on July 10. While he indicated that most of the people of Anatolia were supporting Mustapha Kemal, Chesbrough was fearful of the results of the movement, and believed that Mustapha Kemal was intriguing with his old enemy, Enver Pasha—a fear not well-founded. British troops in the region, about 2,000 men around Baku, did not appear to be sufficient to prevent further massacres of the Armenians, and were soon to be withdrawn, and it was certain that the Italians could never meet the problem. Ravndal was convinced that if these things were true, and no protection were given the Armenians in Azerbaijan and Russian Armenia, they would "doubtless soon be exterminated." The only possible way to check the Turanian movement was to occupy the affected regions with strong Allied forces, arrest and deport the principal Moslem rebels, and disarm "the entire population without regard to race or creed."

American Fears Concerning Turkey

The knowledge of these difficulties and the alarm lest British troops were to leave Batum, as reported, on August 15, worried the United States Government considerably, for it had been advised by the American Commission in Paris that the British withdrawal would probably be followed "by anarchy and massacres in Armenia." Only an American appeal for postponement might alter the British decision to withdraw. As a result Secretary of State Lansing, on August 9, instructed Ambassador John W. Davis to take up the matter with Lord Curzon, the British Foreign Secretary. Two days later Lansing asked Davis to urge London not to withdraw troops from Batum for the time being. Despite further alarming reports, Balfour informed the American Mission in Paris that the long-standing British plans could not be changed, although the Italians had stated that they could not occupy Georgia, and the Americans were not in a position to replace the British.[2]

Davis explained his fears to Curzon, but the British Foreign Secretary insisted that the withdrawal would have to be carried out. He repeated

[1] King Papers: G. B. Ravndal, Commissioner to American Commission, Paris, August 7, 1919.
[2] See Lansing to Davis, August 9, 11, 1919; *U. S. Foreign Relations*, 1919, II, 828. See also American Mission, Paris, to Lansing, August 12, 1919; *ibid.*, 829-830. The Council of Five had had a report from Haskell noting that British withdrawal would endanger 2,000,000 lives and produce anarchy in the Caucasus, and Haskell had asked reconsideration.

that notice of withdrawal had been given, that Italy had declined the task and stated that Great Britain would be highly gratified to see the United States take the Armenian mandate and assume the duties of policing. Davis replied that regardless of future decisions it would be impossible to despatch American troops to the region immediately. By August 13, Lord Curzon informed Ambassador Davis that evacuation of Batum had already begun, although it would not assume "a practical form" until October.[1] Meanwhile, some arrangements which would not let the place "remain without any protection" might be made, and Curzon was inquiring about measures to insure some degree of local security, which would be much easier if the American government were in a position to put troops into the Caucasus or to assure Great Britain that the Armenian mandate would "ultimately be accepted by the United States." He was aware, however, that satisfaction of these conditions was out of the question for the present, and this greatly complicated an issue which was "in itself sufficiently difficult."

By now the Washington government seemed thoroughly alarmed and President Wilson desired Turkish authorities to be warned [2]

> that should they not take immediate and efficacious measures to prevent any massacres or other atrocities being perpetrated by Turks, Kurds, or other Moslems against Armenians in the Caucasus or elsewhere, then all support concerning a secure sovereignty over the Turkish portions of the present Ottoman Empire, under Article XII of his peace terms, will be withdrawn, and that such withdrawal might result in the absolute dissolution of the Turkish Empire and a complete alteration of the conditions of peace.

If the Turks disclaimed control over such developments, they should be advised that if they expected to exercise any sovereignty over any portion of the Empire they should demonstrate that they were not only willing but able "to prevent their conationals and coreligionists from the perpetration of atrocities." Therefore no excuse was to be accepted, and Bristol was to be instructed so to inform the Turkish authorities in Constantinople. A few days later, Lansing urged the American Commission in Paris to discuss the British withdrawal from Batum with the Allied

---

[1] See Davis to Lansing, August 12, 15, 1919; *U. S. Foreign Relations,* 1919, II, 829-831. General Bridges, who had just returned from Batum, told Paris that it would take a month to six weeks to withdraw the 22,000 troops. Bridges agreed that trouble was likely to follow the withdrawal, and remarked that "the thing to do is for us to do the job and you to pay for it." A meeting of the British Cabinet on August 9 had not altered the British position, for Davis noted that the British desire for an American acceptance of the Armenian mandate was as evident as the fear of a pan-Moslem movement.

[2] Lansing to American Mission, Paris, August 16, 1919; *ibid.,* 831-832.

representatives, recommending that "immediate emergency measures be taken" to prevent "all possible bloodshed and other lawlessness."[1]

At the same time, however, Lansing received a statement from Curzon concerning the British position with regard to Armenia.[2] Curzon was anxious to do everything to "satisfy American opinion and to protect the Armenians," but it was difficult to modify the announced British policy of evacuation unless the British knew how long they might be expected to remain and what part the American government was prepared to play. Curzon repeated that Great Britain would welcome any sign of American assistance, and suggested that the United States had even greater interests in Armenia than Great Britain itself. If Great Britain had to remain in the Caucasus beyond the period it had assumed, the burden should be borne by the state which expected to be or was "likely to become the mandatory for the Armenian people." Ambassador Davis, apparently, was not unimpressed with Curzon's note, for he suggested that any answer, other than a positive refusal, should be so worded as to avoid any charge of bad faith in case the United States declined a mandate.

Secretary Lansing discussed the mandate problem with President Wilson and found the situation very difficult. He advised Ambassador Davis on August 23[3] that the United States "would like to appeal officially to the British Government to continue their military control," but unfortunately there were no funds for financial assistance without specific appropriation by Congress, and to obtain the appropriation would complicate further the political turmoil which the treaty of peace had caused. The same thing was true with regard to any future arrangements, because the Senate would bitterly resent the assumption that the United States would accept a mandate. Such action would only add fuel to the flames, in view of opposition to President Wilson in the Senate. In conclusion Lansing urged Curzon to do all he could to continue the generous protection over "a distracted and unhappy race."

On August 26,[4] Davis was instructed to call other considerations "incidentally" to Curzon's attention. Since the United States was not

[1] Same to same, August 20, 1919; *ibid.*, 832.
[2] Davis to Lansing, August 21, 1919; *ibid.*, 832-833. The Curzon note to Davis was dated August 19, 1919. Evidently a similar problem was bothering Polk, for on August 23 he inquired of Lansing: "Before taking the steps you suggest I should be glad to know what reply you wish me to make in case the British or other Allied delegates inquire whether the United States would be willing to pay the expenses of any military assistance that might be sent to Armenia and what are the prospects of the United States accepting a mandate over that country." *Ibid.*, 833-834.
[3] Lansing to Davis, August 23, 1919; *ibid.*, 834.
[4] Same to same, August 26, 1919; *ibid.*, 836-837. For Lansing's own

a signatory either to the Treaty of Paris (1856) or Berlin (1878), it was not responsible, and American action was based purely on humanitarian considerations. Moreover, should Armenian massacres follow the withdrawal of British troops, it might result "in anti-British feeling in American public opinion," which the government would greatly regret. The Armenians and the formation of an Armenian state were considered by the Turks as "serious obstacles" to the realization of their "pan-Turanian and pan-Islamic aspirations." It seemed, therefore, "to be in the interest of Great Britain and the other Allies to help the Armenians and protect them from extermination." If American opinion agreed to the assumption of a mandate over Armenia, it would be because of sympathy for the people and a desire to contribute constructively to their independence. But if further massacres rendered the Armenians unable to "form a Christian state," a strong opposition might develop "against the assumption of any mandate by the United States." Ambassador Davis does not appear to have been too much impressed with the reasoning of the Secretary of State. He could not see Curzon, who was out of town on August 26, but was informed by the acting Secretary of State, Mr. Ronald Graham, that he regretted the situation, but was "in no way surprised," and thought that, perhaps, some measures might be devised to meet it. [1]

Meanwhile Admiral Bristol had conveyed President Wilson's warning to the Turkish Grand Vizier. Damad Ferid Pasha replied by August 25 [2] that the Ottoman Government was doing all it could to maintain order and tranquillity within the borders of the Empire. But the fact that Turkey had just come out of a disastrous war had completely upset the administrative machinery, and it was impossible to keep perfect order with insufficient forces. Damad Ferid declared, however, that it was the

> tragic events of Smyrna which have troubled the peace in Asia Minor and Thrace and exasperated the entire population already upset by the disastrous effects of the late general war. It is again those awful atrocities, unparalleled even in the old conservative times, that brought about a general repentance all over the Empire and causes a deep indignation and exasperation amongst the entire population.

The Ottoman Government could not be held responsible, in any case, for the sad events taking place in the Caucasus. To preserve order, Damad Ferid asked that the government be given the right to increase its soldiers and gendarmerie and requested that the Allies put an end

opposition toward the mandate program, see Lansing, *The Peace Negotiations*, 160.

[1] On August 29, Davis declared that practically all the suggestions in Lansing's despatch had been canvassed in previous conversations. Davis to Lansing, August 26, 29, 1919; *U.S. Foreign Relations*, 1919, II, 837.

[2] Ravndal to Lansing, Constantinople, August 25, 1919; *ibid.*, 835-836.

"as soon as possible to the helplessness" of Smyrna and to the atrocities committed by the Greek forces. He was convinced that only the early conclusion of a definite peace could end the unsettled state of affairs and bring about order and security within the country.

When President Wilson's memorandum concerning the sad state of affairs in Turkey was brought to the attention of the Peace Conference on August 25, Premier Clemenceau complained about the American communication with the Turkish Government, in the name of the Peace Conference and without previous consultation with the Allied High Commissioners. It was explained that the American President was merely stating his own point of view. M. Clemenceau declared that the British had not permitted the French to send troops to Asia Minor, a point with with which Mr. Balfour immediately took issue, remarking that Great Britain had "no objection to the French sending troops" and asking whether Clemenceau would send forces into Armenia. Within two days the French proposed that they would send 10,000 troops for security purposes, and that the troops had to be landed at Alexandretta and Mersina. Mr. Polk, the American representative, considered this more of an attempt to get a footing in Asia Minor than a plan for the protection of the Armenians and asked Balfour if the British Government would consent "to this very palpable attempt to get control of this section of Asia Minor." Balfour merely replied that since the British were withdrawing and the Americans "could not send troops he did not see how the British Government could object." Polk, not unnaturally, wanted to know whether Washington would object to the French plan. [1]

The American Mission in Paris had not long to wait, for on September 2, Secretary Lansing cabled that the United States would welcome the despatch of 10,000 French troops to protect Armenia. The essential thing, after all, was to avoid invasion of Russian Armenia and further massacres, to insure transportation of food by rail from Batum to Erivan, and to demonstrate to the Turks, Kurds and others, that the Allies had not abandoned the Armenians. If French troops were to be sent from France, it seemed more practical to have them land at Batum, instead of Alexandretta or Mersina, to replace the British forces and take immediate control of the railway. In this event, the British should be requested to suspend withdrawal until the arrival of French forces. But within less than two weeks the situation was altered by events which were occurring in other parts of the Near East.

[1] See *PPC*, VII, 839-840, 858-859; *British Documents*, 1919-1939, First Series, I, 508-509, 524. See also Lansing to American Mission, September 2, 1919, *U. S. Foreign Relations*, 1919, II, 838-839. The Department of State had received word on August 30 indicating that the British had evacuated Tiflis on August 29 and would be out of Transcaucasia, including Batum, within two weeks.

Policies Concerning Syria

These events had much to do with the development of policies with regard to Syria, although much else, of course, was also involved. As early as August 11, Mr. Balfour had submitted a basic study, in which he discussed the anxiety which the problem was causing, in view of the misunderstandings which had arisen.[1] The British statesman thought the troubles, basically, had come about because of

> the loudly-advertised policy of self-determination preceded by a Commission of Enquiry—a Commission that began by being international, and ended by being American. This Commission, by the very term of its reference, was to find out what the Arabs of Palestine, Syria, and Mesopotamia desired, and to advise the Powers accordingly. We gave it our blessing, and directed our officers to supply it with every assistance. But this obviously involved, as an inevitable corollary, that the whole future of these regions was still in the balance, and that their destiny depended chiefly on the wishes of their inhabitants. No British officer could possibly think otherwise; yet, if he thus spoke and acted, there is not a Frenchman in Syria—or elsewhere—who would not regard him as anti-French in feeling, and as an intriguer against France in practice.

All this brought into relief "the unhappy truth" that France, Great Britain and the United States had "got themselves into a position over the Syrian problem so inextricably confused that no really neat and satisfactory issue" was "now possible for any of them." According to Balfour five documents were primarily responsible for the difficulties — the promise to King Hussein in 1915, the Sykes-Picot Agreement in 1916, the Anglo-French Declaration of November 1918, the Covenant of the League of Nations, and the directions which had been given to the King-Crane Commission. These documents were "not consistent with each other" and represented no clear-cut policy. The policy which they adumbrated was "not really the policy of the Allied and Associated Powers," although none had lost entirely its validity or could be treated as of merely historic interest. Each could be quoted by the interested parties, and doubtless would be.

Mr. Balfour noted that overlordship was not alien to Middle Eastern peoples, but the scheme as embodied in the Sykes-Picot agreement, for

---

[1] *British Documents*, 1919-1939, First Series, IV, 340-349. See also discussion in The Council of Heads of Delegations, August 11, with special reference to the Armenian situation, in *PPC*, VII, 647-649, when Mr. Polk said that the United States could take no action as to a mandate until Congress acted, and Clemenceau complained "that France could do nothing, Italy could do nothing and, for the present, America could do nothing. It remained to be seen whether, as a result of this, any Armenians would remain." See also ZEINE, *The Struggle for Arab Independence*, 103-104.

example, did seem to him "quite alien to those modern notions of nationality" which were "enshrined in the Covenant and proclaimed in the declaration." Balfour feared that the language of the Covenant might be suitable in the West, but not necessarily in the Middle East, and, after outlining the events in the war which had led to the so-called secret agreements, he indicated that the Covenant falsely assumed that the Middle Eastern peoples were "in the advanced chrysalis independent nations," sufficiently "developed" to demand "provisional recognition," each of which was to be under a mandate until ready to stand alone. Mr. Balfour did not believe this to be so and went on:

> The contradiction between the letter of the Covenant and the policy of the Allies is even more flagrant in the case of the "independent nation" of Palestine than in that of the "independent nation" of Syria. For in Palestine we do not propose even to go through the form of consulting the wishes of the present inhabitants of the country, though the American Commission has been going through the form of asking what they are. The four Great Powers are committed to Zionism. And Zionism, be it right or wrong, good or bad, is rooted in agelong traditions, in present needs, in future hopes, of far profounder import than the desires and prejudices of the 700,000 Arabs who now inhabit that ancient land.
> In my opinion that is right. What I have never been able to understand is how it can be harmonised with the declaration, the Covenant, or the instructions to the Commission of Enquiry.

Balfour did not believe that Zionism would "hurt the Arabs," but they would "never say they want it." According to Balfour, insofar as Palestine was concerned,

> the Powers have made no statement of fact which is not admittedly wrong, and no declaration of policy which, at least in the letter, they have not always intended to violate.

The British statesman, therefore, suggested a number of propositions. First, he contended, the essential principles of the Sykes-Picot Agreement should be maintained, with a French sphere centering around Syria, a British sphere around the Tigris-Euphrates valley, and a Jewish home "in the valley of the Jordan." But, secondly, the Sykes-Picot Agreement should be brought into closer harmony with the Covenant of the League of Nations by the abandonment of special privileges in the so-called "blue" and "red" territories where France and Great Britain had assumed rights "not easily distinguishable from complete sovereignty." Thirdly, economic monopolies should be abandoned. Fourthly, the French zone in Syria should be extended to include Alexandretta and its hinterland, but whether France should also have Cilicia should depend on the arrangement of the Armenian mandate and the Italian claims under the Treaty of London (1915). Finally, Balfour considered that the British zone in Mesopotamia should extend at least as far as Mosul. If Zionism were to influence the world Jewish problem, it should be clear that Palestine should be made available "for the largest number of Jewish immigrants," and it would be "eminently desirable that it should obtain the command of the water-power which naturally belongs to it," whether by extending its borders to the north, or by treaty with the mandatory of Syria. But it should not include the Hejaz Railway, which was "too distinctly bound up with exclusively Arab interests." [1]

The situation was so complicated and confused that David Lloyd George advised Clemenceau on September 11 that it looked as though the question of the Turkish mandates would take longer than had been anticipated, especially in view of the delay in the American decision, and Great Britain could no longer undertake "to maintain an army of over 400,000 men to garrison the Turkish Empire." He proposed to come to Paris the next day to discuss that problem and the Armenian question, and noted that he had invited the Emir Feisal also to come. Clemenceau replied the same day that the definitive settlement had to be delayed until the United States was ready to decide, and declared that it was not possible to separate the problem of Syria "from the other questions connected with the final liquidation of the Ottoman Empire, and to submit it to the Supreme Council independently from those connected with Constantinople, Asia Minor and Mesopotamia." While the relief of British troops in Syria could be settled directly, Clemenceau saw no purpose in having the Emir Feisal come to Paris. [2]

During the meeting of September 13, Lloyd George threatened Clemenceau with an evacuation of British troops from Syria and Cilicia, including the Taurus tunnel. Such action would leave Great Britain in occupation of Palestine from Dan to Beersheba and Mesopotamia, while France would be left at the mercy of the Arabs who were already threatening its position seriously in Syria. Clemenceau was prepared to discuss the boundaries between Syria and Mosul, and he feared that, while Syria and Mesopotamia were under mandate, the Emir Feisal might realize his plans against the French position in Syria. The wisest course, in the French view, was to keep the Sultan in Constantinople, with a French adviser, but Lloyd George insisted that no British Government "could accept any such plan." In the British view, "the only solution

---

[1] On August 17, the Emir Feisal sent Allenby a letter in which he said that the British Government sympathized with him. Feisal was interested in the King-Crane Report, which he credited with "real power." Feisal felt that the British decision to accept a mandate for Palestine involved a division of the Arab countries and a return to the "unjust Agreement [Sykes-Picot] of 1916." The majority of the Arabs, he believed, desired one mandate for both Syria and Mesopotamia. *British Documents*, 1919-1939, First Series, IV, 365-366.

[2] *Ibid.*, 379-381. See also David Lloyd George, II, 1078-1114.

for a government of Constantinople was an American mandate." An agreement in line with Lloyd George's suggestion was reached on September 13, 1919.[1]

The Emir Feisal was much upset by the arrangement, declared that he would never accept it, and indicated that if Great Britain could not be persuaded to give it up, he would appeal to the United States. Should the latter move fail, Feisal felt that he would have no alternative to returning to his people and leading them in armed revolt. As Feisal wrote to Lloyd George, matters had reached "a most dangerous climax." While he was not asking for the fulfilment of promises to his father in officially published statements, he was asking in the name of British honor and "human justice" that the reward of the Arabs for their sincerity and struggles should not be division of their country. He advised that "the future Government of the Arab provinces" would be "the last lesson to be given by Europe to the East," and that if it did not

> turn out to be in accordance with the wishes of the people, confidence will be lost in every future official treatment, and a wide channel opened for intrigues and troubles; the crime will then be duplicated, politically, against the country and morally, against the people themselves.

At the meeting of the Heads of Delegations of the Five Great Powers on September 15, Premier Clemenceau noted that Emir Feisal was scheduled to arrive in Marseilles on the next day and that he had given strict instructions that he "was to be taken straight through to London," since he had understood that Lloyd George had wanted to see him at once.[2] During a discussion of the future of the Peace Conference, Lloyd George declared that, in addition to one or two other big questions, there was still the problem of a Treaty with Turkey, a matter which was being held up until the American position with regard to mandates had been decided. Mr. Polk indicated that the American position might be cleared up in October, a view which Lloyd George considered "rather sanguine," and he doubted that the Conference could be kept in continuous session.

Since it was impossible usefully to discuss the question of mandates, Lloyd George referred to the arrangements for the various military spheres in Turkey, and to his discussion with Clemenceau on September 13 and the *aide mémoire* which he had submitted. After reviewing the arrangement with France, Lloyd George indicated that, in the British

---

[1] See especially Lloyd George Memorandum, September 13, 1919; *PPC*, VIII, 216-217; *Miller Diary*, XVI, 509-513; Polk to Wilson and Lansing, September 16, 1919; *Miller Diary*, XX, 416-419; HOWARD, *The Partition of Turkey*, 241.

[2] *PPC*, VIII, 200-201, 205-208; *British Documents*, 1919-1939, First Series, I, 685-686.

communications with King Hussein, it had always been made clear that, in the British view, "the country west of Damascus, Homs, Hama, and Aleppo was not Arab in character." He hoped to make it clear to the Emir Feisal that the matter had been fully explained to his father, and, in any event, it had been necessary to summon Feisal to Europe, to make the same declaration to him as to the French Government relative to the withdrawal of British forces.

M. Clemenceau declared that the solution of the Turkish problem would have to be considered as a whole, for otherwise great difficulties would be encountered. In the French view "the question of an Arab Empire raised great difficulties," but the pressing problem of the moment was whether French occupation of Syria and Cilicia would be considered not merely as part of the agreement proposed in the British memorandum but as a definite acceptance of the agreement. On the other hand, Clemenceau considered the sending of French troops to Armenia, which he was prepared to do, a "very serious and grave responsibility." But the offer could not constitute a provision of an agreement, "since France was not desirous of going to Armenia and it would involve an enormous burden." Mr. Lloyd George noted that M. Clemenceau would not be committed to the entire agreement by sending troops, the only point being that Great Britain would withdraw its troops from Syria and Cilicia in any event, and hand over their posts to French troops. While Mr. Polk indicated that the discussion was merely an Anglo-French exchange of views, both Lloyd George and Clemenceau considered it necessary to notify the Conference of the arrangement, even if it were not to prejudice the settlement of mandates or boundaries.

The Emir Feisal conferred with Lloyd George in London on Friday, September 19. He was told of the decision to withdraw British forces from Syria and other points, beginning on November 1. The Prime Minister went over the situation, adverting to the 1915 agreement with King Hussein and noting the equally valid agreement with France. Feisal pointed out the prior character of the agreement with the Arabs, noted the faith which they had placed in Great Britain and referred to Arab action in the war. He then put the question:

> Did Great Britain, France and the United States of America, that is to say, the Great Powers, still maintain the words they uttered to small nations, and, more especially, the Anglo-French Declaration of November 9, 1918?

King Hussein wanted to know about a continuation of the subsidy and whether the British Commander-in-Chief would retain his command over the districts from which the troops were withdrawn. Lloyd George replied that Great Britain stood by the agreements with King Hussein, although he knew of no definite treaty with Hussein other than the correspondence of 1915. Lloyd George gave Feisal the *aide-mémoire* of September 13, which he had circulated at the Peace Conference. He indicated that the French would command in the rest of Syria, while Feisal would command in Damascus, Homs, Hama, Aleppo and the whole of that area, Allenby would continue to command in Palestine and Egypt, and General Marshall in Mesopotamia, including Mosul. Lloyd George was in the uncomfortable position of a man who had inherited two sets of engagements from his predecessors, to King Hussein and France, which he was bound to keep. Feisal thought the Prime Minister's first obligation was to Hussein, and

> considered that he himself and the Arab nation were being very badly treated in having a Power thrown on them when it had been promised that they should select for themselves, and he was certain that every Arab would shed his last drop of blood before he admitted the French.... [1]

Feisal wrote to Lloyd George on September 21, that the proposed agreement with the French was "detrimental to the rights of the Arabs and in direct opposition to what they expected from the British and French Governments in particular, and from the civilised world in general." The Sykes-Picot agreement was not officially known to the Arabs and "could never be the basis of any agreement after the Allied and Associated Powers had decided to cancel all secret treaties." Hussein, after learning of the Bolshevik publication of the treaties, from *El-Mustakbal*, had protested vehemently to the British Government. The Arabs, he said, declined to recognize any agreement concluded without their knowledge or participation. Moreover, if British troops had to be withdrawn from Syria, why not withdraw all European troops and leave the responsibility of preserving order to the Arab Government?[2]

Feisal met with Lloyd George again on September 23, and he repeated that he had known nothing of the alleged treaty of October 1915, and neither, evidently, had Sir Henry MacMahon, the British High Commissioner in Egypt. The document represented, it was said, what the Arabs wanted, not what the British Government had accepted. Before going to Europe, according to Feisal, he had "never referred to any agreement with Great Britain or anybody," and had regarded it as a "moral agreement, and had depended on the word of British officials." Lord Curzon indicated that there "never had been any signed agreement

---

[1] *British Documents*, 1919-1939, First Series, IV, 395-404.
[2] *Ibid.*, 406-409, 412-413. Feisal wrote again on September 23, indicating that he had declined to discuss the subject of the evacuation of British forces with the Commander-in-Chief of Allied Forces in Syria and he reminded the Prime Minister that it was "the British forces that lowered the Arab Flag" in Syria.

between His Majesty's Government and King Hussein." Despite his disappointments, Feisal declared that he personally and the Arab nation owed much to Great Britain, but, "on the solution of the Syrian question depended the whole Moslem movement throughout the world."[1]

Feisal talked at length with Col. Cornwallis, his adviser, during the next several days. He desired that Allenby remain in supreme command of evacuated areas, wanted an international commission to consider temporary arrangements pending final decision of the Peace Conference, and urged consideration of the future of the Arab countries at the Peace Conference. Chaim Weizmann had approached him in two discussions, and, in return for Feisal's help in Palestine, was reported to have offered money and advisers to the Arab Government and to be ready to persuade the French "to waive their claims of influence in the interior." Feisal was "strongly inclined" to come to such an agreement.[2]

By September 22, Polk was able to give more detailed information concerning the French offer of troops for Armenia.[3] The proposition involved an expeditionary force of about 12,000 men who were to move into Cilicia and occupy such southern Armenian points as Marash, Malatia, and Urfa, then under British control. Hence the debarkation at Alexandretta and Mersina.

> In pursuance of this plan the British and French agreed on the 15th instant, that the British garrisons in Syria west of the Sykes-Picot line in Cilicia and southern Armenia will be replaced by a French force; that the garrisons at Damascus, Homs, Hama, and Aleppo will be replaced by an Arab force; and that after the withdrawal of the British

---

[1] *Ibid.*, 413-418. For alleged treaty see *ibid.*, 418-419. In it Great Britain was supposed to form an Arab Government with boundaries to the Persian Gulf, the Red Sea, the Egyptian frontiers and the Mediterranean and on the north including Aleppo and Mosul. Aden was outside the boundaries. Basra was to be occupied by Great Britain until the final establishment of the new government. Great Britain was to furnish assistance and advice to the Arab Government.

[2] For Cornwallis Memorandum, September 25, 1919, see *ibid.*, 421-422. See also *ibid.*, 422-424 for letter of T. E. Lawrence to Lord Curzon in which Lawrence indicated that he could probably bring Feisal to agreement on the basis of an elected assembly from Areas A and B, following evacuation, recognition of a new government as promised in November 1918, a free port in Haifa and Tripoli or Alexandretta, and complete evacuation from Areas A and B. See also Col. Meinertzhagen to Curzon (September 26) and the Forbes-Adam memorandum in which the former announces his conversion to Zionism and the latter submits draft proposals for a mandate (*ibid.*, 425-428).

[3] American Mission to Lansing, September 22, 1919; *U. S. Foreign Relations*, 1919, II, 840-841. For convenient text of Memorandum by the Russian Ministry of Foreign Affairs on the Question of Asia Minor, see *ibid.*, 1917, Supplement 2, I, 502.

forces neither the British Government nor the British commander-in-chief shall have any responsibility within the zones from which the army has returned.

This carried out the arrangements contemplated by the Sykes-Picot agreement of 1916, under which the Syrian littoral with Cilicia and southern Armenia were to be occupied and administered by the French. The plan would only protect the few Armenians of Southern Armenia, and would therefore "do nothing to prevent the invasion or the massacring of Armenians in Russian Armenia." Nevertheless joint Franco-American action did not seem possible because Clemenceau had already rejected the sending of any French forces to Russian Armenia via Batum, where the British withdrawal was then being carried out to possible conclusion within ten days. The sending of munitions, supplies and volunteer recruits to the Armenian republic, which Senator John Sharp Williams had proposed, [1] could be assured only if the Batum-Erivan railway could be held by an American force. In that event, the reinforced and equipped Armenian army might be able to withstand the Turks and Tartars successfully.

But no American action was to be taken concerning either the specific Armenian or the other more general Near Eastern problems. American policy was haunted by fear and hesitation in the summer of 1919 and an era of isolationism was soon to set in. Meanwhile, the Turkish nationalist movement was taking definite form and shape and very much substance on the Anatolian plateau under the leadership and direction of Mustapha Kemal, a movement in which the American Commission in Constantinople had been deeply interested. In fact, some of its members had a basic appreciation of its significance, even if it were impossible —for them and for many Turks as well—to see the great possibilities for the future.

The Immediate Aftermath of the King-Crane Report

Meanwhile the King-Crane Report had been very favorably received by the American Delegation at Paris when it was presented on August 28. One copy of the document was left with the Secretary-General of the American Commission to Negotiate Peace, and another was to be transmitted to President Wilson. Mr. Crane himself was "greatly pleased"

---

[1] See Phillips to American Mission, September 20, 1919; *ibid.*, 1919, II, 830, in which he noted that Senator Williams had introduced a resolution proposing to authorize the President to use military forces to protect Armenians. Williams did not trust the French or the obstructionists in the Senate. He was, therefore, in favor "of securing authorization to suspend restrictions against recruiting volunteers for foreign armies in the United States, at the same time securing authorization for the immediate dispatch of arms and ammunition to Armenia."

and thought the Report "solid and sane."[1] Henry White, a member of the American Delegation, and his half-brother, William H. Buckler, who had succeeded Professor W. L. Westermann as head of the Division of Western Asia of the American Commission, were well impressed. Buckler told Captain Brodie that the Report was "a state document of the very first order." Frank L. Polk, who then headed the American Commission, told Dr. King that the rumors concerning the Report already had had "an excellent moral effect" on the French Government, although the press, always active on the subject of Syria, reiterated the French position on the Sykes-Picot agreement.[2]

Delivery to President Wilson

There was another task in connection with the Near Eastern problem which was not yet finished—the preparation of a projected mandate for Turkey. Mr. Buckler had gone over the text of a draft mandate with President Mary Mills Patrick, of the Constantinople Women's College. King and Lybyer studied the project very thoroughly, annotating it throughout, and suggesting a separate article on education, more definite and explicit provision for the secularization of the Turkish state, and abolition of the capitulatory and *millet* system. The projected mandate, in the light of later developments within the territories of the former Ottoman Empire, makes exceedingly interesting reading. Taken as a whole, the project was a fitting model for the "A" mandates.[3]

The work of the King-Crane Commission was clearly and completely at an end and President King and his party sailed for New York from Brest on the *S. S. America* on September 5, with the exception of Mr. Crane, who had gone to Prague to see his son, John Crane, present his credentials as the first United States Minister to the new Republic of

---

[1] Lybyer *Diary*, August 30, 1919. Crane remarked that he had never enjoyed a trip more than he had the one which the Commission had just finished in the Near East.

[2] See especially the Lybyer *Diary*, August 31, September 4, 1919. The Constantinople correspondent of *Eclair* declared that the American Commission had left Turkey without sufficient information to justify a definite conclusion, and added: "Frankly speaking ... the Americans did not receive a very cordial reception in Turkey." The *Echo de Paris* complained that British troops were in the areas investigated and that the American commission made a hurried investigation in the regions where French sentiment was displayed. See also The Springfield *Republican*, September 4, 1919; Washington *Herald*, September 4, 1919, and Cleveland *Plain Dealer*, September 4, 1919.

[3] King Papers: Mary Mills Patrick to W. H. Buckler, Paris, August 2, 1919; A. H. Lybyer to W. H. Buckler, Draft of Suggestions for Mandate in Turkey, September 4, 1919. Carbon copy in Lybyer Papers, original in pencil in King Papers. The suggested changes were embodied in underlined passages in the document. See also the Lybyer and King *Diaries*, September 3-4, 1919.

Czechoslovakia, and Captain Yale, who remained in Paris with the American Commission. During the ten-day voyage, Dr. King wrote a letter to President Wilson in formal transmission of the original copy of the King-Crane Report. He explained: [1]

> Mr. Crane and I have supposed ourselves to be making our report primarily to yourself and to the American Delegation at the Peace Conference, and that you and the Delegation must decide how our report might be further used. But as the American Section of the projected Inter-Allied Commission on Mandates in Turkey, we have aimed so to prepare our report, that (with the exception of the Confidential Appendix to the Report on Syria) it could be put in its entirety in the hands of British, French or Italian representatives, if you so desire.
> Mr. Crane and I have also regarded ourselves as not free to give to the press any statement of our recommendations without your express permission; but have supposed there would be no objection, but might rather be some advantage, in giving some suggestion of the actual conditions found in Syria and Turkey.

In view of the fact that President Wilson already was engaged in his great speaking campaign in behalf of the treaty and the Covenant of the League of Nations ("in which I rejoice"), Dr. King was not going to try to deliver the Report in person, but would send Captain Donald M. Brodie instead. Dr. King promised to do anything the President wished in further clarifying the Report, or in supporting the principles on which it was based. He only hoped that the Report might "help in securing righteous settlements in the Near East."

Captain Brodie delivered the original copy to the White House on September 27, 1919, while President Wilson was still on his "swing around the circle" in behalf of his international principles. When he returned in the autumn, the President was a very sick man, stricken with paralysis. There was never any acknowledgement of the receipt of the Report either from President Wilson or from the American Commission in Paris, and it is doubtful that President Wilson ever saw or read the final Report, for he was almost certainly too ill to study it until after he had retired from the Presidency in March 1921.

Some Attitudes Toward the Report

Thus it was that the King-Crane Report remained entirely confidential, insofar as the general public was concerned, although extracts may have been made available to certain French and British officials. [2]

---

[1] King Papers: Henry C. King to President Wilson, September 10, 1919, *S. S. America* at sea.
[2] King Papers: Mr. W. H. Buckler wrote to Mr. King from Paris on September 8, that the American Commission would "decide how far your report may be confidentially communicated to such men as de Caix. I expect to see him Wednesday." It seems to have been through the

Indeed, on September 21, 1919, Mr. Buckler asked in a meeting of the American Commission whether there were any objection to "the British Commission having a copy of the King-Crane Report," since members of the British Delegation had seen it and "their interest in it was excited." Mr. Polk, however, thought it better that his British colleagues "trust to their memories"—they had read it and he did not doubt that "they made very copious notes of it." [1]

Many reasons for the failure to publish the King-Crane Report have been assigned, including the fact that the Report was late, since the Treaty of Versailles was signed while the Commission was in Damascus. [2] On the other hand, the Treaty of Sèvres with Turkey was not concluded until August 10, 1920, almost a year after the King-Crane Report had been delivered in Paris. Perhaps one reason why the Report was never officially placed before the Paris Peace Conference was that it represented only the findings of the American Section of what had been intended to be an International Commission. No doubt there was a feeling that the frankness of the document, and conclusions concerning the French position in Syria, if published, might have an adverse influence on Franco-American relations. At any rate, David Lloyd George declares that "the Report was so hostile to the French claims in Syria that the President decided not to send it in to the Peace Conference on Turkey...." [3] The British Government, moreover, might have been annoyed by the disclosure of the Palestinian attitudes toward Zionism. Estrangement among the United States, Great Britain and France might have proved a serious setback to the League of Nations, since the United States in particular had refused to approve the Covenant.

Not until three years later was the King-Crane Report to be rescued from the dusty oblivion of the Department of State and published unofficially. Meanwhile, in the months which followed the filing of the document at the White House, there were rumors that both the French Government and the Zionist Organization, and perhaps the British Government, had brought pressure on the American Commission in

---

Department of State that copies reached the British and French Embassies and came to the confidential use of the British and French Governments. Lt. Col. J. K. Watson, British aide to the Commission, may have received a copy. See *British Documents*, 1919-1939, First Series, IV, 272-274, 281-282.

[1] *PPC*, XI, 432-434.
[2] Professor Richard Gottheil, Columbia University, wrote to The New York *Times*, December 12, 1919: "I understand that the committee has returned and has rendered its report. Is there any reason why that report should lie upon some table or in some drawer at the State Department and not be made public? ... We are entitled, I think, to know what these findings were and upon what bases they were built up."
[3] David Lloyd George, II, 1077-1078.

Paris and the Department of State in Washington to suppress the Report.[1] No statement concerning the Report was ever made by the Department of State. It may well be that President Wilson's illness, lack of interest on the part of others, together with the absence of any possibility that the United States would assume any mandate in the Near East, and the feeling that immediate publication would be neither diplomatic nor helpful were the controlling factors in the suppression of the document.[2]

Mr. Crane tells us that he [3]

had never had any discussion with President Wilson about the Mandate Report. I talked with him pretty fully about the work before we went out there. He was much impressed by Howard Bliss' concern that the Arab folk should have an adequate chance to express their feelings which were known to be very profound both in regard to Zionism and a French mandate. He occupied himself very seriously in getting a sound commission organized and under way. But when the report of the Commission came in he was in the middle of very serious problems and could not take it up.

Shortly after his return to Oberlin College, President King received a letter from Mr. W. H. Buckler, containing despatches from the London *Times* dealing with the situation in Syria and Palestine, partly in reply to some articles by the distinguished French publicist, M. Robert de Caix.[4] The *Times* correspondent referred to the "ill-starred Sykes-Picot

---

[1] Henry White "always strongly condemned the temporary suppression of the King-Crane Report on Syria, under pressure from France —the report having stated that a French mandate would be wholly unacceptable to the people. He thought it deplorable that the Syrian preference for American or British supervision should be roughly ignored." Allan NEVINS, *Henry White*, 457-458. The files in the Department of State do not indicate any motives or reasons for failure to publish.

[2] See J. M. N. JEFFRIES, *Palestine: The Reality* (London, Longmans, 1939), 301-302.

[3] Quoted from a letter of Mr. Crane to Mr. Brodie, December 1934.

[4] The London *Times*, September 6, 1919. The despatches are dated August 15, 20, 1919. Colonel Lawrence replied to the *Times* correspondent in The *Times*, September 11, 1919, citing the "secret agreements" with the Arabs. See David GARNETT, *The Letters of T. E. Lawrence*, 281-282. See also Robert de CAIX, "The question of Syria," *The New Europe*, XII, Nos. 150, 151 (August 28, September 4, 1919), 145-149, 169-174. De Caix bitterly resented the developments in Syria, declaring: "We see all this, and at the same time we see the case presented as though the position of France alone could be disputed in the name of the Wilsonian principles. The Americans wished to send a commission of inquiry to the East in order to consult the populations on the question of mandates: and the British press began to speak of a 'Syria Commission' instead of an 'Orient Commission'—as though it were merely a question of making inquiries within the French zone. Even if this unfairly restricted title has been adopted, as we believe, without any ulterior motive, it, at any rate, shows the slope down which the whole policy of Great Britain in the East is being dragged at the expense of France...."

agreement, which assigned Syria to France, indicating that it was indefensible "to dispose of the future of these peoples without reference either to themselves or to our own democracies." There was, according to the *Times* correspondent, a practical program for meeting the situation, approved and fostered by Lord Allenby, establishing

> an Arab kingdom or principality which should include at least O.E.T.A. North, West and East.... Each of these provinces would have a special measure of autonomy under French supervision, so as to secure for example, the position of the large Christian population in Beirut, and the Lebanon. The head of the whole would be Prince Feisal and the mandatory Power France.

Editorially, The *Times*, under H. W. Wickham Steed, supported the sentiments of its correspondent, noting that Lord Allenby had come to London for a short visit in connection with the Syrian problem. The *Times* favored a French mandate for Syria and believed that Great Britain should help France to secure it. Anglo-French friendship, in Steed's opinion, should not be disrupted by misunderstandings concerning Syria. It was essential to secure an understanding between the French and the Zionists, as well as between France and the Emir Feisal, and it should be the concern of the British Government to encourage both.

But Dr. King doubted that Field Marshall Allenby really supported any such program as outlined above:[1]

> It must be remembered that it was partly due to General Allenby's especial urgency that our Commission was appointed and sent. Moreover, in our interview with General Allenby on June 30... I distinctly raised with him the question of Mr. Steed's general policy as to the relation to the French, and his attitude seemed quite different from that of Mr. Steed. He thought, indeed, that the whole of Syria should be united to avoid constant strife between the French and English, but he said that it was clear that the French were not wanted and that unity under France was not possible. He believed that the best solution would be an American mandate over Syria to the borders of Mesopotamia. He also expressed the belief that if France were given the mandate she would be at war with the Arabs within a month, either intentionally or unintentionally, and more likely than not intentionally by French initiative.

There is substantial indication that Dr. King was correct in his analysis of General Allenby's attitude toward the situation in Syria and its

---

[1] H. C. King to W. H. Buckler, October 18, 1919. King felt that The *Times* editorial ignored "entirely the practically unanimous feeling of British officers that the Zionist program, in anything like its full form, could not even be initiated except by force of arms." He noted the moderate tone of American Zionism, "probably on account of the influence of Justice Brandeis." See also the article in *Le Matin*, November 4, 1919, by Stephane Lausanne urging an American mandate over Constantinople. Reprinted in The New York *Times*, November 5, 1919.

potentialities for trouble. Mr. Crane tells us that, when he returned to London from Prague in the autumn of 1919, he showed the Report to Lord Allenby and his aides, and to Mr. David Hogarth, and they "all approved of it. Mr. Hogarth said that he would have been proud to have had his name attached to it." [1]

Another exceedingly favorable comment on the Report came from Professor Edward Elsworth Ross, the distinguished sociologist of the University of Wisconsin, who wrote to Dr. King later in the year: [2]

> It seemed to me that this report was a more perfect example of mathematical demonstration in the field of human relationships than anything I have ever met with. Never have I seen so scrupulous an endeavor to procure measurements of population desires. Your conclusions are wonderfully convincing and your demonstration leaves me an ardent supporter of your entire program.

Professor Ross congratulated the Commissioners on their "superb piece of work" and expressed his "earnest hope" that it would "have its effect on the policy of the government."

Dr. King and Mr. Crane were seriously concerned as to what should be done about their Report. Mr. Crane felt it "most important that it should come out ... and would do much to clear the air." [3] He continued:

> The last two months have seen very dangerous drifting, and the people in Syria do not know what to make of the apparent lack of interest in our work. Everyone who has seen the report has been greatly impressed by it. Howard Bliss, General Allenby and all his aids, and Hogarth were all unqualifiedly for the Report. While in London I was of some service in checking a move to withdraw British soldiers from Syria and substitute French ones—a project that Lloyd George and Clemenceau agreed to one afternoon and ordered put into execution. Fortunately, Allenby was in town, and had the same feeling that I had about the danger of this manœuver.

---

[1] This is from a memorandum supplied by Mr. Brodie.
[2] King Papers: E. A. Ross to H. C. King, November 24, 1919. Mr. Crane had allowed Professor Ross to read a copy of the Report while visiting his daughter at the University of Wisconsin.
[3] King Papers: Crane to King, December 3, 1919. In a letter to Crane on November 18, Dr. King expressed a desire to talk over the situation. He was interested in "knowing whether there is any early intention of releasing our report, so that we might discuss freely its recommendations, for I have the feeling that America would respond a good deal more promptly to a concrete setting forth of the mandatory possibilities than she does to the League of Nations in the abstract. I hope the Senate is not going to take all the meaning out of the League before it gets through with it." Mr. William Chadbourne had written to Dr. King asking if he would be available for conferences with Senators in Washington, but Dr. King wondered if he should not await some word from the President or the Department of State.

The Plan of Captain William Yale

Since Captain Yale had not agreed fundamentally with the recommendations of the King-Crane Report, he wanted to remain in Paris with the American Commission to Negotiate Peace in order to try to work out a solution of the Near East problem.[1] General Tasker H. Bliss had told him that the King-Crane Report was not practical politics, and when Yale saw that the American Peace Commissioners were making no apparent attempt to carry out the recommendations, he began to interest himself in a solution which he thought would meet with acceptance by all four parties concerned—the British, French, Arabs and Zionists.

The Yale Memorandum of September 16, 1919

As early as September 16, Captain Yale prepared a brief memorandum for the American Commission dealing with the recent negotiations between David Lloyd George and the Emir Feisal,[2] following the Lloyd-George-Clemenceau understanding of September 13, under which the British forces were to be withdrawn from Syria by November 1, 1919. Captain Yale pointed out that the Arabs had certain rights under the Covenant of the League of Nations, the Anglo-French Declaration of November 1918, and the secret understandings between King Hussein and the British Government during 1915-1916. The British had indicated that these understandings did not conflict with their engagements to France concerning Syria especially. Under the Covenant the Arabs had

---

[1] Lybyer *Diary*, August 31, September 2, 1919. See also *PPC*, XI, 402, and Yale's letter to the Author, October 17, 1940.

[2] Yale Papers: Captain William YALE, *Emir Feisal's Communication to Lloyd George, September 16, 1919*. See also *PPC*, XI, 427, for meeting of the American Commission, September 23, 1919. Lloyd George explains that the King-Crane Report was "definitely adverse to the French", although neither the Americans nor the British would take a mandate over Syria. Feisal, as already noted, admitted that some power would have to control temporarily in Syria. Under the agreements with the French, France was to have a certain control in Syria, but the British "were equally bound, in an agreement entered into with the French and ourselves, to see that the cities of Damascus, Homs, and Aleppo should be within the Arab sphere. We could not indefinitely keep a large body of troops in a country for which we were not going to undertake any responsibility as a mandatory." Lloyd George therefore "strove to negotiate an understanding between M. Clemenceau and the Emir Feisal which would enable us to evacuate Syria, and to hand over the military occupation to the French, whilst at the same time leaving the Arab garrisons in the cities I have mentioned .... But ultimately an agreement was concluded on September 13th, 1919, by which the evacuation of the British Army in Syria was to be concluded by November 1st, 1919, and the French garrison at Damascus, Hama and Aleppo were to be replaced by an Arab force." Feisal protested against this arrangement as it left the Arabs "at the mercy of greedy imperialistic ideas." Lloyd George, II, 1078-1114.

the right to claim that a primary consideration in the selection of a mandatory should be the wishes of the people, and the people of the Syrian hinterland had made it known "unmistakably" that they did not want France as their mandatory. Furthermore, they had flatly rejected Article XXII of the Covenant of the League of Nations and "would not accept a Mandatory Power unless forced upon them."

Yale rejected the reasoning of Feisal's communication to Lloyd George, which he considered somewhat obscure in its references to the unity of the Arab provinces, especially since Feisal had made an agreement on January 3 [?], 1919, in which he had "recognized" the separation "of Palestine from Syria and the establishment of a National Home of the Jews there." Neither did Feisal, in the Yale view, take into consideration that the inhabitants of Mt. Lebanon desired independence under a French mandate. [1] Yale recognized that the Arabs did have a right to demand "the establishment of an Arab Government in at least part of Syria as well as in Mesopotamia," and to expect that their wishes regarding a mandate should "be taken into consideration." But he did not believe that they had "other rights than these," and questioned the justification of Feisal's claims under "any declarations made either by the Peace Conference, or by England and France jointly," or under the secret agreements between Great Britain and King Hussein.

In Yale's opinion, the Feisal communication to Lloyd George was essentially a threat that if Syria were divided, and the French retained a portion, Feisal would "not be responsible for disorders throughout the country," and he predicted "a general uprising in the Moslem World" and threatened the British "with disturbances throughout their Moslem Empire." This was equivalent to a threat against the British position in Egypt, Palestine and Mesopotamia, and possibly in northern India. There was no question of the gravity of the situation, for the Arabs were excited, rejected the separation of Palestine and Mount Lebanon from Syria, and opposed the acquisition of the country by the French.

Yet it might be possible to make the Arabs see reason and understand that they would be given "the chance to establish an Arab State in the hinterland of Syria with outlets to the sea." If the Arabs could be brought to change their attitude and could be satisfied with "a modest state, a change might be effected in the present status of Syria without danger to the Christian population and without serious disorders in the country notwithstanding the absence of European troops." There was a definite

---

[1] The Arabs deny the binding character of the so-called Weizmann-Feisal Agreement for a number of reasons, including the fact that not all the promises to the Arabs were implemented. See Antonius, 439; William E. HOCKING, *The Spirit of World Politics* (New York, Macmillan, 1932), Appendices I, II, 533-543.

probability of disorder and even anarchy, however, if British troops were withdrawn in accordance with the Lloyd George-Clemenceau understanding of September 13.

Therefore Yale recommended that the British be asked not to withdraw their forces from Damascus, Homs, Hama and Aleppo until a decision had been reached either by the Peace Conference or the League of Nations. The British, in his view, should also be requested not to withdraw until French soldiers had been introduced into the country in sufficient strength to prevent the feared disorders and disturbances.

The Yale Visit to London

Late in September, Captain Yale was ordered to London to secure information on the progress of negotiations between the British Government and the Emir Feisal.[1] He arrived on September 28, Sunday morning, very anxious to see what could be done to prevent "the disastrous explosion of violence" now likely to occur in Syria. Yale believed that the root of the trouble was that

> each of the four interested parties—the Arabs, the British, the French and the Zionists—persisted in exaggerating their own claims, and in minimizing those of the others, as set forth in various treaties, agreements and declarations. Furthermore, I was convinced that the carrying out of the terms of the Memorandum handed to Clemenceau by Lloyd George on Sept. 13th would result in a conflict in Syria between the French and the Arabs: a conflict which would spread rapidly to Palestine and Mesopotamia, and be the cause of a serious situation in the Near and Middle East.

Before leaving Paris, Yale had had interviews with M. Philip Berthelot, of the French Foreign Ministry, M. Jean Gout, M. Robert de Caix, and M. Herbette, the editor of *Le Temps*. Knowing something of the attitude of French officialdom, he thought it would be useful to find out the minimum demands of the British, French, Arabs and Zionists, since he believed that they "offered a basis of settlement, and that it would be advisable personally to aid in bringing about an immediate solution."

Captain Yale called on Ambassador John W. Davis on September 29, and agreed that it would be unwise for the Ambassador to take official

---

[1] Yale Papers: Report in Detail of Interviews in London, September 29 to October 14, 1919. The list of those interviewed was: Colonel Gribbon, British Staff Intelligence; Henry Wickham Steed, Editor of *The Times*; Rustem Haidar, Hejaz Representative; The Emir Feisal; Colonel Cornwallis, Assistant Chief Political Officer of the Egyptian Expeditionary Force, and Col. Sterling, Deputy Chief Political Officer; Dr. Gaster, spiritual head of the Spanish and Portuguese Jews in Great Britain; David Hogarth; Colonel T. E. Lawrence; Lord Robert Cecil; Sir Henry MacMahon; Mr. Garvin, London *Observer*; and Lord Allenby. It should be remembered that Charles R. Crane was also in London at about his time and saw many of the same people.

notice of him. Between September 30 and October 14, when he returned to Paris, Yale saw a number of British, Arab and Zionist leaders, including the Emir Feisal, Colonel Lawrence, Wickham Steed, David Hogarth, and Lord Allenby. Within a week of returning to Paris, he prepared a long memorandum [1] in which he dealt in detail with the Clemenceau-Lloyd George agreement of September 13, his projected solution of the Arab question, the essence of which he had published in *The Times* of London, the necessity for immediate action, and the Mesopotamian oil problem.

Yale believed that the Lloyd George-Clemenceau agreement was "pernicious". Although superficially it represented purely a military arrangement, it seriously compromised the "political future of the Arab Provinces" and also jeopardized the peace of the Near and Middle East. Fulfilment meant establishment of French military and administrative control along the Syrian coast, Cilicia and even "Little Armenia". It also signified direct British military and administrative control over Mesopotamia, and the Arabs, "without being recognized as a provisionally independent government," would be in control of Damascus, Homs, Hama and Aleppo. Those familiar with the conditions—British, French or Americans—were convinced that implementation of the agreement would result in "serious local disorders" which would spread to Kurdistan, Mesopotamia, and Palestine, "and perhaps to the entire Moslem world." The Arabs certainly would resist by force any attempt to carry out the agreement. They might even "throw in their lot with the Turkish rebels" and "in a short time the entire Near East would be engaged in a conflict with the Allies. Such a conflict would cause a most serious reaction in Egypt and in Moslem India." Should the agreement stand, all hope of settling the problems of the Near East, without resort to arms, would vanish. Yale felt that immediate action was, therefore, imperative, and that there was a solution to which the Arabs, British, French and Zionists would agree. The United States could play a constructive role in bringing the parties together and helping them to reach agreement. Further delay could be "the cause for infinite trouble."

While the Emir Feisal was bitterly opposed to the Lloyd George-Clemenceau arrangement, Yale believed that he would accept "any solution imposed upon him by the United States." Under the Yale plan, Feisal could face and control his people if he could "bring them the assurance that a provisional independent Arab Government" both in Syria and Mesopotamia had been recognized by the Allied and Associated Powers. On the other hand, Lloyd George was apparently endeavoring "honestly and loyally" to live up to his understanding with Clemenceau.

[1] Yale Papers: William Yale, Position of the Syrian Question Today, October 21, 1919.

At two Cabinet meetings vain efforts had been made to induce Feisal to agree. The British Government was determined to conciliate the French, although this was not due, in Yale's opinion, to any appreciation of the French position. Men like Allenby, Hogarth, Lawrence and McMahon understood the significance of the French claims, but realized, too, that the British must keep their promises to the Arabs. Indeed, there was considerable sympathy among the British "not only for Emir Feisal and the Arabs of Syria, but also for those of Mesopotamia."

Yale then outlined what he believed to be a plan acceptable to all parties concerned, anonymously published at Wickham Steed's request in the London *Times*, October 8, 1919, which would guarantee to the Arabs a large measure of independence and considerable hope for the future: [1]

> *Palestine* set up as a separate political unit, under the mandate of Great Britain, under whose guidance the Zionists will, with due restraint, be allowed to carry out their projects to make of it a National Home for the Jewish People.
>
> *Mount Lebanon* with a slight increase of territory to the south will be set up as a provisionally independent Lebanon State under French Mandate.
>
> *Syria* from Ma'an and Akaba in the south to be recognized as a provisionally independent state with an Arab Government under Prince Feisal.
>
> This Arab state shall either be under a French Mandate, or shall by a treaty, agreed to by the Peace Conference or the League of Nations, solicit the assistance of France.
>
> *Mesopotamia* shall be divided into two zones, a northern zone, including the vilayets of Mosul and Bagdad, and the southern zone that of Basorah and the Emirate of Mohammederan. The northern zone shall be recognized as a provisionally independent state, with an Arab Government. This State shall either be under the mandate of Great Britain or shall by a treaty agreed to by the Peace Conference or the League of Nations solicit the assistance of Great Britain.
>
> The southern zone shall be under a mandate of Great Britain and shall be given as large a measure of local self-government as may be deemed wise.

This project was almost identical with the recommendations which the King-Crane Commission had found unacceptable. Would it prove more agreeable to the British, the French, the Zionists and the Arabs? Yale believed that he could obtain the support of all the parties concerned. As a matter of fact, a meeting of the British Cabinet was said to have discussed the solution on October 13, but Yale had learned no details except that it had been decided to call together General Bliss, General Gouraud and Lord Allenby to discuss the question of the change of troops in Syria. While he had not discussed his solution with any of the

---

[1] The wording of this proposal differs only slightly from that in Yale's article in the London *Times*.

French leaders, Yale felt he knew the general French attitude and believed the French would accept his project, since they knew the difficulties in Syria and many "would be glad to get rid of it." It was true that men like Jean Gout and certain forces in the French Foreign Ministry and Colonial Ministry did wish to colonize Syria and Mt. Lebanon, but their opposition might be overcome. Berthelot and M. de Caix could be brought to accept the plan, and Gout's antagonism might be overcome with the assistance of M. Tardieu. While the Emir Feisal had not said that he would accept the Yale plan, there were reasons to believe that he might be well "pleased with such an outcome," provided one or two independent Arab Governments were recognized. Although the Zionists might initially protest against limiting Palestine to the land west of the Jordan and south of Mt. Lebanon, many recognized the strength of the Arab nationalist movement, knew that a large Palestine was an impossibility, and, the force of Zionism being spent, would accept a more moderate program.[1]

Yale was convinced that order and peace in the Near East depended on an early solution of the Arab question. Further delay might make any settlement impossible and would threaten, in all likelihood, the peace of the Near East. However, the British, French and Arabs could not reach agreement without assistance, for the three powers were in the position "of three cats perched on three posts, spitting at one another." A common ground, therefore, had to be found, and only the United States could bring the three groups together. Feisal had proposed the first step in this direction, and the British had taken the second in suggesting that Feisal, Allenby and Gouraud meet under the chairmanship of General Bliss. The United States, in any case, would have to act as the mediator, and American representatives would have to assist in realizing a solution. "The Arabs must be protected by America, and assisted in obtaining their just claims in Syria and in Mesopotamia."

The final section of the Yale memorandum dealt with the important problem of Mesopotamian oil, which had already troubled Anglo-American relations and was to prove serious for several years to come.[2]

---

[1] There is considerable doubt, to say the least, that either the Zionists, the French or the Arabs were willing to modify their views, despite the Yale argument.

[2] For documentary sources see especially: Department of State, Division of Near Eastern Affairs, *Mandate for Palestine* (Washington, Government Printing Office, 1927); United Kingdom, Miscellaneous No. 10 (1921). *Correspondence between H. M. Government and the United States Respecting Economic Rights in Mandated Territories.* Cmd. 1226. For backgrounds see also Benjamin SHWADRAN, *The Middle East, Oil and the Great Powers* (New York, Praeger, 1955), Ch. VII; Stephen H. LONGRIGG, *Oil in the Middle East: Its Discovery and Development* (London, Oxford, 1961), Chs. I-III.

It traced something of the history of the Anglo-Persian Oil Company, the Turkish Petroleum Company, and the active interest of the Standard Oil Company of New York, beginning in 1913. Thanks to the reputed wealth of the Mesopotamian resources and the British Government's control of the Anglo-Persian Oil Company and its 50 per cent interest in the Turkish Petroleum Company, the Mesopotamian oil problem became one of primary political significance in which Americans and French as well as British were concerned. Yale believed there was

> the possibility that the French came to an agreement with the British about the exploitation of the petroleum resources of Northern Mesopotamia, when the former consented to give up their political claims to the Mosul area. It was bruited that in the recent agreement between Clemenceau and Lloyd George in September 1919, there were certain stipulations regarding oil which were not included in the copy of the agreement which was given to the American representatives at Paris by Mr. Lloyd George. [1]

Yale had a fundamental appreciation of the necessity of oil for the British Admiralty, but held that there was a basic difference between securing the necessary political control over oil producing regions and obtaining "a monopoly of petroleum resources, a monopoly which would gravely affect the American petroleum industry and the American public in general." He felt that political control of Mesopotamia, with control of the Persian Gulf, "would assure Great Britain that the petroleum supplies of Mesopotamia would in case of war be under her control, no matter who or how many individual interests might develop these resources." To be doubly sure, an arrangement about pipe-lines might be made by which the control of the supply and exports would be absolutely in British hands in case of war. Commercially, north Mesopotamian oil could be brought either to the Persian Gulf or the Mediterranean only through pipe-lines. The pipe-lines could be built by the British Government or by British interests under concession from, and in the interest of the Arab Governments in Mesopotamia and Syria, and could be operated more or less as "common carriers for delivering oil to the coast." Under such an arrangement both the commercial and the Admiralty's interest could be fully served, and fears of a monopoly could be removed. Yale concluded:

> The monopoly of the petroleum resources of Mesopotamia is a question which not only affects one of America's greatest industries and the

---

[1] Howard, 242-243. As early as April 1919, France and Great Britain had signed the Long-Berenger Oil Agreement, which became the basis of the San Remo Oil Agreement of April 24, 1920. By this agreement Great Britain and France delimited their oil interests in Russia and Rumania, British and French colonies, and especially in Mesopotamia. France was allotted a 25 per cent share in the oil exploitation.

American petroleum consumers, but one which affects any decent settlement of the complex questions arising out of the dissolution of the Ottoman Empire and the disposal of the former German colonies of South Africa. The entire question of fair play in international commercial relations and the policy of the "open door" is threatened by the monopoly of the Mesopotamia oil fields contemplated by Great Britain.

Furthermore there is serious danger of disturbing the friendly relations of Great Britain and America, if by unfair political power Great Britain excludes from Mesopotamia American oil interests.

Until the settlement of the Arab Provinces by the Peace Conference, no concessions or rights obtained by any parties since the British Occupation should be respected or recognized; that is to say that any concessions of "rights" which may have been obtained during the British Occupation should not hold as valid.

The Yale "plan" was destined to receive no more favorable attention than the King-Crane Report. Acting Secretary of State Phillips did not permit Yale to get into touch with French officials upon his return to Paris from London and he came to the conclusion that further efforts to bring about a settlement along the lines which he had formulated were futile. So Yale resigned his position with the Peace Commission and asked to be returned to the United States to enter civilian life again. He felt that agreement to a solution which had been drawn up, could have been reached provided only the United States had exerted pressure on its behalf. [1]

The American Military Mission to Armenia

Meanwhile, another attempt on the part of the United States to obtain data on the Near East, somewhat supplementing and even duplicating the work of the King-Crane Commission, was made by sending the American Military Mission to Armenia, under the direction of Major-General James G. Harbord. [2] The mission was appointed on August 13,

---

[1] This is in a note from Professor Yale to the author. See also David GARNETT, *The Letters of T. E. Lawrence*, 287-288. In a letter of October 22, 1929, Lawrence expressed some disagreement with Yale's viewpoint, particularly concerning the Sykes-Picot agreement, which Lawrence indicated, amazed him. Lawrence felt that the Sykes-Picot agreement was a sheet-anchor for the Arabs. While it was absurd in some respects, it did recognize the Syrian claims to self-government and was much better than the settlement which followed. Lawrence felt that the Churchill settlement of 1921-1922 honorably fulfilled the promises made to the Arabs, insofar as the British spheres of influence were concerned. See GARNETT, 670-672; ANTONIUS, 316-319, and T. E. LAWRENCE, *Seven Pillars of Wisdom*, 276 n.

[2] See especially Major General James G. HARBORD, *Conditions in the Near East. Report of the American Military Mission to Armenia.* 66th Congress, 2nd Session, Senate Document No. 266, 44 pp.; also *U. S. Foreign Relations*, 1919, II, 841-874, for text.

following the recommendations of Messrs. Herbert Hoover and Henry Morgenthau, to investigate the political, military, economic and geographical considerations involved in possible American responsibilities in the Near East, and was ordered to proceed immediately to Constantinople.

The Harbord mission sailed from Brest on the *U. S. S. Martha Washington* on August 20, the day before the King-Crane Commission left Constantinople for Paris, and arrived in the Ottoman capital on September 2. After three or four days there, General Harbord divided his party, leaving in Constantinople those members who were to gather information which could best be obtained in that city. Altogether the mission spent thirty days in Asia Minor and Transcaucasia, interviewing representatives of every government [1]

as well as individual Turks, Armenians, Greeks, Kurds, Tartars, Georgians, Russians, Persians, Jews, Arabs, British, and French, including Americans for some time domiciled in the country. It also gave consideration to the views of the various educational, religious and charitable organizations supported by America. In addition to this personal

[1] *The Harbord Report*, 4. The Mission had access to reports of the American Committee for Relief in the Near East, the Food Administration, the mission of Mr. Benjamin B. Moore, sent by the Peace Conference to Transcaucasia, "as well as the very complete library on the region, its geography, history, and governments, loaned by the Librarian of Congress, the American Commission to Negotiate Peace, and others." As to the itinerary: "The Mission proceeded by ship to Constantinople. From there it traveled by the Baghdad Railway to Adana near the northeastern coast of the Mediterranean Sea; the scene of the massacres of 1909, and the principal city of the rich Province of Cilicia, where two days were spent visiting Tarsus, and the ports of Ayas and Mersina; thence continued by rail *via* Aleppo to Mardin; from there by motor car to Diarbekir, Kharput, Malatia, Sivas, Erzinjian, Erzerum, Kars, Erivan, and Tiflis; thence by rail to Baku and Batum. Erivan, Tiflis, and Baku are the capitals of the Republics of Armenia, Georgia, and Azerbaijan, and Batum is the seat of the British military government of the Georgian district of that name. Members of the mission also traveled by carriage from Ula-Kishla to Sivas; from Sivas to Samsun; visiting Marsovan where there is much apprehension among the Armenian population at this time; from Trebizond to Erzerum; by horseback from Khorasan to Bayazid; from Erivan to Nakhichevan, near the Persian border.... The mission traversed Asia Minor for its entire length and the Transcaucasus from north to south and east to west. All of the Vilayets of Turkish Armenia were visited except Van and Bitlis.... The Turkish frontier was paralleled from the Black Sea to Persia. On the return voyage from Batum the mission visited Samsun ... and Trebizond ...." Among others the Mission was assisted by Admiral Bristol, Consuls Ravndal, Jackson, Doolittle, and Colonel Haskell; Dr. Mary Mills Patrick, Hussein Bey (Robert College); Messrs. Barton, Chambers, Christie, Riggs, Partridge, Professor Robert P. Blake, of National University, Mr. Benjamin B. Moore, chief American political intelligence mission to the Transcaucasus, Tiflis; Misses Graffam and Fenanga, and by various other representatives of the Near East Relief and Ottoman government.

contact the mission before leaving Paris was in frequent conference with the various delegations to the peace conference from the regions visited.

The mission returned to the United States *via* France on November 11, 1919, exactly one year after the end of the Great War.

The Report of the Harbord Mission was completed on October 16 on board ship. The first part dealt with the history and present condition of the Armenian people, the second with the political situation and suggestions for readjustment, the third with conditions and problems involved in a mandatory, and the final part with considerations for and against assumption of a mandate over Armenia by the United States. While it is not necessary to give a detailed analysis of all portions of the Report, it is important to consider its basic elements.

In summary but excellent fashion, the Report traced the historical development of the Armenian people. The analysis of the Armenian massacres after 1878 and up to the tragic period of 1916 led to the conclusion that from 500,000 to more than 1,000,000 had been killed. Nevertheless, like the King-Crane Commission, the Harbord Mission was aware that "even before the war the Armenians were far from being in the majority in the region claimed as Turkish Armenia, excepting in a few places" and estimated that there were probably only "270,000 Armenians today in Turkish Armenia." Conditions generally were desperate.

There was much to indicate that when left alone Turks and Armenians had been able to live together peacefully, for co-existence during five centuries unmistakably pointed toward "their interdependence and mutual interest." The Harbord Mission saw nothing which proved that Armenians who had returned to their Turkish homes were "in danger of their lives", although there was a natural apprehension regarding the withdrawal of foreign troops. Like the King-Crane Commission, the Harbord Mission felt that the events at Smyrna had "undoubtedly cheapened every Christian life in Turkey, the landing of the Greeks there being looked upon by the Turks as deliberate violation by the Allies of the terms of their armistice and the probable forerunner of further unwarranted aggression." Foreign powers must accept moral responsibility for the unrest in Turkey, and the Armenians, unarmed at the time of the deportations and massacres, were still unarmed, in a country where everybody else carried a rifle.

In seeking a solution of the problem of Armenia, the first impulse was to find out the possibility of internal reform within the Ottoman Empire, and to ascertain whether the Armenians would accept it, which seemed unlikely. There was also the question of Russian Armenia, with its dominant Russian culture. The League of Nations had contemplated a mandate for the communities formerly belonging to the Ottoman Empire, and the Harbord Mission stressed, as had the King-Crane Commission, that the Turks would prefer a mandatory for the whole Empire to dismemberment and a receivership. Like the King-Crane Commission, the Harbord Mission recognized the difficulties of a purely American mandate:

> A power which should undertake a mandatory for Armenia and Transcaucasia without control of the contiguous territory of Asia Minor —Anatolia—and of Constantinople, without its hinterland of Roumelia, would undertake it under most unfavorable and trying conditions, so difficult as to make the cost almost prohibitive, the maintenance of law and order and the security of life and property uncertain, and ultimate success extremely doubtful. With the Turkish Empire still freely controlling Constantinople, such a power would be practically emasculated as far as real power is concerned. For generations these peoples have looked to Constantinople as the seat of authority. ... Before the war Constantinople was the most important port of Continental Europe, reckoned upon the basis of shipping clearances. There are well-informed business men who believe it is destined to become the third most important commercial city in the world. But, through generations of habit, unless put under a mandatory, Constantinople will continue to be a whirlpool of financial and political currents. Concession hunting, financial intrigue, political exploitation, and international rivalries will center there in the future as in the past. There must be actual control, for responsibility without authority is worse than useless in a land of oriental viewpoints.

If there could be a separate mandate for Armenia and Transcaucasia and one for Constantinople and Anatolia, in the view of the Harbord Mission, it would be most desirable to have such mandates exercised by the same power. The Ottoman Empire had many faults, but it was an "existing institution" and had "some rusty blood-stained political machinery" which could be made to function under strong mandatory control. Many distinguished Turks had favored a general American mandate, as they had also informed the King-Crane Commission:

> It has been very evident to this mission that Turkey would not object to a single disinterested power taking a mandate for her territory as outlined in the armistice with the Allies, and that it would be accomplished with a minimum of foreign soldiery, where an attempt to carve out territory for any particular region would mean a strong foreign force in constant occupation for many years. The aim of the Nationalist, or National Defense Party, as its adherents style it, as stated by Mustapha Kemal Pasha, its head, is the preservation of the territorial integrity of the Empire under a mandatory of a single disinterested power, preferably America. [1]

---

[1] As has been noted earlier, this is a misjudgment of the facts as to Mustapha Kemal's position, although there were some Nationalists who did favor an American mandate. General Harbord saw Mustapha Kemal on September 22, 1919.

The Harbord Mission saw no wisdom in incorporating Turkish territory into Armenia, however, and felt it very unwise to invite trouble which could be avoided by a single mandatory under which Turks and Armenians would be neighbors instead of rivals. Only under a single mandatory could the problem of ultimate boundaries be deferred.

Interestingly enough, the Harbord Mission came to the conclusion that in considering the Armenian problem, there was "something to be said on the part of the Turk." Despite many estimable qualities, generally the Armenian did not endear himself to his neighbors. The Armenian question could "not be settled in Armenia." Again, it could not be solved without answering the questions as to the fate of Turkey and the future of Russia. Pending final solution of these problems, the Mission believed that the power which assumed the Armenian mandate "should also exercise a mandate for Anatolia, Roumelia, Constantinople and Transcaucasia." The divisions of the mandate were an administrative detail to be worked out by the mandatory, although a natural subdivision might be Roumelia, the city of Constantinople, Anatolia, and the Transcaucasian region, without Russian Armenia. It was simpler and more economical to include the whole Ottoman Empire under a single mandatory than to divide it. Moreover, "a plebiscite fairly taken would in all probability ask for an American mandate throughout the Empire." Syria and Mesopotamia were not discussed because they had been excluded from the consideration of the Mission and were actually occupied by France and Great Britain. Whatever nation took the general mandatory should be strong, prepared to carry out a continuity of policy "for at least a generation, and to send its most gifted sons to leadership in the work without regard to political affiliations." A disinterested nation would assume such a mandate only "from a strong sense of altruism and international duty" in "this breeding place of wars and at the unanimous wish of other parties to the Covenant of the League of Nations."

The United States should make its own conditions as a preliminary to consideration of the mandate. There should be specific pledges from France and Great Britain and definite approval from both Germany and Russia of the dispositions made of Turkey and Transcaucasia, and a promise to respect them. Moreover, the mandatory, whoever it was, was to have "absolute control of the foreign relations of the Turkish Empire" and supervision of all concessions. The system of specific assignment of revenues for particular purposes was to be discarded and all foreign control over Turkish finances, such as the Council and Administration of the Ottoman Public Debt, was to cease. All foreign obligations of the Ottoman Empire were to be unified and refunded, with proper allocation, among the succession states.

Unlike the King-Crane Commission, the Harbord Mission submitted arguments for and against American acceptance of a Near Eastern mandate. In favor, it stressed that, as one of the major founders of the League of Nations, the United States was morally bound to assume the responsibilities of a mandatory. The Near East had been a battleground of militarism and imperialism for centuries and world peace must be insured by removing one of the sources of "war infection". The United States had been spending millions of dollars on Near Eastern charities, and had strong missionary and educational ties. The United States was the unanimous choice of the people and the hope of the Armenians, in particular. Acceptance of the mandate would stop the massacres and strengthen American prestige in the Near East. After a period of about five years the mandate might be self-supporting and under any consideration it would be better to spend "millions for a mandate" than "billions for future wars".

On the other side, the Harbord Mission pointed out that the United States, which had in no way contributed to the conditions which had brought about the trouble in the Near East, had prior obligations nearer home and might be weakened for other responsibilities, as in the Americas and the Far East. The first obligations of the United States were to itself and its neighbors. American charities were not limited to the Near East and American missionary and educational institutions would be protected by any mandatory, just as cessation of the massacres and Turkish misrule in general would be assured under any of the Great Powers. The United States would be "put to great expense, involving probably an increase of the Army and Navy." The Mission estimated the cost for the first five years at $ 756,104,000.

In summary, the Mission pointed out that it was difficult, without visiting the region, to realize "even faintly" the respect, faith and affection with which people regarded the United States. Nevertheless, the mandatory burdens might have to be "carried for not less than a generation under circumstances so trying that we might easily forfeit the faith of the world." But if the United States rejected the mandatory, it might be considered as having left unfinished the task for which it entered the war, and as having betrayed its hopes. The decision would have to be made by the American Government and people after weighing all the factors involved.

It is interesting to note the basic agreement between the Harbord Report and the more positive King-Crane Report on all essential elements. Dr. King had a summarized typewritten copy of the Harbord Report, obtained after it had been submitted, but the two commissions did not come into direct contact. The fact of fundamental agreement, however, might help, perhaps, to substantiate the essential soundness of the King-Crane Report.

The Failure of an American Policy

Both the King-Crane Commission and the Harbord Mission posed vital questions for the consideration of the United States. Whatever the decision, the American Government and the American people faced serious risks. Could the problems be solved by evasion or by acceptance of some genuinely constructive role in the world? These appeared to be the alternatives, although they were highly complicated by many other issues. No doubt the activities of Captain Yale in the British and French capitals in the fall of 1919, along with the King-Crane and Harbord Reports, had some influence both in Paris and Washington, but it is well to remember that, after all, the American Government, thanks to opposition at home and on the Paris front, was not prepared to assume the responsibilities either of mediation and pressure or of a possible mandatory, in order to secure some kind of settlement in the Near East. This position toward the specific problem of the Near East characterized the general attitude which was to be assumed toward Europe and even the world as a whole in the period immediately following the World War of 1914-1918.

British Negotiations with Feisal and the French Concerning Syria

Meanwhile, the British Government was still negotiating with the Emir Feisal concerning the situation in Syria and the course of these negotiations serves to illustrate the nature of the problem which also confronted the United States. As already noted, Prince Feisal had been very bitter about the Anglo-French agreement of September 13, and he wrote to Prime Minister Lloyd George again on October 9 noting that [1]

> whatever the merits or demerits of the arrangement, the fact remains that it is regarded by the bulk of the inhabitants with the utmost dismay, and the withdrawal of British troops from Syria is likely to lead to a catastrophe to the whole Arab world and to the common cause which the Allies are defending.

Feisal therefore proposed that the arrangement of September 13 either be cancelled or suspended and that the entire question be placed before the Peace Conference or be considered by a conference of British, French and Arab representatives under an American chairman, which would discuss the question and report to the Peace Conference. At the same time, Lord Curzon wrote to Feisal, once more reviewing the situation, the war agreements, and outlining the British contributions to Arab freedom—at the cost of having 1,400,000 troops in the Middle East and spending some £ 750,000,000. He added that a formal declaration had been made that in no circumstances would the British Government take

[1] *British Documents*, 1919-1939, First Series, IV, 443-444. See also ZEINE, Ch. VI.

the mandate for Syria, as had been stated as early as March 1919. Because of the delay in the United States in deciding whether to take a mandate, there was now

> no prospect of any final peace being made with Turkey until well into next year. In these circumstances His Majesty's Government have decided that it is impossible for them to maintain their troops any longer in Syria, and they have notified the Conference accordingly that they propose to withdraw them on the 1st November 1919.

Insofar as the occupation of a portion of Syria by France was concerned, Feisal was asked to recall that the Arabs owed "their freedom in large measure to the supreme sacrifices made by the French people in the late war." Lord Curzon therefore hoped that Feisal would agree to the proposals set forth on September 13. Similarly, in a letter of October 10, Lloyd George stressed the necessity of British withdrawal from Syria, in view of the burden and the delay in the peace making. [1]

Premier Clemenceau sent the official French reply to the British proposal of October 10, emphasizing that the sole basis of the understanding was that of the Sykes-Picot agreement of 1916 and application of Sir Edward Grey's declarations in 1912. He added that "the situation of France and its relations with the Arabs in its zone can only be identical to the situation of England in Mesopotamia and its relations with the Arabs in its zone." Moreover,

> the questions of Syria and Mesopotamia will be settled definitively at the same time as the fate of the territories of the Ottoman Empire, Constantinople, Asia Minor and Armenia. The traditional rights and interests of England and France in their respective zones cannot be infringed.

Clemenceau noted that the decision of the Council of Heads of Delegations, on September 15, had sanctioned only the principle of withdrawal. Clemenceau then defined the rights of France and the United Kingdom strictly in accordance with the Sykes-Picot Agreement. He added that the question of oil and pipe-lines was bound to the "very important concession of Mosul", and stated that the essential counterpart claimed by French industry and the Parliament was "strict equality in the exploitation of the oil of Mesopotamia and Kurdistan," a point of capital importance because of the French need for oil. Under this reservation, the agreement on the eventual cession of Mosul and all facilities for the construction of pipe-lines crossing the French mandate could be reached. [2]

Prince Feisal had still a third meeting with Lloyd George on October 13, when he pressed his case again, especially for an Anglo-Franco-Arab

---

[1] *British Documents*, 1919-1939, First Series, IV, 444-449, 451-452.
[2] *Ibid.*, 453-454.

conference on the Syrian problem. Feisal finally accepted a proposal that General Gouraud come to London for a talk with him and Lord Allenby, but he hoped the conference would not be confined to military matters, and wanted an American representative. But in view of the illness of President Wilson, Lloyd George thought it "impossible to settle the whole question of the future of Syria now." Allenby indicated that orders had been sent to begin evacuation from the north by November 1, although evacuation from Aleppo would take until the end of the month. [1]

Clemenceau rejected the idea of a conference of military representatives in his reply on October 14, and declared that General Gouraud was not available. Nor would he consent to have the Emir Feisal present, in any event. In Clemenceau's view, only the Peace Conference could take a definitive decision concerning Syria. The British Government should tell Feisal to enter into direct discussions, according to the agreements of 1916. On such a basis, Clemenceau was ready to discuss matters with Feisal during his visit to Paris, if he should desire to see the French Premier. [2] Lloyd George was surprised and deeply regretted the tone of the Clemenceau communication, which he considered "a complete change from the friendly attitude" which Clemenceau had expressed in September. He did not like "the offensive imputation", contended that there were no real conflicts between the Anglo-Arab and Anglo-French agreements, and denied that the British had done anything to injure French interests in Syria or elsewhere in the Middle East. So impressed had the British Government been with the importance of Franco-Arab agreement that the text of Clemenceau's September communication had not been shown to Feisal. In the end, Lloyd George pointed out that even the Sykes-Picot agreement rested on agreement with the Arabs and on the Arab position in Damascus, Homs, Hama and Aleppo. [3]

Feisal wrote to Lloyd George again on October 19 with regard to the proposal for a military conference, indicating that he would endeavor to persuade the French Government to maintain the *status quo* and agree

---

[1] *Ibid.*, 459-60, 461-462. Feisal had written to Lloyd George on October 11, protesting any change in the Government of Syria and referring to the pledges which had been made, and begging that a conference be called to consider the matter. If that were impossible, he would be glad to accept the offer to meet with the British, French and American representatives to consider the problem "involved in the impending withdrawal of British troops from Syria and to give final decision regarding the same."
[2] *Ibid.*, 468-469.
[3] See the Lloyd George communications of October 15, 18, to Clemenceau in *ibid.*, 473-474, 474-476, 479-489. Much of this document is in Lloyd George, II, 1082-1100.

to hold the special conference. But there appeared to be little prospect of success, and on October 20, Lord Derby reported another attack both on the British and Feisal from the pen of Maurice Barrès in *Echo de Paris*. Feisal, who had been in Paris for about fifteen days, wrote Lloyd George on November 6 that he had done his best to keep on good terms with the French Government and had told both Berthelot and Jean Gout that he was ready to write a letter to the French Government guaranteeing "to uphold French interests in Syria," but his procedure had not been approved by Clemenceau. Feisal advised Lloyd George once more that the Arab Syrian Nation would "do everything in their power" to defend their independence and unity, and "make every effort in this connection" and he wondered whether the British Government was "willing to stifle national feeling in Syria and expose the innocent to annihilation." [1]

The Emir Feisal also wrote to the President of the Council of the Heads of Delegations at the Peace Conference on November 6 protesting against the memorandum which Lloyd George had presented to him in London. He objected to changes in the administration of Syria and the withdrawal of British troops from certain Arab provinces, which would not be a permanent arrangement and did not represent the decision of the Peace Conference. Until final settlement, therefore, Feisal objected to a disturbance of the *status quo* and to any division of the country. The "suggested project", based on the Sykes-Picot agreement, was not acceptable. In Feisal's view, the Syrian nation, which had looked toward unity, was "now to be split up and each part put under a separate Government", and he feared that troubles would "begin on the frontiers" and "spread into the heart of the country", and possibly "throughout the Moslem world." [2]

On November 9, Clemenceau thanked Lloyd George for his frank letter of October 18 concerning the French charges against Great Britain, adding that Lloyd George had given proof of good faith when he had

---

[1] *British Documents*, 1919-1939, First Series, IV, 489-490, 490-499, 511-515. Feisal included the correspondence with Clemenceau, who had advised Feisal on November 2, for instance, about the situation in Syria, and on November 5, Feisal declared that if neither the political conditions nor the frontiers were in question, "the public life of the people and the unity and administration of the country" were "gravely compromised." Feisal could not accept the French charge that the Arabs were merely being whipped up by "agitators". Feisal concluded with the remark that the Arabs attached importance to meriting the confidence of the Allies, but that much would now depend on what would be done.

[2] See especially *ibid.*, 517-519; E.S.H. Bulletin, November 15, 1919, Vol. 26, Note from the Hejaz Delegation, November 6, regarding the situation in Syria; II. Note from Prince Feisal to Supreme Council of the Peace Conference, November 6, 1919; George ANTONIUS, *The Arab Awakening*, 298-302.

advised Feisal to come to Paris for discussions. He also professed to share the Lloyd George view as "to the very serious importance of an agreement with the Emir Feisal." But, while the negotiations had been courteous, they had not resulted in agreement, and Clemenceau asserted that the essential difficulty lay "not in the excessive ambitions of France, but in the absolute designs of the Emir," who did not "seem yet really to understand the necessity for the Arabs to accept a French mandate and a British mandate with a view to organizing and developing the Arab States."[1] The Emir Feisal, on the other hand, complained of his treatment in Paris, and advised Lord Derby on November 21 that there not only had been no progress in the negotiations, but that the French Government had made no effort to meet his position and that he had failed to see Clemenceau a second time. Since Clemenceau had refused to see him, Feisal had written a note on November 20 suggesting the maintenance of (1) Arab troops in the limits of the zone they had occupied since the Armistice, (2) British troops in Palestine, and (3) the French in the first zone of the west then under their occupation, and (4) the nomination of a commission composed of British, French and Arab members to settle their differences.[2] There had been no acceptance of this proposal, and Feisal wrote to Lloyd George on November 21 declaring that, despite the British memorandum of September 15, the French intended to occupy the Bekaa, Baalbek, Zebdani, and the area around Homs, Hama and Aleppo and Damascus. He thought the British could not exonerate themselves in view of their agreement.[3]

Matters appeared to have taken a more favorable turn toward the end of the month, however, and on November 27, the Emir Feisal had an interview with Clemenceau during which a provisional arrangement was accepted, stipulating French occupation of the Lebanon and the Syrian littoral to Alexandretta, but not to the Bekaa. The Arab State was to have French assistance and the agreement was to be purely provisional until the final settlement by the Peace Conference.[4]

[1] *British Documents*, 1919-1939, First Series, IV, 520-522, 530-531, which also includes the French note to the Peace Conference, November 17, 1919.
[2] *Ibid.*, 543-545, 546-548.
[3] *Ibid.*, 545-546.
[4] On November 28 Feisal thanked Lord Curzon for his interest in establishing friendly relations with the French Government and he enclosed the correspondence embodying the agreement. But the difficulties did not end, of course, and on December 19, Feisal complained that French troops had attacked in the Bekaa and proceeded to Baalbek. By December 1 a draft mandate for Palestine had been worked out by the British Delegation in Paris and the Zionist Organization. By the middle of December it was clear that the French Government was demanding an equal share in Kurdish and Mesopotamian oil, and at an Anglo-French meeting in London on December 23, there was much

But the Arab portions of the former Ottoman Empire constituted only one set of problems, for there were still all the issues involved in Anatolia, the region of the Straits and Armenia. Sir Eyre Crowe reported to Lord Curzon as early as October 17 that the Harbord Report, which had been completed only the day before, threw no new light on the Near Eastern problem, although it appeared to support the recommendations of the King-Crane Commission in favor of an "integral United States mandate" over Constantinople and the Straits, Anatolia and Armenia. [1] Viscount Grey reported from Washington on October 18 that, while Great Britain would be willing to have an American mandate in Constantinople, delays were causing difficulties, and behind the various projects were some things which he did not like. On October 23 he reported a conversation with Henry Morgenthau, who thought that, after Senate approval of a treaty, it might be possible for him and General Harbord "to create a wave of idealism in favour of Mandate for Constantinople and Armenia." Morgenthau suggested either Anglo-American or International Control of the Straits of Gibraltar to show that the United States was invited into full partnership in the East, and Grey, in turn, indicated that the United States should agree to similar control of the Panama Canal. [2]

The Proposals of the American Commission to Negotiate Peace

Because of the serious concern of some of the American representatives in Paris over the ominous situation in the Near East, one final attempt was made to influence American participation in the settlement. On November 26, 1919, a memorandum was prepared by the American Commission to Negotiate Peace, insisting on the need "of a definite Turkish policy" for the United States. [3] Evidently it was the last significant document dealing with the Turkish problem before the remainder of the American delegation left Paris for home in December 1919. Literally taking a leaf from the King-Crane Report, the memorandum pointed out that "no territorial spoils so large and valuable as the Turkish Empire" had "ever in our time been divided up by Treaty," a fact which might render the liquidation of the Ottoman Empire extremely difficult. It was

---

discussion of the Arab situation, the Turkish problem and Mosul. By January 16, 1920 Feisal and the French Government reached an agreement concerning Syria, under which the French Government engaged to offer its assistance and "to guarantee its independence against every aggression against the frontiers" assigned by the Peace Conference. In general see *ibid.*, 554-603, 624-627.

[1] *Ibid.*, 816-820.
[2] *Ibid.*, 843.
[3] King Papers: American Commission to Negotiate Peace. *Memorandum on the Policy of the United States Relative to the Treaty with Turkey.* Hôtel de Crillon, Paris, November 26, 1919. 6 pp. Mimeographed.

assumed that when Congress met in December 1919 the United States might join the League of Nations and take part "in the negotiation of the Turkish Treaty," not only because of the importance of American interests in Turkey, but because the settlement of the problems raised by the partition of the Ottoman Empire affected "the success of the League of Nations and the peace of the world."

But before the negotiations began the United States should determine "what solution of the Turkish problem" was desired, so that the American representatives helping to prepare the Turkish treaty might "know from the very start" the general outlines of American policy, for otherwise they would be at a serious disadvantage in dealing with the British, French and Italians, all of whom had a definite policy. To guide the negotiators, the United States should decide:

(1) How far it will adopt the recommendations of the Crane-King and Harbord Reports as to the lines on which the Ottoman Empire should be divided;
(2) Whether the so-called "secret" agreements made by other Powers for the partition of Turkey are to be recognized by the United States;
(3) If these agreements are not recognized, whether the United States will be prepared to provide money or troops in order that the territorial and political plans provided for in those agreements may not be carried out;
(4) Whether the United States will be prepared to cooperate in the international control of such portions of Turkey as are not placed under any mandate.

These problems arose in connection with every major division of the Ottoman Empire, as for example, Thrace, Constantinople, and the Straits. It was assumed that Western Thrace would be assigned neither to the Greeks nor to the Bulgars, but would "follow the fate of Constantinople; and that a strip along both shores of the Bosphorus and Dardanelles" would be similarly treated. The League of Nations, without armed forces, could not directly govern this region, but it could not be left independent. If neither the United States nor any other power would assume a mandate over it, the Straits "must be placed under international control," similar to that which would be devised for the Turkish state in Anatolia. Was the United States to remain "aloof from this control," or was it to join in managing the Ottoman Public Debt, or the gendarmerie? If the latter, then it would have to contribute both men and money. The same considerations applied to Anatolia. How far would the United States go in assisting and guiding the government in Anatolia, where the Greek, Italian and French claims would reduce the Turkish area by about fifty per cent? If the United States opposed those claims, which would "Balkanize" Anatolia and Asia Minor, "it must be ready to offer assistance, if necessary, in bringing order to those regions." The problem of Armenia and Kurdistan also offered difficulties. Both the King-Crane and the

Harbord Reports had contemplated a mandate, possibly American, for these regions. But if there were to be no such mandate, the only alternative was "to place the Armenians and the Kurds under some protection." Whether the districts were administered separately or together was not too important, for the main point was "that the control be effective, so as to obviate religious feuds and mutual oppression." Would the United States cooperate willingly with other powers in this task? Finally there were Syria, Palestine and Mesopotamia, the Arab countries which would be divided up according to the secret agreements between Great Britain and France unless the United States objected. And if it did, the United States "must be prepared to support some alternative solution."

What of the aspirations of the various powers to the specific territories claimed under the other so-called "secret" arrangements concluded during the war? The memorandum noted the Greek pretention to Eastern Thrace, but felt it probably would be disallowed. In the vilayet of Aidin, however, the Greeks were occupying a very large region, with some 72,000 soldiers. Expert opinion agreed that they had "no sound ethnic claim and that a continuance of their occupation" would be "ruinous to that region and ultimately to themselves." Great Britain alone favored the Greeks, but since the Peace Conference had permitted them to land at Smyrna, it would be "difficult to turn them out without compensation". "As an inducement to evacuate Smyrna, would the United States loan money to Greece, or bear part of her expenses there incurred?" The Italians had demanded the vilayet of Adalia under the Treaty of London of April 26, 1915, a claim based on no ethnic foundation at all, but merely on the spoils of war, and Great Britain and France were still pledged to the treaty. Financial inducements might be necessary to remove the Italians. Would the United States offer these, if requisite, in order to maintain the integrity of Asia Minor? Under the Sykes-Picot agreement of May 1916, France had claimed territories in Cilicia and Southern Armenia, as well as a protectorate over the native Syrian Kingdom and a portion of the Syrian coast, including Beirut and Mt. Lebanon. While the claim to Cilicia and Armenia might be waived, that to Syria was based on ancient tradition and sentiment as well as interest, although the Syrians rejected a French mandate.

> But to give to the United States, or to any other Power than France, a mandate over Syria would shock French feeling. Any alternative to the French mandate would require steady American effort to carry it through, because England and Italy will not oppose France and because the French army is already in military occupation.

There were also the position and aspirations of Great Britain in both Palestine and Mesopotamia, similar to French ambitions in Syria, except that the Zionists had invited Great Britain to go to Palestine and the Mesopotamian Arabs had not yet "voiced any opposition to her proposed mandate over them." Neither Great Britain nor France, however, had yet consulted the wishes of the local populations. The removal of Great Britain from Mesopotamia would probably be "even more difficult than that of France or Italy from their respective zones." The British position had been set forth in the British memorandum of February 1919. Was the United States "inclined to oppose this British solution of the Turkish problem?" If so, it must be ready "with a well considered alternative plan."

The memorandum, finally, set forth the reasons for American intervention. The altruistic considerations were well known, but for those to whom altruism carried no convictions, two "selfish" arguments were used :

(1) In the interest of peace we ought not to permit a patchwork division of Turkey based on the spoils system and callous to local sentiment, such as will certainly be made if America holds aloof. No Power except the United States can prevent the carrying into effect of those notorious "secret" agreements, which would lead certainly to war and probably to another world war.

We ought therefore to join in the Turkish Treaty, and refuse to permit such a settlement even if the refusal costs us money and trouble.

(2) If the United States takes no part, or an apathetic part, in the settlement of the Near East, its material interests must suffer incalculably. Commercial opportunities in Turkey, as well as in the Ottoman territories placed under mandates, will be lost to the United States if it keeps aloof. The only way to maintain in Turkey our traditional trade policy of the "open door" is to be on the spot and *hold* the door open.

In conclusion, this very important document emphasized that since Turkey had been more completely smashed than any other belligerent, the victors would have to incur "labor and expense" to secure both peace and order within the former Ottoman Empire. Moreover, if the United States would assume no responsibility, it could not "expect to exert influence in securing such a Turkish settlement as it would desire." Thirdly, the expenditure of American money or the promise of some kind of American support would be required in order to render American participation in the Turkish negotiations effective, which might actually "involve temporary American intervention in Turkish affairs." But such treaty should be framed and the negotiations carried out "in close cooperation with the Senate." Hence, the memorandum raised the question whether the Secretary of State could not draft or prepare a definite American policy, somewhat similar to the statement of the British Government in February 1919, which was annexed to the memorandum. This could be submitted to the Senate Committee on Foreign Relations, and when approved, it could be issued to the American negotiators. It seemed clear that unless the American Commission knew in advance how far the United States would co-operate in solving Turkish problems, it would be "heavily handicapped," and American intervention might "after all be sterile."

Few could have stated the basic alternatives before the United States with greater clarity, but the appeal had no effect and the American delegation left Paris early in December 1919. The Treaty of Sèvres of August 1920 was to follow, but peace did not come to the Near East until the Conference of Lausanne finally arrived at a settlement, following the long Greco-Turkish War, on July 24, 1923. It was small wonder that Charles R. Crane complained in his memoirs that while the King-Crane Commission was preparing its report, "carefully studied and approved by the foremost authorities on Eastern Affairs, the countries involved had already been sold to the highest bidders." [1]

Whatever the weaknesses of British or French policy in the Near East, the United States and the American people had their share of responsibility for the failure to bring about an earlier and more just settlement. The bitter partisanship in American politics, along with President Wilson's untimely illness in the fall of 1919, contributed to the rejection of the League of Nations by the United States Senate. The consequent refusal of the United States to accept a responsible place in the peace settlements had repercussions all over the world. Grave damage was done to the prospect of a more healthy settlement in the Near East and in other troubled areas. American cooperation and influence might have altered the course of events and paved the way for a fundamentally sound world order with all nations participating.

---

[1] See also his interview in the New York *Times*, on his return from Europe, December 31, 1919.

CHAPTER IX

The Road to Lausanne

While the Paris Peace Conference was considering all the complex problems raised by the dissolution of the Ottoman Empire and the King-Crane Commission was carrying out its quest for the facts on which to base an equitable and viable settlement in the Near East, the Turks themselves were giving much attention to the fate awaiting their country. Patriotic organizations had sprung up all over the crumbling Empire. Some were groups with legitimate intentions and purposes, while others were thought to be of an unsavory character, led by prominent persons, whose primary desire was to save themselves, often under the protection of some foreign power.

THE TURKISH NATIONALIST MOVEMENT

Members of the King-Crane Commission had come into touch with some of the Turkish nationalist leaders during their interviews at Constantinople in July-August 1919. But if they sensed something of the essence of the movement, they underestimated both its basic and elemental implications and its strength, partly because it was relatively impossible properly to assess it in the old Ottoman capital, partly because it was too early, in 1919, to have the perspective of later years.

Some Anatolian Origins

Not unnaturally, it was in the Anatolian homelands that the Turkish nationalist movement took earliest root and developed strength, insofar as the masses of the Turkish people were concerned.[1] One of the most influential and genuine of the newly organized groups was the Union for the Defense of the National Rights of the Eastern Provinces at Erzerum and El Aziz, with a headquarters also in Constantinople. It was this group which became the nucleus of the Nationalist Congress of Erzerum, headed by Mustapha Kemal, who was to become the great leader of the Turkish nation following the Greek invasion of Smyrna in May 1919.[2] The primary groups in Constantinople were the Ottoman League of

---

[1] For backgrounds of Turkish nationalism see especially Uriel HEYD, *Foundations of Turkish Nationalism: The Life and Teachings of Ziya Gökalp* (London, Luzac [and Harvill], 1950), 174 pp.; Ziya GOKALP, *Turkish Nationalism and Western Civilization*. Translated and edited with an Introduction by Niyazi Berkes (London, Allen and Unwin, 1959), 336 pp.; Altemur KILIC, *Turkey and the World*. Introduction by William O. Douglas (Washington, Public Affairs Press, 1959), 224 pp., especially Chapters I-II; Elaine D. SMITH, *Turkey: The Origins of the Kemalist Movement and the Government of the Grand National Assembly* (1919-1923) (Washington, 1959), 175 pp., *passim*; Bernard LEWIS, *The Emergence of Modern Turkey*, Ch. VIII.
[2] Mustapha KEMAL, *Speech. October 15-20, 1927*. Official Translation. (Leipzig, K. F. Koehler, 1929), 11-12; Gasi Mustapha Kemal Pasha, *Die Dokumente zur Rede* (Leipzig, Koehler, 1920), No. 7, pp. 3-4.

National Unity and the Central Bureau of the National Congress of Turkey, which protested against the Smyrna outrage. But there were others, such as the Ottoman Liberal Party, led by General Sherif Pasha, the Society for the Protection of the Rights of Thrace (Adrianople), the Pasha Ali Society, the Liberal Entente, the Peace and Safety Society, and the Society for the Development of Kurdistan.[1]

In his great six-day speech of October 15-20, 1927, Mustapha Kemal gave us an interesting discussion of the various groups and their aspirations during this period. He noted that they considered [2]

> that the breakdown of the Ottoman Empire was extremely probable. In face of the threatened danger of the dismemberment of their country their first thought was to save Eastern Thrace and later on, if possible, to form a Turco-Mohamedan community that would include Western Thrace. The only way by which they thought they could realize this aim was to put their trust in England or, if this was not possible, in France. With this object they tried to get into touch with certain political personalities belonging to foreign countries. It was believed that their intention was to establish a Thracian Republic.
>
> The object of the "Defense of the National Rights of the Eastern Provinces" Union, on the other hand..., was to use all lawful means to insure the free exercise and development of their religious and political rights for all elements inhabiting these provinces; to defend, if it should become necessary, the historical and national rights of the Mohamedan population of these provinces; to institute an impartial inquiry for the purpose of discovering the motives, the instigators and agitators implicated in the extortions and cruelties committed in the Eastern Provinces, so that the guilty ones might be punished without delay; to do their utmost to remove the misunderstandings that existed between the different elements in the country, and to restore the good relations that had formerly existed between them; and, finally, to appeal to the Government to alleviate as far as it lay in their power the misery resulting from the war.

Mustapha Kemal summarized the three general propositions put forward by the Turks to determine the future status of their country: [3]

1) establishment of a British protectorate; 2) acceptance of an American mandate; and 3) deliverance of the country through regional autonomy under which each district would go its own way. Mustapha Kemal

---

[1] *Dokumente*, 2-4; Mustapha KEMAL, *Speech*, 12-13; *Miller Diary*, V., 134-142, Nos. 337, 338, 339. See also La Société pour l'Étude de l'Histoire Turque, *Histoire de la République* (Istanbul, Devlet Basimevi, 1935), 9-13. A leading member of the Society of the Friends of England was Damad Ferid Pasha.

[2] *Speech*, 10-11.

[3] *Ibid.*, 13-14. See also "Condensed Memorandum Concerning the Organization and Points of View of the League for the Defense of the Rights of Anatolia and Rumelia," Appendix C, Harbord Report on Armenia, *U. S. Foreign Relations*, 1919, II, 875-878; or Report of the American Military Mission to Armenia, by Major-General James G. Harbord, 66th Congress, 2d Session, Senate Document No. 266.

did not feel that any of these proposals could be considered as valid solutions, since, in reality, the Ottoman Empire had been shattered to its deepest foundations. Therefore, "one resolution alone was possible, namely, to create a New Turkish State, the sovereignty and independence of which would be unreservedly recognized by the whole world." It was that resolution which Mustapha Kemal and the Nationalists had adopted before they were forced to leave Constantinople and which they began to put into execution immediately when they set foot on Anatolian soil at Samsun. There were logical arguments to support this high resolve: [1]

> The main point was that the Turkish nation should be free to lead a worthy and glorious existence. Such a condition could only be attained by complete independence. Vital as considerations of wealth and prosperity might be to a nation, if it is deprived of its independence it no longer deserves to be regarded otherwise than as a slave in the eyes of civilized humanity. To accept the protectorate of a foreign Power would signify that we acknowledge that we lack all human qualities; it would mean that we admit our own weakness and incapacity.

The Nationalist Meeting at Erzerum,
July 23-August 17, 1919

The Turkish nationalist movement was thus taking on form and substance on the Anatolian plateau under the leadership of Mustapha Kemal, or, as he was later to be known, Ataturk.[2] Charles R. Crane was much intrigued by and honestly impressed with the nationalists, as he records in his memoirs:[3]

> Perhaps the most significant delegation we saw was a little group which afterwards became the nucleus of the Ankara government. The members appeared before our committee and said, "We are awfully

---

[1] *Speech*, 17-18.
[2] See especially H. C. ARMSTRONG, *Gray Wolf, An Intimate Study of a Dictator* (London, Barker, 1932); H. E. WORTHAM, *Mustapha Kemal of Turkey* (Boston, Little, Brown, 1931); J. DENY, *Souvenirs du Gazi Moustafa Kemal Pacha* (Paris, Geuthner, 1927); Tekin ALP, *Le Kemalisme* (Paris, Alcan, 1937); SMITH, *passim*. See also King Papers: Office of the American Commissioner, Constantinople. *Report on the Political, Military, Commercial and Economic Situation in Trebizond and the Surrounding Vilayets.* Submitted by Ralph F. Chesbrough, American Consul, Class Eight, detailed to Constantinople. Carbon, 13 pp. See also the Chesbrough *Report on the Present Political and Military Status of Batoum, Its Present and Future Commercial and Economical Importance, and the Opportunities it will Offer as a Port of Entry for the Development and Expansion of American Commerce with Armenia, Georgia, Azerbaijan, Persia and Turkestan.* Carbon, 10 pp. Both these reports, sent by Mr. Ravndal to the American Commission at Paris on August 7, are of significance, although Chesbrough misjudged the implications of the nationalist movement.
[3] *Memoirs*, 376. Mr. Crane was somewhat in error as to the attitude of the Anatolian nationalists who, in general, did not appear to favor a mandate.

tired of war; we have had years and years of it; the Italian war, the two Balkan wars, and the Great War and we are very, very tired; we only want peace. If America will take a mandate, not for Syria or Palestine, not for Armenia, but for the whole Turkish Empire, we Turks won't name a single condition. We will throw away our arms and be glad to go back to work; the country won't require much policing, very few soldiers; everyone will be so happy to come under the wing of America."

They were very mellow; you could have done anything with them and the feeling all through the Near East was one of great desire, especially on the part of the Moslem folk, to become reconciled to the western world.

Indeed, Mr. Crane appears to have urged Mr. Louis Edgar Browne, the special correspondent of the Chicago *Daily News*, to go into Anatolia to see Mustapha Kemal and find out what he could—at the grass roots— about the man and the movement which he led and dominated.[1]

On July 23, the very day on which the King-Crane Commission returned to Constantinople, the first Nationalist Congress met at Erzerum in an humble school room. It was composed of representatives of all vilayets, sub-prefectures and districts in eastern Anatolia, and Mustapha Kemal served as Chairman. In a fifteen-day session, the Erzerum Congress perfected an organization, adopted resolutions, and essentially initiated the nationalist program. At the very outset, Mustapha Kemal stressed the basic character of the national movement, noted the dangers of the partition of the Turkish homelands, and declared that "the entire country within its national frontiers" was an "undivided whole", and asserted that if the Empire were to be carved up, the nation would unanimously "resist any attempt at occupation or interference by foreigners."

During the period of the Erzerum Congress there was much talk of the possibility of an American mandate and, as already noted, this was especially true while the King-Crane Commission was in Constantinople. Moreover, some of the Nationalists in Constantinople sought to persuade Mustapha Kemal that this was the only hope of avoiding disaster.[2] But Mustapha Kemal was not persuaded, although he asked

---

[1] Among other things, see Browne's despatches from Konia and Ankara, The Chicago *Daily News*, August 3-5, 1919. On the other hand, a British report to the Foreign Office, dated October 18, was very critical of Browne, "a law unto himself, out for sensation, and with a very superficial judgment of, or regard for facts." It was also noted that journalistic utterances were, moreover, "taken very seriously by the Nationalists and one individual of this breed recently persuaded the Sivas Conference that the Nationalist movement was wholly patriotic, and had the complete endorsement of everyone except England." *British Documents*, 1919-1939, First Series, IV, 820.

[2] *Speech*, 63. Chesbrough noted the apparent results of the Congress as embodied in the decision to sever connections with the Central Government at Constantinople and to resist forcibly any military effort of the Allies to take over the country.

all kinds of questions relative to a mandate. When the Congress finished its work on August 17, it resolved that:

1. The fatherland, within the national frontiers, composes a unified whole, whose parts cannot be separated from each other.
2. In the event of partition of the Ottoman Empire, the nation will resist unanimously, and defend itself against all forms of occupation and intervention.
3. In case the central government be unable to insure the independence and security of the country, a provisional government will be set up for this purpose. The members of this government shall be designated by the National Congress. If such a Congress be not in session, the government shall be appointed by the Representative Committee.
4. It is essential that the national forces take the field and the nation will assert itself.
5. The Christian elements are not to be allowed special privileges compromising our political rights and social equilibrium.
6. No mandate or protectorate shall be accepted.
7. Every effort shall be made to bring about the immediate convening of the National Assembly and placing it in charge of governmental affairs. [1]

The Congress at Sivas,
September 4-11, 1919

Unfortunately, the Sivas Congress did not meet until after the King-Crane Commission had left Constantinople despite some efforts to bring about an earlier convocation. Once more, Mustapha Kemal served as Chairman, despite some opposition. Once more, too, Mustapha Kemal, at the very outset, on September 4, noted the critical situation of the country, with the Greeks in the Smyrna region and penetrating Western Anatolia, the possible inclusion of Thrace in the Greek zone of occupation and a Greek kingdom to be established in the Pontus on the Black Sea, an Armenian state under active consideration and Allied forces in Constantinople. In the face of this tragic situation and its possible consequences, much had to be done if independence were to be achieved. Associations for defense were springing up all over the country. [2]

> In a word, the voice of the nation, which was raised from the west to the east, found an echo resounding in every corner of Anatolia; the national leagues became a single organization, born of the conscience and will of the nation: its aim is not to allow the country to fall under the yoke of the foreigner.

The Sivas Congress considered the problem of an American mandate on September 8. [3] While there was much serious discussion and much reference to the interviews which had taken place with the King-Crane Commission, and a feeling on the part of some that the Turkish nation

---

[1] SMITH, 17-18.
[2] See especially *Die Dokumente zur Rede*, 33-38.
[3] *Speech*, 92-100.

could only survive as an independent entity under a properly administered mandate, Mustapha Kemal was adamant against any such suggestion. In the end the Sivas Congress closed its work on September 11 with a Declaration which foreshadowed the Turkish National Pact of 1920 and constituted the basic political platform upon which Mustapha Kemal and the Turkish Nationalists proposed to rally and defend the country. The Declaration insisted that all the Turkish territory within the frontiers of the Mudros Armistice, inhabited by "a preponderate majority of Turkish population," formed "an undivided and inseparable whole." To insure the national integrity and independence and to preserve the Sultanate and the Caliphate, it was "indispensable to place in action the national forces and the absolute will of the people." Assembled both at Erzerum and Sivas, the Turkish Nationalists were "absolutely resolved to resist and defend" their rights against all intermeddling or occupation on the part of any foreign Powers. While the Turks were willing to permit non-Moslem elements to live within their frontiers on the basis of equality, they were not prepared to give them special privileges— privileges which would tend to disturb their government or threaten their "social equilibrium." The Turks were awaiting the decision of the Paris Peace Conference and hoped it would "conform with right and with such justice" as would reverse the tendencies which were contrary to the historic, ethnic and religious rights of the Turkish people. There were yet hopes that the decision of the Peace Conference would not destroy the unity of the country. The Declaration proclaimed "a just peace" as a national aim, and stated that the Turkish people would "freely accept the economic assistance" of nations without prejudice to their territorial integrity.

The Sivas Declaration called upon the Constantinople Government to submit to the "national will" and urged it to proceed immediately to the convocation of a National Assembly "to save the nation from its present plight." It also called attention to the formation of "The Assembly to Defend the Rights and Interests of Anatolia and Rumelia," of which all Moslem compatriots sharing its sentiments, could be considered as "legitimate members." The Congress selected a Representative Committee to carry out its program. As a compromise with those who favored an American mandate, it was unanimously resolved that "a delegation from the American Congress" be asked to come to Turkey to examine and report upon the actual situation in order to counteract the effect of hostile propaganda in the United States, "before permitting the arbitrary disposal of the peoples and territories of the Ottoman Empire by a treaty of peace." [1]

---

[1] *Harbord Report*, Exhibit E; SMITH, 19-21. Mustapha Kemal remarked: "I remember very well that a document to this effect was drawn up

Some days after the closure of the Sivas Congress, the Harbord Mission came to Sivas, where General Harbord had a long conversation with Mustapha Kemal on September 22 concerning the organization and aims of the Nationalist movement. Asked what he would do if, despite every imaginable effort and sacrifice, the Nationalist movement should end in failure, Mustapha Kemal replied that the nation which exerted "every imaginable effort" and made "every possible sacrifice to secure its freedom and independence" could not fail. If Turkey faltered, he would have to admit that the nation was dead. The possibility of failure, therefore, could not be conceived in the case of a nation full of life and "capable of making every kind of sacrifice." While Mustapha Kemal was somewhat puzzled, he did not "trouble to ascertain what could have been the general's real object" in asking such a question. [1] Mustapha Kemal is reported to have given a statement to General Harbord on October 19, 1919, favoring American assistance: [2]

> The Nationalist Party recognized the necessity of the aid of an impartial foreign country. It is our aim to secure the development of Turkey as she stood at the armistice. We have no expansionist plans, but it is our conviction that Turkey can be made a rich and prosperous country if she can get a good government. Our government has become weakened through foreign interference and intrigues. After all our experience we are sure that America is the only country able to help us. We guarantee no new Turkish violence against the Armenians will take place.

Mustapha Kemal pointed out that the movement rested on the basis of the preservation of Turkish independence and territorial integrity. [3] He expressed faith in the good will and intentions of the American people, feeling that they would "adopt the most efficient, equitable and practical resolutions" concerning the fate of Turkey. The Turks derived "great hope from the Wilsonian Doctrine." While it may be said, therefore, that the Turkish nation generally desired some American assistance, and many people at Constantinople especially wanted an American mandate, there is no evidence, other than the implication of the Harbord Mission, that Mustapha Kemal himself desired such a mandate. Indeed, the Turkish leader insisted in his *Speech* of October 1927 that a logical examination

---

and signed by the Chairman of the Committee, but I cannot remember exactly whether it was sent off or not. In any case, I never attached any particular importance to it." *Speech*, 100. See Dankwart A. Rustow's review of General Ali Fuat Cebesoy's memoirs, *Milli Mücadele Hatiralart* (Vol. I) and *Moskova Hatiralari* (Vol. II) (Istanbul, 1953, 1955), in *The Middle East Journal*, Vol. X, No. 3 (Summer, 1956), 325-326.

[1] *Speech*, 149-150.
[2] See *Harbord Report*, 17.
[3] *Ibid.*, Exhibit C.

of the Sivas Declaration would show no reference to the idea of a mandate, much less "anything ... about asking America to accept it." [1]

American Policy Concerning the Middle East

We have seen that neither the King-Crane Report nor the Harbord Report had much influence on American policy in the Near East. There was never any response, insofar as the records show, to the memorandum of the American Peace Commission of November 26, 1919, which raised the basic questions concerning American policy in the Near East. The primary aim of the Department of State, from the beginning of 1920 to the opening of the Lausanne Conference in 1922, was to follow the customary pattern of safeguarding American interests. American policy was among the fundamental elements preventing a settlement of the problem of the mandates in the Near East for about two and one half years after the end of the so-called First World War.

The "Open Door" in the Near East

From the beginning, the United States took a very strong stand in favor of the principle of the mandates, but it would assume no official responsibility in any of the Near Eastern countries, and very little elsewhere. The United States was especially interested in the principle of "the open door", for the benefit, seemingly, of American oil companies, which actually had or claimed possible concessions in petroleum exploitation in Palestine and Mesopotamia. [2] The American Government felt that the economic resources of mandated territories involved a problem of major principle transcending any particular private or strategic interest, and vigorously objected to the restrictive, exclusive nature of British oil policy, which, however, somewhat paralleled American legislation on the subject in the Western Hemisphere and in the Philippines. The United States also protested against the San Remo Oil Agreement of April 1920 between France and

---

[1] The *Harbord Report, inter alia*, states, 16-17: "A party of distinguished Turks, including a former minister of high standing and a diplomat who for eight years represented his country at one of the European courts, stated that as between the independence of Turkey as it existed in 1914, and a mandate for the Empire given to the United States they greatly preferred the latter, and believed that they spoke for the educated classes of all Turkey." On the other hand, a report of Admiral de Robeck to the British Foreign Office (October 18) noted that members of the Mission appeared to take color from their surroundings, that few had any previous knowledge of the Near East, and that they were " 'green', easy for the Nationalists to spoon-feed, and ready to rise to such catchwords as independence and self-determination." *British Documents*, 1919-1939, First Series, IV, 820.

[2] In general see Howard, 317-28. See also Benjamin Shwadran, Ch. VII; S. H. Longrigg, Chs. II, III.

Great Britain because it did not seem "consistent with the principles of equality of treatment understood and accepted during the peace negotiations at Paris."[1] Thus was developing a fundamental controversy over mineral properties in the Near East—the dangers of which both the King-Crane Commission and the American Peace Commission in Paris had amply warned. This controversy was to continue until the Lausanne Conference, and involved the interests of the Royal Dutch Shell Company, the Turkish Petroleum Company, whose rights the American Government consistently refused to recognize, and various American interests, including the so-called Chester Concession.[2]

Other American Interests

But there were other American interests in the Near East besides oil, some of them of very long-standing. The United States was anxious to preserve the capitulatory rights of American citizens and business interests, not merely in Turkey proper, but in the territories about to be mandated to Great Britain and France.[3] It also expressed concern over the Christian minorities within Turkish territory, especially Greeks and Armenians, although it was not prepared to commit itself to specific measures for their protection. Moreover, the United States developed an abiding interest, which grew with the passing years, in the development of the affairs of the British mandate in Palestine.[4]

Armenia, in whose fate Americans had been professedly concerned for some time, presented an essentially ticklish problem because of its relationship both to Russia and Turkey. The Council of Foreign Ministers at Paris decided in January to recognize Georgia, Azerbaijan and Armenia as *de facto* governments, and American recognition followed on April 23, 1920, but without predetermination of frontiers.[5] Three days later, the Supreme Council, meeting at San Remo, formally asked the United States to assume the Armenian mandate, not because the Powers were seeking to escape a responsibility, it was said,[6]

> but because the responsibilities which they are already obliged to bear in connection with the disposition of the former Ottoman Empire will strain their own capacities to the uttermost and because they believe that the appearance on the scene of a power emancipated from the prepossessions of the Old World will inspire a wider confidence and

---

[1] *U. S. Foreign Relations*, 1920, II, 655, 658-659.
[2] *U. S. Foreign Relations*, 1921, II, 71-94, 99-108, 890-916; 1920, III, 766-774.
[3] *U. S. Foreign Relations*, 1920, III, 757-766.
[4] For the American position relative to minorities see *U. S. Foreign Relations*, 1920, III, 774-809.
[5] *Ibid.*, 774-775, 778; Firuz KAZEMZADEH, *The Struggle for Transcaucasia* (1917-1921), Chap. XVII.
[6] *U. S. Foreign Relations*, 1920, III, 779-783.

afford a firmer guarantee for stability in the future than would the selection of any European power.

The Senate rejected the mandate on June 1,[1] but President Wilson, in accordance with the wishes of the Supreme Council, finally accepted the responsibility of arbitrating the Armenian boundaries, although his decision was not reached until more than three months after the abortive Treaty of Sèvres had been signed.[2] The President recognized that a delimitation of the boundaries would give Armenia at the outset a "population about equally divided between Moslem and Christian elements and of diverse racial and tribal relationship." Wilson felt that the Trebizond vilayet would have to be divided between Armenia and Turkey, the town and harbor to go to Armenia in order to provide access to the sea, while the harbor towns and hinterland of Kerasun and Ordu, strongly Moslem and Turkish, would be left with Turkey. Wilson hoped for the viability of the Armenian nation, and trusted that it would be just with the minorities left under its control.[3]

Before the boundaries could be delimited, or the President could even use his good offices in a "moral" capacity to stop the hostilities still going on in the region, Armenia was suddenly declared a Soviet Republic (December 2) and its fate sealed. Wilson felt that the immediate cause of trouble in Armenia and Turkey was the Treaty of Sèvres. Armenia was now under Moscovite and Soviet domination, and the President saw no possibility of liberation without the moral support of the Great Powers, which held promise "of bringing peace and accord to the contending parties."[4]

The United States and the Treaty of Sevres

The American representatives at the Paris Peace Conference had left for home in December 1919, and hence took no part in the negotiation of the Treaty of Sèvres, but the United States Government was kept informed of the developments and expressed its views unofficially on what appeared to be the pending settlement. In Turkey, in any event, the Nationalist movement was taking an independent course, and on January 28, 1920, the Ottoman Parliament adopted the National Pact, based upon

[1] A statement from Secretary of War Baker on June 2, 1920 indicated that 27,000 soldiers would be needed to police Armenia, although the force might be reduced to 10,000 within three years, with the organization of a native constabulary.
[2] *Ibid.*, 789-795.
[3] See also "Decision of President Wilson Respecting the Frontier between Turkey and Armenia, Access for Armenia to the Sea, and the Demilitarization of Turkish Territory Adjacent to the Armenian Frontier"; *ibid.*, 795-804. November 22, 1920. Also HOWARD, 456, note.
[4] *U. S. Foreign Relations*, 1920, III, 924-926; Firuz KAZEMZADEH, Ch. XIX.

the work of the Erzerum and Sivas Congresses, only to be followed, on April 23, by similar action in the Grand National Assembly in Ankara, after the Allied occupation of Istanbul. [1] Much more fundamental than the diplomatic maneuvers at Paris were the developments on the Anatolian Plateau, however much misunderstood in "the city of light", and, in the end, it was these developments which were to prevail.

American Interest in the Treaty

On March 12, four days before the British occupation of Istanbul, M. Jules Jusserand, the French Ambassador in Washington, advised Acting Secretary of State Frank L. Polk that the work of framing a treaty with Turkey had now gone far enough to warrant "summoning the Turkish delegates at an early date," and he wanted both to learn something of the American attitude and to know whether the United States would participate in the settlement. [2] M. Jusserand's memorandum outlined the European and Asiatic frontiers of Turkey, urged the maintenance of the Sultan in Constantinople, reserved the rights of Allied military occupation in European Turkey and the region of the Straits, and called for establishment of an International Commission of the Straits, composed of representatives of France, Great Britain, Italy, Russia, Rumania, Greece, and Bulgaria, and perhaps of the United States, with administrative and financial authority, to insure freedom of the Straits. Greece was to be given a part of Thrace, and Bulgaria a free port. By a "special arrangement", Great Britain, France and Italy were to have spheres of influence and to furnish "advice and instructors." Armenian independence was to be recognized, under the assistance of the League of Nations, and Turkey was to "relinquish all rights to Mesopotamia, Arabia, Palestine, Syria, and all the islands." Smyrna was to be "administered by the Greeks under the Sultan's suzerainty." A concluding section provided for liquidation of German property in Turkey, maintenance of foreign concessions, creation of a financial commission to control all revenues and expenses, and control of the Ottoman Public Debt.

This was a fairly complete program, not unrelated to plans and projects drawn up and considered at the Paris Peace Conference in 1919. Secretary of State Bainbridge Colby replied frankly on March 24 [3] that the United States opposed "retention of the Turks at Constantinople" and did not believe that the Moslems would resent their expulsion from the Golden Horn. He was certain that the southern frontier with the Arabs was ethnical. He noted "with pleasure" that there was provision

[1] See SMITH, 26-29; HUREWITZ, II, 74-75.
[2] *U. S. Foreign Relations*, 1920, III, 748-750. See also Lloyd GEORGE, II, 1294 ff.
[3] *U. S. Foreign Relations*, 1920, III, 750-753.

for Russian representation on the proposed International Commission of the Straits, and that no arrangement for the government and control of Constantinople and the Straits could "have any elements of permanence" unless Russian interests were "carefully provided for and protected." Mr. Colby thought that Eastern Thrace should be assigned to Greece, with the exception of the northern part, which was "clearly Bulgarian in population," including Adrianople. But he wanted more information concerning plans for spheres of influence in Turkey proper and expressed an interest in Armenia. Mesopotamia, Arabia, Palestine, Syria and the Islands, in Colby's view, should be placed "in the hands of the Great Powers, to be disposed of as those Powers determine." Finally, Mr. Colby thought that a spirit of fairness and a regard for "the commercial interests of victor, vanquished and neutral" would prevail, although the question of concessions raised grave issues and required study. He understood that the territorial arrangements would "in no way place American citizens or corporations," or those of any other country, "in a less favorable situation than the citizens or corporations of any Power party to this Treaty."

The San Remo Agreement

Just one month later, on April 24, the Allies concluded the San Remo Agreement, together with an Anglo-French Oil Agreement, which provided for the maintenance of the Sultan in Constantinople, the right of the Allies to occupy European Turkey and the zone of the Turkish Straits, the creation of an Armenian State, and abandonment by Turkey of Syria, Palestine, Mesopotamia and the Aegean Islands, more or less as outlined in the French memorandum of March 12. [1] Two days later, Ambassador Johnson, at Rome, received the reply of the Supreme Council to Colby, in which the Allies indicated that, while they were glad to have American views, the United States was not participating actively in the peacemaking, and they did not interpret the American desire for information to mean that the Turkish negotiations should be delayed until after exhaustive discussions with the United States. Otherwise "fruitful negotiations" would be "impossible". [2] The Allies rejected the American position concerning ejection of the Sultan from Constantinople, and asserted that the Turco-Arab frontiers were based on ethnic, economic and geographical considerations. They noted the United States position relative to Russian participation in the Straits Commission, but pointed out that it was not to administer Constantinople, and hoped and believed that the United States would accept the provisions concerning freedom of passage through the Turkish Straits. There was agreement concerning

---

[1] See HOWARD, 243. For texts of San Remo Agreements, April 24, 1920 see *U. S. Foreign Relations*, 1920, II, 655-658; *Cmd.* 1226 (1921).
[2] *Ibid.*, 753-756. Johnson to Colby, April 27, 1920, San Remo.

Eastern Thrace, if not Adrianople. The Allies, like the United States, were interested in Armenia, and agreed concerning the Aegean Islands, Mesopotamia, Syria, Arabia, and Palestine, but the problem of Smyrna was causing differences, although the Allies were considering placing it under Greek administration, while retaining Turkish sovereignty until the wishes of the people could be determined. It was felt that the economic provisions were in harmony with the principles embodied in the other treaties, and the United States was assured that equality of opportunity would obtain.

The Turks and Sèvres

A few weeks after the San Remo Conference, on May 11, the Allies presented their terms to the head of the Ottoman Delegation, Damad Ferid Pasha. In a memorandum to Millerand, on June 25, more than a year after his first appearance at the Paris Peace Conference, Damad Ferid protested at length the severity of the terms, involving not only the dissolution of the Ottoman Empire, but a basic infringement of sovereignty. The Turks, he said, could not accept the provisions regarding Constantinople and the Straits, which struck at the heart and paralyzed Turkey's future. Nor could they accept establishment of an International Commission for the Straits, although they were willing to assure commercial freedom of the Straits "to all flags on a footing of complete equality." Similarly they rejected the provisions concerning Smyrna and Armenia, but accepted those relative to the Hejaz, even if adjustments were necessary in Syria and Mesopotamia. [1] The Ottoman Delegation presented a similar protest against dismemberment of the Empire on July 8. [2]

But the protests were of no avail and on July 16, [3] the Allied Powers, recalling Turkish guilt and misdeeds during the war, expressed their firm determination to free the subject nationalities and "put an end forever" to Turkish domination over other nations. If the Ottoman Government refused to sign the Treaty and proved incapable of restoring its authority over Anatolia, the Allies would have to revise the terms concerning Constantinople and expel the Turks from Europe, "this time forever."

Given ten days, until July 27 at midnight, the Ottoman Delegation had little choice, and the abortive Treaty of Sèvres was signed on August

---

[1] *Observations of the Ottoman Empire on the Conditions of Peace.* Ottoman Delegation to the Peace Conference. From Damad Ferid to Millerand, President of the Peace Conference. June 25, 1919. E. S. H. Bulletin No. 637. American Embassy, Paris, July 1, 1920.
[2] *Observations générales présentées par la délégation ottomane à la Conférence de la Paix*, July 8, 1920. 47 pp.
[3] *Reply of the Allied Powers to the Observations of the Ottoman Empire to the Conditions of Peace.* July 16, 1920. E. S. H. Bulletin No. 743, July 21, 1920, Vol. 8, American Embassy, Paris.

10.[1] Under its terms, the Anatolian homelands were left to the Turks, along with Constantinople, the shores of the Marmara and Gallipoli Peninsula, but Turkey had to recognize the separation of Syria, Mesopotamia, and Palestine and their position as mandates under Great Britain and France. The Hejaz was to be independent, and Smyrna to be placed under a five-year Greek administration, after which a plebiscite might be held. The Turkish Straits were to be demilitarized and "internationalized", but actually placed under the Great Powers acting through the Straits Commission, which was to exercise its authority "in complete independence" of the local regime in Constantinople. While the Turkish homelands, theoretically, were to be independent and form the nucleus of a Turkish national state, in reality national independence, with the capitulatory regime still in operation and the country actually divided into spheres of economic influence and interest, would have been a farce.[2] Moreover, Greece and Italy reached a temporary agreement, soon denounced, under which Italy was to retain Rhodes, with the possibility that the rest of the Dodecanese Islands would go to Greece. A final treaty assigned Thrace to Greece, with a provision for a Bulgarian port on the Aegean Sea at Dedeagatch, under a guarantee of the League of Nations.

No doubt the Treaty of Sèvres was both the high point—and the low—in British and Allied imperial policy in dealing with the Ottoman Empire, and it was a policy which violated almost all the fine principles on which the King-Crane Commission had postulated its position. But the treaty never went into effect, despite the signature of the Ottoman Delegation, for the Turkish Nationalists, under Mustapha Kemal, simply refused to have any of it, and continued their historic struggle for independence. Neither the United States nor the Soviet regime liked the Treaty, for it served only to promote turmoil in the Near East, and there were fears in Washington that direct American economic and other interests might be seriously impaired.

The Controversy over Economic Rights

Following the Treaty of Sèvres, the United States carried on a vigorous correspondence with Great Britain and France concerning economic rights in mandated territories. The European Powers saw no reason to

---

[1] See *Treaty of Peace with Turkey, Signed at Sèvres, August 10, 1920.* Cmd. 964. The Ottoman Delegation made a last minute appeal on August 1. See Note from the Ottoman Delegation Requesting Certain Changes in the Conditions of the Turkish Treaty, August 1, 1920. E. S. H. Bulletin No. 820, Vol. 9, 1920.

[2] See Treaty Series No. 12 (1920). *Tripartite Agreement between the British Empire, France, and Italy Respecting Anatolia.* Signed at Sèvres, August 10, 1920. Cmd. 963.

question American rights *per se*, but indicated that the place to discuss the whole question of the mandates was at the Council of the League of Nations, although the problem was complicated by the fact that the United States "had not taken her seat on the Council." [1] The draft mandates for Palestine and Mesopotamia were finally published in August 1921, [2] but were not approved then or in September because of American opposition to consideration without the express, definite and previous approval by the United States, and because of the Greco-Turkish war, and the Anglo-Turkish controversy concerning the Mosul vilayet.

The controversy over the mandates continued into the summer of 1922. By mid-May substantial agreement with Great Britain was achieved, although not until July 17 with France. [3] As the end of the Greco-Turkish struggle approached, and the Lausanne Conference opened, the United States asked that final negotiations concerning the mandates await the signature of the definitive Treaty of Peace. [4] It was not until September 29, 1923 that France's Syrian mandate entered formally into force, while agreement with the United States was finally achieved on April 24, 1924. On December 3 Great Britain and the United States signed an agreement concerning Palestine. [5]

American Policy at Lausanne

The Greco-Turkish tragedy, which had begun in May 1919, ended with a resounding Turkish victory in the signature of an armistice at Mudania on October 11, 1922. [6] For a moment an Anglo-Turkish war threatened, but, a few weeks later, on November 20, the Conference of Lausanne, which was to last until July 1923, opened. It was to bring peace and stability to the Near East during the inter-war period. [7]

[1] See especially HOWARD, 317-327 and notes. See also the correspondence with the League of Nations regarding mandates in *U. S. Foreign Relations*, 1921, I, 87-95.
[2] See Draft Mandates and Other Documents Relating to Territories Under Mandate; *ibid.*, 97-142.
[3] See France: Negotiations to Ensure by Treaty the Rights of the United States in Territories under French Mandate; Great Britain: Negotiations to Ensure by Treaty the Rights of the United States in Territories under British Mandate; *ibid.*, 1922, II, 117-134, 258-310.
[4] See France: Resumption of Negotiations to Ensure by Treaty the Rights of the United States in Syria and the Lebanon; *ibid.*, 1923, II, 1-8; Great Britain, *ibid.*, 218-228.
[5] HOWARD, 326-327.
[6] The text is in Elliott G. MEARS, *Modern Turkey*, 658-659 and *L'Europe Nouvelle*, V, 1366-1367.
[7] See HOWARD, Ch. IX. For the minutes of the Conference see Ministère des Affaires Étrangères. *Documents diplomatiques. Conférence de Lausanne sur les affaires du Proche-Orient* (1922-1923). *Recueil des Actes de la Conférence. Première Série*. Tomes I-IV, Tomes I-II, (Paris, 1923); United Kingdom, Foreign Office, Turkey No. 1(1923). *The Lausanne Conference on Near Eastern Affairs*, 1922-1923. Cmd. 1814.

Formulation of the United States Position

Preparations for the Lausanne Conference had been initiated as early as September 19.[1] The British Government, which had appealed to the United States, among others, to help defend the Straits, also wondered whether there was any possibility that the United States would be represented at the Conference.[2]

Admiral Bristol and others were doubtful about the desirability of American participation, and there was some question as to the character of the representation which Lord Curzon desired. Secretary Hughes advised Ambassador Herrick in Paris on October 27 that the United States was concerned with Near Eastern Affairs and was not disposed to relinquish its rights, although it had not been at war with the Ottoman Empire.[3] Essentially, the United States insisted on: (1) the maintenance of the capitulations, (2) the protection of philanthropic, educational and religious institutions under proper guarantees, (3) appropriate undertakings in regard to freedom of opportunity for commercial enterprise, (4) protection of minorities, (5) freedom of the Straits, and (6) reasonable opportunities for archaeological research and study. Mr. Hughes did not regard the secret treaties of 1915-1917 or the Tripartite Agreements of August 10, 1920 as consonant with the principle of "equality of opportunity" and he desired to assure the "open door" to American interests. At the same time,[4] Hughes told Herrick that the United States would send observers to Lausanne, but since it had not been at war with the Ottoman Empire, the United States would not sign the general treaty. The observers would be present during the negotiations and "ready at any opportunity or critical moment to interpose the necessary word for the protection of American interests." At the first opportunity, the American Observers would be prepared to negotiate a separate treaty with Turkey for the protection of American interests. Mr. Hughes was not disposed to have the United States become involved in commitments relative to the Turkish Straits, but declared that it was a "distinct interest" of the United States

> to obtain effective assurances that the Straits would be open in time of peace for both merchant ships and ships of war to proceed to Constantinople and through the Black Sea. This sea is a highway of commerce and should not be under the exclusive control of Turkey and of Russia.

The memorandum concluded:

[1] Memorandum by Allen W. Dulles, September 19, 1922; *U. S. Foreign Relations*, 1923, II, 879.
[2] *Ibid.*, 880. See also Mr. Hughes' interview in The London *Times*, September 27, 1922.
[3] *U. S. Foreign Relations*, 1923, II, 881-882, 884 ff.
[4] *Ibid.*, 887-889.

While it is neither natural nor desirable that we should participate in the peace conference or become involved in the negotiations regarding policies and aims in which we have no share it is essential that the Department should be constantly in command of adequate information, keen for the protection of American interests, ready to throw the full weight of our influence to obtain assurances for the freedom of the Straits and the protection of minorities, candid as to our views and in a position at any suitable time to make the separate agreement which at some time must be made with the Turkish Government recognized by the Powers. No point of advantage should be forfeited, no just influence lost, no injurious commitments made. We should maintain the integrity of our position as an independent power which has not been concerned with the rivalries of other nations which have so often made the Near East the theater of war.

The United States Position on the Eve of the Lausanne Conference

At the same time, the British Government officially invited United States participation in the conference, in a capacity similar to that at San Remo, or more actively, in the discussions of the Straits question.[1] On October 28, Secretary Hughes designated Ambassador Richard Washburn Child to head the delegation, on which Minister Joseph C. Grew and Admiral Mark Bristol were also to serve. Lord Curzon denied Lenin's claim to representation, but he believed that the United States, "as a maritime power in her own interest as well as in common interest ought to participate to the full in the Straits convention." Curzon hoped that the United States Government and the American people would "appreciate the propriety, wisdom and obligation of this sharing of responsibility for maintaining a great open waterway as a wide-open door." Curzon's views concerning the capitulations were substantially similar to those of the United States.[2]

The General Board of the United States Navy, in a very significant memorandum of November 10, fully supported the principle of freedom of the Straits, but it also contended that no solution which imposed "an artificial barrier between so great a power" as Russia "and the sea" could "contain within it the elements of permanency—of stability." The General Board insisted that the United States should "with full justice insist on equal rights," but could not claim special rights. Likewise, the General Board thought there should be "complete freedom of navigation of the Straits for all vessels of war." It recognized no "parallel between

---

[1] *Ibid.*, 889-890.
[2] Later on, on December 13, Hughes wrote to Sir Auckland Geddes, the British Ambassador, that he had instructed the American representatives to impress on the Turks the danger of antagonizing world opinion unless they made it clear they did not intend to "drive out over a million people under conditions of extraordinary hardship, suffering and loss of life." *Ibid.*, 1922, II, 965-966.

the status of the Dardanelles and that of the Panama Canal"—it was by no means unique in this attitude. In the light of experience with Ottoman control of the Straits, the General Board favored "international control," with equal representation for the United States on any international board which might be established.[1]

Substantially on the eve of the Lausanne Conference, the British Ambassador, Sir Auckland Geddes, called upon Secretary of State Hughes to discuss the delicate situation in the Near East following the Turkish victory,[2] to find out especially the extent to which Great Britain could rely on the United States to thwart a possible Turkish attempt to drive the Christian population from Constantinople. Hughes indicated that the United States would use diplomatic pressure "to the utmost extent," but was unwilling to threaten war, unless it were ready to go to war. Evidently there was much straightforward language:

> The Ambassador then referred to the relation of the United States representatives to Turkish matters at the peace conference. He said that the Secretary had no idea of the influential position that President Wilson had occupied; that it was in deference to his wishes, who was the spokesman for the United States, that the Allies had deferred making settlement with Turkey; that the Allies had desired to go ahead, but that they delayed for months, because of hope of American support; that the present difficulties were the result of that delay. The Ambassador said that the British had not desired mandates. The whole mandate idea was Mr. Wilson's idea and . . . the British had deferred to his views in the hope of American cooperation. The Secretary asked, if they did not wish the mandates, whether they desired the territories or whether the Ambassador meant to imply they did not wish any territories at all as a result of the war. The Ambassador did not directly meet this question. He said he was in the Cabinet at the time and knew that these territories would be a burden and that the British had taken up their share of the burden in the expectation that America would take its share and now they feared that they were being left alone.

There was much truth in the statement of the British Ambassador. Mr. Hughes wanted no controversy, however, concerning the Peace Conference and merely stated that the United States "would never accept a mandate over the Near East," and that the American conception was quite different from the British, and he denied any American responsibility for the existing situation. What troubled "the dreams of British statesmen," in the Hughes view, "was their maintenance of their

---

[1] *Ibid.*, 1923, II, 893-897. "American Policy as to Freedom of Navigation of the Dardanelles". The Senior Member Present of the General Board, Department of the Navy (W. L. Rodgers) to the Secretary of the Navy (Denby). For convenience see also HUREWITZ, II, 117-119.

[2] Memorandum by the Secretary of State (Charles Evans Hughes), November 10, 1922; *ibid.*, 1922, II, 952-955.

imperial power"—a matter with which the United States was not concerned.[1]

The United States Position at Lausanne

Although it was subject to change in detail, the American position seemed fairly well outlined when the Lausanne Conference opened on November 20, 1922. At the outset, Ambassador Child announced that the United States Delegation would take no part in the negotiations, sign no documents or assume any obligations, but would be present at all discussions, and expected to be treated on a footing of perfect equality with other delegations.[2] While the United States Delegation felt that Western Thrace should go to Greece and the Adrianople area to Bulgaria, it was interested in this problem and that of the Aegean Islands only as they affected the disposition of Constantinople and the Turkish Straits.

Essentially there were three basic proposals concerning the Straits: (1) the British proposal, with which the United States somewhat sympathized, to guarantee freedom under some kind of international control; (2) the Turkish proposal to maintain Turkish sovereignty, with restricted rights of navigation; and (3) the Soviet proposal, which would preserve Turkish sovereignty, but close the Straits to warships, with the Black Sea remaining a Russian lake. Mr. Hughes instructed the United States Delegation to stand for freedom of navigation, and insisted that there could be no proper comparison between the Turkish Straits and the Panama Canal. He noted that there could be no assurance, in view of "the traditional American policy," that the United States would participate in an international commission of the Straits.[3] Secretary Hughes advised the Delegation that the United States desired to assure freedom of passage for commercial vessels and warships "by proper treaty provisions without an international board of control," since such a board would only "provide an opportunity for busybodies and be a constant source of irritation." Ambassador Child took this position in the Conference on December 6.[4]

By the end of December[5] it appeared that an agreement on the Straits would soon be realized; on January 31, 1923 a draft convention was ready, and on February 4, Ismet Pasha accepted it. The United States favored the regime of freedom for commercial vessels, which the new draft convention guaranteed, and was not opposed to the restrictions

---

[1] *Ibid.*, 955-958. Secretary of State Hughes' Memorandum, November 13, 1922.
[2] *Cmd.* 1814, p. 11; see also HOWARD, 285-297.
[3] *U. S. Foreign Relations*, 1923, II, 910-913.
[4] *Ibid.*, 914-917, 920. See also HOWARD, 288.
[5] *Ibid.*, 931-933.

on warships, but it would not become a party to the convention or accept membership on the International Commission of the Straits.[1]

The United States was also much concerned with the preservation of the capitulations, economic and financial rights, and the privileges of minorities in Turkey. In the end, abolition of the capitulatory regime and the provision of a satisfactory substitute proved so difficult that the Conference largely broke up over this question and basic agreement was reached only with the conclusion of the treaty in July 1923.[2] Similarly the economic and financial problems, involving the issue of the "open door", were not settled until the last moment.[3] Finally, too, agreement was reached concerning the protection of educational, philanthropic and religious institutions, and the Greek problem was settled through the compulsory exchange of Greek and Turkish populations. But there was no possibility of solving the Armenian question, and the problem of an Armenian homeland had to be dropped.[4]

After numerous crises, the first period of the Lausanne Conference came to an end on February 4, 1923, when the Turkish Delegation refused to sign the general draft treaty which the Allied Powers presented on January 31. As Admiral Bristol recorded, the failure to reach agreement was "due to a lack of unanimity among the Allies, to Curzon's disregard of Turkish nationalism, and to the perseverance of the Turks."[5]

Ismet Pasha explained the Turkish position to Admiral Bristol on the Orient Express out of Venice on February 6 and made it clear that he wanted a settlement on the basis of the Turkish National Pact. The United States, he was advised, desired to defer its own treaty until after a definitive peace had been signed.[6] There was much feeling against Great Britain in Ankara but, because of the American open door policy, the more moderate view concerning the capitulations, and the position on the Straits, the United States was regarded in a more favorable light. On March 31, the Department of State advised the British Embassy of its opposition to the economic and financial clauses in the draft treaty, since they served to uphold the old concessions.[7]

[1] *Ibid.*, 935-936; HOWARD, 290-297. See also Erik BRÜEL, *International Straits* (London, Sweet and Maxwell, 1947), II, 359-380.
[2] *U. S. Foreign Relations*, 1923, II, 931-933; HOWARD, 304-307.
[3] HOWARD, 308-313.
[4] *U. S. Foreign Relations*, 1923, II, 902-903, 946-947. Dr. George R. Montgomery, an adviser on the staff of the King-Crane Commission, represented the so-called Armenia-America Society at Lausanne, and propagated the idea of a large Armenia.
[5] *Ibid.*, 966-967. See also Joseph C. GREW, *Turbulent Era*, I, Chaps. 18-20; R. H. DAVISON in G. A. CRAIG and F. GILBERT, *The Diplomats*, Ch. 6.
[6] *U. S. Foreign Relations*, 1923, II, 966-967.
[7] *Ibid.*, 970-971.

Much happened between February 4 and April 23, 1923, when the Lausanne Conference reconvened.[1] On March 6 the Grand National Assembly rejected the draft treaty because it conflicted with the Turkish National Pact, although it decided, in principle, to reopen negotiations with the Allies. The new treaty was to be based upon the complete abolition of the capitulations, postponement of the Mosul question and the economic clauses, abandonment of the Turkish claim to the Thracian boundary, insistence on Greek reparations, acceptance of all other points settled at Lausanne, and immediate evacuation of territories occupied by the Allies. The Allies indicated on April 1 that they were willing once more to confer.

Meanwhile, the United States was entering the drama somewhat more directly through its support of the Chester Concession,[2] which Secretary Hughes had rather vigorously contested earlier in 1921. Mr. Hughes was still anxious to avoid the impression of favoring one American firm over another. Evidently with a view to securing American assistance and splitting the Allies, the Grand National Assembly approved the Chester Concession on April 9.[3] But the Chester Concession soon faded from the picture and the Standard Oil Company more or less took its place.

On the eve of the reopening of the Conference, Mr. Allen W. Dulles, Chief of the Near Eastern Division of the Department of State, wrote to Secretary Hughes that the Allies had not taken the United States into their confidence and expressed anxiety about the conflict of economic interests, especially in view of French antagonism toward the Chester Concession.[4] Quite evidently the Allies were loath to abandon their claims, based on existing agreements. When Joseph C. Grew proceeded to Lausanne on April 19, he was instructed to undertake no pledges concerning the Straits, and it appeared that Washington did not want to close the door to an American legal adviser, if the capitulatory regime were to be abolished.[5] Economic and financial concessions continued to be the stumbling block at the conference.

But by July 24 the Treaty of Lausanne was signed. The last of the great treaties following World War I, it confirmed the mandate system by which Great Britain and France acquired their respective positions in Syria, Palestine and Iraq. It recognized the British position in Egypt and the annexation of Cyprus, as well as the Italian position in the

---

[1] *Ibid.*, 872-874.
[2] See especially *U. S. Foreign Relations*, 1923, II, 1172-1252, for Chester Concession. See also *ibid.*, 1921, II, 919-920, for attempts to influence situation.
[3] On March 10, 1925, Admiral Bristol cabled that the Chester Concession, as negotiated in 1923, was dead. See *ibid.*, 1251-1252.
[4] Dulles to Hughes, April 4, 1923; *ibid.*, 974-980.
[5] *Ibid.*, 981-987.

Dodecanese Islands. The problem of Mosul remained to be settled in 1926, when Great Britain finally retained that rich and strategic vilayet. Constantinople and Eastern Thrace went to Turkey. The Lausanne Treaty had signaled the death knell of the Ottoman Empire, but it had symbolized the advent of the new Turkish national state, which was freed of the chains of the hated capitulatory regime. A new convention of the Straits had been written, placing those historic waters under an international control, while necessarily preserving the reality of British sea power. On the other hand, Armenia was forgotten, and the Bulgarian Government was to claim that it had been given inadequate access to the Aegean Sea. In the end, the Turks had won their independence after more than 10 years of struggle. They were now to move along the revolutionary paths of Nationalism, Industrialism and Secularism under the banner of Mustapha Kemal's Turkish Republic.[1]

THE AMERICAN TREATY OF LAUSANNE

The United States did not sign the general Treaty of Lausanne or adhere to the convention of the Straits, although its Delegation concluded a treaty with Turkey shortly after the end of the Lausanne Conference.[2] The treaty was to follow the general pattern, providing for protection of philanthropic and religious enterprises, a substitute for the capitulatory regime, "free navigation of Dardanelles and Bosphorus," adjustment of claims, safeguarding of minorities, regulation of naturalization, and archaeological research.

The Negotiations

When the Lausanne Conference resumed in April 1923, the American negotiations took on more form and substance, with concrete discussions carried on by the experts. The question of the capitulations remained serious, and Admiral Bristol felt that American rights, along with those of other nations, were being "gradually but surely worn away," since the Turks consistently acted on the assumption that the capitulations were gone forever. Bristol added:[3]

> Everybody recognizes that the cause of the Capitulations is lost since no Power will take any radical action to insure their retention even in modified form, but at the same time the fiction of the existence of the Capitulations still has a considerable effect upon the situation, not upon the Turks certainly, but upon the efficiency of the High Commission in dealing with the difficult problems that come up in every way.

---

[1] See HOWARD, 313-314. See also Lloyd GEORGE, *Where Are We Going?* (New York, Doran 1923), 322-328, with its interesting comment that the Treaty of Sèvres was much better than the Treaty of Lausanne.
[2] *U. S. Foreign Relations*, 1923, II, 1040-1052.
[3] *Ibid.*, 1049-1050. March 21, 1923. See also Nasim SOUSA, *The Capitulatory Regime of Turkey: Its History, Origin, and Nature* (Baltimore, Johns Hopkins, 1933), Ch. XII.

THE MIDDLE EAST AFTER LAUSANNE 1923

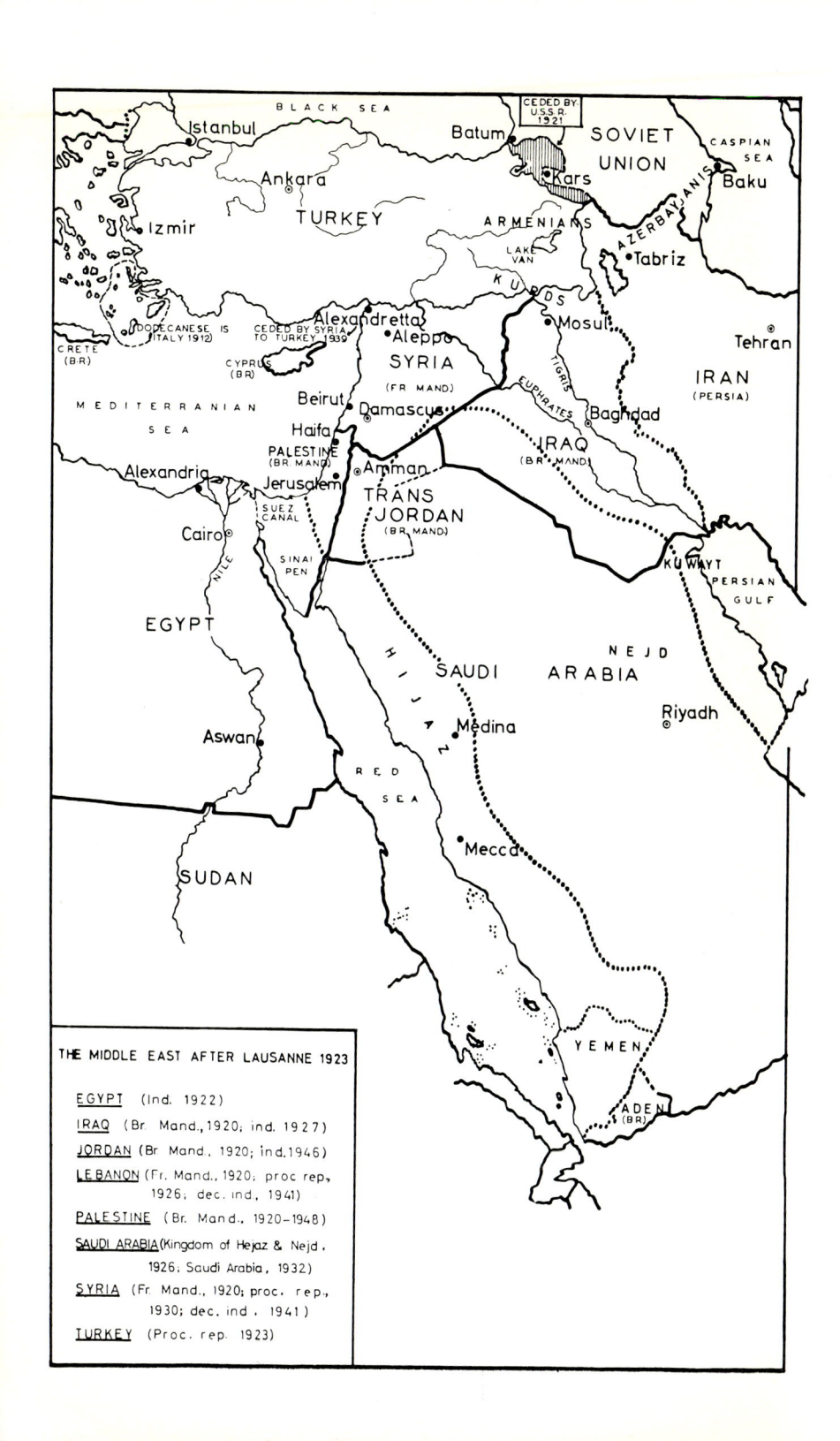

EGYPT (Ind. 1922)
IRAQ (Br. Mand., 1920; ind. 1927)
JORDAN (Br. Mand., 1920; ind. 1946)
LEBANON (Fr. Mand., 1920; proc rep,
1926; dec. ind., 1941)
PALESTINE (Br. Mand., 1920-1948)
SAUDI ARABIA (Kingdom of Hejaz & Nejd,
1926; Saudi Arabia, 1932)
SYRIA (Fr. Mand., 1920; proc. rep.,
1930; dec. ind., 1941)
TURKEY (Proc. rep. 1923)

Secretary of State Hughes also knew that the regime of the capitulations would have to go and was not disposed to demand their unqualified retention. With proper diplomacy, some agreement could be achieved without substantial loss to American rights.[1] By the end of May, Hughes indicated that the United States could consent to the abrogation of the capitulations, to become effective when the new treaty was ratified.[2] An American draft, forwarded to Washington on June 2, provided for resumption of diplomatic and consular relations, the adjustment of disputes, most favored-nation treatment, and "freedom of commerce and navigation." Mr. Hughes warned, however, that American public opinion might not approve a treaty which did not make some provision for the protection of minorities and the American schools.[3]

The differences did not seem irreconcilable, however, and Ismet Pasha had a long discussion with Mr. Grew on July 21 concerning all the points under consideration. But there were no mutual concessions. While the Turks were willing to study further the American proposal concerning the Straits, they would not discuss minority articles or change the declaration regarding the legal regime. The negotiations continued into August, with a few adjustments of position on both sides, and finally on August 6 a Turco-American treaty was signed, with letters concerning schools, and declarations on judicial and sanitary matters. The Americans agreed to Ismet's proposition that "every sort of capitulation no matter what might be its origin" was abolished. Mr. Grew explained that "the ships and aircraft of the United States would not be obliged to conform to the rules established by the Straits Convention," except when they were in force "at any given moment." Moreover, the United States was not obligated to adhere to the Straits Convention, although Ismet Pasha hoped that it would do so "at the first opportune moment."[4]

Grew cabled Hughes[5] that the treaty was far from what he had desired, but more favorable terms were impossible. Throughout the negotiations, the Mission had "all felt that the Turks were essentially honest." In a note of December 8, 1923,[6] Bristol wrote of an informal gathering of American business and professional people in Istanbul, in which they all favored ratification of the treaty, because failure to ratify would complicate political, economic and cultural relations between the two countries.

---

[1] *U. S. Foreign Relations*, 1923, II, 1051-1052.
[2] *Ibid.*, 1061-1063.
[3] *Ibid.*, 1087-1088.
[4] *Ibid.*, 1121, 1138-1142.
[5] *Ibid.*, 1148-1150.
[6] *Ibid.*, 1150-1151.

The several texts of the American treaty arrived in Washington on February 18, 1924.[1] The agreement provided for the renewal of normal relations between the United States and Turkey under a treaty of friendship and commerce, in general following the same lines as the Treaty of Lausanne. It completely abolished the capitulations and recognized Turkey's full equality with other nations. But the resumption of diplomatic relations under the new treaty required American action, and the question of ratification became a political and even religious issue in the United States Senate, involving the Armenian issue, and the treaty was not approved. American relations with Turkey were put on a formal basis only by the *modus vivendi* reached between Admiral Bristol and Tewfik Rustu Aras, on February 17, 1927, and regular diplomatic representation was resumed only on October 12 of that year, when Ambassador Joseph C. Grew presented his credentials to President Ataturk.[2]

[1] *Ibid.*, 1151-1171.
[2] See especially Leland GORDON, *American Relations with Turkey*, 363-369. A new treaty of commerce and navigation was not proclaimed until April 25, 1930.

CHAPTER X

Was the Experiment Worth While?

The Publication of the King-Crane Report

For more than three years the King-Crane Report remained a "secret" in the files of the Department of State in Washington. It was not, indeed, until 1922, when Ray Stannard Baker was preparing his volumes on *Woodrow Wilson and World Settlement*, one of the early monumental studies of President Wilson's participation in the Paris Peace Conference, that portions of the Report finally came to be published. Mr. Baker had expected to find a copy in President Wilson's personal files, along with other pertinent papers, but none was found, perhaps because the President's copy, delivered at the White House the day after Mr. Wilson had collapsed on his speaking tour of the country in the fall of 1919, was transmitted to the Department of State.[1] Baker wrote to Dr. King on May 4, 1922, asking for a copy of the Report. He had "never heard exactly" what had become of it and wanted to know about its present status. Had "any part of it ever been published?"[2] President King replied two days later:[3]

> The State Department have never published any part of [the Report], and seem to have adopted the policy of not giving anyone access to it. Under those circumstances Mr. Crane and I have felt that about all we could do was to say to those who inquired of us about it, that so far as we were concerned we were perfectly ready to have the report seen by any inquirer, but that we did not feel at liberty to publish our findings until the State Department had released the report, although a few individuals had seen the report.

Mr. Crane thought that one of the primary reasons for refusing to make the Report public had been "the opposition of the Zionists," and President King, too, wondered whether Zionist opposition had not been a factor.

Mr. Baker felt that publication of the Report would bring to light much needed information concerning the Near East and he wondered whether King and Crane could give him permission to use it in connection with his work on *Woodrow Wilson and World Settlement*. Crane had previously urged Dr. King to take up the matter with President Harding, although he doubted that "a Republican Administration would be willing to release the Report."[4] But something might be done through

---

[1] From a memorandum by Donald M. Brodie. Mr. Baker confirmed its accuracy in a letter to Brodie on May 10, 1927.
[2] King Papers: Baker to King, May 4, 1922.
[3] King Papers: King to Baker, May 6, 1922. King had been forced to deny a request of Dr. Stephen P. Duggan in 1920 to see the Report. Mr. Crane made two trips to the Near East during 1922, in the spring to Syria, among other places, and in the fall to Istanbul, Egypt and Jidda.
[4] King Papers: Baker to King, May 8, 1922; King to Baker, May 23, 1922.

Secretary of State Hughes. It was realized, of course, that the value of publishing the Report now would not be anything like what it might have been had it been promptly released when it was prepared in 1919. Dr. King personally was inclined "to put the whole Report" in Baker's hands and let him follow his "own wisdom in the use of it," but he did not feel justified in doing so until he had talked with Mr. Crane, who would be returning from Europe soon.[1] The two former Commissioners met in July and referred Baker's request to former President Wilson, who stated that he had "no objection to Baker's making public the Report." Indeed, he thought it "a very timely moment for its publication." Baker, therefore, received a copy a few days later, and was able to use it immediately.[2]

Ray Stannard Baker thus published the first excerpts of the King-Crane Report in Chapter XXV of his volumes on *Woodrow Wilson and World Settlement*, and they appeared serially in the *New York Times* on December 3-4, 1922.[3] Mr. James Wright Brown, the proprietor of *The Editor and Publisher*, the oldest publishers' and advertisers' journal in the United States, had followed the development of President Wilson's foreign policy with considerable interest and, when he read the extracts in the *New York Times*, he wanted to have the complete Report made available to the press as a "sound basis for editorial judgment." Late in September he was granted permission by Mr. Wilson to secure a copy from Mr. Baker and publish it in full. Dr. King and Mr. Crane first learned of this publication through a form letter which was sent to a number of men interested in the Near East.[4] When the Report was published in this convenient form, Mr. Crane and his associates

---

[1] King Papers: Baker to King, May 25, 1922. King drew Baker's attention to Professor A. H. Lybyer's article on "Turkey under the Armistice" in the April 1922 issue of *The Journal of International Relations* which contained a good deal of the material which had come into the hands of the King-Crane Commission.

[2] Crane Papers: Woodrow Wilson to C. R. Crane, July 6, 1922. Baker received permission at about the time that the American Congress voted a joint resolution confirming the Balfour Declaration, which President Harding signed on September 21, 1922, and when the Council of the League of Nations was approving the Palestine Mandate (July 24, September 21, 1922). Dr. F. I. Shatara, an Arab who had testified before a Congressional Committee, wrote in the New York *Times*, December 16, 1922, that his request for publication of the Report had been "disregarded by the same forces that had suppressed it till now."

[3] Reflecting the views of President Harding, a White House statement of December 6, 1922 expressed pleasure that "the government had not undertaken the responsibility for any Turkish territory." The United States "would not take on responsibility for the affairs of the rest of the world."

[4] King Papers: Fenton Dowling to Dr. King, November 21, 1922.

distributed some 20,000 copies to universities and libraries and to individuals interested in the problems of the Near East throughout the world.

Some Estimates of the King-Crane Report

The publication of the excerpts of the King-Crane Report attracted wide attention, and when the full Report appeared in *The Editor and Publisher* there was considerable comment. Although the Report had no official standing outside the United States Government, it was an interesting and important document, extolled by the Arabs as a generally objective account of conditions prevailing in the Middle East during 1919, and equally condemned by Zionists because it did not support the Zionist program in Palestine.

The Press

The *New York Times*, on August 20, 1922, editorially praised the Report for its analysis of a most difficult problem, but pointed out that it had no influence on the settlement of the questions with which it dealt "because no use was made of it by our representatives at Paris:"

> There are sufficient reasons for its suppression. By the time it was made, our Government had definitely withdrawn from active participation in settlements affecting Turkey; and, furthermore, the situation at home regarding the peace was shaping up in such a fashion that to have put out a program of American mandates over almost all the former Turkish lands, as the Commission recommended, would have been a totally futile proceeding. But the report has slumbered too long. It demands at least consideration in the determination of our policy toward these quests.
>
> The settlement in Asia Minor we are now expected to approve as to mandates goes counter to the findings of our Commission in three principal respects. It divided Palestine from the rest of Syria, it goes very far toward meeting the Zionist program in the former region, and it places France in control of Syria. America has not, of course, entered the League of Nations, but cannot regard without interest any tampering with the religious, educational and humanitarian work of her people in this region, and she will inevitably have to bear her full part in the consequences of the actions of the other great powers in the Near East, if they should lead to another Great War.

An editorial in the New York *Evening Post*, on August 31, 1922,[1] by Dr. Edwin F. Gay, rightly insisted that it would have been wise to have published the document when it appeared in 1919, even though "the trend of political events at home made it impossible to dream of carrying out its recommendations." Because of the "deep practical concern" of the United States in the problems raised by the division of the Ottoman

---

[1] Gay raised the question of the "minority report" of Captain Yale, wondering why it was not published, thereby contributing to a tempest in a teapot. See Donald M. Brodie's letter to The New York *Evening Post*, September 1, 1922.

lands, "the facts and opinions offered by men as sincere and disinterested as Mr. Crane and President King must be welcome." The editorial further stated :

> ... The days of the Paris Conference were magnificent days, when almost anything seemed possible and when many alleged impossibilities did indeed come to pass. But France had for years been the spokesman of the Christians in Syria (as the Sykes-Picot treaty of 1916 recognized) and Lord Balfour had committed Great Britain to the establishment of a national home for the Jews in Palestine. Moreover, though the dream of a great Pan-Arab State stretching from the Mediterranean to Persia is attractive, the hard fact is that the Arab tribes, loosely organized and politically backward, could not now bring it to realization.
>
> Reports of abuses by the French administration and of disputes between Arabs and Jews and British officials in Palestine make clearer than ever the necessity for carrying through, in the spirit as well as in the letter, the mandate terms under which considerable supervisory authority was given to the League of Nations. These mandates were granted only a few weeks ago, and their form offers every necessary safeguard. The League has a corporate responsibility in the matter from which it is not relieved, because, for example, individual member states are opposed to its taking any action. It seems ungracious to appeal to an agency of which we as a nation almost ignore the very existence, but it is nevertheless true that with the League lies the next step.

In a warm appraisal of the Report, the *Editor and Publisher*, following publication of the complete text in the issue of December 2, 1922, referred to it as "one of the great suppressed documents of the peace-making period," and noted that the text made clear "why the Report should have been rigorously concealed by a then spineless State Department":

> Yet, if it had been published promptly, as intended, it would completely have altered the current of events in Turkey; and possibly also have changed the whole American attitude toward post-war international responsibilities. Certainly it would have freed us from a flood of unfounded propaganda; and it might easily have saved the lives of possibly a million persons, needlessly sacrificed since the war.
>
> There would have been no need of a Lausanne Conference, or of a Graeco-Turkish war, or of a disruption of allied co-operation in the Near East, or of any of the tragic and tremendous events there which now threaten the wreck of civilization, if the King-Crane Report had been published.

The Report was needed by every editorial writer, all students of history, missionaries and business people who were interested in the problems and prospects of the Near East, as well as by the statesmen in and out of Congress who should have information concerning that vital region. While not all the conclusions of the Report were applicable at the time of publication, nevertheless the Report itself was a "journalistic triumph" which revealed how a small group of American reporters, or investigators, took an assignment to find out the bed-rock facts upon one of the most clouded and intricate international situations in the world. They went about their task with all the canniness, caution and courage of good correspondents. Moreover, they not only fearlessly discovered the facts and clearly set them forth, but they also followed them to their conclusions.

There were varying reactions abroad. While the British and European press, in general, did not concern itself too much with the Report, it is interesting to note that two Cairo journals, *Muqattam* and *Karmel*, published it, the former in full. As Charles R. Crane, who was in the Near East at the time, wrote to Woodrow Wilson on January 23, 1923: "The Report is looked upon as a serious, careful, sympathetic effort to apply the principles you had enunciated and for which America went into the war." [1]

The French considered the Report very unfair and biased, condemned the way in which the investigation had been carried on, and pointed out that the King-Crane Commission had not visited Anatolia, Armenia or Mesopotamia. [2] A London journal, *The Near East*, declared on January 25, 1923, that the publication was "too belated to arouse more than passing curiosity at this juncture," and after outlining the essentials of the Report, it captiously noted that "a Commission of this nature, consisting of two people of the same nationality," was almost worthless, "because it was inevitable that the majority of the people whom they questioned on the spot should try to say what they thought the Commissioners desired." *The Near East* admitted that the Report itself, and especially the Confidential Appendix, was not without some interest, although it was "most unkind of the Commissioners to suggest that this appendix should be for American consumption only." *The Manchester Guardian* [3] of December 8, 1922, noted that the Report had been published

---

[1] Woodrow Wilson Papers-X6: Crane thought that "the introductory comment of the editor who published the Report was admirable" and noted that it was "being widely quoted and discussed." Crane to Wilson, Tor, Harbor of Sinai, January 12, 1923. See also *Oriente Moderno*, II (February 15, 1923), 528-529.

[2] See especially R. de GONTAUT-BIRON, *Comment la France s'est installée en Syrie*, 262-282; Michel PAILLARES, *Le Kémalisme devant les Alliés* (Constantinople, 1922), 1-31.

[3] *The Round Table*, XIII (December 1922), No. 49, pp. 1-29, commented on the general situation: "The withdrawal of the United States from active participation in the Near Eastern arrangements was much more than a cause of delay; it added enormously to the difficulty of devising a settlement which would work. An American mandate for Armenia and Constantinople would have ensured both the safety of the minorities and the freedom of the Straits. No other Power could have held the Dardanelles and still have been thought disinterested, and none could have carried the financial burden imposed by a mandate for

as a part of a movement to force the United States Government to take a larger share of responsibility in the Near Eastern settlement, but its effect was "more likely to influence the growing anti-French feeling than to encourage more active participation in the Lausanne Conference...."

Conflicting Opinions

Sir Ronald Storrs, who had become the British Military Governor of Jerusalem shortly before the King-Crane Commission arrived in that region, was somewhat caustic in his estimate of the Americans and their work. He felt that the proposal for such an investigation "could only have emanated from or been acceptable to a person without knowledge of or interests in the Near East." Moreover, when it was recalled that "to the anticipating Eastern mind the nationality of the Commission ... predetermined that of the Mandatory," it would "be understood that these findings were more favourable to Great Britain than would be gathered from a literal reading of the text." Storrs was somewhat incensed at the suggestion of possible British pressure on some of the witnesses who appeared before the Commission. [1]

Some comments were particularly bitter. Jacob de Haas, [2] a Zionist who felt that the King-Crane Commission had produced endless trouble in Syria and Palestine without bringing any benefits, thought that "the official suppression of the King-Crane Report was probably the only way of ending the situation created by the appointment of the commission." Perhaps the most unjustified comment came from the pen of Samuel Untermyer, the distinguished lawyer who, as President of the Palestine Foundation Fund, was much interested in the fate of the Jewish

Armenia. It is well known that President Wilson desired and expected his countrymen to undertake this trust, and, indeed, that the Turkish treaty was deferred so that he could obtain their consent.... American repudiation of the President's policy in this matter has had consequences in the East comparable to those which followed in Europe on the failure to ratify the Anglo-American guarantee to France. The defeat of the altruist in politics means more than the overthrow of an individual: it denotes the eclipse of a political philosophy. When a great nation shrinks from its own ideals, others are emboldened to jettison positive obligations, and the world exchanges with relief moral enthusiasm for the simpler claims of self-interest."

[1] Sir Ronald STORRS, *The Memoirs of Sir Ronald Storrs*, 375-376. Although Mr. Crane wrote only one line of the Report, Storrs considered him primarily responsible for its character.

[2] Jacob de HAAS, *Palestine: The Last Two Thousand Years*, 491. See also Elie KEDOURIE, *England and the Middle East: The Vital Years, 1914-1921*, 147, who remarks: "The King-Crane Commission manifested itself and went away. The report of the two commissioners was as ill-informed as its influence on policy was negligible. But their enquiry was the occasion of turbulence and unsettlement. It raised false hopes, and gave rise to intrigue and intimidation. It exacerbated political passions and thereby made a peaceful settlement immeasurably more difficult."

National Home in Palestine. Untermyer sought to discredit the Report altogether: [1]

With its forty thousand words, its countless figures, its marshalling of evidence, and its apparent efforts at impartiality, the report does, on the surface, produce the effect of a serious and valuable contribution to the world's knowledge of conditions in Asia Minor. At first glance one is tempted to accept without further parley the conclusions of the American Commission, and it certainly would be easier to do so than to wade through thirty closely-printed newspaper columns in order to arrive at an independent conclusion. *However, one who, like myself, is vitally and peculiarly interested in at least one of the problems dealt with in the Report*, with respect to which he has a high public duty, and who cannot therefore afford to accept the conclusions ready-made, must check carefully the material submitted.

A close and detailed examination of the whole report inevitably leads to the conclusion that the Crane-King Report is without value when judged by the standards applicable to such a document and to the character of the investigations on which it should be based, *i.e.*, impartiality of the inquirer, validity of the evidence and accuracy of observations.... The Crane Report, on the contrary, is based on inadmissible facts, supported by valueless evidence and conceived in a biased spirit. It is trivial by reason of its inaccuracies and is disingenuous in its reasoning.

Mr. Untermyer was an attorney arguing a case. It was, perhaps, a sample of his evidence that he cited a New York newspaper to prove that there were only 400,000 Arabs and some 120,000 Jews in Palestine. The Commission, he contended, had merely "created opinions as it went along...."

An ESCO Foundation study, in 1947, considered the Report biased, and its recommendations unworkable and self-contradictory. But it admitted that "the opinions echoed by the Commissioners undoubtedly reflected the prevalent political attitude in Syria and Palestine". The primary fault in the Palestine section lay not so much with the investigatory procedures as with "the whole approach to the problem." A truly objective approach, in this Zionist view, required [2]

giving equal consideration to the Jewish problem, together with the needs and views of the native inhabitants. Under the circumstances,

---

[1] Samuel UNTERMYER, "Zionism and the Crane Report," *The Forum*, Vol. LXIX, No. 1 (January 1923), 1120-1136. Italics supplied. See also Frank E. MANUEL, *The Realities of American Palestine Relations*, 244-254.
[2] The ESCO Foundation for Palestine, *Palestine: A Study of Jewish, Arab and British Policies* (New Haven, Yale, 1947), I, 212-213. ESCO is an acrostic for Ethel S. Cohen. Italics supplied. The material on the King-Crane Commission is similar to that in I. B. Berkson, "The Abortive King-Crane Recommendations — Science or Propaganda," *Hearings Before the Committee on Foreign Affairs, House of Representatives, Seventy-Eighth Congress, H. Res. 418 and 419 (1944)*, pp. 213-223.

it is questionable whether the wishes of the majority of the population could *at that time* be taken as the sole determining factor....

But, if not in 1919, when were the wishes of the majority of the people to be the determining factor?

There were those who did not adopt the Zionist view of the Report. As already indicated, Commander David Hogarth, the distinguished authority on the Middle East, Lord Allenby and others were very favorably impressed with the work of the Commission. Professor E. A. Ross, the sociologist of the University of Wisconsin, as already noted, remarked that he had never "seen so scrupulous an endeavor to procure measurements of population desires" and became "an ardent supporter" of the entire King-Crane program. In his survey of the history of the Paris Peace Conference of 1919, Professor H. W. V. Temperley indicated that the Report may have been suppressed because it was "too plain spoken and likely to embarrass both the American Government and the Peace Conference if published," although the "general purport of their findings soon became known, official secrecy notwithstanding." While it had no practical results, Temperley felt that the Report probably presented an accurate picture of the situation in Palestine and Syria.[1] Professor Arnold J. Toynbee, an outstanding authority on the Near East, confirmed the Temperley view that the King-Crane Report "tallied with certain antecedent facts which were not open to dispute...."[2]

Perhaps it was natural that Mr. George Antonius, the well-known Arab authority on the Near and Middle East, should be charitably inclined toward the King-Crane Commission, but in any case, his comments are worth recording:[3]

---

[1] H. W. V. TEMPERLEY, *A History of the Peace Conference of Paris*, VI, 148-149. See also Stephen Hemsley LONGRIGG, *Syria and Lebanon Under French Mandate* (London, Oxford, 1958), 89-93. Longrigg notes: "Men of integrity and good sense, and representing a nation totally devoid of ambitions in the Levant," the Commission "spent the most patient efforts in discovering the facts of public opinion in every community .... But the Report in any case had no influence upon the decisions to be taken in Europe; submitted by its authors in Paris on August 28, it was studied (as far as appears) by nobody and was completely ignored by all statesmen among the responsible peacemakers."

[2] Arnold J. TOYNBEE, *The Survey of International Affairs*, 1925. Vol. I. *The Islamic World Since the Peace Settlement* (London, Oxford, 1927), 387. J. M. N. JEFFRIES, *Palestine: The Reality*, 299-300, considered the Report "a full document and a frank one, amply argued. The recommendations are well presented and perfectly feasible...." See also Quincy WRIGHT, *Mandates Under the League of Nations* (Chicago, University of Chicago, 1930), 45-46, and W. E. HOCKING, *The Spirit of World Politics* (New York, Macmillan, 1932), 254-255.

[3] George ANTONIUS, *The Arab Awakening*, 296. See also William R. POLK, David M. STAMLER, and Edmund ASFOUR, *Backdrop to Tragedy*:

The King-Crane Report is a document of outstanding importance. It is the only source to which the historian can turn for a disinterested and wholly objective analysis of the state of feeling in Arab political circles in the period immediately following the War. The investigation carried out by the American commissioners was the only attempt made on behalf of the Peace Conference to establish the facts relating to Arab aspirations by actual ascertainment on the spot: in that alone, their findings merit special attention. But it added greatly to the value of the inquiry that it was undertaken by a body with no national ambitions to promote, who approached their task with open minds, and that it was conducted by two men of recognized independence of judgment in whom the qualities of insight and sanity were remarkably combined. Of that, the Report bears ample evidence throughout: perhaps the most outstanding characteristics are the shrewdness of its findings and the unmistakable honesty of its recommendations.

Neither Dr. King nor Mr. Crane ever wavered in their conviction that the Report was based on an impartial investigation of the facts, although Dr. King did not feel called upon forever to defend it either in the public press or the public forum, a position which Professor Lybyer also shared. The Report would simply have to stand or fall as an historical document describing the situation in the Near East as the King-Crane Commission found it in the spring and summer of 1919.[1]

On the occasion of the exercises at Oberlin College in June 1927 in honor of President King, reference was made to the work of the Commission, both by Admiral Mark Bristol, the former High Commissioner in Turkey, who had so ably assisted the Commission, and by Mr. Crane,

---

The Struggle for Palestine (Boston, Beacon, 1957), p. 266, to the effect that "subsequent events" had shown "that the report was in all its essentials correct." For a recent estimate see James B. GIDNEY, "The King-Crane Commission: An American Policy for the Middle East," XXXVI *Middle East Forum* 8 (October 1961), 26-33.

[1] Professor William Yale, who served with the Commission, but disagreed with some of its methods and conclusions, wrote in 1958: "The work of the commission might justly be criticized as that of amateurs with no experience in the highly technical job of 'self-determination.' It can be said that the commission without ulterior motives private or political endeavored to do as thorough and unbiased a job as limitations of time and trained personnel made possible. Historical events since 1919 in Palestine, Syria, and Lebanon demonstrate conclusively that the investigation revealed with considerable accuracy the actual wishes of the principal religious and cultural groups in the area and that the commission's report, exclusive of its politically impractical recommendations, gave a reasonably accurate analysis of the situation as it existed in the summer of 1919." William YALE, *The Near East*, 336. Professor Yale wrote to the author on July 2, 1941 that he had always considered the Report "a very fine document, honest, scholarly, thorough," although he disagreed with the authors and felt that Dr. King and Dr. Lybyer did not understand the eastern mentality. But "the report *per se*" was "an admirable piece of work which" redounded "to the credit of King, Crane, Lybyer, and Brodie."

who was represented by Donald M. Brodie.[1] Among other things, Admiral Bristol remarked that

> ...the King-Crane Report, which was not for some years published, is probably as just, fair and extensive a report of the people of the Near East, of those countries which they visited, as ever has been prepared, or probably will be prepared for many years to come. This report has been utilized, I know, by our Americans abroad, and, if foreigners do not admit it, I am sure they have used it to the great advantage of their relations with that part of the world.

Mr. Brodie, reading the message of Charles R. Crane, noted that

> ...The report brought to light several perfectly definite principles. The Allies did not see fit to carry out the perfectly obvious recommendations of that report. The high hopes of the Arab people, both Moslem and Christian, have been disappointed. The strain between the Arab and the western peoples has greatly increased, but all the Arab folk, as I have reason to know, into the remotest oasis, revere that report, for which President King was so largely responsible. They believe that it is the charter of their freedom. They are going to use it as the foundation of their position, toward the mandatory powers, never compromising its principles. There is nothing that gives me more pride than to have been associated with President King and his inspiring work.

An Evaluation of the King-Crane Report

Essentially, the King-Crane Report may be evaluated from two basic points of view: (1) as a technique in the art of peace-making, regardless of the temporary character of some of the specific recommendations, made in the light of the situation existing in the Near East during 1919 as determined by the investigations of the Commission; (2) in the light of the developments in the years which followed the Peace Conference of 1919.

The Recommendation Concerning Palestine

Let us take first the recommendations concerning Palestine. It is well to recall that, while the Commissioners rejected the extreme Zionist program, they proposed to maintain the unity of Syria-Palestine, under a British or American mandate, with provision for a limited Jewish National Home. They did not act on the basis of so-called anti-Jewish prejudices. They made their recommendations simply on the basis of the facts as they found them in Palestine at the time, when only about ten per cent of the population appeared to be Jewish. Developments within Palestine since 1919 would seem, in part at least, to justify the recommendations of the Commission, since Palestine became a battleground

---

[1] From Oberlin College: *Ninety-Fourth Anniversary Exercises in Honor of President Henry Churchill King*. 2:30 P. M. June Twentieth Nineteen Hundred and Twenty-Seven (Cleveland, Earl H. Pendell and Associates, Shorthand Reporters and Associates, 1927), 75. Typewritten.

among the forces of Zionism and Arab nationalism and British imperialism, centering around the control of the Suez Canal and the eastern Mediterranean sea. Zionism, evidently, was not to consider the limited size and poverty of Palestine, and was to flower at the very time that a genuine and vigorous Arab nationalism was coming into bloom. Hans Kohn has well stated the problem: [1]

> In the midst of their startling successes, some Zionists—not always well informed—have come to regard the Palestinian Arabs and their problems as of only secondary importance and Palestine as exclusively the country of the "manifest destiny" of the Jewish people. Some Jewish and non-Jewish observers, fascinated by the historical appeal of the land and by the desire for a largescale solution of the "Jewish problem", have not always taken into full account two factors inherent in the situation: the limited absorptive capacity of the country, which is very small, with only few fertile districts and no important natural resources, and the existence of a relatively very large Arab population, which since the beginning of the World War has become strongly conscious of its national aspirations.

These difficulties continued throughout the inter-war period, into the Second World War and afterward, and ultimately eventuated in the struggle which led to the partition of Palestine and the establishment of the State of Israel during 1947-1949. [2]

The Recommendations Concerning Syria

In the case of Syria, the Commission proposed a united country under the constitutional rule of Prince Feisal, with either the United States or Great Britain as the mandatory. It overestimated the force of Arab nationalism at the time, and underestimated the strength of religious identification. It was pointed out that any attempt to force a French mandate on the unwilling Arabs would lead to difficulties, might produce an Anglo-French quarrel, a Franco-Arab struggle, and force "a dangerous

---

[1] Hans KOHN, *Revolutions and Dictatorships* (Cambridge, Harvard, 1939), 321-322. See also H. F. FRISCHWASSER-RA'ANAN, *Frontiers of a Nation: A Survey of Diplomatic and Political History Relative to the Palestine Problem* (London, 1955), 168 pp.; J. C. HUREWITZ, *The Struggle for Palestine* (New York, Norton, 1950), *passim*. Sir Ronald STORRS, *Zionism and Palestine* (Pelican, 1940), 107, wrote: "From the Jewish point of view Zionism, involving many sacrifices, is an idealistic movement. For the inhabitant of Palestine it is entirely materialistic, nationalistic, acquisitive, and non-religious. The injunction, oft repeated, to Arabs 'to work with Jews to develop their common country' is a mere irritation, for it is only their common country by virtue of a bond which those most affected there have not yet accepted."

[2] Among other things, see Royal Institute of International Affairs, *Great Britain and Palestine*, 1915-1945. Information Papers No. 20 (London, Oxford, 1946); George KIRK, *The Middle East in the War*, 1939-1946 (London, Oxford, 1952), 5-30, 228-250, 306-333; George KIRK, *The Middle East*, 1945-1950 (London, Oxford, 1954), Pt. III.

alternative" upon Great Britain. The Commission was aware of the long-established French connections with Syria, but it feared the consequences of a French mandate. Again, it rejected the Syrian claim to the region of Cilicia.[1] Much in the history of Syria since 1919 would appear to justify many of the suggestions of the King-Crane Commission. There were constant troubles of an administrative, economic, political and social nature in the years after 1919, with armed uprisings in 1920, when Feisal was dethroned, 1925 and 1936. Altogether there were no less than eighteen revolts in Syria between 1919 and 1941. A Franco-Syrian treaty of September 8, 1936 promised Syria independence within three years, but consummation was frustrated, French politics aside, by the coming of the war in 1939. While independence was promised after the conquest of Syria by British Imperial and Free French Forces in September 1941, it was not until the end of the war, in 1945, that independence was really achieved.[2]

The Recommendations Concerning Iraq

In accordance with the King-Crane Report, Mesopotamia, or Iraq, was placed under British mandate. A careful study of the development of modern Iraq during the inter-war years would appear to justify the King-Crane proposal. Likewise, it is interesting to observe that the vilayet of Mosul became a part of the Iraq mandate in 1925, as the King-Crane Commission had suggested in 1919.

Iraq became independent in 1927 and entered the League of Nations as a sovereign state in 1932. The outbreak of a Nazi-Fascist inspired rebellion against the British in April 1941 during the struggle for the eastern Mediterranean Sea and the control of the Near and Middle East, however, was indicative of continued antagonisms and difficulties in Iraq and the Arab lands as a whole. Similarly, the Iraqi revolt in July 1958 and the events which followed were symptomatic of continued unrest.[3]

Arab federation, as had been proposed, for very natural reasons, was not achieved, although the British Government indicated its readiness to work

[1] Note the Franco-Turkish difficulties during 1936-1939. See especially: *La question d'Alexandrette et d'Antioche*, I-IV (Ankara 1936); *La Société de l'Indépendance de Hatay* (1936); *Le Sandjak lutte pour son Indépendance* (1936); *Le Calvaire du Hatay* (1936).
[2] See especially S. H. Hemsley LONGRIGG, *Syria and Lebanon Under French Mandate*, passim; A. K. HOURANI, *Syria and Lebanon: A Political Essay* (London, Oxford, 1946), passim.
[3] Among other works see Philip IRELAND, *Iraq: A Study in Political Development* (New York, Macmillan, 1938), 510 pp.; H. A. FOSTER, *The Making of Modern Iraq* (Norman, University of Oklahoma, 1935), 219 pp.; Majid KHADDURI, *Independent Iraq: A Study in Iraqi Politics since 1932* (London, Oxford, 1951), 291 pp. For the earlier period see H. St. John B. PHILBY, *Forty Years in the Wilderness* (London, Robert Hale, 1957), Chs. IV, V.

in that general direction during the spring of 1941. On March 22, 1945 the League of Arab States was formed, and years later, on February 22, 1958, Egypt and Syria established the United Arab Republic. Subsequently, with the adherence of Yemen, the United Arab States was formed. The Syrian Arab Republic broke away from Egypt in September 1961, and the extent to which union or federation or confederation among the Arab States would be achieved—or how—remained to be seen. [1]

The Turkish Nation

The King-Crane Commission had proposed a general American mandate for the whole of Turkey, and had rejected all Greek or Italian claims to any portion of Asia Minor. In the case of Turkey proper, the Commission underestimated the resurgent strength of a rejuvenated Turkish nation under the able leadership of Mustapha Kemal, or Ataturk. Certainly the Turkish chieftain, and, for the most part, those around him, did not want a mandate of any kind, although the Turkish nationalists were well disposed toward Americans, and did not outlaw the prospect of some sort of political, economic and educational assistance from abroad which would not infringe on Turkish independence or sovereignty. In the end, few could deny that Turkish independence had worked out better than a mandate, granted the vicissitudes of time and circumstance. Indeed, as a whole, it might be argued that the Turks achieved for themselves almost exactly what a mandate might have accomplished along the road of secularization, nationalism and industrialization. A type of internationalization of the Turkish Straits was realized in the Lausanne Conference in July 1923, although this Convention came to an end in the Montreux Convention of July 1936, when Turkish sovereignty was restored over the Straits. [2] Armenian independence did not materialize. Even the limited recommendation of the King-Crane Commission, thanks to the exigencies of world politics, proved impossible of realization.

[1] See especially The Arab Information Center, *The Arab League: Its Origin, Purposes, Structure and Activities*. Information Papers No. 1 (New York, 1955), 31 pp.; *Basic Documents of the League of Arab States*. Document Collections No. 1 (New York, 1955), 40 pp.; B. Y. BOUTROS-GHALI, *The Arab League*, 1945-1955 (New York, International Conciliation, No. 498, May 1954); Paul E. ZINNER, *Documents on American Foreign Relations 1958* (New York, Harper, 1959), 378-381. See also Fayez A. SAYEGH, *Arab Unity: Hope and Fulfillment* (New York, Devin-Adair, 1958), 272 pp.; John MARLOWE, *Arab Nationalism* (London, Cresset, 1961), 236 pp. For documents on Arab League and Arab unity see Muhammad Khalil, *The Arab States and the Arab League* (Beirut, Khayats, 1962), II, Pts. 1 and 2.

[2] See especially Harry N. HOWARD, *The Problem of the Turkish Straits*. Department of State Publication 2752, Near Eastern Series 5 (Washington, U. S. Government Printing Office, 1947), 68 pp.

The Validity of the King-Crane Recommendations

In view of the failure of the United States to assume any mandatory responsibilities in the Near East, one may raise the general question of the validity of the Commission's recommendations—for after all, the King-Crane Commission postulated American membership in the League of Nations and the assumption of a mandate in Syria and Asia Minor.[1] Certainly, however, the King-Crane Commission is not to be held responsible for the American failure to assume international obligations in the post-war world. It could be argued that the basic failure was that of the American people in rejecting the Wilsonian program of international cooperation under the League of Nations, including the assumption of a mandate in the Near East. The King-Crane Commission warned against cynicism and disillusionment which in the form of political isolationism and economic nationalism was to contribute much to the breakdown in 1939. In the light of another era, following the end of World War II, when the United States assumed obligations of an almost universal character, whether military, political or economic, the recommendations made in 1919 seem mild, indeed. But, the scene had vastly changed, and the United States became involved in all the far corners of the world, with little possibility of disentanglement.

The Question of Method

But one may evaluate the work of the King-Crane Commission and its experiment in peace-making from another angle, somewhat divorced from these temporal considerations. Recommendations of any commission are subject to political application, and there is a primary responsibility of political leaders and governments to decide on what is to be done. With time, even a very short period of time, some proposals become impracticable — as, for example, the King-Crane recommendations concerning Turkey. But these considerations have little or nothing to do with the problem of the general validity of this type of investigation.

The King-Crane Commission had been sent because President Wilson and others in authority believed that this was the best way to obtain the information necessary for setting up a sound post-war system in the Near and Middle East. President Wilson rejected the notion, held by some Americans at Paris, that all the necessary information was easily available in the French capital. This would seem to be a thoroughly sound position. It is one thing to gather information from books, pamphlets, documents

---

[1] "If it is not certain that the United States will accept a mandate in those regions, it is misleading to present the United States as one of the possible advisers. Unless there is some possibility that those choices shall count, the work of such an inquiry as that of the King-Crane Commission can hardly be other than mischievous." W. E. HOCKING, *The Spirit of World Politics*, 255.

WAS THE EXPERIMENT WORTH WHILE? 325

and conference, or even from diplomatic and other sources from the field, but such information, however gained, can best be attested by actual investigation on the spot. In some instances direct investigation is the only means of attestation. It is still a valid, scholarly and scientific procedure even if it proves nothing either positively or negatively over and above what was known in the beginning, for such an affirmation or negation is itself a part of the testing of the knowledge necessary as a foundation for any procedure of investigation.

The methods which the Commission used were those of balancing common sense with expert knowledge. Before going out to the Near East the Commission studied thoroughly the basic literature on the subject, including the "full and varied reports and material" of the office of the Western Asia Division of the American Commission to Negotiate Peace. The quest in Syria, Palestine and Turkey proper was carried on in the light of that background. In Syria and Palestine care was taken to see that all shades of opinion were duly represented in interviews, conferences and petitions. Numerous foreigners in official and unofficial positions were interviewed. While the Commission spent forty days in the Syrian region, it was not able to visit extensively in Anatolia, Armenia or Mesopotamia. But it was able to make recommendations concerning these regions, for much information had been gathered, using Constantinople as the center to which delegations came from a wide range of places. The Harbord Mission, which did spend some time in Anatolia and Armenia, generally substantiated the King-Crane conclusions, although without making positive recommendations.

It is true that the Inter-Allied Commission on Mandates in Turkey, as originally conceived, never materialized, for only the American Section was ever sent to the Near East. This was, from some points of view, quite obviously a misfortune. In the first place, a genuine Inter-Allied Commission might have made recommendations which would have had more possibility of acceptance by the Peace Conference. Secondly, the Commission should have been definitely an official body representing all the Powers at the Peace Conference. But it was not an unmixed harm that the Inter-Allied Commission did not go, for it may well be that the American group obtained a fairer, more objective impression and presented a more unbiased report than a so-called international commission would have formulated. Nevertheless, the fact that only the American group went to the Near East did give rise to charges of partiality, of unfairness, and even of ignorance and naïveté, particularly since only Palestine, Syria and Constantinople were investigated directly on the spot.

It has been pointed out, too, that the King-Crane Commission went to the Near East too late effectively to accomplish its mission. It is interesting to note, however, that, as late as July 5, 1919, a number of distinguished British subjects urged the appointment of expert commissions to study a series of problems in Southeastern Europe and the Near East. [1] These gentlemen declared that "any disadvantages that delay may involve would be slight as compared with the evils of making under pressure of weariness and impatience hasty and perhaps ill-informed decisions which would leave rankling resentments and the seeds of war behind." Again, one may point out that whereas the King-Crane Commission began its work in June 1919, the Harbord Mission did not arrive in Armenia until mid-September and did not complete its work until the middle of October. But the delay in sending the King-Crane Commission, in any event, was hardly the fault of its members, who were ready to leave Paris by the middle of April and anxious to begin their work on the spot. The fact that they did not get away until the end of May was to be explained by the opposition of the French Government to any Commission going to Syria and, in part, by Zionist objections to an investigation in Palestine. In addition, the British Government failed to press the matter, and some Americans at Paris opposed the despatch of the Commission on the ground that all the necessary information was available in Paris and they believed that such a Commission might unduly arouse the emotions of the Near Eastern peoples among whom it might work.

As a result of the delay, the Treaty of Sèvres was sufficiently advanced to be presented to handpicked Ottoman delegates before the Commission returned to Paris. But since it was not until August 10, 1920 that the treaty was signed, there was ample opportunity, as the American Delegation indicated in November 1919, for the application of the King-Crane Report. This would have been particularly true had the Peace Conference been organized, as originally intended, into a *preliminary conference* to impose a preliminary treaty on the vanquished states, and then taken more time to negotiate the final treaties of peace. [2]

There can be little question concerning the qualifications of the members of the King-Crane Commission, although neither Dr. King nor Mr. Crane was an expert on Near Eastern problems. Both were men of intelligence and independence, whose honesty and impartiality were unassailable. Professor Lybyer, Dr. Montgomery and Captain Yale were all acquainted, both by residence and knowledge, with the problems of the Near East, whatever their specific limitations. [3]

---

[1] See the letter to the London *Times*, July 5, 1919, signed by Lord Crewe, Lord Carnock, Viscount Bryce, Sir George W. Buchanan, Frederick Kenyon, Arthur J. Evans, and Sir William M. Ramsay.
[2] See Harold NICOLSON, *Why Britain Is At War* (Penguin 1939), Ch. X.
[3] Captain Brodie's work as Secretary-Treasurer of the Commission was outstanding, as was Laurence Moore's work in handling the finances, about $ 20,000.

WAS THE EXPERIMENT WORTH WHILE?

The King-Crane Commission represented one of the first and most unusual attempts to ascertain the wishes of a people in an effort to accord them justice. The Commission was similar to the various Royal Commissions which the British Government has sent out to different regions for purposes of investigation. It may even be compared with some types of Congressional committees which have been used to investigate numerous problems, especially where expert staffs are used. It was a prototype of the Commissions of Investigation which the Assembly and Council of the League of Nations—and the later United Nations—used to excellent advantage in the investigation of problems. [1]

The procedures employed were not only perfectly legitimate and valid, but very often were the only types of investigation which could determine the necessary elements in the situation. Moreover, the use of the Commission raises the wider problem of the introduction of expert information and recommendation, not only in the immediate conduct of foreign relations, but in the planning of foreign policy.

It is in the light of this long-range vision that the work of the King-Crane Commission should be considered. In sending the Commission President Wilson made a genuinely constructive and challenging contribution to the technique of peace-making. His confidence in the group was justified by its diligent work and careful report.

---

[1] Compare the investigation of the King-Crane Commission with the work of the League of Nations Commissions which inquired into the problem of Mosul and the Sino-Japanese conflict in Manchuria. See League of Nations, *Question of the Frontier Between Turkey and Iraq* (C. 400. M.147.1925.VII) and Appeal by the Chinese Government. *Report of the Commission of Enquiry* (The Lytton Commission) (C.663.M.320.1932.VII. 12). Compare also with the various UN Commissions and Special Committees.

A SELECTED BIBLIOGRAPHY

Insofar as the King-Crane Commission, specifically, is concerned, this study is based primarily on manuscripts which came into the possession of the various members of The American Section of the Inter-Allied Commission on Mandates in Turkey and which were made available to the author, as stated in the preface. While detailed reference need not be made to all the items from these varied sources, enough are listed to indicate their importance. A brief but suggestive bibliography of printed materials is also being listed. The bibliography has been generally classified as follows: (I) *Sources*, (A) Manuscript and other Materials from the King-Crane Commission, and (B) Other Manuscript Materials; (II) *Printed Documentary Sources*; and (III) *Books Concerning the Near and Middle East*.

I. SOURCES

(A) MANUSCRIPT AND OTHER MATERIALS FROM THE KING-CRANE COMMISSION

   a. *The Papers of Captain Donald M. Brodie (Secretary)*

In addition to numerous Arabic petitions, the following items are of special interest:

La Communauté Grecque Orthodoxe de l'Indépendance de Tripoli de Syrie. A Messieurs les Délégués de la Conférence de la Paix. Tripoli, le 15 Mai 1919. 2 pp.

Charles R. Crane to President Wilson, July 10, 1919, Beirut, Syria, with enclosure of same date; Copy of partial report of Commission cabled in code, July 10th; Statement of Emir Feisal to American Commission; Statement of Syrian National Congress, Damascus, July 2, 1919; Résumé of Syrian Situation by Dr. A. H. Lybyer. The latter documents are also in the files of the Department of State, Washington, D. C.

Ligue de l'Unité Nationale, Statement of Principles. Constantinople, August 12, 1919, 2 pp.

An Armenian statement to the King-Crane Commission. August 10, 1919. 1 p. Signed by about 300 people.

Conseil National Assyrien, Constantinople, August 20, 1919. Statement of principles presented to Charles R. Crane. 5 pp. (French).

Committee of Thrace, Constantinople, August 21, 1919. Statement of Principles. 2 pp.

The Accounts of the King-Crane Commission, compiled by Laurence S. Moore.

Captain Donald M. Brodie, Memorandum Concerning the King-Crane Commission. 31 pp. Written late in 1919 or early in 1920.

—, Mr. Crane's Visit to Syria, April 1-9, 1922. 7 pp. Prepared in August 1940 from notes made shortly after the events.

—, Memorandum Regarding the Suppression and Publication in 1922 of the King-Crane Report on Mandates in Turkey. Prepared on August 28, 1940. 1 p.

Charles R. Crane to Donald M. Brodie, November 30, 1934. A brief memorandum of Mr. Crane's memories of the King-Crane Commission.

b. *The Papers of Charles R. Crane*

The unpublished *Memoirs* of Charles R. Crane, especially pp. 369-380, which deal with the experiences of Mr. Crane as a member of the King-Crane Commission. The memoirs were dictated in the later years of Mr. Crane's life.

c. *The Papers of Dr. Henry Churchill King*

1. *Manuscript Materials*

Letters and Diaries

The *Diary* of Henry Churchill King, January 1, 1919-December 31, 1919. A small *Notebook* of Dr. King, dealing with the Near and Middle East. Letters dealing with the appointment of the Commission:

Joseph C. Grew to H. C. King, April 29, 1919.

Robert Lansing to H. C. King, April 30, 1919; two letters containing appointment of King as Commissioner, with instructions for Commission embodying copy of memorandum on "Future Administration of Certain Portions of the Turkish Empire under the Mandatory System".

Grew to King, May 5, 8, 1919.

King to Colonel House, May 21, 22, 1919.

Grew to King, May 22, 27, 31, 1919.

Commission Letters:

Charles R. Crane to President Wilson. Cable, Constantinople, July 29, 1919.

H. E. Pears to G. R. Montgomery, August 21, 1919.

W. H. Buckler to H. C. King, September 8, 1919.

H. C. King to President Wilson, from U. S. S. *America*, September 10, 1919.

Memoranda, Despatches and Statements

American Commission to Negotiate Peace. Future Administration of Certain Portions of the Turkish Empire under the Mandatory System. SM-140. Mimeographed, 3 pp. Secret, annotated by Dr. King.

—, Memorandum on the Policy of the United States Relative to the Treaty with Turkey. November 26, 1919. Mimeographed, 6 pp.

British Delegation to the Peace Conference. Statement by the British Government for the Peace Conference Concerning the Settlement of the Middle East. February 7, 1919. 12 pp.

Interallied Commission on Mandates in Turkey, American Section. The Dangers to the Allies from a Selfish Exploitation of the Turkish Empire. May 1, 1919, 4 pp.

—, Report of the King-Crane Commission. Typewritten.
Near Eastern Division, American Commission to Negotiate Peace. Syrian Aspirations. A Report on the Aims and Aspirations of the Syrian Moderate Party. From the Office of Professor W. L. Westermann. 5 pp.
A. H. Lybyer, The Balkan Policy of the Peace Conference. March 22, 1919. 19 pp.
—, Persia, 1906-1914. 24 pp.
—, Projected Organization of the King-Crane Commission. April 24, 1919. 3 pp.
—, Suggestions in Regard to the Turkish Situation. May 20, 1919. 2 pp.
—, Statement on Mandates in the Near East. September 4, 1919. 14 pp. In communication to W. H. Buckler.
French Claims to Syria. 3 pp. No date, no author.
Reports from Admiral Mark Bristol, February 7-August 1919; Conditions in the Near East. Copies of reports and telegrams from the Senior U. S. Naval Officer and U. S. High Commissioner in Constantinople. Some 60 cables.
A number of Arabic memoranda dealing with the Syrian-Palestine Situation.
II. The Southern or Arab Area. Description. No date or author. 5 pp.
Apostolic Delegate, Beirut, A la Commission Américaine d'enquête pour la Syrie. July 5, 1919.
Howard Crosby Butler, Report on the Proposals for an Independent State or States. 42 pp.
Velid Eluzzia, Memorandum Presented to American Commission of Inquiry by the Ottoman Press Association. August 3, 1919. 7 pp.
Ahmed Emin Bey [Yalman], Memorandum Presented to the American Section of the International Commission for Mandates in the Near East. By Ahmed Emin (Ph. D., Sociology Department, Columbia University, New York), formerly professor of statistics at the University of Constantinople, now [1919] publisher and editor of *Vakit* [Times]. August 15, 1919. 7 pp.
Office of the American Commissioner [G. B. Ravndal]. Report on the Present Political and Military Status of Batoum, Its Present and Future Commercial and Economical Importance, and the Opportunities it Will Offer as a Port of Entry for the Development and Expansion of American Commerce with Armenia, Azerbaijan, Persia and Turkestan. August 3, 1919. 10 pp. Paraphrase of telegram sent to Washington, August 7, 1919. 2 pp. By Ralph F. Chesbrough, Consul.
—, Report on the Political, Military, Commercial and Economic Situation in Trebizond and the Surrounding Vilayets. Submitted by Ralph F. Chesbrough, American Consul, Class Eight, detailed to Constantinople. Constantinople, August 3, 1919. 13 pp.
—, Address of M. André Mandelstam, Reported by Gabriel B. Ravndal, October 1, 1919. 2 pp. The Soul of the Turk. Extracts of Speech by

M. Mandelstam, formerly Chief Dragoman of the Russian Embassy at Constantinople, later Professor of International Law at Petrograd. Reported by Consul General Ravndal, in Doc. 91, October 1, 1918. 2 pp.

George R. Montgomery, Memorandum of Interview with Commissioner [Gabriel Bie] Ravndal. August 5, 1919. 2 pp.

George E. White to the American Commissioners, August 16, 1919. 2 pp.

Mary Mills Patrick, Fourteen Reasons for an American Mandatory over Turkey. 2 pp.

2. *Printed Materials*

A large number of news clippings from American, British, French and other journals dealing with the Commission.

A number of printed copies of the *Report* of the King-Crane Commission (Editor and Publisher).

MOON, Parker T., *The Principal Declarations Respecting Terms of Peace by President Wilson and by the Secretary of State*. Prepared by the Section of Territorial, Economic and Political Intelligence. American Commission to Negotiate Peace. February 10, 1919 (Paris, 1919). 61 pp.

American Commission to Negotiate Peace. *Handbook "A": A Collection of Recent Political Information, October 14th to November 27th*. Paris, 1919. 78 pp.

Preliminary Peace Conference. *Report of the Commission on the League of Nations* (Paris, 1919). 20 pp.

The Plan of the *"New Syria National League" for the Future Government of Syria*. 1 p.

The Armenian Delegation to the Peace Conference. *The Armenian Question before the Peace Conference* (Paris, 1919), 28 pp., 2 maps.

Robert de CAIX, "The Question of Syria", *The New Europe*, XII, Nos. 150-151 (August 28, September 24, 1919), 145-149, 169-174.

3. *Maps*

Large map of Syria, Palestine and Part of Iraq, with pencil markings, in color, showing Arab, Jewish, British and French positions.

Map of Eastern Turkey in Asia, Syria and Western Persia (Ethnographical). Published by the Royal Geographical Society, 1910, railways inserted to November 1917.

Map showing the present political and Military Situation in Syria. March 1919.

Turkey. Political Divisions showing Vilayets and Independent Sanjaks. The Divisions are drawn in with pens of blue and red for railways.

Syria. Homs-Beirut. Geographical Section, General Staff. No. 2321. For official use only. War Office, 1910.

Zones of Influence of Territorial Acquisitions in Western Asia. According to the "Secret Treaties". Small map.

Anatolia and Armenia. Black and White Map with divisions drawn in.

Carte de la République du Pont (Euxin).
Turkey. Racial and religious groups according to sanjaks.
Arabia. Small photostat of map.
Délégation nationale arménienne. Arménie.
Bartholomew's War Map of Asia Minor, Arabia, Persia, etc.

4. Postal Cards and Snapshots

Dr. King had a very large number of postal cards of Palestine, Syria and Turkey proper. He also had a quite large collection of snapshots showing the Commission at work, delegations interviewed, etc.

d. The Papers of Professor Albert Howe Lybyer
1. Manuscript Materials

Letters and Diaries
The *Diary* of Albert Howe Lybyer, January 1-September 15, 1919.
Notes taken in Paris, May 1919; *Notes* at Constantinople.
Caleb F. Gates to A. H. Lybyer, April 12, 1919. 3 pp.
Lybyer to Joseph C. Grew, April 16, 18, 1919; Grew to Lybyer, April 19, 1919.
Lybyer to Grew, April 23, 1919. 3 pp. Description of Commission.
E. G. Forbes Adam to Lybyer, May 8, 14, 1919.
Felix Frankfurter to Woodrow Wilson, May 8, 14, 1919.
Woodrow Wilson to Felix Frankfurter, May 13, 16, 1919.
D. G. Hogarth to Lybyer, May 20, 21, 1919.
Grew to Lybyer, May 27, 1919. Appointment.
Crewe to the Editor of The [London] *Times* on Commissions for Completing Peace, signed by Crewe and six others. July 5, 1919. 2 pp.

Memoranda and Statements
Memorandum noting interchange between Venizelos and Orlando on Mediterranean problems. January 1, 1919.
Instructions for the Commissioners. March 25, 1919.
American Commission to Negotiate Peace. Minutes of the Meeting of April 18, 1919. Mission to Syria. 3 pp.
A. H. Lybyer, Preliminary Project of Itinerary for the Interallied Turkish Commission. Memorandum to H. C. King. April 1919. 2 pp.
—, Notes of Conversation with Admiral Grayson, April 15, 1919.
—, Two Short Memoranda, with Information from De Caix and Maurice Long. May 1, 1919.
—, Suggestions in Regard to the Turkish Situation. May 20, 1919. 2 pp.
—, The Apparent Situation in Syria. July 1, 1919. 4 pp.
—, Additional Observations on Syrian Situation. Constantinople, July 24, 1919. 4 pp.
—, Brief Historical Sketch of the Visit to Syria, Palestine and Cilicia of the American Section of the Interallied Commission on Mandates

in Turkey. Constantinople, August 1, 1919. Annotated and revised by Dr. King. 20 pp.
—, Draft Suggestions for Mandate in Turkey. To W. H. Buckler, September 4, 1919.
Interallied Commission on Mandates to Turkey. American Section. General Instructions. April 30, 1919.
—, Data Gathered; Data Still Desired. May 1, 1919. Prepared by Dr. King.
—, Condensation of Instructions, May 1, 1919.
—, Supplementary Instructions, May 1, 1919. 2 pp.
—, The Dangers to the Allies from a Selfish Exploitation of the Turkish Empire. May 1, 1919. 4 pp.
—, Who's Who of King-Crane Commission: (1) Henry Churchill King, (2) Charles R. Crane, (3) Albert H. Lybyer, (4) Laurence Shaw Moore, (5) George R. Montgomery, (6) William Yale, (7) Sami Haddad, (8) Michail Dorizas, (9) Ross Lambing, (10) Paul Oscar Toren.
—, Plan of Internal Organization of Commission.
—, Commission Schedule, June 10-13, 1919.
—, Memorandum of Interview between Delegations from Ludd, Ramleh, and neighboring villages. A. H. L. and D. M. B. Jaffa, Palestine, June 11, 1919.
—, Henry Churchill King and Charles R. Crane to Woodrow Wilson, June 12, 1919. Jaffa, Palestine. Copy of Cable.
—, Members of the Zionist Commission in Palestine. June 16, 1919.
—, Statement to the Interallied Commission on Mandates in Turkey. American Section. By Zionist Commission to Palestine. June 16, 1919. Signed by Harry Friedenwald.
—, Moslem Memorandum, Jerusalem. June 16, 1919. 8 pp.
—, Memoranda of Meetings in Palestine: Ramallah et al, Nablus, Jenin, Nazareth, Es-Salt, Acre. June 21, 1919.
—, Memorandum of Meeting at Haifa, June 23, 1919.
—, Demands of People of Coast, now found in Damascus. Distributed in Bazaars of Damascus at 3.40 P. M., Wednesday, June 25, 1919.
—, Program at Damascus, June 26, 1919.
—, Statement to the Press of Damascus, June 26, 1919.
—, Interview of Commissioners, Advisers present, of the Kadi, Mufti, and six others of the Ulema at Damascus. June 26, 1919. 1 p.
—, Notes on Interview of Commissioners, Advisers present, with General Gabriel Pasha, Chief of Police and Gendarmerie, Damascus, 3.30 P. M., June 27, 1919. 1 p.
—, Statement of the Emir Feisal to the American Commission. Damascus, July 1, 1919. 4 and 7 pp.
—, Confidential Letter to Commission (Very Secret). Damascus. July 1, 1919. 4 pp.

—, Statement of Syrian Conference, Damascus, July 3, 1919. Damascus Program. 2 pp.
—, Address of Moslem Women of Beirut to Commission, signed by Ibtihaje Kaddourah. July 8, 1919.
—, Telegram of Commission to President Wilson. Beirut, July 11, 1919.
—, Cable of Commission to President Wilson, July 10, 1919.
—, Petition of Turkish Women to the Commission. Original and Translation. August 1, 1919. 2 pp.
—, Turkish Statement. August 1, 1919. 2 pp.
—, American Mission in Paris to King and Crane, August 17, 1919. Suggesting return.
J. B. Jackson (Consul), Report to Department of State on Commission's Visit. Aleppo, Syria, July 21, 1919. 3 pp.
Michel Lotfallah, A Monsieur Clémenceau, Président de la Conférence de la Paix. Undated. Memorandum. Copy, 2 pp.
George R. Montgomery, Questions on Zionism. July 1, 1919. 4 pp.
—, Adana. 1 p.
Mary Mills Patrick, Memorandum on Education in Turkey. To W. H. Buckler, August 2, 1919.
Captain William Yale, Strong National Feeling. July 1, 1919. 3 pp.
—, Letter from Captain Yale to Professor Westermann describing conditions in Syria and Palestine. Beirut, July 8, 1919. 4 pp.
—, A Report on Syria, Palestine and Mount Lebanon for the American Commissioners, prepared by Captain William Yale, Technical Advisor to the American Section of the International Commission on Mandates in Turkey. July 26, 1919. Constantinople. 34 pp. Signed copy. Annotated by Dr. King.
—, Recommendations as to the Future Disposition of Palestine, Syria and Mount Lebanon, Prepared by Captain William Yale, Technical Advisor to the American Section of the International Commission on Mandates in Turkey. Constantinople. July 26, 1919. 11 pp. Signed copy. Annotated by Dr. King.

Interviews and Notes on Specific Topics

Anatolia: Draft of Opinion (A. H. L.).

Armenia- Interviews: (1) Hagopian, January 24, 1919; (2) Armenian Patriarch and others, August 1, 1919; (3) Mr. Dahtadjian; (4) The Tashnakists; (5) the Armenian Democratic Party; (6) the Armenian Hunchakists; (7) Armenian Delegates from Eastern Provinces, August 6, 1919; (8) Miss Graffam; (9) Dr. Tavitian, August 11, 1919; (10) Ovhannes Pasha Couyoumjian, August 11, 1919; (11) Bezian, etc.

Notes: (1) Statement of *Ligue de l'Unité Nationale*, August 12, 1919; (2) Statistics of Armenian Population from *Encyclopedia Britannica*, 11th Edition; (3) Proposed Boundaries of Turkey and Armenia, Prepared by Professor David Magie; (4) Estimates of the Population of an

Armenian State (A. H. L.); (5) Map Prepared under Westermann (?), showing percentages in Turkish Provinces; (6) Armenian Bibliography, by W. W. Rockwell; (7) Notes on Armenia, the Massacres, and Kurdistan, taken by A. H. L.; (8) Memoir to Commission by K. K. Krikorian, August 2, 1919; (9) Reflections as to Armenia, A. H. Lybyer, August 19, 1919; (10) Estimates for Armenia on Large Plan of Westermann and Small Plan of Lybyer; (11) Reasons for forming a Large Armenia, by K. K. Krikorian, August 8, 1919; (12) Statistics of Present Armenian Population, by Armenian Patriotic Association, August 6, 1919.

Cilicia:

Document on the Province of Adana. Prepared by Turks. 3 Parts, with notes. 16, 2, and 8 pp.
Albert H. Lybyer, Brief Memorandum on Cilicia.
Conversation of A. H. Lybyer with M. Jean Gout at Quai d'Orsay, April 10, 11, 1919.

Kurds:

Study on Kizilbasch-Kurds. Memoir Presented to Col. Haskell, probably in summer of 1919.
Claims of Kurds and Assyrians.

Mesopotamia:

Memoir Presented to the Commission at Aleppo, July 1919.

Smyrna:

Copy of Report on Consul Ralph F. Chesbrough, May 25, 1919.
Letter from H. E. Peers to G. R. Montgomery, August 21, 1919.

Turkey:

Résumé of Confidential Letter [from Ravndal] to Department of State, October 1, 1919.
Résumé of Report on Turkish Wilsonian League, January 7, 1919.
Statement on Conditions in Turkey by Dr. George Washburn.
Program of Commission, Constantinople, July 31, 1919.
Interview with Jemal et al, July 31, 1919.
Interviews with Mustapha Rauf Bey, Ahmed Emin Bey [Yalman], Irfi Bey, Ali Kemli Bey, Ahmed Riza Bey et al, Essad Pasha et al. Committee for the Protection of Thrace, Committee for Protection of Oriental Provinces.
Memoirs from League of Ottoman National Unity, August 12, 1919.
Turkish-made Map of Region around Antioch, with Suggested Boundary Lines.

Supplementary Interviews:

(1) August 1, 1919: Greek Patriarch et al; Greek Smyrna Committee; Greek Thracian Committee; Committee of Pontus; (2) August 6, 1919:

Turkish Social-Democratic Party; Chaldean Clergyman (Assyrian); (3) August 11, 1919: Bulgarian Commission; Mr. Yantis; Kurdish Democratic Party; Georgian Representatives; (4) August 12, 1919: Jemal Pasha, Prefect of City, et al; Chefik Rizia; Nunib Effendi, and Teha; Mazhar Bey; Abdul Medjid, and Bedri Bey; Hassim Tami Bey and Ali Emiri Effendi; Mr. Bambahas; Sheikh Riza Effendi et al; Shemseddin Bey; Museffa Zia; Jelal Bey; Assyrian Group.

2. *Printed Materials*

Documents Upon Which is Based the Right of the People of Syria to be Consulted as to Their Political Future Before any Government is Imposed Upon Them by The Peace Conference. 1 p.

HALL, William H., Editor, *Reconstruction in Turkey. A Series of Reports Compiled for The American Committee of Armenian and Syrian Relief.* 1 Madison Avenue, New York City. For Private Distribution Only. 1918. 243 pp. Compiled by a Sub-Committee appointed in October 1917 and submitted to Dr. James L. Barton, Chairman.

HATCH, Harold A., and HALL, William H., *Recommendations for Political Reconstruction in the Turkish Empire.* For Private Distribution. November 1918. 7 pp. [Lybyer's Copy was received November 27, 1918. Marked Confidential].

KRIKORIAN, K. K., *The Mandate for Armenia* (Constantinople, 1919), 18 pp.

La Vérité sur la question syrienne. Publié par le Commandement de la IVme Armée [Jemal Pasha] (Stamboul, 1916). 168 pp., with Arabic facsimiles.

e. *The Papers of Captain William Yale*

Captain William Yale, A Report on Syria, Palestine and Mount Lebanon for the American Commissioners, prepared by Captain William Yale, Technical Advisor to the American Section of the International Commission on Mandates in Turkey. Constantinople, July 26, 1919 34 pp. Copy. Hoover Library on War, Revolution and Peace, Stanford University.

—, Recommendations as to the Future Disposition of Palestine, Syria, and Mount Lebanon, Prepared by Captain William Yale, Technical Advisor to the American Section of the International Commission on Mandates in Turkey. Constantinople, July 26, 1919. Copy. 11 pp. Hoover Library.

—, American Commission to Negotiate Peace. Emir Faisal's Communication to Lloyd George. Paris, September 16, 1919. 3 pp.

—, The Arab Problem: Suggestions for Settlement. Peace of the East. The London *Times*, October 8, 1919.

—, Report in Detail of Interviews in London. September 27-October 14, 1919. 13 pp.

—, Position of the Syrian Question Today. Paris, October 21, 1919. 15 pp.

(B) OTHER MANUSCRIPT MATERIALS

a. *The Papers of General Tasker H. Bliss*

The Minutes of the Daily Meetings of the Commissioners Plenipotentiary. Bliss Papers, Box 101, File 30 A. The Division of Manuscripts, the Library of Congress. These are the minutes of the American Commission to Negotiate Peace. Used especially for the period of February 1 to September 25, 1919.

b. *The Papers of Colonel E. M. House*

The Minutes of the Daily Meetings of the Commissioners Plenipotentiary. From the House Collection at Yale University.
The Diary of Colonel E. M. House. Selected passages from the unpublished Diary. Yale University.

c. *The Papers of Robert Lansing*

Certain materials from the Papers of Robert Lansing, in the Division of Manuscripts, Library of Congress, have been used, as cited.

d. *The Papers of Professor W. L. Westermann*

Photostatic copies of the following papers from Professor Westermann's files are in the Hoover Library on War, Peace and Revolution at Stanford University:

Great Britain, British Delegation. Statement of British Policy in the Middle East for Submission to the Peace Conference (if required). Draft. February 18, 1919. 18 pp.

—, Statement by the British Government for the Peace Conference Concerning the Settlement of the Middle East. First Proof for Revision. February 7, 1919. 17 pp.

—, Maps Illustrating Memorandum Respecting the Settlement of Turkey and the Arabian Peninsula.

—, Appendix on Previous Commitments of His Majesty's Government in the Middle East.

—, Memorandum on British Commitments to King Hussein.

—, British Draft Map of Projected Situation in Arab Countries before the San Remo Agreement.

—, Europe.

—, The Settlement.

e. *The Papers of President Woodrow Wilson*

The Papers of President Wilson are on file in the Division of Manuscripts in the Library of Congress. Only the major materials dealing with the King-Crane Commission are here cited.

The Emir Feisal, Memorandum. January 1, 1919 (WWP 13 [IX-A]).
Memorandum on Syria. February 8, 1919. (WWP 25)
Howard Bliss to President Wilson, February 7, 11, 1919. (WWP 25)
R. S. Baker to President Wilson, March 21, 1919. (WWP 32)

A SELECTED BIBLIOGRAPHY 339

Emir Feisal to President Wilson, March 24, April 20, 1919. (WWP 33, 45)
E. M. House to Woodrow Wilson, April 21, 1919. (WWP 45)
Robert Lansing to Woodrow Wilson, April 28, 1919. (WWP 48)
H. C. King to Col. E. M. House, May 6, 1919. (WWP 51)
Felix Frankfurter to Woodrow Wilson, May 8, 14, 1919. (WWP 54, 55)
Woodrow Wilson to Felix Frankfurter (May 13, 16, 1919)
Edwin S. Montague to President Wilson, May 17, 1919. (WWP 56)
The Hedjaz Delegation to Colonel House, Paris, May 20, 1919. Transmitted to President Wilson. (WWP 56)
Henry Morgenthau, Sr., William H. Buckler, Professor Philip Brown, The Future Government of Asia Minor. May 21, 1919. (WWP 56)
Henry White to the President, May 22, 1919. (WWP 57)
Henry C. King to Mr. Close, May 28, 1919. (WWP 58)
The President to Dr. King, May 29, 1919. (WWP 59)
Charles R. Crane to Wilson, June 9, 1919. Cable. Constantinople.
Inter-Allied Commission on Mandates in Turkey, American Section. The Dangers to the Allies from a Selfish Exploitation of the Turkish Empire. May 1, 1919. (WWP 75)
American Commission to Negotiate Peace. Division of Western Asia. Abstract of Memorandum Which Accidentally Came into Our Hands, Presumably intended for the French Foreign Office, on the Syrian Matter. [From Mr. Frazier's Office. Memorandum for the President]. Undated, but probably about April 17, 1919. (WWP 75)
Memorandum for President Wilson Upon the Settlement of the Northern Portion of the Turkish Empire. Prepared by David Magie and W. L. Westermann. (WWP 75)
A British Solution for the Turkish Problem. An undated memorandum in the Wilson Papers. (WWP 75)
Copy of Crane-Wilson letter, July 10, 1919; telegram of July 10, 1919; Feisal Statement, Lybyer's Summary, July 1, 1919; Syrian Congress, July 3, 1919. Covering letter by Donald M. Brodie. President Wilson's handwriting: "Syrian Congress". (WWP File II-B)
Emir Feisal to President Wilson, July 9, 1919. (WWP VI-A, Folder 40, Box 5)
Charles R. Crane to Woodrow Wilson, January 12, 1923. (WWP X 6)
Baker-Bolling Correspondence, July 24, 25, October 2, 1922. (WWP X 4)

d. *The National Archives, Washington, D. C.*

There are relatively few papers on the King-Crane Commission as such in The National Archives. Pertinent materials may be found in American Commission to Negotiate Peace, 1918-1919, Vol. 157 Vols. 382, 383, 384 and 385 contain some basic material on the Middle East and the Ottoman Empire, along with much Zionist propaganda material.

II. PUBLISHED DOCUMENTARY SOURCES

ADAMOV, E. E. (Editor), *Konstantinopol i Prolivy*. 2 volumes (Moscow, 1925-1926). Authoritative Russian source on the question of Constantinople and the Straits during the war of 1914-1918. French translation: *Constantinople et les Détroits*. 2 volumes (Paris, Les Éditions Internationales, 1930-1932).

—, *Razdel Aziatskoi Turtsii* (Moscow, 1924), 383 pp. The partition of Asiatic Turkey according to secret documents of the former Imperial Russian Foreign Ministry.

BAKER, Ray Stannard, *Woodrow Wilson and World Settlement* (New York, Doubleday Page, 1922), 3 volumes. Volume II is especially valuable for documentary materials on the Paris Peace Conference.

France. *Documents diplomatiques. Conférence de Lausanne sur les affaires du Proche-Orient* (1922-1923). *Recueil des Actes de la Conférence* (Paris, Imprimerie nationale, 1923). Première série. Tome I contains the protocols of the first commission; Tome IV, documents on the negotiations of February 1 to April 22, 1923. *Deuxième Série*, Tome I, *procès-verbaux* and documents on second part of Conference, April 23-July 24, 1923. Tome II contains final acts of Conference.

Great Britain, Foreign Office, Turkey No. 1 (1923). *Lausanne Conference on Near Eastern Affairs, 1922-1923. Records of Proceedings and Draft Terms of Peace* [*With Map*]. Cmd. 1814.

—, Treaty Series No. 16 (1923). *Treaty of Peace with Turkey, and Other Instruments Signed at Lausanne on July 24, 1923*. Cmd. 1929.

—, Miscellaneous No. 3 (1939). *Correspondence between Sir Henry McMahon, G.C.M.G., G.C.V.O., K.C.I.E., G.S.I., His Majesty's High Commissioner at Cairo and the Sherif Hussein of Mecca. July 1915-March 1916*. With a Map. Cmd. 5957.

—, Miscellaneous No. 4 (1939). *Statements made on behalf of His Majesty's Government during the year 1918 in regard to the Future Status of certain parts of the Ottoman Empire*. Cmd. 5964.

—, *Reports of a Committee Set up to Consider Certain Correspondence between Sir Henry McMahon (His Majesty's High Commissioner in Egypt) and the Sherif of Mecca in 1915 and 1916*. March 16, 1939. Cmd. 5974.

—, *Documents on British Foreign Policy*, 1919-1939. Edited by E. L. Woodward and Rohan Butler. First Series, Vols. IV-VIII (1919-1920) (London, H. M. S. O., 1952 ff). Cited as *British Documents*, 1919-1939. Indispensable for British policy.

HUREWITZ, J. C., *Diplomacy in the Near and Middle East. A Documentary Record*, Volume I, 1535-1914; Volume II, 1914-1956 (New York, D. Van Nostrand, 1956). A very useful and convenient collection of documents.

"King-Crane Report on the Near East. A Suppressed Official Document

A SELECTED BIBLIOGRAPHY 341

of the United States Government," *Editor and Publisher*, LV, No. 27 (December 2, 1922), i-xxvii.

MILLER, David Hunter, *My Diary at the Conference of Paris, with Documents* (New York, Appeal Printing Company, 1928) 22 volumes. The authoritative documentary source on the Paris Conference until publication of the Department of State's volumes.

MUSTAPHA KEMAL [Atatürk], *A Speech delivered by Ghazi Mustapha Kemal, President of the Turkish Republic. October 1927* (Leipzig, K. F. Koehler, 1929), 724 pp. Indispensable for an understanding of the Turkish position.

—, *Dokumente zur Rede* (Leipzig, Koehler, 1929), 270 pp. Documents with Mustapha Kemal's *Speech*.

Ottoman Delegation to the Paris Peace Conference. *Observations of the Ottoman Empire on the Conditions of Peace*. From Damad Ferid to Millerand, President of the Peace Conference, June 25, 1920. E. S. H. Bulletin No. 637. American Embassy, Paris. Hoover Library on War, Revolution and Peace.

—, *Observations générales présentées par la délégation ottomane à la Conférence de la Paix*. 8 juillet 1920. A Turkish document of 47 pages presenting a scathing denunciation of the Treaty of Sèvres.

—, *Reply of the Allied Powers to the Observations of Ottoman Empire to the Conditions of Peace*. Spa, July 16, 1920. E. S. H. Bulletin No. 743, July 21, 1919. American Embassy, Paris. Hoover Library.

United States. Senate Document No. 266, 66th Congress, 2nd Session. *Conditions in the Near East*. Report of the American Military Mission to Armenia, by Major General James G. Harbord.

—, Department of State, Division of Near Eastern Affairs. *The Mandate for Palestine* (Washington, Government Printing Office, 1927). The correspondence between the United States and the United Kingdom over Palestine and Mesopotamia, with treaty. See also Great Britain, Foreign Office, *Correspondence between H. M. Government and the United States Respecting Economic Rights in Mandated Territories*, Miscellaneous No. 10 (1921), Cmd. 1226.

—, Department of State, *Papers Relating to the Foreign Relations of the United States*. Especially the volumes, as cited, covering the years 1920-1923 (Washington, U. S. G. P. O., 1936-1938). Cited generally as *U. S. Foreign Relations*.

—, Department of State, *Papers Relating to the Foreign Relations of the United States. The Paris Peace Conference 1919*. Vols. I-XIII (Washington, U. S. G. P. O., 1943-1947. Volume XII, pp. 745-863, contains the published materials relative to the King-Crane Commission, the Report of which is in pp. 751-863. Cited as *PPC*.

The Zionist Organization. *The Jewish People and Palestine. Statement made before the Palestine Royal Commission in Jerusalem, on November 25th, 1936* by Dr. Chaim Weizmann, President of the Zionist Organization and of the Jewish Agency for Palestine. Issued by the Head Office of the Zionist Organization, Jerusalem. 30 pp.

III. SELECTED WORKS CONCERNING THE NEAR AND MIDDLE EAST

ANTONIUS, George, *The Arab Awakening. The Story of the Arab National Movement* (Philadelphia, Lippicott, 1939; Beirut, Khayat's Book Store, 1955, 1961), 471 pp. Classic account of the development of Arab nationalism.

BAKER, Ray Stannard, *Woodrow Wilson and World Settlement* (New York, Doubleday Page, 1922), 3 volumes. Chapter IV, Vol. I, is especially useful.

DUGDALE, Blanche E. C., *Arthur James Balfour, First Earl of Balfour, K. G., O. M., F. R. S.* (New York, Putnam's, 1937), 2 volumes. Authoritative discussion of origins of the Balfour position on Palestine and Zionism.

EDIB, Halidé, *The Memoirs of Halidé Edib; The Turkish Ordeal, Being the Further Memoirs of Halidé Edib* (New York, Century, 1928), 2 volumes. Memoirs of the distinguished Turkish writer. An excellent personal account of her reflections on the King-Crane Commission.

The ESCO Foundation for Palestine, Inc., *Palestine, a Study of Jewish, Arab, and British Policies* (New Haven, Yale, 1947), 2 volumes. A valuable, scholarly Zionist study.

GARNETT, David, *The Letters of T. E. Lawrence* (New York, Doubleday, Doran, 1939), 896 pp. Many of these letters throw an interesting light on the development of British policy in the Near and Middle East.

GEORGE, David Lloyd, *The Truth About the Treaties* (London, Gollancz, 1938; *Memoirs of the Peace Conference* [New Haven, Yale, 1939]), 2 vols.

DE HAAS, Jacob, *Palestine: The Last Two Thousand Years* (New York, Macmillan, 1934), 523 pp. A general history which loses much of its perspective in its treatment of the post-World War I years.

HOCKING, W. E., *The Spirit of World Politics. With Special Studies of the Near East* (New York, Macmillan, 1932), 571 pp. Some excellent chapters on the Near East.

HOUSE, E. M., and SEYMOUR, Charles, *What Really Happened at Paris. The Peace Conference* (New York, Scribners, 1921), 528 pp. See especially Professor W. L. Westermann's Chapter VIII on "The Armenian Problem and the Disruption of Turkey."

HOWARD, Harry N., *The Partition of Turkey, 1913-1923: A Diplomatic History* (Norman, University of Oklahoma Press, 1931), 486 pp.

—, "An American Experiment in Peace-Making: The King-Crane Commission", *The Moslem World*, Vol. XXXII, No. 2 (April 1942), 122-46.

A SELECTED BIBLIOGRAPHY 343

JEFFRIES, J. M. N., *Palestine: The Reality* (London, Longmans, 1939), 728 pp. An anti-Zionist treatise.

KOHN, Hans, *A History of Nationalism in the East* (New York, Harcourt, Brace, 1929), 476 pp.

—, *Revolutions and Dictatorships. Essays in Contemporary History* (Cambridge, Harvard, 1939), 437 pp. Excellent Chapters XI and XII on "Revolution in the Desert" and "Zionism".

MANUEL, Frank E., *The Realities of American-Palestine Relations* (Washington, Public Affairs Press, 1949), 378 pp. Pro-Zionist treatise.

MARLOWE, John, *The Seat of Pilate* (London, Cresset, 1959).

—, *Arab Nationalism and British Imperialism* (London, Cresset, 1961), 236 pp.

MASON, Alpheus Thomas, *Brandeis: A Free Man's Life* (New York, Viking, 1946), 713 pp. Ch. XXIX, on "International Justice and the Jews, 1912-1921", is particularly important.

NICOLSON, Harold, *Peace-Making. 1919. Studies in Modern Diplomacy* (New York, Harcourt, Brace, 1939), 378 pp.

POLK, William E., STAMLER, David M., and ASFOUR, Edmund, *Backdrop to Tragedy: The Struggle for Palestine* (Boston, Beacon, 1957), 399 pp. Balanced study.

Royal Institute of International Affairs, *Great Britain and Palestine, 1915-1946.* Revised Edition (London, Oxford, 1946), 177 pp. Excellent handbook.

SHOTWELL, James T., *At the Paris Peace Conference* (New York, Macmillan, 1937), 444 pp. An informative diary.

SMITH, Arthur D. Howden, *Mr. House of Texas* (New York, Funk and Wagnalls, 1940), 381 pp. Journalistic biography.

SMITH, Elaine, *Turkey: Origins of the Kemalist Movement and the Government of the Grand National Assembly* (1919-1923) (Washington, 1959), 175 pp. Excellent brief treatise.

SPEISER, E. E., *The United States and the Near East* (Cambridge, Harvard, 1947), 263 pp. General treatise on United States policy.

STEIN, Leonard, *The Balfour Declaration* (London, Vallentine, Mitchell, 1961), 681 pp. Indispensable for Zionist background and development of the Balfour Declaration. The author was Political Secretary of the World Zionist Organization (1920-1929), was President of the Anglo-Zionist Association (1939-1949), and advised the Jewish Agency in presenting its case before both the Palestine Royal Commission (1936) and the Woodhead Commission (1938).

STORRS, Sir Ronald, *The Memoirs of Sir Ronald Storrs* (New York, Putnam's, 1937), 563 pp. Memoirs of the former British Military Governor of Jerusalem.

TAYLOR, Alan R., *Prelude to Israel: An Analysis of Zionist Diplomacy, 1897-1947* (New York, Philosophical Press, 1959), 136 pp. Brief treatment.

TOYNBEE, Arnold J., *The Survey of International Affairs*. 1925. Volume I. *The Islamic World Since the Peace Settlement* (London, Oxford, 1927), 611 pp.

—, "The Modern West and the Islamic World", *A Study of History*, Vol. VIII, 216-272.

—, "The Modern West and the Jews", *ibid.*, 272-313.

WEIZMANN, Chaim, *Trial and Error: The Autobiography of Chaim Weizmann* (New York, Harper, 1949), 498 pp. Indispensable for any study of the problems of Zionism and Palestine.

ZEINE, Zeine N., *Arab-Turkish Relations and the Emergence of Arab Nationalism* (Beirut, Khayats, 1958), 156 pp. Brief account, with essential corrections of the Antonius thesis.

—, *The Struggle for Arab Independence: Western Diplomacy and the Rise and Fall of Faisal's Kingdom in Syria* (Beirut, Khayats, 1960), 297 pp. An excellent study of the subject, with primary interest in the Peace Conference and attendant developments in the Middle East.

Appendix
THE RECOMMENDATIONS OF THE KING-CRANE COMMISSION

[Excerpted from Department of State, *Papers Relating to the Foreign Relations of the United States. The Paris Peace Conference* 1919 (Washington, U. S. Government Printing Office, 1947), XII, 787-799, 799-802, 841-848.]

I. SYRIA AND PALESTINE

The Commissioners make to the Peace Conference the following recommendations for the treatment of Syria:

1. We recommend, as most important of all, and in strict harmony with our instructions, that whatever foreign administration (whether of one of more powers) is brought into Syria, should come in, not at all as a colonizing Power in the old sense of that term, but as a Mandatary under the League of Nations, with the clear consciousness that "the wellbeing and development" of the Syrian people form for it a "sacred trust".

(1) To this end the mandate should have a limited term, the time of expiration to be determined by the League of Nations, in the light of all the facts as brought out from year to year, in the annual reports of the Mandatary to the League or in other ways.

(2) The Mandatary Administration should have, however, a period and power sufficient to ensure the success of the new State; and especially to make possible carrying through important educational and economic undertakings, essential to secure founding of the State.

(3) The Mandatary Administration should be characterized from the beginning by a strong and vital educational emphasis, in clear recognition of the imperative necessity of education for the citizens of a democratic state, and the development of a sound national spirit. This systematic cultivation of national spirit is particularly required in a country like Syria, which has only recently come to self-consciousness.

(4) The Mandatary should definitely seek, from the beginning of its trusteeship, to train the Syrian people to independent self-government as rapidly as conditions allow, by setting up all the institutions of a democratic state, and by sharing with them increasingly the work of administration, and so forming gradually an intelligent citizenship, interested unselfishly in the progress of the country, and forming at the same time a large group of disciplined civil servants.

(5) The period of "tutelage" should not be unduly prolonged but independent self-government should be granted as soon as it can safely be done; remembering that the primary business of governments is not the accomplishment of certain things, but the development of citizens.

(6) It is peculiarly the duty of the Mandatary in a country like Syria, and in this modern age, to see that complete religious liberty is ensured, both in the constitution and in the practice of the state, and that a jealous care is exercised for the rights of all minorities. Nothing is more vital than this for the enduring success of the new Arab State.

(7) In the economic development of Syria, a dangerous amount of indebtedness on the part of the new State should be avoided, as well as any entanglements financially with the affairs of the Mandatory Power. On the other hand the legitimate established privileges of foreigners such as rights to maintain schools, commercial concessions, etc., should be preserved, but subject to review and modification under the authority of the League of Nations in the interest of Syria. The Mandatory Power should not take advantage of its position to force a monopolistic control at any point to the detriment either of Syria or of other nations; but it should seek to bring the new State as rapidly as possible to economic independence as well as to political independence.

Whatever is done concerning the further recommendations of the Commission, the fulfillment of at least the conditions now named should be assured, if the Peace Conference and the League of Nations are true to the policy of mandatories already embodied in "The Covenant of the League of Nations". This should effectively guard the most essential interests of Syria, however the machinery of administration is finally organized. The Damascus Congress betrayed in many ways their intense fear that their country would become, though under some other name, simply a colonial possession of some other Power. That fear must be completely allayed.

2. We recommend, in the second place that the unity of Syria be preserved, in accordance with the earnest petition of the great majority of the people of Syria.

(1) The territory concerned is too limited, the population too small, and the economic, geographic, racial and language unity too manifest, to make the setting up of independent states within its boundaries desirable, if such division can possibly be avoided. The country is very largely Arab in language, culture, traditions, and customs.

(2) This recommendation is in line with important "general considerations" already urged, and with the principles of the League of Nations, as well as in answer to the desires of the majority of the population concerned.

(3) The precise boundaries of Syria should be determined by a special commission on boundaries, after the Syrian territory has been in general allotted. The Commissioners believe, however, that the claim of the Damascus Conference to include Cilicia in Syria is not justified, either historically or by commercial or language relations. The line between the Arabic-speaking and the Turkish-speaking populations would quite

certainly class Cilicia with Asia Minor, rather than with Syria. Syria, too, has no such need of further sea coast as the large interior sections of Asia Minor.

(4) In standing thus for the recognition of the unity of Syria, the natural desires of regions like the Lebanon, which have already had a measure of independence, should not be forgotten. It will make for real unity, undoubtedly, to give a large measure of local autonomy, and especially in the case of strongly unified groups. Even the "Damascus Program" which presses so earnestly the unity of Syria, itself urges a government "on broad decentralization principles."

Lebanon has achieved a considerable degree of prosperity and autonomy within the Turkish Empire. She certainly should not find her legitimate aspirations less possible within a Syrian national State. On the contrary, it may be confidently expected that both her economic and political relations with the rest of Syria would be better if she were a constituent member of the State, rather than entirely independent of it.

As a predominantly Christian country, too, Lebanon naturally fears Moslem domination in a unified Syria. But against such domination she would have a four-fold safeguard: her own large autonomy; the presence of a strong Mandatary for the considerable period in which the constitution and practice of the new State would be forming; the oversight of the League of Nations, with its insistence upon religious liberty and the rights of minorities; and the certainty that the Arab Government would feel the necessity of such a state, if it were to commend itself to the League of Nations. Moreover, there would be less danger of a reactionary Moslem attitude, if Christians were present in considerable numbers, rather than largely segregated outside the state, as experience of the relations of different religious faiths in India suggests.

As a predominantly Christian country, it is also to be noted that Lebanon would be in a position to exert a stronger and more helpful influence if she were within the Syrian State, feeling its problems and needs, and sharing all its life, instead of outside it, absorbed simply in her own narrow concerns. For the sake of the larger interests, both of Lebanon and of Syria, then, the unity of Syria is to be urged. It is certain that many of the more thoughtful Lebanese themselves hold this view. A similar statement might be made for Palestine; though, as "the holy Land" for Jews and Christians and Moslems alike, its situation is unique, and might more readily justify unique treatment, if such treatment were justified anywhere. This will be discussed more particularly in connection with the recommendation concerning Zionism.

3. We recommend, in the third place, that Syria be placed under one Mandatory Power, as the natural way to secure real and efficient unity.

(1) To divide the administration of the provinces of Syria among

several mandataries, even if existing national unity were recognized; or to attempt a joint mandatary of the whole on the commission plan: — neither of these courses would be naturally suggested as the best way to secure and promote the unity of the new State, or even the general unity of the whole people. It is conceivable that circumstances might drive the Peace Conference to some such form of divided mandate; but it is not a solution to be voluntarily chosen, from the point of view of the larger interests of the people, as considerations already urged indicate.

(2) It is not to be forgotten, either, that, however they are handled politically, the people of Syria are there, forced to get on together in some fashion. They are obliged to live with one another — the Arabs of the East and the people of the Coast, the Moslems and the Christians. Will they be helped or hindered, in establishing tolerable and finally cordial relations, by a single mandatary? No doubt the quick mechanical solution of the problem of difficult relations is to split the people up into little independent fragments. And sometimes, undoubtedly, as in the case of the Turks and Armenians, the relations are so intolerable as to make some division imperative and inevitable. But in general, to attempt complete separation only accentuates the differences and increases the antagonism. The whole lesson of the modern social consciousness points to the necessity of understanding "the other half", as it can be understood only by close and living relations. Granting reasonable local autonomy to reduce friction among groups, a single mandatary ought to form a constant and increasingly effective help to unity of feeling throughout the state, and ought to steadily improve group relations.

The people of Syria, in our hearings, have themselves often insisted that, so far as unpleasant relations have hitherto prevailed among various groups, it has been very largely due to the direct instigation of the Turkish Government. When justice is done impartially to all; when it becomes plain that the aim of the common government is the service of all classes alike, not their exploitation, decent human relations are pretty certain to prevail, and a permanent foundation for such relations to be secured — a foundation which could not be obtained by dividing men off from one another in antagonistic groups.

The Commissioners urge, therefore, for the largest future good of all groups and regions alike, the placing of the whole of Syria under a single mandate.

4. We recommend, in the fourth place, that Emir Feisal be made the head of the new united Syrian State.

(1) This is expressly and unanimously asked for by the representative Damascus Congress in the name of the Syrian people, and there seems to be no reason to doubt that the great majority of the population of Syria sincerely desire to have Emir Feisal as ruler.

(2) A constitutional monarchy along democratic lines, seems naturally

APPENDIX 349

adapted to the Arabs, with their long training under tribal conditions, and with their traditional respect for their chiefs. They seem to need, more than most people, a King as the personal symbol of the power of the State.

(3) Emir Feisal has come, too, naturally into his present place of power, and there is no one else who could well replace him. He had the great advantage of being the son of the Sherif of Mecca, and as such honored throughout the Moslem world. He was one of the prominent Arab leaders who assumed responsibility for the Arab uprising against the Turks, and so shared in the complete deliverance of the Arab-speaking portions of the Turkish Empire. He was consequently hailed by the "Damascus Congress" as having "merited their full confidence and entire reliance." He was taken up and supported by the British as the most promising candidate for the headship of the new Arab State — an Arab of the Arabs, but with a position of wide appeal through his Sherifian connection, and through his broad sympathies with the best in the Occident. His relations with the Arabs to the east of Syria are friendly, and his kingdom would not be threatened from that side. He undoubtedly does not make so strong an appeal to the Christians of the West Coast, as to the Arabs of the East; but no man can be named who would have a stronger general appeal. He is tolerant and wise, skillful in dealing with men, winning in manner, a man of sincerity, insight, and power. Whether he has the full strength needed for his difficult task it is too early to say; but certainly no other Arab leader combines so many elements of power as he, and he will have invaluable help throughout the mandatory period.

The Peace Conference may take genuine satisfaction in the fact that an Arab of such qualities is available for the headship of this new state in the Near East.

5. We recommend, in the fifth place, serious modification of the extreme Zionist Program for Palestine of unlimited immigration of Jews, looking finally to making Palestine distinctly a Jewish State.

(1) The Commissioners began their study of Zionism with minds predisposed in its favor, but the actual facts in Palestine, coupled with the force of the general principles proclaimed by the Allies and accepted by the Syrians have driven them to the recommendation here made.

(2) The Commission was abundantly supplied with literature on the Zionist program by the Zionist Commission to Palestine; heard in conferences much concerning the Zionist colonies and their claims; and personally saw something of what had been accomplished. They found much to approve in the aspirations and plans of the Zionists, and had warm approbation for the devotion of many of the colonists, and for their success, by modern methods, in overcoming great natural obstacles.

(3) The Commission recognized also that definite encouragement had been given to the Zionists by the Allies in Mr. Balfour's often quoted

statement, in its approval by other representatives of the Allies. If, however, the strict terms of the Balfour Statement are adhered to — favoring "the establishment in Palestine of a national home for the Jewish people," "it being clearly understood that nothing shall be done which may prejudice the civil and religious rights of existing non-Jewish communities in Palestine"—it can hardly be doubted that the extreme Zionist Program must be greatly modified. For "a national home for the Jewish people" is not equivalent to making Palestine into a Jewish State; nor can the erection of such a Jewish State be accomplished without the gravest trespass upon the "civil and religious rights of existing non-Jewish communities in Palestine." The fact came out repeatedly in the Commission's conference with Jewish representatives, that the Zionists looked forward to a practically complete dispossession of the present non-Jewish inhabitants of Palestine, by various forms of purchase.

In his address of July 4, 1918, President Wilson laid down the following principle as one of the four great "ends for which the associated peoples of the world were fighting": "The settlement of every question, whether of territory, of sovereignty, of economic arrangement, or of political relationship on the basis of the free acceptance of that settlement by the people immediately concerned, and not upon the basis of the material interest or advantage of any other nation or people which may desire a different settlement for the sake of its own exterior influence or mastery." If that principle is to rule, and so the wishes of Palestine's population are to be decisive as to what is to be done with Palestine, then it is to be remembered that the non-Jewish population of Palestine—nearly nine-tenths of the whole—are emphatically against the entire Zionist program. The tables show that there was no one thing upon which the population of Palestine were more agreed than upon this. To subject a people so minded to unlimited Jewish immigration, and to steady financial and social pressure to surrender the land, would be a gross violation of the principle just quoted, and of the peoples' rights, though it be kept within the forms of law.

It is to be noted also that the feeling against the Zionist program is not confined to Palestine, but shared very generally by the people throughout Syria, as our conferences clearly showed. More than 72 per cent — 1350 in all — of all the petitions in the whole of Syria were directed against the Zionist program. Only two requests—those for a united Syria and for independence—had a larger support. This general feeling was only voiced by the "General Syrian Congress", in the seventh, eighth and tenth resolutions of their statement:

7. We oppose the pretentions of the Zionists to create a Jewish commonwealth in the southern part of Syria, known as Palestine, and oppose Zionist migration to any part of our country; for we do not acknowledge their title, but consider them a grave peril to our people

from the national, economical, and political points of view. Our Jewish compatriots shall enjoy our common rights and assume the common responsibilities.

8. We ask that there should be no separation of the southern part of Syria known as Palestine nor of the littoral western zone which includes Lebanon from the Syrian country. We desire that the unity of the country should be guaranteed against partition under whatever circumstances.

10. The fundamental principles laid down by President Wilson in condemnation of secret treaties impel us to protest most emphatically against any treaty that stipulates the partition of our Syrian country and against any private engagement aiming at the establishment of Zionism in the southern part of Syria; therefore we ask the complete annulment of these conventions and agreements.

The Peace Conference should not shut its eyes to the fact that the anti-Zionist feeling in Palestine and Syria is intense and not lightly to be flouted. No British officer, consulted by the Commissioners, believed that the Zionist program could be carried out except by force of arms. The officers generally thought that a force of not less than fifty thousand soldiers would be required even to initiate the program. That of itself is evidence of a strong sense of the injustice of the Zionist program, on the part of the non-Jewish populations of Palestine and Syria. Decisions, requiring armies to carry out, are sometimes necessary, but they are surely not gratuitously to be taken in the interests of a serious injustice. For the initial claim, often submitted by Zionist representatives, that they have a "right" to Palestine, based on an occupation of two thousand years ago, can hardly be seriously considered.

There is a further consideration that cannot justly be ignored, if the world is to look forward to Palestine becoming a definitely Jewish state, however gradually that may take place. That consideration grows out of the fact that Palestine is "the Holy Land" for Jews, Christians and Moslems alike. Millions of Christians and Moslems all over the world are quite as much concerned as the Jews with conditions in Palestine, especially with those conditions which touch upon religious feeling and rights. The relations in these matters in Palestine are most delicate and difficult. With the best possible intentions, it may be doubted whether the Jews could possibly seem to either Christians or Moslems proper guardians of the holy places, or custodians of the Holy Land as a whole. The reason is this: the places which are most sacred to Christians—those having to do with Jesus—and which are also sacred to Moslems, are not only not sacred to Jews, but abhorrent to them. It is simply impossible, under these circumstances, for Moslems and Christians to feel satisfied to have these places in Jewish hands, or under the custody of Jews

There are still other places about which Moslems must have the same feeling. In fact, from this point of view, the Moslems, just because the sacred places of all three religions are sacred to them, have made very naturally much more satisfactory custodians of the holy places than the Jews could be. It must be believed that the precise meaning, in this respect, of the complete Jewish occupation of Palestine has not been fully sensed by those who urge the extreme Zionist program. For it would intensify, with a certainty like fate, the anti-Jewish feeling both in Palestine and in all other portions of the world which look to Palestine as "the Holy Land".

In view of all these considerations, and with a deep sense of sympathy for the Jewish cause, the Commissioners feel bound to recommend that only a greatly reduced Zionist program be attempted by the Peace Conference, and even that, only very gradually initiated. This would have to mean that Jewish immigration should be definitely limited, and that the project for making Palestine distinctly a Jewish commonwealth should be given up.

There would then be no reason why Palestine could not be included in a united Syrian State, just as other portions of the country, the holy places being cared for by an International and Inter-religious Commission, somewhat as at present, under the oversight and approval of the Mandatary and of the League of Nations. The Jews, of course, would have representation upon this Commission.

6. The Recommendations now made lead naturally to the necessity of recommending what Power shall undertake the single Mandate for all Syria.

(1) The considerations already dealt with suggest the qualifications, ideally to be desired in this Mandatory Power: First of all it should be freely desired by the people. It should be willing to enter heartily into the spirit of the mandatory system, and its possible gift to the world, and so be willing to withdraw after a reasonable period, and not seek selfishly to exploit the country. It should have a passion for democracy, for the education of the common people and for the development of national spirit. It needs unlimited sympathy and patience in what is practically certain to be a rather thankless task; for no Power can go in, honestly to face actual conditions (like land-ownership, for example) and seek to correct these conditions, without making many enemies. It should have experience in dealing with less developed peoples, and abundant resources in men and money.

(2) Probably no Power combines all these qualifications, certainly not in equal degree. But there is hardly one of these qualifications that has not been more or less definitely indicated in our conferences with the Syrian people and they certainly suggest a new stage in the development of the self-sacrificing spirit in the relations of peoples to one another.

The Power that undertakes the single mandate for all Syria, in the spirit of these qualifications, will have the possibility of greatly serving not only Syria but the world, and of exalting at the same time its own national life. For it would be working in direct line with the high aims of the Allies in the war, and give proof that those high aims had not been abandoned. And that would mean very much just now, in enabling the nations to keep their faith in one another and in their own highest ideals.

(3) The Resolutions of the Peace Conference of January 30, 1919, quoted in our instructions, expressly state for regions to be "completely severed from the Turkish Empire," that "the wishes of these communities must be a principal consideration in the selection of the Mandatory Power." Our survey left no room for doubt of the choice of the majority of the Syrian people. Although it was not known whether America would take a mandate at all; and although the Commission could not only give no assurances upon that point, but had rather to discourage expectation; nevertheless, upon the face of the returns, America was the first choice of 1152 of the petitions presented—more than 60 per cent—while no other Power had as much as 15 per cent for first choice.

And the conferences showed that the people knew the grounds upon which they registered their choice for America. They declared that their choice was due to knowledge of America's record: the unselfish aims with which she had come into the war; the faith in her felt by multitudes of Syrians who had been in America; the spirit revealed in American educational institutions in Syria, especially the College in Beirut, with its well known and constant encouragement of Syrian national sentiment; their belief that America had no territorial or colonial ambitions, and would willingly withdraw when the Syrian state was well established as her treatment both of Cuba and the Philippines seemed to them to illustrate; her genuinely democratic spirit; and her ample resources.

From the point of view of the desires of the "people concerned", the Mandate should clearly go to America.

(4) From the point of qualifications, too, already stated as needed, in the Mandatary for Syria, America, as first choice of the people probably need not fear careful testing, point by point, by the standard involved in our discussion of qualifications; though she has much less experience in such work than Great Britain, and is likely to [show less patience; and though her definite connections with Syria have been less numerous and close than those of France. She would have at least the great qualification of fervent belief in the new mandatory system of the League of Nations, as indicating the proper relations which a strong nation should take toward a weaker one. And, though she would undertake the mandate with reluctance, she could probably be brought to see, how logically the taking of such responsibility follows from the purposes

with which she entered the war, and from her advocacy of the League of Nations.

(5) There is the further consideration, that America could probably come into the Syrian situation, in the beginning at least, with less friction than any other Power. The great majority of Syrian people, as has been seen, favor her coming, rather than that of any other power. Both the British and the French would find it easier to yield their respective claims to America than to each other. She would have no rival imperial interests to press. She would have abundant resources for the development of the sound prosperity of Syria; and this would inevitably benefit in a secondary way the nations which have had closest connection with Syria, and so help to keep relations among the Allies cordial. No other Power probably would be more welcome, as a neighbor, to the British, with their large interests in Egypt, Arabia, and Mesopotamia; or to the Arabs and Syrians in these regions; or to the French with their long-established and many-sided interests in Beirut and the Lebanon.

(6) The objections to simply recommending at once a single American Mandate for all Syria are: first of all, that it is not certain that the American people would be willing to take the Mandate; that it is not certain that the British or French would be willing to withdraw, and would cordially welcome America's coming—a situation which might prove steadily harassing to an American administration; that the vague but large encouragement given to the Zionist aims might prove particularly embarrassing to America, on account of her large and influential Jewish population; and that, if America were to take any mandate at all, and were to take but one mandate, it is probable that an Asia Minor Mandate would be more natural and important. For there is a task there of such peculiar and world-wide significance as to appeal to the best in America, and demand the utmost from her, and as certainly to justify her in breaking with her established policy concerning mixing in the affairs of the Eastern Hemisphere. The Commissioners believe, moreover, that no other Power could come into Asia Minor, with hands so free to give impartial justice to all the peoples concerned.

To these objections as a whole, it is to be said, that they are all of such a kind that they may resolve themselves; and that they only form the sort of obstacles that must be expected, in so large and significant an undertaking. In any case they do not relieve the Commissioners from the duty of recommending the course which, in their honest judgment, is the best course, and the one for which the whole situation calls.

The Commissioners, therefore, recommend, as involved in the logic of the facts, that the United States of America be asked to undertake the single Mandate for all Syria.

If for any reason the mandate for Syria is not given to America, then the Commissioners recommend, in harmony with the express request of the majority of the Syrian people, that the mandate be given to Great Britain. The tables show that there were 1073 petitions in all Syria for Great Britain as Mandatary, if America did not take the mandate. This is very greatly in excess of any similar expression for the French. On the contrary—for whatever reason—more than 60 percent of all the petitions, presented to the Commission, directly and strongly protested against any French mandate. Without going into a discussion of the reasons for this situation, the Commissioners are reluctantly compelled to believe that this situation itself makes it impossible to recommend a single French mandate for all Syria. The feeling of the Arabs of the East is particularly strong against the French. And there is grave reason to believe that the attempt to enforce a French Mandate would precipitate war between the Arabs and the French, and force upon Great Britain a dangerous alternative. The Commissioners may perhaps be allowed to say that this conclusion is contrary to their own earlier hope, that—because of France's long and intimate relations with Syria, because of her unprecedented sacrifices in the war, and because the British Empire seemed certain to receive far greater accessions of territory from the war—it might seem possible to recommend that France to given the entire mandate for Syria. But the longer the Commission remained in Syria, the more clear it became that that course could not be taken.

The Commissioners recommend, therefore, that if America cannot take the mandate for all Syria, that it be given to Great Britain; because of the choice of the people concerned; because she is already on the ground and with much of the necessary work in hand; because of her trained administrators; because of her long and generally successful experience in dealing with less developed peoples; and because she has so many of the qualifications needed in a Mandatory Power, as we have already considered them.

We should hardly be doing justice, however, to our sense of responsibility to the Syrian people, if we did not frankly add some at least of the reasons and misgivings, variously expressed and implied in our conferences, which led to the preference for an American mandate over a British mandate. The people repeatedly showed honest fear that in British hands the mandatory power would become simply a colonizing power of the old kind; that Great Britain would find it difficult to give up the colonial theory, especially in case of a people thought inferior; that she would favor a civil service and pension budget too expensive for a poor people; that the interests of Syria would be subordinated to the supposed needs of the Empire; that there would be, after all, too much exploitation of the country for Britain's benefit; that she would never be ready to withdraw and give the country real independence; that she did not really believe in universal education, and would not provide adequately for it; and that she already had more territory in her possession—in spite of her fine colonial record—than was good either for herself or for the world. These misgivings of the Syrian people unquestionably largely explain their demand for "absolute independence", or a period of "assistance" of only twenty years, their protest against Article 22 of the Covenant of the League of Nations, etc. They all mean that whatever Power the Peace Conference shall send into Syria, should go in as a true mandatary under the League of Nations, and for a limited term. Anything else would be a betrayal of the Syrian people. It needs to be emphasized, too, that under a true mandatary for Syria, all the legitimate interests of all the nations in Syria would be safeguarded. In particular, there is no reason why any tie that France has had with Syria in the past should be severed or even weakened under the control of another mandatory power, or in an independent Syria.

There remains only to be added, that if France feels so intensely concerning her present claims in Syria, as to threaten all cordial relations among the Allies, it is of course possible to give her a mandate over the Lebanon (not enlarged), separated from the rest of Syria, as is desired by considerable groups in that region. For reasons already given, the Commissioners cannot recommend this course, but it is a possible arrangement.

Respectfully submitted,

CHARLES R. CRANE
HENRY C. KING

II. MESOPOTAMIA

In view of the Resolutions, passed by the Peace Conference on January 30th, 1919, and of the Anglo-French Declaration of November 9th, 1918 —on the eve of the Armistice—both of which documents class Syria and Mesopotamia together to be treated in the same way, and make to them the same promises and assurances, the Commissioners recommend that the Peace Conference, adopt for Mesopotamia a policy in general parallel to that recommended for Syria, in order that the Anglo-French Declaration may not become another "scrap of paper".

1. We accordingly recommend, as most important of all, and in strict harmony with our Instructions, that whatever foreign administration is brought into Mesopotamia, should come into Mesopotamia, not at all as a colonizing power in the old sense of that term, but as a Mandatary under the League of Nations, with clear consciousness that "the well-being and development" of the Mesopotamian people form for i_t a "sacred trust". To this end the Mandate should have a limited term, the time of expiration to be determined by the League of Nations, in the light of all the facts as brought out from year to year, whether in the annual reports of the Mandatary to the League or in other ways.

The entire text of the first recommendation for Syria, with its subordinate recommendations, applies point by point to Mesopotamia as truly as to Syria.

If the Peace Conference, the League of Nations, and the appointed Mandatory Power loyally carry out the policy of mandataries embodied in the Covenant of the League of Nations, the most essential interests of Mesopotamia would be fully safeguarded — but only so.

2. We recommend, in the second place, that the unity of Mesopotamia be preserved: the precise boundaries to be determined by a special commission on boundaries, after the mandate has been assigned. It should probably include at least the Vilayets of Basra, Bagdad, and Mosul. And the Southern Kurds and Assyrians might well be linked up with Mesopotamia. The wisdom of a united country needs no argument in the case of Mesopotamia.

3. We recommend, in the third place, that Mesopotamia, be placed under one Mandatary Power, as the natural way to secure real and efficient unity. The economic, political, social and educational development of the people all call for such a unified mandate. Only waste, confusion, friction, and injury to the people's interests, could come from attempting a division and "spheres of influence" on the part of several nations. But this implies that the Mandatary Power shall not itself be an exploiting power, but shall sacredly guard the people's rights.

4. Since it is plainly desirable that there be general harmony in the political and economic institutions and arrangements of Mesopotamia and Syria; and since the people themselves should have chief voice in determining the form of government under which they shall live, we recommend that the Government of Mesopotamia, in harmony with the apparent desires of its people, be a Constitutional Monarchy, such as is proposed for Syria; and that the people of Mesopotamia be given opportunity to indicate their choice of Monarch, the choice to be reviewed and confirmed by the League of Nations. It may be fairly assumed that the 1278 petitions from Syrians for the independence of Mesopotamia —68.5 per cent of the total number received—reflects the feeling in Mesopotamia itself; and such contact as we have been able to secure with Mesopotamians confirms the assumption, and leads to the belief that the program, presented at Aleppo by representative Mesopotamians, headed by Jaafar Pasha, Military Governor of the Aleppo District, and practically parallel to the Damascus Program, would be generally supported by the Mesopotamian people. Whether this support extends to each item in the program alike, and so to the naming of a King from the sons of the King of the Hedjaz, we have not sufficient data to determine, and so have recommended that a plebiscite be taken upon that point; although there is British evidence that many Mesopotamians have expressed themselves in favor of one of the sons of the King of the Hedjaz as Emir.

5. The Mesopotamian Program expresses its choice of America as Mandatary, and with no second choice. Undoubtedly there has been a good deal of feeling in Mesopotamia against Great Britain, and the petitioners specifically charge the British authorities in Mesopotamia with considerable interference with freedom of opinion, of expression, and of travel,—much of which might be justified in time of military occupation. But feeling so stirred might naturally breed unwillingness to express desire for Great Britain as Mandatary. On the other hand, the material in the pamphlet called "Copies and Translations of Declarations and Other Documents relating to Self-Determination in Iraq" (Mesopotamia) was called out by an attempt on the part of the British Government in Mesopotamia to secure the opinions of leading men of all groups concerning "self-determination". This material, just because reported directly to British officials, is doubtless somewhat more favorable to the British than it would otherwise be; but it gives unquestionably good evidence of much opinion likely to choose a British mandate. And after all, the range of choice of a mandatary, of sufficient power and experience and of essential justice, is decidedly limited, and it is by no means improbable that if the Mesopotamians were confronted by a refusal of America to take a mandate for Mesopotamia, they would make Great Britain at least second choice, as the majority of the Syrians did. There is supplementary evidence also upon this point.

Now it seems so unlikely that America could or would take a mandate for Mesopotamia, in addition to the possible consideration of Syria and Asia Minor, that the Commissioners recommend that the Peace Conference assign the mandate for Mesopotamia to Great Britain: because of the general reasons already given for recommending her as mandatary in Syria, if America does not go in there; because she is probably best of all fitted for the particular task involved, in view of her long relations with the Arabs; in recognition of the sacrifices made by her in delivering Mesopotamia from the Turks, though with no acknowledgement of right of conquest, as her own statements expressly disclaim; because of the special interests she naturally has in Mesopotamia on account of its nearness to India and its close connections with Arabia; and because of work already done in the territory.

These reasons make it probable that the largest interests of the people of Mesopotamia as a whole will be best served by a British Mandate, in spite of the fact that from the point of view of world-interests, in the prevention of jealousy, suspicion, and fear of domination by a single power, it were better for both Britain and the world that no further territory anywhere be added to the British Empire. A British Mandate however, will have the decided advantage of tending to promote economic and educational unity throughout Mesopotamia and Syria whether Syria be under Great Britain or America—and so will reflect more fully than ever before, the close relations in language, customs, and trade between these parts of the former Turkish Empire.

In a country as rich as Mesopotamia in agricultural possibilities, in oil, and in other resources, with the best intentions, there will inevitably be danger of exploitation and monopolistic control by the Mandatory Power, through making British interests supreme, and especially through large Indian immigration. This danger will need increasingly and most honestly to be guarded against. The Mesopotamians feel very strongly the menace particularly of Indian immigration, even though that immigration should be confined to Moslems. They dread the admixture of another people of entirely different race and customs, as threatening their Arabic civilization.

Respectfully submitted,

CHARLES R. CRANE
HENRY C. KING

III. ASIA MINOR

The recommendations, dealing with mandates in the Asia Minor portion of the former Ottoman Empire, follow naturally upon the preceding discussions of pertinent action already taken by the Peace Conference; of dangers arising from a selfish division and exploitation of Turkey; of considerations looking to a proper division of Turkey; and of problems naturally resulting. For the recommendations built directly on foundations already laid by the Peace Conference: They aim to prevent a selfish exploitation and division of Turkey. They intend not less surely to ground such division of Turkey as is recommended solely upon considerations of justice and the good of all| men. And in this spirit they endeavor honestly to face the grave problems arising, and to seek their solution in the light of the full discussion which precedes. That discussion has been so full, that the Recommendations of the Commissioners need do little more than summarize conclusions, except upon two points,—the reasons for a general American Mandate, and the conditions upon which such a mandate might be taken by America.

The Commissioners recommend:

1. The formation, under a Mandatary, of an Armenian State, completely separated from Turkey....

It is consequently recommended that Cilicia should not be separate from Anatolia at present.

2. The similar formation, under a Mandatary, of an International Constantinopolitan State, completely separated from Turkey....

3. The appointment of a Mandatary for the continued Turkish State, in line with the apparent wishes of the majority of the Turkish people;

the major terms of the Mandate to be defined by the Peace Conference or the League of Nations, and further adjustments to be arranged between the Mandatary and Turkey....

4. That ... no independent territory be set off for the Greeks; though local autonomy be granted to that portion of the sanjak of Smyrna which has a decided majority of Greeks, but under the general mandate for Turkey.

5. That a commission or commissions on boundaries in Asia Minor be appointed to study on the ground and to exactly define the boundaries of the states named in the first three recommendations, and the precise limits of any locally autonomous area in Smyrna. The definition of the boundaries of the Turkish State would require the study and definition of the northern boundaries of Syria and Mesopotamia as well, with special reference to allowing to the Kurds a measure of autonomy under close mandatary rule, possibly in connection with Mesopotamia, and with the clear understanding that the rights of the Syrians, Chaldean, and Nestorian Christian minorities in this whole region shall be carefully guarded.

6. A general single mandate for the whole of Asia Minor (not assigned to Mesopotamia or Syria) to include under it the mandate for Armenia, the mandate for the Constantinopolitan State, and the mandate for the continued Turkish State, each with a governor of its own to ensure full attention to its particular interests, besides a governor-general over the whole. The various interrelations and common concerns of the constituent states would thus be studied and cared for, as well as their individual needs....

7. That the United States of America be asked to take this general single mandate together with its inclusive mandate for the Armenian State, the Constantinopolitan State, and the continued Turkish State. This recommendation is made for the following reasons which need to be developed in full:

(1) As already pointed out, it seems to be generally desired that America should take the mandate for Armenia....

(2) America is also the most natural Power to take the mandate for the International Constantinopolitan State, as well as for Armenia; for the simple reason that she is the only Great Power territorially and strategically disinterested....

(3) It is to be added that America is also the most natural Power for the Mandate over the new Turkish State, because the Turkish people want her, and generally trust her, as the evidence previously given indicates; and because America is peculiarly prepared to meet the needs of the Turkish people in this crisis in their history, as the reasons to be given for a general American mandate will later bring out....

(4) The best solution for mandates in Asia Minor would seem then

to be, to combine all three mandates in a composite mandate, which would be put in the hands of America as the single Mandatary....

(5) Considerations on which America would be justified in taking a composite general mandate for Asia Minor. Those conditions are: that she is really wanted by the Turkish people; that Turkey should give evidence that she is ready to do justice to the Armenians, not only by the allotment of the territory within her borders, recommended for the Armenian State, but also by encouraging the repatriation of Armenians, and by seeing that all possible just reparation is made to them as they return to their homes; that Turkey should also give evidence that she is ready to become a modern constitutional state, and to abolish military conscription; that Russia should be ready to renounce all claims upon Russian Armenia; that the Allies should cordially welcome America's help in the difficult situation in Turkey; and especially that all plans for cutting up Turkey, for the benefit of outside peoples, into spheres of influence and exploitation areas should be abandoned. These conditions are necessary to a successful solution of the Turkish problem. Unless they are fulfilled, America ought not to take the mandate for Asia Minor. And the Commissioners do not recommend that the mandate be given to America if these conditions cannot be essentially met.

Respectfully submitted,

CHARLES R. CRANE
HENRY C. KING

Index

Abdullah, Emir, 118
Adalia, 2, 20, 32, 66, 86, 215, 283
Adana, 27, 42, 62, 140
Aden, 43
Adrianople (Edirné), 192, 299
Adriatic, question of, 22
Aegean Islands, 22
Aga Khan, 66
Aharonian, 26
Ahmed Riza Bey, 166-167
Aidin, 65, 283
Aintab, 42
Akaba, 17
Aleppo, 3, 17, 32, 42, 137, 148, 253-254, 264, 278
Alexandretta (Hatay), 3, 23, 27, 42, 136, 197, 248, 250, 255
Ali Kemal Bey, 166
Allenby, General Sir Edmund H. H. (Field Marshal Lord), 8, 32, 51, 82-84, 91, 105-106, 111, 135, 149, 254, 261-262, 266, 278, 318
American Commission to Negotiate Peace, 10-11 (Report of Intelligence Section), 26, 32, 37, 55, 263, 281-285 (proposals of)
American Jewish Congress, 73
American policy, failure of, 276-285
American Relief Committee, 52-53
Amman, visit of King-Crane Commission to, 111-113
Anatolia, 2, 6, 11, 18, 20, 32, 34, 35, 62, 63, 64-65, 67-68, 78, 192, 197, 214-216, (disposition of), 236, 282, 278-294, 299
Anglo-French Declaration, (November 8, 1919), 8, 24, 34, 84 fn, 221, 227, 249, 263
Anglo-French Entente, 43
Anglo-Persian [-Iranian] Oil Company, 268
Anglo-Russian Accord, (March 12, 1915), 1
Antonius, George, 318-319
Arabia, 12, 20-23, 43, 61, 75, 76, 80
Arab confederation, 2, 11
Arabian Peninsula, 17

Arabs, 2, 16-17
Aras, Tewfik Rüstü, Turkish Foreign Minister, 310
Archer, Msg. J. F. Gioranimous, 127
Ardahan, 27
Arizona, U.S.S., 65
Armenia, problem of mandate, 2, 6, 7, 11, 13, 15, 20, 21, 26-27, (Armenian case at Peace Conference), 32, 34, 42, 43, 45, 46, 48, 53, 58, 62, 64-65, 67, 69-70, 74, 79, 80, 158, 164-167 (Turkish views), 169, 175, 182-185, 187-190, 211-213, 215-216, 231-232, 239-241, 242-243, 255, 256, 270-275 (American [Harbord] Military Mission), 283, 290-291, 295-296, 299
Asia Minor, 6, 21, 22, 52, 58, 61, 62, 65, 68, 70, 72, 75, 243, 271, 282
Atatürk, Kemal (Mustapha Kemal Pasha), 193, 234, 243-244, 256, 273, 287, 288-289, 290-294, 310
Augagnard, Senator, 43, 85
Azerbaijan, 15, 16, 244, 295

Baghdad, 3, 18 (railway), 42, 64, 91, 227
Baker, Ray Stannard, 36, 37, 74, 82 fn, 311-313
Baku, 16
Balfour, Arthur James (First Earl of Balfour), 33, 34, 51, 65, 66, 68 fn, 111, 157-158, 248, 249-251
Balfour Declaration, (November 2, 1917), 4-5, 11, 27, 37, 73, 74, 91, 94, 96, 99, 120
Barnard, U.S.S., 87
Barrès, Maurice, 279
Barton, Dr. James L., 6, 24
Basra, 3, 227
Batum, 16, 244, 248
Beirut, 3, 17, 42, 53, 126
Bell, Lady Gertrude, 35
Berthelot, Philippe, 265, 279
Bitlis, 27, 172

Black Sea, 11, 27
Bliss, Dr. Howard, President, Syrian Protestant College (American University of Beirut), 24, 25, 26, 32, 84
Bliss, General Tasker H., 26, 45, 49, 218, 263, 267
Bliss, W.T., 129
Boghos Nubar Pasha, 26
Bohn, W.F., 46
Bolshevik Revolution, 4, 19
Bosphorus, 11, 14, 213, 233, 282
Brandeis, Justice Louis D., 99
Brenier, Henri, 35
Briand, Aristide, 9
Bristol, Admiral Mark L., 52, 66, 69, 81, 84-85, 87, 88, 155-156, 162, 186, 216, 236-244, 245, 247, 302, 303, 308, 309, 319-320
Brodie, Donald M., 41, 90-91, 109-110, 129, 144, 209, 219, 220, 257, 258, 320
Brown, James Wright, 312-313
Brown, Philip Marshall, 67 fn
Browne, Louis Edgar, 290
Buckler, W.H., 67 fn, 257, 259, 260
Bulgaria, 8, 75, 162
Butler, Crosby, 211
Brusa (Bursa), 60, 62, 80
Bryce, James, 78

Cairo, 51
Caix, Robert de, 35, 43, 45, 48, 51 fn, 85, 260, 265, 268
Cambon, Paul, 105
Caucasus, 63, 67, 247
Cecil, Lord Robert, 10
Chambers, Dr. W.N., 140
Chesbrough, Ralph Y., 69, 244
Chester Concession, 295, 307
Child, Richard, W., 303, 305
Chirol, Sir Valentine, 35
Cilicia, 2, 9, 11, 21, 27, 32, 46, 52, 58, 67, 70, 71, 140-141, 161, 215, 250, 255, 283
Clayton, General Sir Gilbert, 77 fn, 84, 91-92, 106
Clemenceau, Georges, 9, 26, 31-33, 34, 44, 53, 54, 62, 64, 65, 68, 72, 76, 82, 83, 84, 85, 168, 159, 161, 248, 251, 255, 256, 263, 266, 269, 277-281
Colby, Bainbridge, 298
Commission of Inquiry, case for, 24-26
Congress of Liberal Turks, 28
Constantinople, 6, 10, 13, 14, 19, 32, 42, 43, 44, 47, 48, 50, 52, 53, 60, 62, 63, 64, 65, 67, 68, 69, 70, 74, 78, 79, 158, 161, 179, 192, 213-214 (Constantinopolitan State), 216-217, 232-233, 235, 280, 282, 297, 297-298, 299
Coolidge, Professor Archibald Cary, 39
Council of Four, 20-22 (Resolution of January 30, 1919), 45, 63, 64, 65, 66, 83
Crane, Charles R., 25, 36, 37, 38, 39, 41, 47-50, 51, 53, 54, 75, 77, 78, 80, 81, 82, 87, 89, 99-100, 111, 126, 129, 133, 137, 141, 154, 162, 167, 168, 169, 186, 187, 195, 208, 209, 216-220, 256-257, 258, 260, 262, 285, 289, 290, 311, 312, 315, 319-320, 326
Crawford, Stuart, 111
Curzon, Marquess of Kedleston, 51, 66, 105, 106, 244-247, 254, 276, 277, 280, 302-303
Cyprus, 64 fn

Daghestan, 15
Damad Ferid Pasha, 69, 156-157, 247-248, 299
Damascus, 3, 8, 17, 32, 42, 46, 53, 105, 253, 254, 278, 280
Damascus Program, 128-129, 135, 143, 144, 145, 146, 150, 223
Dardanelles (see also Bosphorus, Constantinople, Straits, etc.), 11, 14, 179, 213, 233, 282
Davis, John W., 244, 265-266
Day, Clive, 10
Derby, Lord, 279
Diarbekir, 27, 42
Dodecanese Islands, 1, 14, 19, 63, 64, 307-308

INDEX

Dominian, Dr. Leon, 24, 72
Druse, 123
Dulles, Allen W., 307
Dupont, U.S.S., 217

Eder, M.D., 96
Edib (Adivar), Halidé Hanum, 167-169
Editor and Publisher, 312-313
Egypt, 6, 43, 46, 102
Eleuzzia, Velid, 170
Elizabetpol, 27
Ellis, W.T., 96, 101, 104
Entente Libérale (Turkey), 166, 242, 288
Epirus, Northern, 22
Erzerum, 27, 42; Congress of, 172, 287, 288-291, 297
Erzinjan, 42
ESCO Foundation, 317-318
Essad Halil, Dr., 166

Feisal, Emir, 8, 22, 23, 25, 26, 35, 43, 49, 51, 53, 75, 77, 82, 84, 97, 105, 117, 119, 120, 121, 124, 131, 146, 150, 203-204, 221, 251, 252, 253, 254, 255, 263, 264, 266-267, 268, 276-281
Fiume, 62, 63
Forbes-Adam, Eric, 82
Fourteen Points (Wilson), 5-6, 12
France, 6, 8, 9, 22, 25, 32, 43-45, 49, 52, 61, 62, 64, 65, 67, 69, 75, 76, 80, 82-84 105, 108-109, 110, 111, 122, 145-148, 149, 161, 197, 210, 226-227, 248, 249, 253-254, 259, 261, 264, 283, 294-295, 301
Frankfurter, Professor Felix, 37, 55, 73-74, 99
Friedenwald, Harry, 96

Gabriel, Lt. Col. V., 89
Galli, Signor, 45, 85
Gates, Caleb F., 52-53, 60, 71, 72, 84, 185, 187, 188, 189-190, 216
Gauvain, Auguste, 35
Gay, Dr. Edwin F., 313-314
Geddes, Sir Auckland, 303-304, 305
General Syrian Congress, 118-123
Georgia, 15, 184, 242, 244, 295

Germany, 12, 20
Gibraltar, Straits of, 280
Glazebrook, American Consul, 89, 95
Gouraud, General Henri J.E., 267
Gout, Jean, 43, 44, 45, 54, 85, 265, 268, 279
Graffam, Mary, 184-185
Grayson, Rear Admiral Cary T., 47
Grey, Sir Edward, 277
Grew, Joseph C., 47, 49, 50, 52, 53, 68, 81, 129, 303, 307, 309, 310
Great Britain, 2, 6, 9, 11, 13, 16, 18, 19, 49, 59, 61, 62, 63, 66, 67, 75, 76, 80, 96, 105, 108, 122, 144, 149, 151, 210-211, 226-227, 228, 248, 249, 253-254, 259, 264, 269, 279, 283, 294-295, 300-301
Greece, 6, 9, 11, 14, 34, 63, 64, 65, 67, 68-69, 79, 162, 179-181, 214, 229, 234, 283, 291

Haas, Jacob de, 7, 316
Haddad Pasha, General Gabriel, 109
Haddad, Dr. Sami, 41, 129
Hagopian, A. der, 28
Haifa, 42
Hall, William H., 6, 7
Hama, 3, 17, 32, 148, 253, 254, 265, 278, 280
Harbord, Maj. Gen. James, G. (American Military Mission to Armenia), 241, 270-275, 276, 282, 292-293, 294
Harput, 2, 27, 42, 52
Haskell, Col. W.N., 241
Hazelwood, U.S.S., 141, 153
Heck, 70
Herrick, Myron T., 302
Hejaz, Kingdom of, 15, 23, 61, 75, 76, 91, 123, 138, 299
Hogarth, Commander David, 4, 5, 43, 47, 50, 76, 82, 85, 262, 266, 267, 318
Holy Places, 9, 12, 13, 18, 61, 103, 127
Homs, 3, 17, 32, 137, 148, 253, 254, 264, 278, 280

INDEX

Hoover, Herbert, 96, 160-161, 240, 241, 271
Hoskins, Captain Halford L., 40
House, Col. E.M., 10, 31, 33, 35, 36, 37, 49, 50, 71, 72, 73, 75, 76, 77, 80, 84
Howe, Frederick, 24
Hughes, Charles Evans, 240, 302, 303, 304, 305, 307, 309, 312
Hunchakist Party (Armenia), 183
Hussein, King of Hejaz, 2, 3, 8, 19, 43, 61, 138, 151, 249, 253, 254, 255, 263
Hussein Bey, Professor, 28

Ibn Saud, Emir, 3, 16
India, 3, 60
Inter-Allied Commission on Mandates in Turkey, American Section (King-Crane Commission), 26, 32, 36-52, 75, 81, 82, 85, 86, 105
Inonu, Ismet, 305-306
Iraq (Mesopotamia), 23, 322-323
Istanbul Women's College, 81, 186, 217
Italy, 2, 61, 62, 63, 64, 65, 67, 79, 80, 83, 159, 283
Izzet Pasha, 68

Jaafar Pasha, General, 138
Jackson, Consul J.B., 138, 139
Jaffa, 42, 91, 92, 95
Jamil Bey, 164-165
St. Jean de Maurienne, Treaty of, 2, 159
Jemal Pasha, 70, 149
Jerusalem, 99
Jewish National Home (Commonwealth, State), 11, 27, 31, 73, 93, 97-98, 101, 103, 120, 151, 199, 205
Jews, 5, 12, 23, 61, 73
Judson, Dr. H.P., 24
Jusserand, Jules, 297

Kars, 27
Kayseri, 14
Kemal Bey, 164-165
Kerasund, 14

Kerner, Prof. Robert J., 39, 40, 48, 50, 81, 82
King, Henry Churchill, 11, 36, 37, 38, 39, 40, 41, 42, 45, 46-48, 49, 50, 51-54, 56, 59, 60, 71, 74-76, 77-79, 80, 81-82, 89, 101, 107, 111-112, 125, 126, 129, 135, 137, 140, 141, 153-154, 162, 165, 169, 179, 186, 195, 199, 208, 209, 218, 219, 243, 257-258, 260, 261-262, 275, 311, 319-320, 326
King-Crane Commission, 8, 26, 36 (Instructions), 36-52 (Appointment), 59-62 (first report), 69, 71, 73, 74, 75, 81, 84-86 (departure), 87, 161 ff; 195-237 (report), 256-262 (Aftermath), 311-313 (publication), 313-320 (estimates of), 320-327 (evaluation)
Kitchener, Field Marshal Lord, 2
Knox, Philander C., 39
Konia, 65, 66
Kurdistan, 2, 21, 70, 171, 197, 215, 277, 283, 288

Lansing, Robert, 5, 21, 26, 45, 49, 55, 69, 81, 245, 246, 248
Lausanne, Conference of, 301-308
Lausanne, Treaty of, 9, 285, 307-308, 308-310
Latakia, 17, 136
Lawrence, Col. T.E., 3, 10, 35, 36, 43, 71, 92, 266
League of Nations, 7, 13, 14, 16, 18, 20, 21, 22, 25, 34, 38, 44, 48, 50, 55, 61, 75, 79, 89, 107, 117, 120, 121, 138, 145, 151, 174, 175, 200, 218, 222, 226, 236, 249, 250, 258, 259, 263, 267, 274, 275, 282
Lebanon, 9, 17, 42, 84, 115, 125-129, 130-133, 143, 146 ff, 150, 200-208, 210, 223-227, 264, 267, 268, 280, 283
Lewin-Epstein, E.W., 96
Lloyd George, David, 4, 5, 6, 20, 21, 31, 32, 33, 34, 43, 46, 50, 51, 53, 54, 62, 63, 64, 65, 66,

INDEX

67, 68, 76, 82, 83, 84, 86, 119, 158, 159, 160, 251, 252, 253, 254, 259, 263, 264, 266-267, 269, 276-281
London, Treaty of, 1, 32, 63
Long, Maurice, 88
Luce, U.S.S., 88
Lybyer, Albert Howe, 10, 28, 39, 40, 41, 42, 43-47, 49, 50, 51, 52, 53, 54, 57, 71, 75, 81, 82, 87, 89, 92-93, 94, 107, 115-118, 128, 129, 133-134, 139, 141, 145-148, 162, 169, 186, 193, 195, 209, 210-220, 257

Macedonia, 162, 213-214
Magee, David, 70, 84
Mahmud Pasha, 166-167
Mandates, 21, 61, 62, 76, 216-217
Mandelstam, André, 191
Marash, 27, 42
Mardin, 42, 52
Marmara, Sea of, 11, 14, 233
Maronites, 92, 109, 125, 135, 150
Marshall, General, 254
Marshall, Louis, 31
Martha Washington, U.S.S., 271
McCormick, Vance, 36
McMahon, Sir Henry, 2, 47, 50, 85, 254
Mecca, 16
Mediterranean Sea, 17, 62
Mersina (Mersin), 2, 3, 14, 42, 153, 248, 255
Mesopotamia (see also Iraq), 11, 12, 17, 18, 20, 21, 32, 33, 48, 58, 59, 61, 66, 69, 79, 80, 83, 158, 202, 211, 227-228, 241, 250, 267, 268, 269, 277, 283, 284, 299
Middle East, 8, 11, 51, 52, 294-301
Miller, David Hunter, 6, 10, 11, 27
Millet, Philippe, 35
Money, General Sir Arthur, 91, 95
Montagu, Rt. Hon. Edwin S., 66, 67, 157
Montgomery, George R., 40, 41, 84, 87, 92, 101-102, 128-129, 138, 140, 195-198, 209
Moore, Laurence S., 41, 129

Morgenthau, Henry, Sr., 41, 67, 240, 271, 280
Mosseri, Jack, 96
Mosul, 9, 17, 42, 227, 250, 277
Mudania, Armistice of, 301
Mudros, Armistice of, 8, 292
Mustapha Arif Bey, 165
Mustapha Kemal Pasha (See Atatürk)

Nabi Bey, 166-167
Nablus, 100
National Liberal Party (Milli Ahrar) of Turkey, 164, 167, 177, 288
Near East (see also Middle East), 26, 42, 49, 53, 58, 71, 73, 75, 76, 77, 78, 86, 294-295 ("open door")
Near East Relief, 6, 90, 149, 186
Nejd, 3, 23
Nicolson, Sir Harold, 10, 64, 65, 66

Oberlin College, 38
Orlando, Vittorio Emanuele, 65, 83
Ottoman Delegation to Peace Conference (see also Damad Ferid Pasha), 68, 156-157
Ottoman Empire, 3, 5, 6, 7, 8, 10, 11, 12, 13, 14, 15, 16, 18, 20, 22, 27, 29, 43, 44, 52, 55, 58, 59-62 (dangers of selfish exploitation), 63, 64, 65, 66, 67, 69, 71, 74, 80, 81, 133, 152, 163, 165, 166, 170, 219, 221, 228-231 (non-Arabic portions), 243, 251, 282, 284, 287, 288, 289, 308
Ottoman League of National Unity, 166-167, 174, 176, 177, 287-288
Ottoman Liberal Party, 288
Ottoman Press Association, 170-171

Palestine, 4, 5, 6, 9, 11, 12, 18, 20, 21, 23, 27, 32, 33, 37, 43, 46, 48, 51, 58, 66, 69, 73, 76, 80, 81, 83, 88, 90, 130-133, 195-198, 221-227, 250-251, 264, 267, 268, 283, 284, 299, 320-321

INDEX

Pallavicini, Capt., 54, 85
Panama Canal, 280, 304
Pasha Ali Society (Turkey), 288
Patrick, Mary Mills, 87, 186, 190, 257
Peace Conference, Ch. I, 23, 53, 92, 98, 102
Peace and Safety Party (Turkey), 165, 288
Pears, H.E., 194
Peet, Dr. William W., 88, 162, 186
Percy, Lord Eustace, 10
Persian Gulf, 3, 12, 269
Petitions (King-Crane Commission), 142-145
Petroleum, Yale memorandum, 58
Pichon, 9, 32, 43, 221
Picot, Georges, 2, 84, 99-100, 105, 126
Polk, Frank L., 218, 248, 252, 255, 257, 259, 297
Pomaks, 162
Port Said, 43
Postlethwaite, Lt. Col. F. J. M., 89, 91

Qatif, 3

Ravndal, Gabriel Bie, 87, 162, 186, 191-193, 217, 244
Red Sea, 12
Reed, Major, 95
Reshid Saadi Bey, 166-167
Rihany, Abraham M., 72
Riza Bey, 171
Robert College, 52, 236
Romilly, Col. B., 100
Ross, Edward Alsworth, 262, 318
Royal Dutch Shell Co., 295
Rublee, George, 36
Russia, 4, 15, 67, 70, 161, 211, 295

Safidin, 166
Samsun, 14, 173
San Remo, 294-295 (oil agreement), 295-296 (conference), 298-299 (agreement)
Saracen, 152
Scala Nuova, 64
Secret Treaties, Inter-Allied, 1-2

Sèvres, Treaty of, 9, 269, 296-301, 326
Shahbender, Dr., 107
Shefik Bey, 171
Sherif Pasha, General, 28
Sidon, 14, 17
Sivas, Congress of, 172, 174, 291-294, 297
St. Joseph University, 128
Smith, Heathcote, 193
Smyrna (Izmir), 2, 11, 14, 18, 20, 22, 42, 63, 64, 65, 68, 69, 81, 86, 164, 216, 229, 242, 243, 283, 287, 291
Sola Pool, David de, 96
Standard Oil Co. of New York, 269
Steed, Henry Wickham, 35, 54, 261, 267
Storrs, Sir Ronald, 94, 95, 316
Straits, Turkish (see also Bosphorus, Constantinople, Dardanelles, Marmara), 10, 13, 14, 18, 19, 53, 60, 66, 67, 69, 80, 158, 160, 161, 192, 214, 232-233, 280, 282, 297-300, 303-304, 305-306, 307-309
Suleiman Nazif Bey, 169
Supreme Council, 22, 25, 27, 75
Sykes, Sir Mark, 2
Sykes-Picot Agreement, 2, 49,1 20, 122, 149, 249, 250, 254, 256, 257, 260-261, 277, 279, 283
Syria, 3, 6, 9, 12, 17, 20, 21, 22, 24, 25, 26, 32, 33, 35, 36, 42, 43, 46, 48, 49, 50, 51, 53, 58, 61, 69, 77, 79, 80, 83, 84, 85, 88, 90, 102, 105-154 (Syrian problem), 158, 195-198, 198-209, 210, 221-227, 249-256 (policies concerning), 264, 267, 268, 269, 276-281, 283, 284, 299, 321-322

Tabbit, Selim Bey, 125
Tachnakists (Armenian Federation Party), 182-183
Taft, William Howard, 39
Tardieu, André, 268
Temperley, H.W.V., 318

Tewfik Dejani Effendi, 91
Thrace, 13, 18, 19, 22, 192, 213, 232, 243, 291, 299
Thrace, Committee for the Protection of the Rights of, 168, 288
Tiflis, 27
Toynbee, Arnold J., 12-20, 42, 43, 47, 85, 318
Trans-Caucasia, 15, 271
Trebizond (Trabzon), 2, 11, 27
Tripartite Agreement, (April 26, 1916), 1
Tripoli, 17, 135
Turkey (see also Ottoman Empire), 3, 7, 11, 13, 14, 15, 21, 28-29, 33, 44, 46, 48, 52, 55, 60, 61, 62-69, 71, 74, 75, 77, 78, 79, 86, 155-156, 162, 163-179, 191-193, 211, 233-234, 239, 240, 242, 277, 284, 295, 323
Turkish Nationalist Movement, 287-294
Turkish National Pact, 292, 296-297
Turkish Petroleum Co., 268, 295
Turkish Social Democratic Party, 170
Turkish Wilsonian League, 28

Union and Progress, Committee of, 71, 166
Union for Defense of National Rights of Eastern Provinces, 287
Untermyer, Samuel, 316-317
United States, 35, 46, 48, 53, 58, 59, 61, 62, 63, 64, 65, 67, 68, 70, 75, 76, 79, 86, 108, 113, 132, 134, 149, 158-159, 174, 178-179, 192-193, 197, 200, 210, 226-227, 235-237, 243, 246-247, 248, 249, 253-254, 259, 266, 268, 274, 283, 284, 285, 290-294, 296-301, 301-308
United States Navy, General Board of, 303-304

Van, 27, 173
Venizelos, Eleutherios, 22, 64, 65, 162
Versailles, Treaty of, 159, 162, 259

Watson, Lt. Col. J.K., 91, 93
Weizmann, Chaim, 23, 27, 73
Westermann, W.L., 26, 36, 40, 41, 43, 45, 47, 48, 49, 52, 54, 69, 78, 82, 84, 85, 94, 102, 129, 257
White, George E., 187-188
White, Henry, 26, 37, 45, 49, 77, 161, 257, 260
Williams, Senator John Sharp, 256
Wilson, Woodrow, 5, 6, 8, 13, 20, 21, 24, 25, 27, 31-34, 35, 36, 37, 40, 47, 48, 50, 51, 53-54, 55, 58, 59, 60, 62, 63, 64, 65, 66, 67, 68, 72, 73, 74, 76, 77, 78, 79, 80, 81, 82, 84, 85, 86, 90, 92, 106, 129-134, 149, 157-161, 162, 167, 174, 175, 186, 217, 218-220, 225, 241, 245-248, 256-257, 260, 285, 296, 311, 312, 324, 327
Wise, Rabbi Stephen S., 23, 31

Yale, William, 40, 41, 58, 70, 84, 88, 90, 92-94, 102, 111, 113-115, 126, 128, 129, 130-133, 139, 148, 162, 195, 198-209, 210, 258, 262-270, 276, 326
Yalman, Ahmed Emin [Bey], 165-166, 174, 176, 177
Yemen, 23
Young Turks, 73

Zeinel Abeddin Irfani Bey, 166
Zionism, 8, 13, 18, 28, 46, 53, 72-74, 79, 81, 87-104 (inquiry into), 130, 143, 150, 196, 250, 251, 259, 261, 264, 267, 268, 313
Zionist Organization, 23, 27-28, 50, 86, 96-98 (Zionist Commission), 143, 224-226, 259, 280, 313

13